TURNING THE TIDE

The Life of Lady Rhondda

Angela V. John is a widely published historian and biographer based in Pembrokeshire. For many years she held the chair in History at the University of Greenwich, London. She is now an Honorary Professor at Swansea University. Her previous biographical subjects include Lady Charlotte Guest, Elizabeth Robins, Henry W. Nevinson and, most recently, Evelyn Sharp. She is a vice-president of Llafur, the Welsh People's History Society.

TURNING THE TIDE

The Life of Lady Rhondda

Angela V. John

Parthian
The Old Surgery
Napier Street
Cardigan
SA43 1ED

www.parthianbooks.com

First published in 2013

ISBN 978-1-909844-72-8

Editor: Francesca Rhydderch
Cover design by www.theundercard.co.uk Typeset
by typesetter.org.uk
Printed by Lightningsource.com

The publisher acknowledges the financial support
of the Welsh Books Council.

British Library Cataloguing in Publication Data

A cataloguing record for this book is available from
the British Library.

CONTENTS

ACKNOWLEDGEMENTS

At an early stage in my research I spent a summer's afternoon with the historian Ryland Wallace exploring the village of Llanwern in south-east Wales. This was where the Thomas family had lived. A chance meeting with helpful local resident Sharon Burgess proved to be a catalyst for much more. It led to interviews with Coral Westcott and the late Barbara Hollingdale, both very knowledgeable about the area and the family. Through them I got to know descendants on Margaret's mother's side and descendants of D.A. Thomas, her father.

I have been aided immensely by these family members. One of my greatest debts is to Frankie Webber, Margaret's god-daughter and cousin who also worked for *Time and Tide*. Her reminiscences in numerous letters and telephone conversations, and her welcome in Ireland have helped to transform my understanding. Anne Eliza Cottington has been wonderfully supportive and generous, and has given me access to sources as well as introducing me to Pen Ithon Hall and the wider family. Rosie Humphreys and Clare Davis have kindly let me use family papers and provided valuable insights for which I am also much indebted. Jamie Cottington's expertise has been especially valuable. I am also very grateful to Susannah Bower and Nicholas Wightwick. Ann Salusbury has illuminated several puzzles. Thanks also to Daisy Greenwell, Astrid Treherne and Mrs R.P.D. Treharne for their correspondence.

I have received great kindness and assistance from those living in Margaret's former homes. John Knight and his family could not have been more welcoming. The same goes for Angela and Hugh Ellingham. I'm also grateful to Ian and June Burge and Peter Collacott. Others have been generous with written material. Deirdre Macpherson has kindly shared her research on the Archdale family. Paula Bartley, Ellen Wilkinson's new biographer has, as always, willingly provided me with information. The Winifred Holtby scholar Gill Fildes has been ever ready to supply references, and discussions with her have aided me greatly.

At the Palace of Westminster, Baroness Gale of Blaenrhondda, Mari Takayanagi, Jessica Morden, Melanie Unwin and Dorothy Leys have been very helpful. I am indebted also to Anthony Lejeune and Catherine Gladstone for their memories of *Time and Tide* and to Catherine Clay, author of a forthcoming literary study of the paper. Denise Myers has kindly shared material on Llanwern and Gerard Charmley on D.A. Thomas. Richard Clark was most helpful. Ryland Wallace helped to kickstart much research and he and Lucy Bland read draft material. I am grateful to Richard Keen for accompanying me on research trips from Donegal to New York.

Although it is not possible to name all who have contributed in some way, I wish to mention the following: Jane Aaron, Deirdre Beddoe, David Berguer, Katherine Bradley, Handa Bray, Laurence Clark, Sioned Davies, Martin Durham, Shirley Eoff, Neil Evans, Hywel Francis, Emelyne Godfrey, Lesley Hall, Nicholas Hiley, Carolyn Jacob, Simon James, Aled Jones, Elin Jones, Julia Jones, Louise Knight, Thomas Lloyd, Ceridwen Lloyd Morgan, Mair Morris, Peter Mountfield, Nicola Phillips, June Purvis, Imogen and Steve Roderick, Jenny Rudge, Marion Shaw, Michael Sherborne, Angela Tawse, Pam

Thurschwell, Norman Watson, Chris Williams, Emma Williams, Huw Williams, Sian Williams and Judith P. Zinsser.

I am grateful to the archivists/librarians of Aberystwyth University; the BBC Written Archives Centre, Caversham Park, Reading; Bodleian Libraries, University of Oxford (Department of Special Collections); Bristol Record Office; British Library; British Library of Political and Economic Science (Archives Division); CADW; Cardiff University Archives; Columbia University in the City of New York (Rare Book and Manuscript Library); PEN International; Eton College Archives; Fales Library and Special Collections, New York University; Gwent Record Office; Harry Ransom Center, University of Texas at Austin; HMCS (York Probate – Sub Registry); Houghton Library, Harvard University; Hull History Centre; University of Illinois at Urbana-Champaign (The Rare Book and Manuscript Library); Imperial War Museum; Institute of Directors; Mary Evans Picture Library; McMaster University (William Ready Division of Archives and Research Collections); Merthyr Tydfil Central Library; The National Archives, Kew; National Portrait Gallery, London; The National Trust (Records and Archives, Heelis, Swindon); Newport (Gwent) Museum and Art Gallery; Newport (Gwent) Reference Library; New South Wales State Library; the Palace of Westminster Collection; The Parliamentary Archives; University of Reading Special Collections Service; Schlesinger Library, Radcliffe Institute, Harvard University; Somerville College Library, University of Oxford (and the Principal and Fellows of Somerville College); Royal Commission on the Ancient and Historical Monuments of Wales; South Wales Miners' Library, Swansea University;

SPR Archives, Cambridge University Library; St Leonards School Archives; Surrey History Centre; University of Sussex; West Glamorgan Archives and the Women's Library, now the Women's Library @LSE.

Special mention must be made of Llyfrgell Genedlaethol Cymru/National Library of Wales for the unfailing helpfulness and friendliness of staff, from those who hauled heavy volumes of *Time and Tide* week after week, to individuals who provided all sorts of advice and expertise.

I have benefited from the opportunity to try out some of my ideas at the following: Ursula Masson annual memorial lecture, University of Glamorgan 2011; the House of Lords; the annual Women's History Network lecture at the Women's Library, London 2012; the Women's History Network Conference, Cardiff University; the PENfro Book Festival; Port Talbot Historical Society; 'The Aftermath of Suffrage', International Conference, Humanities Research Institute, University of Sheffield and the NAASWCH Conference, Bangor University.

Every effort has been made to contact copyholders. I thank the Society of Authors (on behalf of the Bernard Shaw Estate and as the Literary Representative of the Estate of Virginia Woolf), the Michael Ayrton Estate (Henry W. Nevinson and Evelyn Sharp Papers), the British Library (Phyllis Deakin recording), Hull City Council (Winifred Holtby), Independent Age, formerly RUKBA (Elizabeth Robins Papers). Quotations from published and unpublished Vera Brittain material are included by permission of Mark Bostridge and T.J. Brittain-Catlin, Literary Executors for the Estate of Vera Brittain 1970. The quotation from Glyn Jones is by permission of the copyright holder Literature Wales. The verse from John

Betjeman's poem 'Caprice' is reproduced by permission of John Murray (publishers).

I was fortunate to be given an Authors' Foundation grant by the Society of Authors which enabled me to carry out research at Harvard and New York Universities and, like many writers, have received excellent advice from this society. A Small Literary Commission Grant by the Welsh Books Council helped me to complete research within the UK.

I have benefited from the wisdom and expertise of my editor Francesca Rhydderch. Working with the Parthian team has been a delight and I thank all involved, especially Richard Davies.

ILLUSTRATIONS

Front cover: Margaret at her Desk by E.O. Hoppé (copyright c. 2012 Curatorial Assistance, Inc./E.O. Hoppé Estate Collection)
Back cover: Young Margaret reading.

18. Stonepitts, Kent
19. Helen Archdale (on left) at the *Time and Tide* office (Deirdre Macpherson)
20. A front page of *Time and Tide* in the first year (Llyfrgell Genedlaethol Cymru/National Library of Wales)
21. Margaret shakes hands with Alice Paul in 1925 (The Schlesinger Library, Radcliffe Institute, Harvard University)
22. Margaret with Winifred Holtby and George Bernard Shaw at the Malvern Festival 1935 (Hull History Centre, Hull City Council)
23. Churt Halewell, Surrey in the 1940s
24. The Drawing Room, Churt Halewell
25. Margaret in the garden at Churt Halewell
26. Theodora Bosanquet in 1930 (SPR Archives, Cambridge University Library)
27. Sidney George Strube plays on the popular Pear's soap advertisements 1 April 1922 in D.A. Thomas Papers, Scrapbook C8, p.73 (Llyfrgell Genedlaethol Cymru/National Library of Wales; Express Newspapers)
28. Alice Burton's painting of Viscountess Rhondda, now in the House of Lords (Copyright House of Lords WOA7177 http://www.parliament.uk/, with grateful thanks to the House of Lords)
29. The elderly Margaret on the steps of the *Time and Tide* office (7AMP/O/061, 1949, Women's Library @LSE)
30. The Llanwern Memorial to the Thomas/Rhondda family

Figure in text:
Page xx From the *Daily Herald* 28 April 1927 (Llyfrgell Genedlaethol Cymru/National Library of Wales; News International; Unite the Union).

The front and back cover images and all others are from private collections unless otherwise indicated.

LIST OF ABBREVIATIONS

BFUW	British Federation of University Women
CCWO	Consultative Committee of Women's Organisations
D.A.	David Alfred Thomas, Viscount Rhondda
EPRCC/ERGECC	Equal Political Rights Campaign Committee/Equal Rights General Election Campaign Committee
ILP	Independent Labour Party
NSD	National Service Department
NUSEC	National Union of Societies for Equal Citizenship
NWP	National Woman's Party
NUWSS	National Union of Women's Suffrage Societies
SPG	Six Point Group
SPR	Society for Psychical Research
WAAC/QMAAC	Women's Army Auxiliary Corps/Queen Mary's Army Auxiliary Corps
WIL	Women's Industrial League
WRAF	Women's Royal Air Force
WRNS	Women's Royal Naval Service
WSPU	Women's Social and Political Union

LADY RHONDDA'S LIFE

1883	Born in London
1887	Moves to Wales. Lives at Llanwern House, Monmouthshire
1899	To Boarding School in Scotland
1904	To Oxford University
1908	Marries Humphrey Mackworth
1909	Secretary of Newport, Monmouthshire's suffragette society (till 1914)
1913	Arrested and briefly imprisoned in Usk Gaol
1914	Becomes Lady Mackworth
1915	Survives the sinking of the *Lusitania*
1917	Women's National Service Department Commissioner for Wales
1918	Chief Controller of women's recruitment in Ministry of National Service
	On death of father becomes the second Viscountess Rhondda
	Founds Women's Industrial League
1919	By now Director of 33 companies
1920	Establishes *Time and Tide* in London
1921	Founds Six Point Group
	Publishes memoir of father
1922	Rhondda Peerage Claim is accepted then rejected
	Meets Winifred Holtby and Vera Brittain
1923	Divorces
1925	Moves to Stonepitts, Kent with Helen Archdale
1926	Becomes editor of *Time and Tide*

	Elected first female President of the Institute of Directors
	Chairs equal rights societies (from 1926-8)
1933	Publishes autobiography
1937	Moves to Churt Halewell, Surrey with Theodora Bosanquet
	Publishes book of essays
1943	President of Women's Press Club
1943-5	Writes *Time and Tide* pamphlets
1955	Receives honorary doctorate from the University of Wales
1958	Dies in London

INTRODUCTION

Looking for Lady Rhondda

Margaret Haig Thomas, who became the Second Viscountess Rhondda in 1918, was one of the movers and shakers of British society during the first half of the twentieth century. She is probably best remembered for having founded, funded and edited *Time and Tide,* an innovative, imaginative and adaptable weekly paper that dazzled readers with its cutting edge perspectives. From its start in 1920 until her death almost four decades later she was at its helm, helping to shape this mouthpiece for the intelligentsia. It described itself as 'the paper which is trying not merely to talk but to think'.[1]

Although never written exclusively by or for women, its pioneering all-female board and the serious attention it paid to women's rights gave newly enfranchised women in particular a voice and a confidence. When asked what inspired her feminism, the journalist Mary Stott explained that she 'ingested it from the *Manchester Guardian* and *Time and Tide*.[2] By the 1930s it had transmuted into a

13

Bloomsbury-based literary journal showcasing the emerging and leading writers of the day, including Sean O'Casey, Rebecca West, D.H. Lawrence and Rose Macaulay. After the publication of *The Years* in 1937, Virginia Woolf wrote of her relief – not only was her book praised by the *Times Literary Supplement* but also '*Time and Tide* says I'm a first rate novelist and a great lyrical poet'.[3] By 1945 the paper had reinvented itself once more as a leading political review.

For this vision and enterprise alone, overseeing what Anthony Lejeune has called 'this stupendous ocean of ink',[4] and refusing to toe official lines, Margaret deserves recognition. Yet her achievements did not start or end there. She had gained notoriety in pre-war Wales as a suffragette. She was the long-term secretary of the Newport branch of the militant Women's Social and Political Union (WSPU). In 1913 she was briefly imprisoned and went on hunger strike. She was not, however, the classic rebel woman reacting against a narrow Victorian upbringing. Although her eminently quotable autobiography tells how women's suffrage was 'the very salt of life' and came 'like a draught of fresh air into our padded, stifled lives',[5] in truth she had been much less stifled than most women.

Margaret's remarkable family included redoubtable figures on her mother's side: female Haig relatives who were already deeply committed to suffrage activism. Her father, the industrialist and Liberal politician David Alfred Thomas (known as D.A.) became internationally renowned as a highly successful and wealthy industrialist. He was Margaret's sounding board and she was devoted to him. She had been to university (briefly) and although her decision to marry Humphrey Mackworth, a local country squire, was a recipe for restlessness, she had greater latitude than many of her contemporaries and pursued a career in business.

The bond between Margaret and her father was cemented by the terrifying ordeal they endured in 1915 when they both survived – just – the sinking of the *Lusitania*. D.A.'s premature death three years later had huge repercussions. It meant that Margaret inherited his business empire, his title and responsibility for his natural children. The story of D.A.'s parallel family forms an important and intriguing part of his legacy and Margaret's life, yet until now it has been missing from historical accounts of both figures.

In contrast, Margaret's career as an industrialist was widely recognised at the time. In 1927 the *New York Tribune* called her 'the foremost woman of business in the British Empire'.[6] Inheriting her father's coalmining, shipping, newspaper and other interests made her a very wealthy woman. By 1919 she was sitting on 33 boards and chairing seven of them. She held more directorships than any other woman in the UK in the 1920s and in 1926 became the first and, to date only, female president of the Institute of Directors. The *Daily Herald* described her as one of the five most influential individuals in British 'Big Business'.[7] But she had to learn to operate in an overwhelmingly masculine environment that was wary of female entrepreneurs. And the timing was disastrous. Her father's fortunes had been made in heavy industry. The depression and long-term decline in the demand for coal posed new challenges.

Margaret had held weighty posts during the First World

War, first in Cardiff, then London, where she was chief controller of women's service within the Ministry of National Service. In 1921 she founded and chaired the Six Point Group (SPG), which sought to complement women's newly-won political emancipation with equal social and legal rights. Through this group she promoted equal rights in Europe. Her involvement in international feminist politics in the 1920s included publicly endorsing at home and abroad the views of the militant American National Woman's Party.

In the 1920s she was one of the leading figures in the battle for women under thirty to receive the vote. This important yet neglected final piece of the women's suffrage jigsaw receives due attention here. At the same time she became embroiled in a sustained and inventive battle for hereditary peeresses to take their seats in the House of Lords. Tenacious to the last, she persisted in her claim for forty years and was largely responsible for their belated victory.

To date much that has been written about Margaret Rhondda has understandably focused on her as an important equal rights figure in Britain. Dale Spender's volume of extracts from *Time and Tide* concentrates on the 1920s, telling the feminist part of the story of Margaret's paper.[8] The subtitle of American historian Shirley Eoff's valuable 1991 study of Margaret is *Equalitarian Feminist*. She explained that her intention was not to present a complete biography but 'to illuminate Lady Rhondda's struggle for equal rights and social justice in modern Britain'.[9] In her account, the spotlight is firmly trained on the twenties and thirties.

Catherine Clay's *British Women Writers 1914-1945*

(2006) examines networks of friendship enjoyed by women writers. Margaret and her paper are writ large here.[10] But we need also to consider Margaret's later years when she does not so easily fit the role of either feminist icon or non-party progressive. Her specific focus on women's rights had receded by the late 1940s and 1950s and her political outlook shifted to the right.

Clay does, however, help to redirect us to some of Margaret's significant friendships, most notably that with Winifred Holtby, who became *Tide and Tide's* youngest director and was an invaluable member of the writing staff until her tragically early death in 1935. In Holtby's most famous novel *South Riding* her headmistress heroine Sarah Burton has her senior girls read Lady Rhondda's autobiography *This Was My World* as their Easter holiday homework.[11] Holtby's life – and death – is important for understanding Margaret. Vera Brittain's name has long been associated with Holtby and she too played a significant part in Margaret's story but in a markedly different way.

George Bernard Shaw was another key figure in Margaret's life. She enjoyed socialising with him and they sustained a fond and frank correspondence. His *Time and Tide* articles were much appreciated. Margaret's many contributions to her paper included thoughtful critiques of Shaw's plays. Much less forgiving were her attacks on the writings of H.G. Wells, who could not be called a friend.

Margaret was divorced in 1923. She had moved from Wales to London and made a home in Kent. She lived first with Helen Archdale, who edited *Time and Tide* in its early days, then spent the last twenty-five years of her life in London and Surrey with Theodora Bosanquet. Theodora[12] became the paper's literary editor. She had been Henry James's amanuensis and this and her own writing have recently received attention. She knew James's biographer Leon Edel and features not only in his work but also, for example, in David Lodge's *Author, Author*.[13]

Margaret was the subject of a poem by her disgruntled employee the poet John Betjeman and appears in an unpublished play by Holtby. She features prominently in *Clash*, a novel about the General Strike of 1926 by the socialist politician Ellen Wilkinson.[14] The two women were good friends. Wilkinson's character is a wealthy but compassionate socialite. Margaret spent much of her life challenging the belief that being rich connoted idleness. She worked hard and spoke and wrote about the problems of 'The Leisured Woman', but her love of luxury and appetite for travel also undermined her assertions when so many were living in poverty.

A study of Margaret's long life needs to consider what Wales meant to her. She spent her formative years at Llanwern in south-east Wales and at Pen Ithon Hall (her mother's family home) in mid-Wales. Her father's and (subsequently) her own wealth came from the south Wales valleys. In later years she re-engaged with her Welsh roots, not least through an increased attention to questions of Welsh identity in the columns of *Time and Tide*.

Although Margaret's achievements were largely unsung in the second half of the twentieth century, there is now evidence of renewed interest in her life. In 2003-4 an online poll (with 41,223 nominations) to identify the top hundred Welsh heroes 'of all time' ranked her 66th.[15] The

list contained a mere ten women and was led b'
Zeta Jones at number thirteen. Margaret was
a groundbreaker and 'The Welsh Boadicea'.
historian Deirdre Beddoe has pronounced her 'without
doubt the most prominent Welsh woman of the twentieth
century'.[17]

When the Addidi Inspiration Award for Female
Entrepreneurs was launched for UK businesswomen in
2009, Margaret was selected as one of the five nominees.[18]
This wealth management group had decided to honour
female entrepreneurs from a time when 'it was not common
for women to be running businesses and creating wealth'.
Each nominee was championed by a modern successful
businesswoman. Margaret's was the online strategist Shaa
Wasmund, who applauded her business acumen and desire
to improve life for other women.

In line with my other biographies, Margaret's life story is
told here in a broadly chronological fashion but structured
so that individual chapters examine specific interests.
Some follow aspects of her public life. Others adopt a
more personal focus. To aid the reader, the main events
of her life are outlined on pp. 11-12.

The first three chapters examine Margaret's years in
Wales as a daughter, wife and suffragette. There follow
three chapters on her war work and dramatic experiences,
from the sinking of the *Lusitania* to a scandal concerning
the Women's Royal Air Force. The next two chapters show
how she reconstructed her life in London after the war in
personal and public terms following the death of her
father and the consequent responsibilities she secretly had
to shoulder.

Margaret was unusual in that she brought together the often divergent worlds of business and the arts. Chapter 9 follows her fortunes as a businesswoman, while Chapter 10 assesses the significance of the first two decades of *Time and Tide*. Chapter 11 looks at her woman-centred social world, considering both how she was viewed by others and her personal relationships, including her friendship with Holtby. Margaret's feminist politics at home and internationally are the focus of Chapter 12. An assessment of her writings follows in Chapter 13. Chapter 14 tells how she fought for a seat for women in the House of Lords. The last two decades of Margaret's life and the shifting political and financial fortunes of *Time and Tide* are explored in the final two chapters. They also consider the influence of Theodora Bosanquet and of the Second World War on Margaret and examine how she adjusted to the 1950s.

Biography can be deceptive. It supplies a rounded, composite figure, imposing a suspicious order and linear development on a life. It risks over-estimating the significance of an individual in her or his society. It is tempting to reduce the subject to hero or villain status, to provide worryingly neat solutions and so undervalue the protean nature of peoples' motives and actions.[19] The wish to empathise or to provide a definitive account can encourage generalisations and a rejection of descriptions that do not fit our dominant, invariably subjective images. It can suggest impossibly consistent lives. In practice we are all prone to be contradictory and fickle, presenting varying faces to different – and even the same – people in the present, let alone over a long period of time. Appreciating how others view 'our' subject means recognising a parallax: understanding that perspectives can shift, depending on audience, circumstances, experiences and personal predilections.

Statements that might at first appear contradictory can, however, be usefully reconciled rather than refuted. They can help to reveal aspects of the multiple identities individuals both construct and have constructed for them. Even basic descriptions of physical appearance can vary enormously. In 1922 the American press described Margaret as 'a rather magnificently big and sturdy looking woman'.[20] The explorer Freya Stark remembered first meeting her at lunch with the archaeologist Gertrude Caton-Thompson in 1936. Stark saw her as 'a powerful person with a really beautiful face, with kind and amused mouth and strong broad forehead and square hands – all square and small and strong she is'.[21] The journalist Malcolm Muggeridge, who contributed to *Time and Tide*, recalled Margaret as 'plump and curly'.[22] Such apparently contradictory comments are revealing about time and the person who made them, but memory, gender, culture, environment, potential readers and even fashions in hairstyle (Margaret had her hair shingled) also helped to influence and inflect such perceptions.

This biography includes a number of visual representations of Margaret. These photographs and paintings suggest change over time and her catholicity of interests. We can track the young schoolgirl at St Leonards, watch her engage in street politics as a suffragette in 1913 and contrast this with Solomon J. Solomon's portrait of the elegant young lady. We see Margaret turn into the reflective businesswoman-cum-journalist in Hoppé's photograph. The international campaigner is captured as she meets the

American Alice Paul in London with other members of the International Advisory Committee of the National Woman's Party in 1925. A formal portrait painted by Alice Burton six years later reveals a dignified woman, carefully dressed and displaying the turquoise-and-diamond brooch, set in gold, that her mother had given her. Margaret still wears her wedding ring here (and would continue to do so) although she had been divorced for almost a decade.

But just as representative, albeit less stately, is an informal snap of Margaret in the garden of her Surrey home, Churt Halewell. Here she is casually dressed in corduroy trousers and a cashmere sweater bought for her by cousins after she had treated them to a skiing holiday. An image of an older, somewhat weary-looking Margaret standing on the steps of the Bloomsbury offices of *Time and Tide* reminds us of her final years. After decades of propping up her paper, the money began to run out, the venture to which she had dedicated much of her life was threatened and her health gave way.

The various names Margaret used are indicative of the different roles she played. Young Margaret Haig Thomas was known to her cousins as Daisy (Marguerite) but to the villagers of Llanwern she was 'Her Young Ladyship'. When she married she became Mrs Mackworth and then Lady Mackworth but these marks of her marriage were left behind in 1918 when she inherited her father's title and became the second Viscountess Rhondda. Too often in pictures and print she was (and remains) confused with her mother Sybil Margaret, the Dowager Viscountess. Formal communications were signed 'Rhondda' but MR or Margaret was how she ended letters to her friends.

Letters form an important part of this biography,

whether correspondence with Holtby or those in which *Time and Tide* contributors such as Brittain and St John Ervine discuss Margaret. Then there are sensitive family letters, including Margaret's correspondence with D.A.'s mistress and children and some heartrending personal letters to Helen Archdale. Inevitably there are also some tantalising gaps. For example, Humphrey Mackworth remains a shadowy figure due to a lack of written material. We may speculate but there is no reliable explanation as to why Margaret and Humphrey did not have children. Mere scraps of evidence alert us to what he might have felt about his wife's activities and there is no record of how he reacted to her *Lusitania* ordeal.

D.A.'s papers in the National Library of Wales contain two large scrapbooks of press cuttings about Margaret. Although she left no diary,[23] two volumes written in the thirties by her mother Sybil have been discovered recently. Valuable perspectives can also be gleaned from the diaries of the former actress and suffragette Elizabeth Robins, a founder member of the board of *Time and Tide* and of the SPG. Theodora also kept a diary and we can glimpse the last fifteen years of Margaret's life refracted through her entries.[24]

Time and Tide itself has been central to this project. Margaret wrote hundreds of articles, many for her paper, and several books. Her autobiography, published as early as 1933, has been used by historians and literary critics. But it is a misleading, albeit fascinating, source, as significant for what it conceals as for what it discloses about her past, let alone her present. Other 'ego documents' survive, such as an unpublished autobiography by Helen Archdale as well as specialist collections that throw light on Margaret's war work, business dealings, radio broadcasts and much more. Oral testimony has been especially helpful, particularly that of Margaret's god-daughter and relative Frankie Webber who also worked for *Time and Tide*.

Biography may pose some problems but when such rich sources are considered, its potential far outweighs them. Indeed, the biographer occupies a crucial vantage point, since only with time and distance can the broad patterns of a life be effectively traced. Biography is also increasingly appreciated for what Barbara Caine has recently described as 'the capacity of an individual life to reflect broad historical change'.[25] Exploring the life of a pivotal twentieth-century figure such as Lady Rhondda can make this possible.

CHAPTER ONE

Margaret Haig Thomas

In a quiet country lane on the edge of the little Welsh village of Llanwern in Gwent, there is a church dedicated to St. Mary. A tall memorial stone with a pedestal is prominent in the churchyard. It commemorates the lives of three people. The first is David Alfred Thomas, Viscount Rhondda of Llanwern (1856-1918), privy councillor, MP for 22 years, president of the Local Government Board and Food Controller in the Great War. 'He counted not his life dear unto Himself' is his epitaph. 'Blessed are the pure in heart' are the words chosen for his wife Sybil Margaret (née Haig, 1857-1941).

The ashes of their only child, Margaret, are also buried here. She is described as 'Proprietor and Editor of Time and Tide for 31 years' and a simple 'Rest in Peace' follows. It *is* a peaceful setting, although from the 1960s the Spencer Works, Britain's first wholly oxygen-blown integrated steelworks, would dominate the landscape. Yet this was an appropriate legacy for a family whose wealth had been based on heavy industry.

Across the fields from the church stood Llanwern House. Here the Thomas family lived from the end of 1887. Although Margaret claimed that it was built in William and Mary's reign, later stating that it was a Queen Anne building, it was probably constructed in or soon after 1760 on the site of an older house.[1] Demolished in the early 1950s, the three-storey building enjoyed a commanding position on a hilltop about 200 feet above sea level and overlooking what is known as the Caldicot Levels. On a clear day it was possible to look across the Channel to Clifton Suspension Bridge.

Llanwern Park's two hundred acres of rolling land were covered with elm, beech and lime trees. There was an Italian sunken garden, lily pond, fan garden and underground ice house as well as a large walled kitchen garden. The rectangular, slightly austere, pale red-brick house with a stone parapet was at the end of a long winding drive and seemed less attractive than the landscape. The lack of ornamentation gave it a somewhat utilitarian appearance and it was readily dismissed by one French governess as '[more] like a factory than a house'.[2] Yet one side boasted a vast flowering magnolia, reputed to be the tallest in Britain. A gardener travelled from Kew Gardens just to prune it. Large elms helped to screen the building from view. It faced west and when the setting sun was reflected in its many windows the house looked as though it were on fire.

It was just a few miles from Caerleon and Newport and convenient for D.A. Thomas – D.A. – to travel by train to his office in Cardiff. And although the London train was not scheduled to stop at Llanwern station, it did so for the Thomas family. At first Llanwern Park was rented but D.A. purchased it in 1903 and the interior of the house was restored to its former splendour by Oswald Milne, assistant to the great architect Lutyens.[3] It had large, somewhat formal rooms with elaborate plasterwork and a few Chinese features.[4] Llanwern is close to Magor where D.A.'s grandfather had been a yeoman farmer before moving to work in the Merthyr pits. Llanwern (the church in the alders or, less romantically, the church on swampy land) was where Margaret grew up.

Both of her parents had a huge influence on her as a child and adult. D.A.'s decision to involve his daughter in his business empire and to hand his title to her says a lot about him, though this was not as straightforward as the historical record suggests. Margaret's book about her father exceeded three hundred pages and was slightly longer than her own autobiography. The latter appeared when she was fifty but reads as the account of a dutiful daughter. At the same time the contrast between her opportunities and those of her mother speaks volumes about the changes in early twentieth-century British society.

The life of Margaret's mother, known as Mrs D.A. Thomas (later Dowager Viscountess Rhondda) seems, like her mode of address and the experiences of many Victorian women, to have been primarily defined through others. When she died in March 1941, *The Times* obituary said little about her. Practically all the information was about whose widow she was and who her daughter Margaret had become. It was also pointed out that she was a member of an ancient Scottish Border family with an impressive lineage: the Haigs of Bemersyde in Berwickshire. The distinguished soldier and founder of the British Legion, Earl Haig, was a cousin. Sybil boasted seventy-two first cousins.

Here was an impressive extended family with a very long history proudly traced back to Petrus De Haga of the twelfth century. Its members knew – and still know and celebrate – their third and fourth cousins and have not infrequently married them. Haigs put family connections first. An acquaintance described the clannish family as 'a regular maelstrom... if you entered into friendly relations with them you had to become a Haig'.[5] Margaret described her Haig relatives as the 'endlessly ramified cousins'.[6] They were all part of the Haig 'cousinage'. They would come 'in shoals'[7] to stay at Llanwern – Sybil's diary in the mid-1930s records cousins young and old – and throughout her life Margaret retained a loyalty to them.

Sybil had been born in Brighton on 25 February 1857,[8] the fourth daughter in a family of ten children that, like the offspring of Lady Charlotte Guest (who also married a wealthy Welsh industrialist) divided neatly into five boys and five girls.[9] Her father George Augustus Haig had been born and raised in Dublin. The son of a distiller, he became a successful agent in England for the sale of Scotch and Irish spirits and then set up his own business as a wine merchant in London, where he also owned property.

In 1858 he purchased 2,548 acres of land with eleven farms near the village of Llanbadarn Fynydd, between Llandrindod Wells and Newtown. Here, on gently sloping land in this beautiful hill country, he designed and had built in 1862, Pen Ithon Hall, named after the River

Ithon. This two-storeyed house followed the Irish practice of having a central hall from which the main rooms radiated and, like his family home Roebuck, a front entrance with Doric columns in the Irish Georgian style.

George Augustus Haig became High Sheriff for the county as well as a magistrate. He stood (unsuccessfully) in several elections as a parliamentary candidate. Margaret's grandmother Anne Eliza (née Anne Elizabeth Fell) was, she felt, gentle, humorous and rather more tolerant than her grandfather. She died when Margaret was eleven. The pretty lych-gate in the churchyard at the local church is dedicated to her memory. George Augustus Haig, who boasted luxuriant mutton-chop whiskers, lived on until 1906.

The daughters were artistic. Like her eldest sister Janet, Sybil painted miniatures and later exhibited some of her work in London galleries. One of her brothers, Alexander W. Haig, was a student at Cambridge in the late 1870s and friendly with two Welsh brothers, John Howard (Jack) and the younger David Alfred Thomas. Jack had visited Pen Ithon where he had met Rose Helen, Sybil's elder sister. They became engaged and in the summer of 1880 Rose and Sybil, accompanied by Mrs Haig, visited Jack's home, a stuccoed mansion called Ysgyborwen, outside Aberdare in Glamorgan. This was how Margaret's parents met. Despite old Mr Haig's reservations about D.A.'s credentials, he and Sybil were engaged in July 1881. D.A. was christened. On 27 June 1882 they were married by special licence in Pen Ithon's billiard room.

D.A. had been born at Ysguborwen on 26 March 1856. His was an even larger family than his wife's. He was the fifteenth of seventeen children born to Samuel Thomas and his second wife Rachel when she was eighteen and he was forty. Tragically only five of their children survived infancy (Samuel's first wife and their child had also died young). As with her account of her Haig grandparents, Margaret's depiction of the Thomas household plays on the contrast between husband and wife. She stresses her paternal grandmother's sociability and generosity in contrast to her older, somewhat taciturn and stern husband. She tells how he once burned a new fur coat on which she had lavished sixty pounds – a huge expense in the late nineteenth century – without his permission.

According to Margaret, she then spent a further sixty pounds on another coat and said she would go on buying if need be. Samuel Thomas let her keep this coat.

Margaret was keen to paint a picture of a self-made man, a devoted nonconformist and strict disciplinarian. It helped to form a contrast to the idyllic life she sought to convey when describing her own upbringing as the sole child of loving parents. She nevertheless conceded that D.A. was proud of his father and was his favourite child. He followed in his footsteps. Samuel is reputed to have muttered on the day D.A. was born, 'I see nothing for him but the workhouse'. Although highly conscious of the precariousness of building a fortune and reputation – Samuel was close to bankruptcy at the time of his son's birth – he prospered. Originally a grocer in Merthyr Tydfil, he became a very successful mining entrepreneur and laid the basis for his granddaughter's riches. Yet Sybil was seen as marrying beneath her. Ignoring the fact that it was D.A. who gave his wife her title, when interviewed an elderly former inhabitant of Llanwern village explained that: 'Lady Rhondda was *Lady* Rhondda and the man she married was just D.A. Thomas'.

Margaret's autobiography is somewhat dismissive of Rachel Thomas's achievements. She conceded that her grandmother possessed 'a good deal of artistic instinct' but added that 'she did not make very much impression upon me'. She portrayed her as charming but rather inconsequential and 'though quite shrewd in her way, quite unintellectual... She was a kind and a nice woman, but never probably a very interesting one'.[10]

Yet this description is at odds with other evidence: Rachel Thomas was highly regarded in Welsh literary circles. She was a member of the Gorsedd[11] and her bardic name was Rahil Morganwg. She was active in the prestigious Honourable Society of Cymmrodorion and knowledgeable about genealogy. She was described in the press as the natural successor to Lady Llanover, the renowned patron and promoter of Welsh cultural life.[12] Widowed young, she then divided her time between Wales and England. She lived at the magnificent Blunsdon Abbey near Swindon with her daughter (Margaret's cousin Louisa Mary) and spent the London season at their house off Park Lane. When she died in her seventy-third year in 1896, three special trains were laid on from Cardiff (via Pontypridd), Llwynypia and Merthyr to bring people to the public funeral in Aberdare. In his account of D.A.'s election as Merthyr's MP in 1888, the former Liberal MP Llewelyn Williams suggested that her popularity in the constituency helped to ensure D.A.'s selection as a candidate.[13] Admittedly, Margaret was only twelve when Rachel Thomas died, but her portrayal is nonetheless skewed. It may reflect her desire to emphasise her father's independent achievements, but it suggests too a lack of interest in Welsh-language culture.

At first Dai, as her father was then called, spoke only Welsh at home. A nurse from England taught him English. When he was nine he was sent to school at Manila Hall, Clifton. He spent a year abroad before reading mathematics at Cambridge University where his chief occupation seems to have been sports. Yet, unlike many of his fellow entrepreneurs, he was and remained fascinated by ideas and books throughout his life. It is interesting, though, in the light of his daughter's truncated time at university, to see that although he initially won a scholarship to Jesus College, it was later taken from him because he did no work. However, he was suffering from ill-health and so took what today we would call a 'gap year', travelling abroad. A second scholarship was awarded at Gonville and Caius College. David Evans's hagiographical memoir claims that D.A. was 'one of the most promising mathematical scholars who ever left that great seat of learning'.[14] But he was awarded only a second class degree, of which he was ashamed.

D.A. started reading for the Bar, but once his father died in 1879 he turned his attention from the legal profession to the family business. He had inherited a personal fortune of £75,000, Ysguborwen Colliery and a share in the Cambrian Collieries. These Rhondda collieries were run by the firm Thomas, Riches & Co (J.O. Riches and O.H. Riches had been Samuel Thomas's partners).

A new deed of partnership was drawn up. D.A. and his elder brother Jack (always the more conservative of the two and now married to Sybil's sister) agreed to manage the collieries with the Riches brothers. D.A.

worked in the sales department and then literally learned his trade at the coalface at Clydach Vale. Margaret's account of her father's life, which includes extracts from his letters, emphasises that he was more ambitious and ready for change than his three partners. After marrying Sybil in June 1882 and living for six months in Cardiff, they left Wales for London. According to Margaret, D.A. spent much of his time reading at the British Museum before embarking on a new career in a stockbroker's office.

In December 1882 D.A. and Sybil rented a property at 76 Prince's Square, Bayswater in west London. It was here at a tall stuccoed house that Margaret was born on 12 June 1883. She later wrote: 'My father was disappointed: he wanted a boy'. D.A. was to remain disappointed in that Margaret was their only child. Yet he delighted in his fair-haired, blue-eyed daughter. In many respects he was enlightened and liberal. Later he and the young Margaret would discuss books and ideas together. They spent Sundays walking in the Brecon Beacons or climbing the Sugar Loaf Mountain near Abergavenny (owned by the family). D.A. paid Margaret the compliment of declaring that they were 'not like father and daughter; we are butties' (a term that in Wales suggests both friend and work mate and also the timber props used at the coalface).[15] Nevertheless, it would be Sybil who would suggest that their daughter enter the business.

Two months after Margaret's birth the family moved to Kent. They rented Ovenden House (she misspelled it as Ovendon in her autobiography). It was the former dower-house of Lady Stanhope, on an old estate in Sundridge near Sevenoaks. Margaret spent her early years there and in the 1920s would live in the area again. Her father took up bee-keeping and commuted to the City. As a partner in a private firm he could not join the London Stock Exchange. His attempt to persuade his partners to change this by making the firm a limited company was rejected by them. But the death of O.H. Riches in 1887 altered the situation. That December the family returned to Wales. D.A. took over as manager of the sales agency of the Cambrian Collieries and they moved to Llanwern.

Llanwern House was a somewhat formal home with large rooms. It had eight bedrooms on the first floor and a further four on the second. The most striking room was the oblong saloon with a beautiful rococo-style plaster ceiling. Oak panelling in the dining room and other rooms made it seem quite dark. Margaret did not see it as a comfortable place. It seemed to reflect something of the slightly austere character of Sybil. 'Spartan' is the word that Margaret often used to describe her mother.

Yet she was at pains to stress that she grew up in a happy home where up to twenty guests could be accommodated easily, cared for by a resident cook and a number of domestics. The family took its responsibilities seriously and Margaret was used to entertaining from a young age. For example, in the summer of 1895 when she was twelve, members of the Loyal Cambrian Lodge of Freemasons came from Merthyr by special train 'with their lady friends' to Llanwern. D.A. was the Worshipful Master. After a formal reception Margaret helped to serve the picnic that preceded games of cricket, tennis and bowls.[16]

She was taught by European governesses (French then German) and taken to church by her mother on Sundays. One way of entertaining herself was to make up stories when she went to bed. Margaret would use her imaginative powers in this way for many a year, only breaking the habit 'with a big effort' in her mid-thirties.[17]

In contrast to the adult world of Llanwern, the six weeks of summer holidays spent at Pen Ithon were portrayed in Margaret's autobiography as a passport to freedom and an opportunity to have company of her own age. To be an only child must have been especially disappointing in an era when large families were the norm. Although family size was declining, the average was still six living children when Margaret was small. She longed to have a large family of her own. Cousins were an important substitute for siblings and it is perhaps no coincidence that Margaret's autobiography opens not with an account of her own home but with a glimpse of Pen Ithon in the heart of the Radnorshire countryside. Here she revelled in playing outdoors with her cousins, roaming the hills and moors on pony and by foot. Although one of Sybil's brothers had died in his teens, the others survived and they and their children descended on Pen Ithon for their holidays.[18]

Here too were beloved and unconventional aunts. The senior aunt was the beautiful Janetta (Janet Boyd) widow of a deputy Lord Lieutenant of County Durham. Aunt Janetta, like George Bernard Shaw, advocated Jaeger garments. She dressed in white and dried her handkerchiefs on window-panes to save ironing. She took the young ones on walks collecting toadstools which, she maintained, were as edible as mushrooms. When they appeared on the dinner table 'the children whooped for joy, but the other mothers sat in the deepest anxiety'.[19] They were gobbled up but nobody appeared to suffer.

Janetta was a talented miniaturist and exhibited annually at the Royal Academy and in Paris. She later became an ardent Theosophist. When a cousin died she sent a funeral wreath with a card saying 'Heartiest congratulations'. Margaret's favourite aunt, also her god-mother, was, however, Aunt Lottie[20] (Charlotte) Sybil's unmarried sister who, along with many women of her day, sacrificed her desire for a profession to stay at home and look after her widowed father. Aunt Lottie enjoyed long hikes and was adored by the nieces and nephews who spent their summers at Pen Ithon. D.A. had the Thatched Cottage in Llanwern built for her. This four-roomed house was also designed by Oswald Milne and enabled Lottie to be close to her relatives in her later years. She wrote 'No Vote, No Census' on her 1911 census form.

Margaret had fourteen Haig first cousins. They featured much more prominently in her life than did her first cousins on her father's side. With the exception of Peter Haig-Thomas, who was a double cousin so also part of the Pen Ithon clan, the seven children of D.A.'s sister Jemima are conspicuous by their absence from her autobiography, as is Eira, daughter of his brother Samuel.

Another change of scenery would occur at election time when the family decamped to Ysguborwen. Not content with being a businessman, much of D.A.'s career was spent in pursuing politics.[21] Neither father nor daughter could be accused of narrow, single-minded business interests. In the autumn of 1887 he had been asked to stand for Merthyr Boroughs as the Liberal candidate in a by-election. He was returned unopposed and remained one of its two MPs until 1910, heading the poll in contested elections in 1892 (when Wales's most populous

constituency returned him with a record 11,948
majority), in 1895 and 1900. In 1906 he received over
three and a half thousand more votes than his fellow MP,
the founder of the Independent Labour Party (ILP), Keir
Hardie. D.A.'s family home was in the centre of his
constituency.

During the 1892 election Margaret did daily lessons
with her governess at Ysguborwen then, in time-honoured
fashion, was used in winning electoral support. She was
taught a sentence of Welsh which meant 'Please vote for
Father, everybody' and had to utter this at the many
nightly meetings. D.A. was renowned for being an
uninspiring speaker. Elizabeth Phillips put it nicely in her
history of pioneers of the Welsh coalfield: 'he had not the
gift of facile oratory'.[22] Even his biographer, Rev. Vyrnwy
Morgan, generally extravagant in his praise for D.A.,
admitted this weakness. He explained that D.A. never
brought a good speaker with him when addressing
electors. Allowing Alfred Thomas MP (later Lord
Pontypridd) to talk first was a deliberate foil since D.A.
knew that audiences would be even more bored by the
opening speaker and that in comparison he would fare
better.[23] D.A. tended to repeat his speeches in each
location and read them out. So his little daughter's
intervention perhaps helped to provide some
entertainment.

D.A. now had Parliamentary business to attend. The
family had a London flat at 122 Ashley Gardens, Victoria
and from the age of thirteen the young Margaret Thomas
– for that is how she was known at this time – attended
Notting Hill and Bayswater High School, run by the Girls'
Public Day School Trust. It had opened in Norland Square

in 1873 as the second of these important schools designed to give girls a good academic education. Margaret's headmistress was Harriet Morant Jones. Starting with ten pupils, there were 400 by 1900, a number of whom won university places.

Notting Hill High had been D.A.'s idea but, perhaps due to her wish to board, Margaret persuaded her parents to let her go much further away, to St Leonards School for Girls in the medieval coastal town of St Andrews, Fife. She started there in the autumn of 1899 when she was sixteen and stayed until Easter 1902. The brainchild of the Ladies' Educational Association, St Leonards had been founded in 1877 and was initially known as St Andrews School for Girls. Three of its first six mistresses were Girtonians. Its first two headmistresses, Louisa Lumsden and Frances Dove, were both made Dames. Experience of the strict regime at another academic boarding school, Cheltenham Ladies' College, where both women had taught, had convinced these pioneers that 'freedom and responsibility' mattered as much as study.[24] There were no petty rules. Margaret's headmistress was a former St Leonards pupil, Julia Grant.

Underpinning the school was a belief that girls should have as good as, if not a better, education than their brothers. It was the first school in the world to play women's lacrosse (each house had a team), and staff encouraged a competitive spirit in sport and study, though as Margaret's housemistress stressed, this was directed at the honour of the school and house rather than personal glory.[25] Margaret was not sporty, but the ethos was that girls could and should excel in whatever they undertook. It provided a challenging academic education that included Latin, modern languages and science. There was a debating society and girls enjoyed walks along the cliffs. Writing about the women of her time Janet Courtney asked 'Did any other girl's [sic] school in the 'nineties leave its pupils so free that they could wander at will like this?'[26]

Whereas Margaret's years at Notting Hill High are dismissed in a few sentences of her autobiography, three and a half chapters are devoted to the few years she spent at St Leonards. This is described in glowing terms. The fact that the school had, by the time of writing, acquired quite a reputation for attracting girls who later became very successful, may have influenced this retrospective account. Catherine Marshall, a Liberal who became a key figure in suffragist and Labour politics, was at St Leonards with Margaret, though she was three years younger than her. The eminent Cambridge historian Ellen McArthur and the pioneer doctor Louisa Garrett Anderson, also suffrage activists, had been pupils before Margaret's time. Mona Chalmers Watson (née Geddes) who worked with Margaret in the First World War then chaired the board of *Time and Tide*, was also a former pupil, as was Helen Archdale.

Margaret's autobiography grew out of an attempt to record her gratitude to her former housemistress Miss J.C.E. Sandys when the old lady was elderly and seriously ill. She died three years before the book appeared. One chapter is devoted to her. Presenting a striking, stylish figure who also managed to be kind and generous, Margaret suggested that she was adored by her charges and that they never felt patronised by her. At a time when many educationalists were sticklers for authority, Julia

Sandys appears as a remarkable figure. She arrived at St Leonards for a temporary post and stayed for twenty-two years, first as a housemistress at Bishopshall East and then from 1896 as founding housemistress of St Rule East. Her recognition of the need for her charges to express individuality did not always endear 'the Sandys' to other members of staff and thus ensured unstinting loyalty from those in her house.[27] The House system was similar to boys' boarding schools and each house had its own colours, traditions and loyalties. Houses also entertained the whole school with plays. Margaret acted in 'Alice in Wonderland' for her house, playing the part of the Duchess.

Margaret was by no means alone in stressing the value of a role model at her girls' school. The writer and suffragette Evelyn Sharp, for example, saw her head-mistress in London as a vital inspiration.[28] Margaret found a lifelong friend in Edith Mary Pridden, nicknamed Prid. She was eight months younger than Margaret and the daughter of the head of a preparatory school in Surrey. The two girls began at St Leonards at the same time. They walked round the school playground in the early evenings in their hooded cloaks, earnestly discussing Renaissance and Reformation Europe, literature and politics. Prid, who was head of house in her last year, became a teacher and from 1922 to 1944 was a St Leonards housemistress at Bishopshall West. Another friend – for life – was the extravagantly named Beatrice Hestritha Gundreda Heyworth (known as Gundreda), from a military family living in Suffolk. She hailed, however, from Risca in Monmouthshire.

Recollecting her happy time in Scotland, Margaret

called it 'that very perfect present'.[29] She was not an outstanding pupil academically and one former pupil had a somewhat negative recollection of her as 'very silent and rather vague'.[30] Her best subject was French, which she had studied at home for many years. Her appreciation of St Leonards was primarily for the way it took girls seriously, teaching and allowing them to think for themselves, though it is interesting to note that in the early 1920s at least, she was critical of the school's failure to encourage girls to enter the professions.[31] The former pupil and later lawyer and educationalist, Betty Archdale, recalled that on their visits to St Leonards to see her, her mother Helen and Margaret 'always made nuisances of themselves' and 'would speak out about the school, suggesting it should be pushing the girls more'.[32]

Nevertheless Margaret returned to St Leonards to speak at several alumnae events and to visit Prid. She was appreciative of the way that she 'had learnt a freedom of initiative' and 'a freedom of mental development'. At a time when women lacked the vote and many basic rights, Margaret's home and schooling had, in contrast to the later experiences of many girls from a similar background, been considerably more progressive than the society she now entered.

On leaving school Margaret became a debutante. Her mother had also 'Come Out' when she was Margaret's age. Sybil Thomas was imbued with a strong sense of duty and appropriate behaviour so became convinced that this was the correct step for her daughter. The saloon at Llanwern was the venue for a number of balls. But, as Margaret put it, 'One might as well have tried to put a carthorse into a drawing-room as turn me into a young lady at home'.[33] For three long months from May to July for three years, she endured the London season. Her afternoons involved polite tea parties. Evenings were taken over by dances interspersed by occasional At Homes. At all of these events she was chaperoned by Sybil.

Although photographs suggest a poised young lady, Margaret was by her own admission awkward, plump and excruciatingly shy. She found the whole experience painful and pointless. She would have been happy to discuss political ideas or literature but had no appetite for small talk and quickly became 'an inarticulate lump of diffidence'.[34] The only time that balls were bearable was when cousins appeared: 'Cousins were people one could talk to. Cousins were people one really liked'.[35]

Writing about the experience thirty years later, Margaret roundly condemned this archaic method of securing suitable marriage partners, though conceded that at the time she enjoyed the finery and had not actually rebelled against the social round that she found so uninspiring. Depicting the world of the debutante as a form of imprisonment she now denounced

> The falsity and unreality of all its values, the cheapness and vulgarity of its standards and indeed of the whole atmosphere that pervades it, the stupidity of the conversation of its inmates are such it seems to me as no sane person should be asked to endure.[36]

She even felt that it was partly responsible for a discernible decline in western civilisation. In 1932 E.M.

Delafield's novel *Thank Heaven Fasting* exposed the absurdity of the system's single-minded pursuit of a husband. Drenched in irony, it was dedicated to Margaret 'for it has sprung out of many conversations that we have held together'.[37]

Yet unlike most young debutantes Margaret then read History at Somerville College, Oxford. She chose to do this and was well prepared for higher education. The founder of St Leonards, Louisa Lumsden, had been a pioneer student at Emily Davies's College for Women established in 1869 at Hitchin, the basis for what became Girton College, Cambridge. For Lumsden it had been a liberating experience. Like Margaret, she had been '[s]ick to the soul' of balls and croquet and an empty life. Now she worked, read and 'learned the worth of friendship'.[38] For many young women fortunate enough to attend one of the new colleges, university also meant a realisation of ambition and comradeship.

Not so for Margaret, who declared 'Somerville was certainly not my spiritual home'.[39] *This Was My World* skirts over her time there. Her account says nothing about academic study or even what subjects she was studying (Responsions, the preliminary examinations in basic Latin, Ancient Greek and Mathematics). Her reports do not suggest that she had any difficulty intellectually. She was described as '[i]nteresting and thoughtful' at the end of her first term in 1904. Her essays were 'always pleasant to read and she shows considerable ability. Very promising'. The report for the next term noted that she was 'original and independent in thought'. It also described her writing and spelling as somewhat original. She was untidy and, in contrast to her later years, 'not perhaps a remarkably hard worker'. Nevertheless Margaret was judged once more to be 'very promising' with 'real intellectual power and a vivid imagination'. Yet at Easter 1905 after only two terms at Oxford University, she abandoned her studies. The college Register simply states that she left 'to live at home'. At this point her love affair with the man she would marry prevailed.

Had she gone straight from school to university, perhaps her reactions would have been different but, unlike those seduced by the beauty and buildings of Oxford, Margaret focused on the limitations of her college: 'Somerville smelt frousty to me'. She suggests that she had, by the age of twenty-one, outgrown the girls' boarding school atmosphere, particularly since neither her boarding school nor home had been stifling. Margaret had been given her own car – a rare and very privileged symbol of freedom – and was long used to discussing politics and business with her father. Female students at Oxford did not enjoy equal status with men (they sat examinations but were denied degrees) though the woman who would become so passionate about equal rights was, at this point, unconcerned about such matters. 'Dowdy' is the word that best summarises Margaret's view of the dons and students she encountered.

Winifred Knox (later Lady Peck) was a History student at Lady Margaret Hall and had also been at St Leonards – 'that windswept corner of Fife' – with Margaret. She recalled Margaret asking her 'if I liked going on with "this schoolgirl business"'.[40] The former debutante, accustomed to wealth and privilege, could not bear 'the cloisterishness of the place' and was irritated by the air of forced brightness and virtue that hung about the cocoa-cum-missionary-party-hymn-singing girls, and still more the self-conscious would-be naughtiness of those who reacted from this into smoking cigarettes and feeling really wicked.[41]

In March 1914, young Vera Brittain, who later knew Margaret well, also found her first encounter with Somerville College somewhat off-putting. Sitting the Somerville Scholarship paper, she noticed 'the dowdiness of dinner frocks, and shuddered to see the homely food and piles of emptied soup-plates in the hatches'.[42] Women's colleges were poor relations compared to the well-endowed and long-established men's colleges. Brittain's first few weeks as a student proved, however, to be a revelation: 'I had never known anything so consistently stimulating as that urgent, hectic atmosphere'.[43]

No such sense of exhilaration accompanied Margaret's reminiscences of Somerville even though she was there when its principal was Agnes Maitland who, it was said, 'quite frankly wanted Somerville to inherit the earth'[44]. Maitland was transforming the college, and was responsible for the development of its library. Margaret acknowledged how much she enjoyed John Stuart Mill's work[45] yet she made no reference to the fact that the Somerville Library contained 2,000 of his own volumes. She did, however, admire Miss Maitland and her tutor Miss Beatrice Lees. And she would presumably have known, in advance of going up to Somerville, the vice-principal. She was the Hon. Alice Moore Bruce, daughter of the former Home Secretary Lord Aberdare (H.A. Bruce) and Senior Trustee of the Dowlais Iron Company. He had been, like D.A., Liberal MP for Merthyr Tydfil and her mother was a campaigner for secondary and higher education for women.

Nevertheless, Margaret would support her former college financially in years to come and she became treasurer to the Oxford Women's Colleges' Fund, which sought through fundraising to raise endowments for the women's colleges between 1921 and 1925.[46] In 1924 she was invited to participate in a debate held by the Oxford Women's Debating Society at Lady Margaret Hall. She opposed the contention that 'the academic woman is a mistake'.[47] Margaret also became a patron of the fund established by the British Federation of University Women (BFUW) to develop Crosby Hall, Chelsea as an international residential hostel for graduate women in London.

When she addressed a conference held by the International Federation of University Women in Norway she discussed the issue of whether it was preferable for business women to be university trained. She suggested that it was desirable for the majority of those with positions of responsibility in the higher branches of industry and commerce – hardly surprising given her audience – but she did stress that 'I should *not* like to see a university training regarded as a sine qua non (or anything approaching it) in business'.[48] She conceded, though, that it was wise to get a university training if possible because of the broad view of life it could provide. A trained mind should aid balanced and unbiased judgement and give confidence, something especially important for women.

Margaret's choice of words is interesting: it was a 'university training', not a university degree that supplies these qualities. As for a degree, she emphasised that there was the danger of it being looked upon as a substitute for brains 'which it is not'. She pointed out that 'the average university professor mistrusts, dislikes and despises' those in business.

Margaret's decision to leave Oxford ensured some ambivalence about the value of graduates. In a letter to Winifred Holtby in 1933 she told her that she was '[s]o glad you've got a secretary & that she's non-university!!!'[49] Brittain, who was active in Margaret's Six Point Group and wrote for *Time and Tide* in the 1920s, later disparaged Margaret's dismissal of Oxford, stressing that she left no bequest to the women's colleges. However, Margaret spent time fund-raising for them. She also became a governor of the London School of Economics and was the first woman president of the forerunner of Cardiff University (to which she left a bequest).[50] Today Somerville College displays a portrait of Margaret.

When Brittain first went to university much of her energy was spent worrying about her beloved Roland who went to the Front on 31 March 1915. Margaret too was caught up in a romance when she was a first-year student, though not in such difficult circumstances. Her autobiography suggests that by the time she went up to Somerville in 1904, she was already 'more than half in love'.[51] But she then qualifies this by adding that this was 'almost entirely the effect of suggestion' arising from a conventional desire to marry and to be wildly in love.[52] There followed a brief period of conformity for a young woman who would, before long, emerge as far from conventional.

CHAPTER TWO

Mrs Mackworth: Marriage and Suffrage

There is one garment of clothing that neatly captures the symbolic and actual restrictions and constrictions that young ladies used to have to endure: the corset. When Margaret's mother broached the subject one summer holiday, her daughter reluctantly but obediently donned great whale-boned stays. Margaret was never dainty. Aged fifteen she was five feet six and a half inches tall and weighed over twelve stone. She wore her corsets (after removing the side bones) until she reached the liberating age of twenty-one, then they were abandoned. When, however, she became engaged, she put them on once more. This did not last: 'I only paid a year's deference to my husband's wishes'.[1] After less than three months of marriage she 'cast them for good and all'. Her husband lasted a little longer but in time he too was ultimately cast aside.

Margaret had met a number of young men at London balls and social events, but they had not impressed her.

When Sybil and an acquaintance with an eligible stepson planned a day at Henley for the two of them she was not pleased. She felt he was too old for her. He had already stayed with her family and showed far more interest in her cousin Dorothy than herself (this was Aunt Edith's daughter whose name was changed to Violet in *This Was My World*). Margaret did relent, but after waiting just six minutes at Paddington for her hosts she glimpsed a couple of cousins and promptly trooped off to Henley with them instead. The man she jilted that day was the founder of the scouting movement Robert Baden-Powell. Twenty-six years older than Margaret, he had recently returned from South Africa.

The man she married was Captain (later Major) Humphrey Mackworth. Margaret's autobiography, written a decade after they divorced, portrays a romantic young lady. She suggests that she had been very willing to marry Humphrey who was well-suited in social terms. She sought to make marriage her career. He was slim, five feet eleven inches tall, balding and, unlike her clean-shaven father, sported a moustache. Despite differences in intellect, interests and age – he was twelve years older than Margaret – he does not appear to have circumscribed her activities. Indeed, she was at pains to suggest in her autobiography that a period when she had lacked direction and purpose now gave way to a much more contented time.

Born in 1871 in Aldershot, Humphrey was the eldest surviving son and heir of Colonel Sir Arthur William Mackworth Bart CB, the sixth baronet of his line, and Lady Mackworth, formerly Alice Kate Cubitt. The Mackworths were one of Monmouthshire's principal landowning families. An earlier eponymous ancestor, Sir Humphrey Mackworth MP (1657-1727) had married the heiress to the Gnoll estate, Neath, in Glamorgan and become a pioneer of the south Wales copper industry. Another illustrious predecessor was Herbert Francis Mackworth, H.M. Inspector of Mines for the South Western region in the mid-nineteenth century. Margaret's husband was the second of twelve children. At the time of his marriage his parents lived in the centre of Caerleon at The Priory, a former twelfth-century Cistercian monastery, later a nunnery, that had been more or less rebuilt in about 1800.

One of Humphrey's five sisters ran a local Church of England Home for 'waifs and strays'. The family prided itself on its military heritage. A Mackworth was said to have fought at the battle of Poitiers in the Hundred Years' War and Humphrey's father had been in the army practically all his life. All but one son went into the armed forces. Humphrey was a former Lieutenant in the 3rd Battalion Queen's (Royal West Surrey) Regiment and had been a Captain in the Royal Monmouth Royal Engineers (Special Reserve). Although over a decade older than Margaret, he was still in his thirties.

The couple were engaged in late 1907. Humphrey's family was staunchly Conservative. However, although conformist, he was not really a political animal. We might well wonder what D.A. thought of this match.

Once engaged, according to her autobiography, Margaret obediently withdrew from the local branch of the Liberal Social Council, which she had only joined because of her father's position. However, at a WSPU meeting held in Cardiff in October 1909 she provided another reason for leaving the party her father represented. She declared that it was because of the Liberal government's opposition to women's suffrage and that she 'would not support that party again until they decided to help the women's movement'.[2]

Yet more than politics divided this married couple. Margaret summed it up thus:

> Humphrey held that no one should ever read in a room where anyone else wanted to talk. I, brought up in a home in which a father's study was sacred, held, on the contrary, that no one should ever talk in a room where anyone else wanted to read.[3]

Humphrey did not spend time reading. The Master of the Llangibby (Llangybi) hounds (he described his occupation as Master of Fox Hounds), he saw himself as a man of action. Margaret was, however, a bookworm.

They were married on 9 July 1908 at Trinity Church, Christchurch, midway between the family homes.[4] Margaret was twenty-four. It was a stylish wedding. The young guests wore King Charles costumes. 'The dresses', declared the *Western Mail* 'were a feast'.[5] Prominent Liberals were there, along with a host of Haigs. There was a reception at Llanwern then a honeymoon in Norway. A photograph taken in front of Llanwern House shows the bride and bridegroom standing suspiciously apart from each other.

They lived until at least the end of 1911 at Llansoar House, close to Caerleon, an ivy-clad sixteenth-century grey, stone building in a secluded wooded valley: 'We settled down there very happily,' wrote Margaret years later.[6] Meanwhile their own home was being built for them: Oaklands in nearby Ponthir (Llanhennock). It was her parents' wedding gift. This attractive stone house with a pantiled roof was designed by Oswald Milne. He exhibited his design at the Royal Academy in 1909.[7] The Mackworths had a cook, housemaid and parlour maid and no financial worries.

Margaret had adopted the role of the dutiful wife but she thought it patronising to get involved in societies such as the Mothers' Union, which involved teaching village women about household and child management. With no children of her own to manage she was painfully aware that these women knew far more about the subject than she did. She may have shared a belief in women's suffrage with the veteran suffragist and Primrose Leaguer Mrs Elizabeth Harcourt Mitchell, who lived at nearby Llanfrechfa but the latter's establishment of a missionary society for girls was simply not her style. Margaret thought it an 'unpardonable impertinence' to be a 'do-gooder'.[8]

She did, however, stress that her mother-in-law (who did good works with local nursing associations and mothers' groups) was both wise and kind. Lady Mackworth presented the young Mrs Mackworth at Court. There were dinner parties and other social events but Margaret appears to have taken these in her stride. She hunted regularly, finding it both exhilarating *and* frightening, also (at least by the 1930s) uncivilised. Her autobiography suggests that Humphrey was dull but not demanding, asking only 'to be left in peace to potter about the kennels'.[9] He became a director of the Naval Collieries (D.A. was chairman and managing director) and of L. Guéret Ltd (D.A. was its deputy chairman).

Yet married life with Margaret was to become anything but peaceful. Although many late Victorian ladies found a purpose and usefulness in helping and writing about the urban poor of Britain, especially in East and South-east London, Margaret opted for suffrage rather than slums. She became a militant suffragette and was imprisoned for the cause. Newspaper accounts mentioning Mrs Mackworth at the local hunt gave way to accounts of her at suffrage meetings. However, although they provided an excitement previously lacking in Margaret's life, it was hardly a novelty for her family.

Sybil had long been an active, law-abiding suffragist and involved in politics more generally. As the wife of a longstanding Liberal MP, she was active in promoting Liberal politics. She was president of the Aberdare Women's Liberal Association within her husband's constituency of Merthyr Boroughs (where he was the more senior of the two MPs) from its creation in late 1891 to 1907. Sybil hosted one of its first committee meetings at Ysguborwen House. Ursula Masson has noted how she was especially assiduous during election years.[10] Indeed, the Aberdare society was formed when D.A. was facing his first contested election and he spoke at its formal inaugural meeting in February 1892. At its height it boasted 600 members and was the second largest such association in Wales.

Sybil was also president of the Abergavenny Women's Liberal Association and Aunt Lottie was president of the Newtown branch. From 1895 to 1900 Sybil presided over the Welsh Union of Women's Liberal Associations. She and its first president, Pembrokeshire-based Nora Philipps (Lady St. Davids from 1908), advocated feminist and pro-suffrage policies within and beyond Welsh Liberal circles. Both sat on the executive of the Women's Liberal

Federation. They lobbied hard for support for Faithful Begg's women's suffrage bill that recorded a breakthrough in February 1897 with its comfortable pro-suffrage majority of 71 (before being talked out at the committee stage five months later). Sybil had been on the executive of the Central National Society for Women's Suffrage since the mid-1890s, along with prominent radical Liberals such as Jane Cobden.

D.A. was not the only one to use his daughter in political propaganda. Sybil also recognised the value of family support. For example, on 11 November 1895, the twelve-year-old Margaret accompanied her mother on to the platform for the first of a series of monthly meetings held by the Aberdare Women's Liberal Association at Carmel Hall in which they sought to 'combine entertainment and instruction'.[11] Sybil delivered what the press called 'a brief and effective address'.

Familial support within women's suffrage was not restricted to the Pankhursts. It was particularly evident amongst the daughters of pro-suffrage parents. The Professor of Celtic Studies at Oxford University, Sir John Rhys, chaired Oxford's first public meeting for women's suffrage. His pro-suffrage wife Lady Elspeth was a key figure in the Oxford branch of the Women's Liberal Federation. Their daughters Myfanwy and Olwen sat on the executive committee of the Oxford Women's Suffrage Society. Sir John Rhys was its president.[12] In his study of women's suffrage in Wales, Ryland Wallace notes that both Victorian suffragists and members of the Women's Freedom League (formed in 1907 after a split in the WSPU) included a number of family members, female and male.[13]

Margaret's commitment to women's suffrage was, according to her autobiography, triggered by one of her many older second cousins, the portrait artist Florence Eliza Haig.[14] In her early fifties she and her younger sister Evelyn (known as Eva), also an artist, formed an Edinburgh branch of the Pankhursts' WSPU, the suffrage organisation that became renowned for its militancy. Florence was both a WSPU organiser in Chelsea by the time of the 1910 election and branch secretary, a position she held until 1916. This branch attracted a number of artists, and they made some of the movement's colourful banners in the basement of its Kings Road shop.[15] Their parents supported women's suffrage. Their father James Haig was a barrister (as were a number of male suffrage supporters) and a third sister, Cecilia Wolseley Haig, was also a militant activist. She and Eva had earlier been active in the Edinburgh Ladies' Debating Society and they, like Sybil, joined the Central National Society for Women's Suffrage.

Florence Haig was one of the first women to be imprisoned for suffrage militancy. On 11 February 1908, when Parliament sat, the third Women's Parliament was also held in Caxton Hall. Florence and another Chelsea portrait artist, Marie Naylor, moved the motion to carry the resolution to the prime minister. In what became known as the Trojan horse incident or pantechnicon raid, a group of women, including Florence and artist friends the sisters Marie and Georgina Brackenbury (who acquired enough Welsh words to embarrass Lloyd George at public meetings), hid in a horse-drawn furniture van that took them to the door of the House of Commons, where they leapt out brandishing petitions. A sentence of six weeks in Holloway, the first of several prison sentences, followed. One prisoner who had smuggled in a pencil wrote her own version of 'Sing a Song of Sixpence' published in the *Daily Mail*:

> Sing a song of Christabel's clever little plan
> Four and twenty Suffragettes packed in a van
> When the van was opened they to the Commons ran
> Wasn't that a dainty dish for Campbell-Bannerman?[16]

Florence was invited to Llanwern to recuperate and to satisfy the curiosity of the Thomas family. The picture of suffrage painted by this artistic relative whose hair was so long that it allegedly almost reached her ankles, seems to have persuaded Margaret that she should join the suffrage demonstration in London's Hyde Park on 21 June 1908. Called 'Women's Sunday', this brought together suffragettes from across Britain just over a week after the law-abiding National Union of Women's Suffrage Societies (NUWSS) had staged its own vast procession.

The conversion experience is a familiar tale in narratives of suffrage. But whereas reaction against family is often an ingredient in the rebellion that creates the suffragette, in Margaret's case the Thomas family was carefully and centrally implicated in her story. Her vital step was triggered from within – literally within the family home – but it enabled her to move forwards to a lifestyle that would also challenge her new Mackworth identity. In practice the shift may not have been quite as smooth as Margaret's recollection suggests. Conversion narratives make compelling reading and are a valuable means for writers to point up events that, retrospectively at least, are seen as symbolic and even heroic. Margaret's life story was crafted in the inter-war years when she had a particular feminist agenda to promote and when an acceptable model of the suffragette past was carefully cultivated.[17] Nevertheless, the frequency with which dramatic conversions feature in suffrage recollections of all kinds – not just the written autobiography – and the drama of the movement in these years does suggest that they had some real meaning at the time.

And Margaret had certainly chosen a spectacular event for her first suffrage outing. The WSPU newspaper *Votes for Women* claimed that it was the largest gathering at one spot in the history of the world, although, like the massive Kennington Common demonstration of the Chartists on 10 April 1848, hyperbole from supporters needs to be understood in relation to the huge symbolic effect of such events and the numbers involved in policing them.[18] Even *The Times* conceded that between a quarter and half a million attended that June day. Seven vast processions marched through London converging on Hyde Park. It was the first time the suffragette colours of purple, white and green were deployed – there were 700 banners in these colours – and participants were advised to wear white or cream, perhaps with a touch of purple and green to enhance the banners. More than 10,000 scarves were sold on the two days before the demonstration.

An excursion train from Cardiff conveyed 365 women to London. Although Newport did not yet have a WSPU or NUWSS branch, a photograph shows a banner (made of purple silk) at Hyde Park sporting the word 'Newport'.[19] The Welsh contingent gathered at Paddington station behind the former mill-worker Annie Kenney. They were joined by those from the Midlands and the West of England. Margaret was 'thrilled with this chance for action'.[20]

This demonstration took place just two and a half weeks before her wedding. She had persuaded her future husband that there was no harm in attending. Her mother, who combined progressive beliefs with Victorian propriety and rectitude, was with her. Sybil's suffrage convictions were, however, accompanied by concern that her daughter should not walk 'unchaperoned through the gutter'. For Margaret the day signified a point of no return. She summed up beautifully the sentiments of many women of her era when she explained the effect that militant suffrage had on her and her generation:

> It gave us release of energy, it gave us that sense of being of some use in the scheme of things, without which no human being can live at peace. It made us feel that we were part of life, not just outside watching it.[21]

Elsie McKenzie, who became an organiser for the WSPU in Cardiff, felt a similar sensation. After standing on a chair to address an audience in Barry – she spoke for two hours – she told a friend: 'I do not know what is happening to me. I seem to be changed into somebody else'.[22]

Unlike many, including Sybil, who proceeded cautiously from constitutional, moderate suffragism to more militant beliefs, Margaret read avidly about women's rights and embraced the suffragette creed from the outset. She was not sidetracked into other political organisations but single-mindedly pursued women's suffrage. She argued that militancy was needed because '[t]he crust of custom and prejudice was too thick' for anything else to succeed.[23] She made a nice distinction between the constitutionalist approach and that of the WSPU: 'instead of asking gently for help, accepting the crumbs offered', the suffragettes 'demanded a Government measure' and made it clear that they would bring 'what pressure might be necessary' to ensure their demands were met.[24]

Her father had some reservations about Margaret joining the WSPU. She prevaricated for three months then decided that 'he could be no judge of a matter which concerned one primarily as a woman'.[25] In the autumn she and her old school friend Prid went 'full of excitement' to the WSPU headquarters at Clement's Inn and committed themselves.

D.A. voted in Parliament for women's suffrage and believed in free speech, but he objected to militancy. His speeches to the Aberdare Women's Liberal Association in the 1890s suggest that at this stage at least, he had some way to travel in terms of understanding the struggle for women's equality. In February 1892 he told what a local newspaper called 'a bevy of fair ladies, with a small admixture of gentlemen' that 'doubtless, some there, *like himself* [my emphasis] felt they would rather not have seen the women take part in politics' but they had no option in the matter since the Tory Primrose League was already extremely active.[26] He did, however, later moderate his views.

D.A. was no stranger to controversy and political rebellion. He had been a Liberal whip in 1888 and 1892, but he and three other Welsh MPs refused the whip in

1894. He turned his back on Lloyd George, who wanted the Welsh Liberal Federation to amalgamate with Cymru Fydd (Young Wales). In the spring of 1908 the anti-suffrage H.H. Asquith became prime minister and Liberal MPs came under increasing pressure from both their party and from suffragettes. The WSPU adopted a policy of opposing all Liberal parliamentary candidates, regardless of whether or not they were sympathisers.

In July 1910 D.A. was one of twenty-one Welsh MPs who voted for the second reading of the Women's Franchise Bill (eight voted against it and there were five abstentions). That October and November he spoke in Cardiff in favour of the Conciliation Bill which proposed to extend the vote to women who possessed the local government vote.[27] Yet these utterances need to be understood in context. Since January 1910 he had been MP for Cardiff (his predecessor was anti-suffrage), but he was about to give up his seat and the new Liberal candidate, Sir Clarendon Hyde, was a known 'Anti'. Welsh women Liberals were split on the issue of whether to confine their efforts to women's suffrage and support only those Liberals who endorsed the Conciliation Bill, a position upheld in public by Sybil at the national conference of Welsh Liberal Women in Cardiff.

The following year D.A. declared that if the men of Wales and nonconformist ministers who had been preaching religious equality for years had been prepared to make similar sacrifices to those made by the Suffragettes, they would not still be waiting for a Disestablishment Bill.[28] And in November of that year (almost a year after he had ceased to be MP for Cardiff) he became a vice president of the Men's League for

Women's Suffrage, the largest and most respected of the men's support groups.[29] This society had been founded in London by a barrister in March 1907 and was a powerful pressure group, largely composed of lawyers, academics, clergymen, journalists and businessmen (twenty per cent of its first 300 members were in finance and commerce). These were men who already had voting rights and could therefore exert pressure in places of public power. The Men's League also had its own monthly newspaper. A fellow vice-president was Sir Alfred Mond, the powerful Liberal and founder of the Mond Nickel Company of Clydach, the largest nickel works in the world. D.A. would have understood Mond's language. He called women's suffrage 'an effort at co-partnership'.[30]

Already bruised personally from political battles and slights, most notably Campbell-Bannerman's refusal to give him office in 1905, D.A. was well aware what a commitment to a political cause would mean for his daughter. He was also conscious of what she might face at the local level in a society that prided itself on its masculine public culture and consequent domestic environment for women.

In November 1909, on the day before Margaret made a dramatic personal appearance on the suffrage stage, D.A. saw how unpleasant suffrage meetings could be for speakers. An open-air meeting was held on behalf of the Women's Freedom League at Cardiff docks. This group, which had been formed after a split within the WSPU in 1907, was popular in towns such as Swansea. It advocated more resistance than the law-abiding NUWSS and deployed imaginative forms of passive resistance. Australian-born Muriel Matters was its south Wales organiser (at the opening of Parliament she had flown over Westminster in an airship painted with 'Votes for Women'). She was one of three women attempting to address an increasingly raucous crowd of about 1,000 from a trolley.

Cat-calls, handfuls of rice, and music hall ditties were forcing her to end the meeting when, according to the *Western Mail*, suddenly D.A. 'forged his way through the immense gathering, and mounted the trolley'. The paper was used to criticising his politics but now it was his manliness that was deemed paramount. Its account of the chivalrous man intervening in the nick of time helped to counteract the charges of emasculation voiced by hecklers. They responded to D.A.'s intervention by chanting 'Put me amongst the girls' and 'Oh! Oh! Antonio'. He stood for ten minutes, hat in hand, enduring taunts such as 'Stick to your party and put your hat on' and 'If you are a man come down'. Although he was even less successful than Muriel Matters in getting a hearing and a lighted squib was soon afterwards placed on the trolley, the paper's headline declared 'Mr D.A. Thomas goes to the Rescue'. An editorial carefully pointed out that the women had done 'some silly things in their advocacy of the suffrage' but it deplored meetings being broken up.[31]

The next day another headline in the paper announced: 'Mr D.A. Thomas's Daughter Shouted Down'. Reporting Margaret's hostile reception at a meeting in Aberdare, it added that D.A. had apparently received 'a gentle hint' that his daughter would not be allowed a hearing and had chosen to 'laugh off' such threats.

Back in the summer of 1909, members of Aberdare Liberal Club had visited Llanwern Park where Margaret made what was considered 'a very fine speech' on women's suffrage. So, according to her autobiography, she was asked to address the club on women's suffrage. The *Western Mail's* version was that she 'gently dropped the hint' that she would be pleased to speak. Margaret stated that she would like to bring a lady with her. Soon afterwards she made it clear that her companion would be the West of England WSPU organiser, Annie Kenney. Although many of the committee were opposed to this militant suffragette appearing in their club, their president was the speaker's father and their MP so no formal objection was made. The meeting eventually went ahead on 18 November, though it was decided not to endorse proceedings by using club premises. It was held instead at the Bowen Jenkins Memorial Hall and, to minimise disruption, it was ticketed (members were allowed two tickets). There was a run on these tickets and the hall was crowded out well in advance.

The first organised public meeting on women's suffrage in Wales had taken place nearby in June 1870. Rose Mary Crawshay, who had married into the wealthy and infamous Crawshay dynasty of ironmasters based at Cyfarthfa Castle, had organised, chaired and spoken at the gathering in Merthyr's Temperance Hall. Women's suffrage in Wales was intrinsically linked (as Chartism had been) to the wider British movement. It reflected Margaret's wider bifurcated agenda and lifestyle that straddled Wales and England, though it would also reveal some cultural and linguistic patterns that distinguished it from its English counterpart.

The 1909 meeting took place at a moment when relations between women Liberals and the Liberal party were deteriorating. It was becoming apparent that although suffrage was a priority for many, this was not so for the government.[32] The Aberdare district had witnessed heated meetings on subjects such as Welsh disestablishment. Election campaigns could also foment trouble but the press called this gathering '[t]he most rowdy meeting' held in the town for at least thirty years.[33]

The previous week the suffragette Theresa Garnett had been charged with assaulting Winston Churchill when he arrived at Bristol railway station before speaking at the Colston Hall. She had approached him with a riding whip in her hand but the popular impression was that he had actually been whipped. She was sentenced to a month in prison. He asked for the whip as a souvenir. Annie Kenney was based in Bristol.

Aberdare was part of D.A.'s Merthyr Boroughs constituency. Kenney was linked with the politics of its other MP, Keir Hardie. She had campaigned in Merthyr for Hardie's election in 1906. Ladies were in the majority in the Aberdare audience but scattered throughout the hall were 'young men bent on mischief, and the fun was fast and furious' claimed the *Merthyr Express*. The original chairman had withdrawn and been replaced by Maria Richards, a member of the local board of guardians. A stalwart of the Aberdare Women's Liberal Association, she was a moderate suffragist. When she introduced Margaret she was interrupted by the sound of bells, whistles and trumpets.

Margaret was received with cheers, boos and whistles. She first explained the WSPU's main aim since Annie Kenney had advised her always to state what she wanted and why, followed by how she meant to obtain it. But there followed such a cacophony of sounds – hoots, shouts, a shrill blast from a trumpet, cat-calls, a policeman's whistle and a rattle – that her words were drowned. She persevered, mentioning Asquith (cheers followed) and remarking that she could not understand 'how any Liberal true to his principles can object to the vote being granted women on the same terms as men'. During a temporary lull she appealed to her audience's beliefs: 'Even if you object to our methods very strongly, you must, if you are Liberals and true to your principles, approve of our claims to the vote'. But 'unseemly gestures', the singing of comic songs and the noise from outside where a crowd scratched the rough glass windows, ensured that little more could be said.

The three women attempted to restore the peace but herrings, ripe tomatoes and cabbages were hurled onto the platform. Even Kenney, a seasoned campaigner, had great difficulty in being heard. The audience was seeking revenge for the infamous occasion in Manchester's Free Trade Hall three years earlier when Annie Kenney and Christabel Pankhurst had interrupted Sir Edward Grey as he was appealing for the return of a Liberal government. At that stage of the movement such an intervention – the first instance of the tactic of intervening at cabinet ministers' meetings – had appeared outrageous to many. The customary deference leading politicians expected was often undermined in practice by opponents, but such behaviour was deemed especially shocking when it emanated from ladies.

The Aberdare meeting rapidly got out of control. Dead mice were hurled onto the platform and live mice set loose in the body of the hall, along with sulphurated hydrogen gas, snuff and cayenne pepper (producing loud sneezes). Window panes were smashed, many chairs were broken and 'some fear was entertained of something approaching a panic'. Although initially refusing to give up, after ten more minutes of attempting in vain to be heard, even Kenney surrendered. The women walked out slowly from the back of the platform into the gymnasium and escaped in a cab.

The event demonstrated the hostility between many Liberal men and suffragettes. Elizabeth Andrews (who, in 1919, became the Labour Party's first Women's organiser for Wales) later recalled the reception given to Elsie McKenzie and Florence Haig's friend Marie Naylor when they visited Pentre to speak to the local branch of the ILP the month after this Aberdare meeting.[34] Young Liberals gathered outside the café where they were speaking, threw rotten fruit, shouted slogans and broke the window. The speakers escaped down a ladder to the riverside and fled to the next village for their train.

The Aberdare attack also revealed splits between local Liberal women. One of Sybil's former committee members, Mrs R.H. Miles, handed the press a statement declaring that she had been refused permission to put a proposal at this meeting. She approved of what were called 'genuine efforts' to secure the vote for women, but viewed with 'the utmost contempt' the 'antics' of the Pankhursts. They were 'calculated to do irreparable injury to the cause of woman'. The meeting anticipated responses that would become common after the suffragettes adopted a deliberate policy of militant action from late 1911.

Margaret's association with the suffragettes distanced her from her father's constituents, although only a matter of weeks later he ended his long stint representing the district. The *Aberdare Leader* suggested that Margaret deserved a 'respectful hearing if only for the sake of her respected father' though a letter signed 'Another of the Boys' commented that if D.A. Thomas treated MPs as suffragettes did, he too would receive such treatment.[35] The Liberal Club expressed regret that he had not discouraged the visit.

The timing of Margaret's public appearance and D.A.'s move is interesting. In early October he had spoken at the annual dinner for the Liberal Registration agents of the Aberdare valley and suggested that his constituents might well feel like a change after nearly twenty-two years.[36] He also joked that his fellow member, Keir Hardie, would receive far more support from his wife and daughter than he would himself. Hardie was deeply involved with women's suffrage and associated with Sylvia Pankhurst.

Margaret and her mother ensured some public confrontation. At one election meeting for D.A., an under-secretary of state was due to speak. Local suffragettes occupied the front row, to the consternation of D.A.'s agent, who wanted to turn them out. However, D.A. was ill with influenza so could not attend. Sybil replaced him and threatened to walk off the platform if the women were ejected. They remained.

By the time Margaret wrote about the Aberdare meeting in her autobiography, she was able to make light of it. She implied that she had been relieved not to have to make a speech that anyone could hear and that she was 'pleasantly exhilarated by the whole affair'.[37] She described this occasion as her first experience of public speaking for the cause.[38] This was not the case, though it is difficult to tell whether her account can be attributed to faulty memory (she also stated that it took place at Merthyr rather than Aberdare), or whether she sought to increase the dramatic effect by suggesting the ordeal faced by an ingénue.

Margaret, Annie Kenney and the pioneer doctor and Mayor, Elizabeth Garrett Anderson, had already addressed a 'well attended' WSPU meeting at the Park Hotel Cardiff on 13 October where Margaret had explained why she supported militancy. A week later she chaired a further meeting in Cardiff.[39] Nearly 200 people heard the trio speak at a Newport 'At Home' on 14 October, one of those neat suffrage subversions of society functions that suggested how the public world might challenge the home. Margaret also organised Caerleon's first suffrage meeting in the same month (chaired by her mother).[40] Nevertheless, the 'suffragette baiting' and reception Margaret received at Aberdare must have been intimidating and humiliating for her, even though the press described the attack as 'refined ruffianism'. She offered to pay for the damages.

If anything, though, Margaret was more determined than ever to persevere. She was young, her life now seemed to have some purpose and, as she wrote years later, there was something to work for that 'we believed in with all our hearts. What more could anyone want?'[41] One week after the Aberdare encounter she chaired a volatile meeting closer to home in the schoolroom of London Street Congregational church, Maindee. It was the second meeting of the day held in the Newport area to listen to Marion Wallace-Dunlop who had initiated suffrage hunger striking that summer by fasting for ninety-one hours in prison. Once again there was pandemonium. Sulphur was burned, squibs and crackers were thrown and lights extinguished. Margaret closed the meeting after a bag of flour hit the speaker. Another speaker was Elizabeth Harcourt Mitchell who had signed the famous women's suffrage petition of 1866.

Margaret wrote in her autobiography that Newport suffragettes became organised as a consequence of the infamous Aberdare meeting and 'the conviction on my part that it was essential that our local town, Newport, should be converted to suffrage'.[42] Here again her record is misleading. The meeting in Newport's Temperance Hall (which held 1100 people) which she described as following her maiden speech actually took place in April 1909, more than six months before the infamous Aberdare meeting. Margaret had chaired it.[43] Christabel Pankhurst had declined an invitation but her mother Emmeline had accepted. 'Every young hooligan in the town threatened joyously to come and break up the meeting' recalled Margaret. But she and they had not reckoned on 'the power of a great speaker'. Mrs Pankhurst 'held that audience in the hollow of her hand' and effectively silenced those who had come to jeer.[44]

It is Annie Kenney who deserves the credit for getting Newport's WSPU organised. She had come to Wales in early May 1909 from Bristol on a mission: determined to turn Cardiff and Newport into flourishing WSPU centres. Margaret chaired the first At Home in Newport the following month and both of her parents were in the audience. A working committee was formed soon after this and a meeting held in the Savoy Hotel. A WSPU shop was opened in September and Gabrielle Jeffery (who later formed the Catholic Women's Suffrage Society) became a paid WSPU organiser in Newport.

The Anti-Suffrage League was mobilising too, though some of its key figures seem to have been more conspicuous by their absence. Mrs Harcourt Mitchell's sister-in-law Lady Llangattock (president of the Newport and Monmouthshire branch) was absent from a meeting of 'Antis' in June that she had been due to chair because she was on her yacht at Syracuse. Ivor Guest, MP for Cardiff from 1906 until D.A. defeated him in 1910, was another 'Anti' who could not attend. Ironically he was a grandson of one of the nineteenth century's most eminent women achievers: Lady Charlotte Guest. In that same month another of Charlotte Guest's grandchildren, Mildred Mansel (prominent in WSPU activities in the West Country) was arrested for breaking windows at the War office and sent to Holloway. Such divided loyalties were very different from the Thomas family. Ivor Guest's mother Lady Wimborne had been a signatory to the famous anti-suffrage Appeal in 1889.[45] Guest (who became Lord Wimborne in 1910) was secretary, then treasurer, of the Women's National Anti-Suffrage League.

The Newport branch of the WSPU was chaired by Sybil. Margaret later claimed that Sybil was never actually a member of the Union though the local newspaper stated that mother and daughter were members.[46] It is likely that whilst D.A. was an MP (until the end of 1910) it was thought expedient for her not to be a member. She may simply never have joined after that date, although if this is the case her active public commitment and generous financial support question the importance of actual membership. For example, she contributed to George

Lansbury's by-election at Bow, where he stood unsuccessfully as a women's suffrage candidate, and she supported the WSPU's prisoners' fund. Mary Richardson (the suffragette renowned for slashing the 'Rokeby Venus' in London's National Gallery) recalled how the WSPU till was kept full by generous gifts from Sybil and a few other wealthy women.[47]

Sybil hosted annual suffrage garden parties at Llanwern Park. The 1909 reception honoured two suffragettes who had been imprisoned after breaking windows at the Treasury then went on hunger strike: Lillian Dove-Willcox and Cardiff-born Mary Allen.[48] The family welcomed about 150 people including Kenney. Interestingly, Humphrey and his mother were present, as were unlikely figures such as Colonel Lindsay, the Chief Constable of Glamorgan. Sybil pointed out that she did not like stone-throwing tactics but that they must agree on doing their best to get the vote.

Sybil presided over some of the meetings held by the non-militant suffragist Cardiff and District National Union, the largest suffragist society outside London by 1912. However, she also chaired a reception held in honour of Mrs Pankhurst at Newport's Westgate Hotel (where Prid performed 'dainty pianoforte solos').[49] Sybil's involvement in suffrage at this time bears out Krista Cowman's evidence for Merseyside that at the local level there was not necessarily a rigid division between suffrage societies when it came to individual support.[50] In 1912 Sybil presided at a Pontypool WSPU meeting where she reportedly declared that if some 'did not like the militant side of the movement they themselves were to blame for the position in which they found themselves because they should have done more work themselves'.[51] Reflecting on suffrage after the First World War, Margaret wrote, 'My mother and I were both strongly in favour of militancy'.[52]

Margaret became the honorary secretary of Newport's WSPU branch, which soon boasted a hundred members. From the spring of 1910 weekly meetings were being held in addition to mid-week At Homes. The branch, which seems to have been predominantly composed of middle-class ladies, sported its own banner made of green linen with painted purple irises and white lilies and the portcullis symbol of the House of Commons in the middle. Declaring 'How Beggarly Appear Arguments Before A Defiant Deed', it affirmed the WSPU motto 'Deeds Not Words'. It was made by a Miss Brown in time for the vast 'Prison to Citizenship' demonstration in London in June 1910 where the west of England and south Wales contingent was accompanied by a band paid for by Sybil. At the July demonstration Newport's new organiser – the Carmarthenshire-born science graduate Rachel Barrett – chaired the Welsh platform at Hyde Park. During September Barrett (who spoke Welsh) was busy recruiting members in north Wales, so Margaret ran the shop on Friday afternoons.

But, like other suffrage activists, Margaret did not restrict her activities to her home patch. She presided in February 1911 at a gathering of Cardiff suffragettes addressed by Mrs Pankhurst who predicted (inaccurately) that the imminent payment of Members of Parliament – one of the original six points advocated by the Chartists in the 1830s – would be accompanied by votes for women. That autumn Margaret spoke at two meetings in south Pembrokeshire[53] and in July 1912, at a Saturday evening WSPU meeting in Cardiff's Llandaff Fields, she argued that granting women the vote in New Zealand had beneficial effects on infant mortality.[54]

Margaret devoured classic writings on women's rights. She later described Olive Schreiner's *Woman and Labour* as 'almost a bible to the pre-war generation of young women'.[55] She was also impressed by *Marriage as a Trade* by Cicely Hamilton who became a director of *Time and Tide*. Reading armed her for public speaking and when the WSPU sent instructions that branch secretaries should send articles about suffrage activities to the local press, she embarked on a path that would provide her with some of the experience needed for her later career.

As so often, her father was crucial here. Not only did he give her a typewriter for her birthday but he also introduced her to the editor of Wales's leading daily, the *Western Mail* and this led to Margaret penning regular features on women's suffrage and related issues for Welsh newspapers 'in praise of militancy'.[56] In effect she was supplying information, much of which was by her own admission from the leading WSPU organ, *Votes for Women*. From late April 1912 for three months she wrote a weekly column entitled 'Woman's Cause' in the *Monmouthshire Weekly Post*.[57] Most weeks she covered two or three aspects of the movement, addressing topics such as how close Mrs Pankhurst had come to losing her life as a result of her hunger strike, forcible feeding, the 'Antis', differential prison treatment accorded to men and women, and the position of women in Japan.[58] She signed her column Mrs M.H. Mackworth but when she made news rather than reporting it, the paper headed its account of her court appearance 'Mrs Humphry [sic] Mackworth'.[59]

Margaret's reading had included George Bernard Shaw's self-styled 'unpleasant' play of 1894, 'Mrs Warren's Profession'. Its witty exploration of the ambitions and social networks of the eponymous brothel-keeper exposed the economic basis of prostitution and capitalism's role in perpetuating this profession. An article Margaret wrote for the *Western Mail* in August 1912 focused on a related subject that interested her, her mother[60] and wider society: the organised international trafficking of innocent young women to continental brothels. Known as white slavery, this was causing something of a moral panic.[61]

Legislation in 1885 in the wake of a sensational press campaign spearheaded by W.T. Stead had increased the age of consent from thirteen to sixteen. Many women had continued to press for tightening the part of the law that dealt with streetwalkers and brothel keepers. Literature such as Olive Malvery's *The Soul Market* (1907) argued for the age of consent to be eighteen. Now a new Criminal Law Amendment Bill garnered support from the Liberal government. The Women's Liberal Federation was increasingly disillusioned with the latter's failure to grant women's suffrage, and by mid-1912 the organisation was warning that continued good relations with the Liberal Party could not be guaranteed. The government thus sought to appease those Liberal women known to feel strongly about the white slave trade. Stead, whose death was as dramatic as his journalism exposing white slavery, had been on the *Titanic*. Margaret suggested in her 'Woman's Cause' column that effective legislation against the white slave trade would be the best memorial to Stead.[62]

Margaret's concern was that the bill was being emasculated by amendments at the committee stage. It sought to make procuration a felony (with white slavers liable to immediate arrest) instead of merely a misdemeanour. But now it had been amended on the grounds of the liberty of the subject so that only specially detailed sergeants could make an arrest. Margaret did not deny that this was an important principle, but questioned why the liberty of a putative slave trader should be perceived as more important than that of a supposed burglar. Due to pressure, the more straightforward arrest without warrant was reinstated as part of the legislation passed in December 1912. Procuration therefore became a much more serious offence than it had been. In August Margaret also used this case to demonstrate to the *Western Mail's* readers the urgent need for women to have political power, not least because here was an issue about women's lives and one about which more women than men cared.[63]

Margaret was by now advertising suffrage in the streets of south Wales, a shocking fact to polite society. The audacity of suffragette appropriation of public space was met with astonishment. Women might inhabit streets. Ladies did not. A photograph from 1913 shows Margaret, Aunt Lottie and Miss Lawton parading through Newport wearing sandwich boards advertising a WSPU meeting. The press was careful to stress who Mrs Humphrey Mackworth and Miss Haig were.

Suffragettes advertised and sold their propaganda across Britain. The writer and suffragette Evelyn Sharp recounted (in a series of witty vignettes based on her work for the Kensington branch of the WSPU) the indignities of

'Patrolling the Gutter'. She described 'a band of naturally timorous ladies, girt with sandwich-boards' issuing forth into a strong south-west wind, London drizzle and thick mud underfoot.[64] The Newport ladies also glimpsed the daily life and indignities of those who regularly pounded the streets. It was something that Margaret enjoyed, a break from being Mrs Mackworth. But although it was an eye-opener for her and other ladies, their actions were not always appreciated. The postman who watched the Kensington women retreat into the suffrage shop shouted out, 'Votes for a few rich women, that's all you're after!'

In April 1910, during a week promoting the WSPU newspaper *Votes for Women* nationally, Margaret and Rachel Barrett spent a day selling the newspaper on the Cardiff streets. Some miners who had been canvassed by the WSPU during the recent mid-Glamorgan by-election bought the paper from Margaret. On Saturday mornings she stood in the gutter in Newport's High Street selling *Votes for Women* (the references to the gutter in suffrage accounts were not for effect: standing on pavements meant they could be moved on for contravening by-laws about obstruction).

One day, to her consternation, Margaret glimpsed her mother-in-law's chestnut horse rounding the corner. Before the carriage and its occupant – 'a lady of considerable presence and the rustling silk type of dignity' – could reach her, she dived into the nearest side street. Margaret later turned this episode into a sketch called 'Her First Experience' (signed MHM) for *Votes for Women*. With 'pink cheeks and thumping heart', it suggests the trepidation she felt on first announcing in a shaky voice that grew stronger in the face of taunts: 'This week's *Votes for Women* one penny!' The moral of her story is that she must not be so cowardly in future.[65]

Yet, as Margaret admitted, the Mackworths did not attempt to curb her activities. Indeed, they even attended some of her meetings. In mid-April 1910, the radical war correspondent and suffrage activist Henry W. Nevinson participated in a 'fairly large' meeting held by Newport WSPU in the Temperance Hall. His speech lasted for about forty-five minutes and was well received. He noticed that many Mackworth family members were also present. Sir Arthur Mackworth talked to him at the end. Nevinson had known Sir Arthur's eldest son and Humphrey's brother, Digby Mackworth, in Ladysmith during the Second Anglo-Boer War (Digby had lost his life there). Nevinson took tea 'with a young Mrs Mackworth [Margaret] & others'.[66]

Humphrey used to meet the excursion train from London at 3am, armed with a flask of hot soup, and drive his wife home from London demonstrations such as the 'Coronation' procession of June 1911, where Welsh costume was worn.[67] He did, however, baulk at having members of the Pankhurst family to stay. He could maintain form so long as suffragette action did not literally come home. Mrs Pankhurst was put up instead at Llanwern, as were a number of other prominent suffragettes.

Humphrey attended some events at the more genteel end of the movement, such as a reception at the Royal Hotel Cardiff in November 1909 organised by the Women's Freedom League. An orchestra played, Muriel Matters spoke on the League's objectives, and Cicely Hamilton and Christopher St. John's witty one-act farce 'How the Vote Was Won' was performed.[68]

Margaret's friend Prid was now a teacher and the treasurer of Bournemouth WSPU. The two women spent early September 1910 seeking converts in the West Country. This was part of the holiday campaign advocated by the WSPU. *Votes for Women* suggests that meetings in Devon towns such as Barnstaple and Bideford were large and successful, but Margaret's account conveys a somewhat different impression. The women thought Barnstaple was ripe for conversion, but it was to be another year or so before even a NUWSS branch was established there.

They hired a lorry and chalked pavements, announcing their meeting in the market place. A decent-sized crowd listened with good humour to their 'anxiously prepared' speeches, and it was only later that they discovered that somebody had hung above them a placard declaring 'Blokes for Women'.[69] In Sherborne, Dorset, where Lady Frances Balfour's presence had prompted the formation of a suffrage society in 1909, their audience was mainly small boys who pelted them with rotten tomatoes. Their open-air meeting on the outskirts of Bournemouth and close to Prid's home resulted in some people buying *Votes for Women,* but apples and manure were thrown at their lorry.

They faced further indignities in the Monmouthshire mining village of Risca.[70] When they arrived at the station a crowd awaited them and they were 'severely hustled'. Margaret's hat and purse were dislodged and her hair pulled down her back. They managed to reach the square and used a lorry for a temporary platform. Rotten eggs were thrown and they were pursued. They climbed hedges and railings. At the last moment Sybil materialised with a posse of policemen and the chauffeur-driven car. Such a pursuit *and* such a rescue speak volumes.

Rather than pose problems for her father, Margaret decamped to Scotland during the election campaign of January 1910. The prime minister declared in his East Fife constituency: 'I have always been an opponent of woman [sic] suffrage. It is not good either for women or for the state'.[71] Margaret encountered him on his way to address a meeting at St. Andrews Town Hall at which no women were to be admitted. Margaret, her relative Cecilia (from that remarkable trio of Haig sisters) and another Scotswoman were undeterred.[72] Margaret jumped onto the running-board of Asquith's car and addressed him. As she described it, he leaned back into the corner 'looking white and frightened and rather like a fascinated rabbit'. The crowd pulled her away – 'very indignant they were' – and she and the women were pursued by youths. Their hats were tugged off, their clothes torn and their hair pulled down. Their attempt to hold a meeting in the street was futile (St. Andrews had a branch of the Anti-Suffrage League). They were rescued by three young golf caddies and sought refuge in a smart golfers' hotel close to the links before creeping back to their lodgings.

Years later, the Communist Lewis Jones, ex-Cambrian Collieries pit boy from Clydach Vale, wrote in his novel *Cwmardy* (1937) that Lord Cwmardy (a thinly-disguised D.A.) had become 'so wealthy that his daughter could afford to travel the country demanding rights for women'.[73] This remark underplayed the connections that at times existed between some members of the WSPU (though, emphatically, not Margaret) and militant socialists in the mining communities of south Wales.[74] It also dismissed the commitment of women like Margaret who could easily have sat at home in comfort instead of risking ridicule and imprisonment.[75] But it does remind us too of the gulf that persisted in terms of both gender and class between Margaret and the world of the Rhondda miner.

Chapter Three

'To Prison while the Sun Shines'[1]

The autobiography of the playwright, novelist and art critic Laurence Housman includes reminiscences of the time when he and his artist sister were active supporters of women's suffrage. He comments on the spirit of the 'aboundingly brave' women brought up in repressive Victorian society who confounded expectations by embracing militant suffrage. He tells several stories about such women. One of them was Margaret.

Housman (who sat on the executive of the Men's League) spoke on women's suffrage across England and Wales. On one occasion his hosts were the Thomases of Llanwern:

At dinner the increase of militancy was being discussed, and, in certain of its forms, condemned. Only that week a local letter box had been set on fire; it was the latest form that militancy had then taken; and in that high social circle it was not approved: it was hoped that the perpetrators would be caught and punished. My host's daughter was sitting next to me: she gave me a soft nudge. 'I did it', she said.[2]

Housman's story is both revealing and misleading. Margaret is presented (though not named) as the daughter who has had a bit of a lark, unknown to her parents. She does not sound like a thirty-year-old married woman. D.A. and Sybil's views on militancy were not synonymous: mother and daughter were more in agreement on this issue than were husband and wife. And when Margaret famously set a letter box on fire in 1913, her parents were thousands of miles from their dinner table. Nevertheless, Housman's anecdote served its purpose, suggesting that militant suffragettes could be found in the most unlikely places.

Margaret devoted three chapters of her autobiography to women's suffrage. The first was modestly called 'On the Outskirts of the Suffrage movement'. There followed a chapter on meetings and cabinet ministers. The third chapter was starkly entitled 'Prison', suggesting the apogee of suffragette commitment. This was in line with how suffragette memoirs were told in the inter-war years.[3]

Margaret was not the only Welsh woman to go to gaol for the suffrage cause. Welsh women were amongst those who volunteered to take part in unlawful protests in London in 1906-7. They were subsequently incarcerated. The militancy of November 1911 in London resulted in two Newport women and Aunt Janetta being imprisoned.[4] In March 1912 Agnes Jacobs (née Williams) was sentenced to one month's imprisonment and hard labour after smashing windows at Earls Court Post Office with a hammer. An attached label read 'To Mr Lloyd George. A Protest from a Welsh Woman against repression'.[5] Rachel Barrett served time in Holloway and Canterbury the following year, after which she adopted disguises and a pseudonym to prevent re-arrest.[6]

Within Wales, James Grant held weekly open-air meetings in the summer of 1913 in Treorchy where he sold over 100 copies of the *Suffragette*. He was arrested for obstruction; he refused to pay his fine and spent five days in Cardiff Gaol.[7] There were also English suffragettes who were detained in Welsh gaols.[8] Yet Margaret seems to have been the only Welsh woman sentenced to prison within Wales for suffrage activities. Her crime and conviction prompted a disproportionate amount of public attention.

In November 1911 Asquith announced that there would be a new reform bill which could be amended to include women's suffrage. Lloyd George, the chancellor, had been campaigning against the latest Conciliation Bill (introduced earlier that year) that would have granted women a limited vote. It had already passed its second reading (with a larger majority than its 1910 equivalent) and had even been translated into Welsh. The prospect of a new government Franchise Bill now posed something of a dilemma. Many felt that it deliberately threatened the future of the Conciliation Bill. The WSPU chose to end its truce and a new campaign of militancy ensued.

The Member of Parliament for North Monmouthshire was the Home Secretary Reginald McKenna, whose selection in 1885 had been supported by D.A.[9] Three members of the Pontypool and Griffithstown branch of the WSPU went on a deputation to see McKenna towards the end of 1911. He made clear his opposition to their aims. Barrett therefore responded with a challenge: 'Then we may go back to your constituents and tell them that you oppose votes for women' to which he is said to have replied with a smile, 'Yes, certainly, and that it is open to them to convert me.'[10] In July 1912 Labour Party members in his constituency passed a resolution protesting against the forcible feeding of suffrage prisoners and demanded that they be treated as political prisoners. They called on McKenna to vote against any reform measures that did not include women.[11]

Women across Monmouthshire rallied. The suffragettes' methods of getting McKenna's attention were not, of course, the ones he wanted and the press made the most of this. In the summer of 1912 it was reported in the London press that he had been 'violently shaken' by a 'Woman in Pink' when laying the foundation stone of Monmouthshire training college at Caerleon. Margaret took offence at what she saw as gross exaggeration. She had been present, and she protested to the *Western Mail* that the suffragette had merely caught hold of the Home Secretary's lapel. Turning the tables, she stressed that this woman was 'a frail, fragile little person', who had been suffering from heart strain ever since because of 'the violent way she was caught hold of when hurled down the steps'.[12] The pink silk frock and matching floppy hat belonged to Margaret and had been worn by the London suffragette. Suitably attired and accompanying 'one of our men sympathisers', she had gained access to McKenna.

The New Year produced a Manhood Suffrage Bill without women's enfranchisement. The Speaker ruled out amendments (though pro-suffrage cabinet members such as Sir Edward Grey tried to promote them). The government had succeeded in further alienating the militants and now moderate suffragists looked to Labour rather than the Liberals.

In 1935 George Dangerfield's seminal publication *The Strange Death of Liberal England* claimed that these pre-war years were part of a general crisis, of which the women's rebellion was a crucial component. Historians have long debated his thesis (which stretched the meanings of the words 'Edwardian' and 'England' to encompass the period that ended in war and involved challenges to English dominance). Whether or not accepting the idea of *a* crisis of Liberalism (or liberalism), it remains the case that all parties faced fundamental challenges and 'Labour Unrest' as well as the struggle over Irish Home Rule. Such turbulence inevitably affected the fortunes of women's suffrage.[13]

Florence Haig was alert to the gendered use of language in the way the press described militant action, neatly declaring that '[r]aid is the feminine of deputation'.[14] If a group of men protested, it was described as a deputation but female composition rendered it a raid. Within Wales, issues of nationalism, labour relations and religion (particularly church disestablishment) commanded attention alongside women's suffrage. The inter-connectedness of suffrage and labour militancy is noticeable, not least in terms of timing and the demands on the police in industrial Wales. The fluctuating fortunes of the crises and their competition for attention can be seen in the topical cartoons by the prolific political commentator J.M. Staniforth in the *Western Mail*.

Some of the most pressing matters of the day had a direct link to Margaret and her family. At the same time as Margaret and Sybil were immersing themselves in women's suffrage, D.A. was facing the Cambrian Combine dispute in mid-Rhondda and both issues were reported with some fervour in the Welsh press. The Cambrian Combine was D.A.'s creation: a consolidation of colliery combines dating from 1908 which eight years later controlled two-thirds of the coal output of the Rhondda valleys. A lack of agreement over piece-rates in the autumn of 1910 was followed by wholesale stoppages involving at least 11,000 men and the Tonypandy Riots. The protracted strike lasted until late summer 1911. Pitted against D.A. and the Combine – characterised by Chris Williams as 'the epitome of capitalist combination and progressiveness'[15] – were men who had their own combine committee. They too displayed progressiveness and modernity, albeit in a somewhat different form, through their developing ideas about workers' control.

Early in 1912 British miners went on strike nationally for a minimum wage. Every pit in south Wales closed. The outcome was a compromise measure, but nevertheless a Minimum Wage Act was passed. There now appeared what Kenneth O. Morgan has called 'probably the most famous document of industrial revolt ever produced in the Welsh or any other coalfield', *The Miners' Next Step*.[16] It declared its faith in industrial unionism, aiming to achieve workers' control of industry and 'real democracy' through direct action. This syndicalist declaration (from Noah Ablett and members of the Unofficial Reform Committee of the South Wales Miners' Federation), which put the focus on the producer, sent a shiver down many a spine. D.A. was far from being an old-style coal master. He could see the value of organised labour and believed in collective bargaining and a minimum wage. But as Morgan has stressed, his fear was that syndicalism fostered disunity and challenged his vision of one coalfield united by common interests.[17] For the *Western Mail* the syndicalist message was anathema. On 27 February 1912 the paper called it an 'amazingly wicked proposal'.

The next day Sybil and Edith Pilliner (treasurer of Newport WSPU and married to a JP) held an At Home at Newport's Westgate Hotel, scene of the famous Chartist Newport Rising of November 1839. Lady Isabel Margesson told the large gathering that about ninety-five per cent of sweated workers were female because they lacked the protection of the vote. Women had, however, learned the lessons of militancy and 'the next thing they touched would be property... Militant methods must go on, and the suffering must be endured'.[18] Militant had multiple meanings in the heady atmosphere of 1912.

In London 150 militants were arrested after what the *Western Mail* called 'an insane attack on shops'. Christabel Pankhurst declared that '[t]he fact that the miners are going to get legislation because they have made themselves a nuisance is a direct incitement to women to endeavour to obtain a similar privilege'.[19]

Margaret meanwhile used the Welsh press to deplore the government's 'useless pledges, evasions and procrastinations'. In her 'Woman's Cause' column, she was especially critical of the way McKenna managed to 'dodge' rather than answer parliamentary queries about the treatment of women in prison. As for his attitude towards these rank and file prisoners, it was 'frankly impossible to understand'.[20]

In her view, the Liberal government had reneged on their promises to the women in a way that would never have happened to men with votes. Was it surprising, she asked in the *Western Mail*, that, having been so goaded, some were now 'in a reckless and even dangerous mood'? She quoted the moderate Lady Betty Balfour who had pointed out the government's hypocrisy of crying shame at suffrage acts while applauding Sir Edward Carson when he declared that he was prepared to break every law in Ireland to oppose Home Rule.[21]

The government's inconsistency in dealing with different types of militancy prompted a number of letters from Margaret. In 1914 she criticised the way that, unlike suffragette action, threats of civil war in Ulster provoked government responses. Was it therefore 'more wicked to destroy property than life'?[22] Nevertheless, it is noticeable that, despite her excoriating words about the government, D.A.'s daughter did not participate in the election and by-election campaigns within Wales where suffragettes did their best to ensure the defeat of Liberal candidates. At the end of 1909 Lloyd George stayed at Llanwern and was photographed on the lawn with its owners. The *Western Mail* called the family 'passive suffragettes'.[23]

This paper included some positive information about suffrage. An account praising Rachel Barrett's considerable organisational abilities and portraying her as an untiring worker for the cause was possibly written by Margaret.[24] But in its editorials, Parliamentary reports and its use of adjectives, the paper, like the local NUWSS, made clear its distaste for the direction in which the WSPU was moving.

Staniforth's cartoons were unequivocal. 'The Sane and the Insane Sisters' contrasted a wild woman with a bomb and a law-abiding moderate.[25] In the same issue there was a report on the arrival of the south Wales contingent of the NUWSS marchers in the Suffrage Pilgrimage to Hyde Park, describing them as 'anti-outrage' women. An earlier cartoon had depicted suffragette census resisters hiding on census night 1911. Barrett had found an unoccupied building in Albany Road, Cardiff where about fifty women gathered, as *Punch* quipped, 'to take leave of their census' as part of the tactics of passive protest that were particularly popular with the Women's Freedom League.[26] The *Western Mail* repeatedly spelt Annie Kenney's name incorrectly. At the end of 1912 it mentioned that 'Dark stories' were circulating about new, sensational militant methods ahead.[27]

The press was torn between the wonderful stories provided by these imaginative publicity-conscious activists and the distaste that many readers would feel for the cause.[28] As 'suffragette outrages' increased in frequency, so more space was devoted to them, especially since Wales was providing plenty of incidents by 1913. Stories were carefully positioned within the paper. A report of suffragette action on 21 March 1913 was followed in the same column by an account of an Englishman shot by a Spaniard in Paris.

Margaret was ready to correct misrepresentation by journalists. In a letter in the *Western Mail* in April 1913 simply signed M.H. Mackworth, she reacted against an account of a meeting held at the Temperance Hall, Newport, at which she had been present. Chillingly polite at the outset: 'I feel convinced that you would not for one moment intentionally misrepresent what happened', she then weighed in, suggesting that a false impression had been given of what was actually a crowded and successful meeting. She denied that any missiles had been directed anywhere near the speakers though the editor responded, stressing that eggs had been thrown outside the hall, one having landed at the feet of their informant.[29]

Margaret also ridiculed Winston Churchill's record on suffrage, declaring that he had been a supporter in 1908 when he needed votes in the by-election in Manchester, but had soon changed his tune. She outlined his shifting positions and his recent opposition to the women's suffrage amendments to the Franchise Bill. This daughter of the erstwhile Liberal MP and industrialist ended her letter suggesting that 'Members of the Government not only sit on the safety valve: they seem determined to stoke up the boiler fires as well'.[30] She had particular reason to single out Churchill for attack.

Five months after writing these words Margaret was arrested. Her shift from verbal to incendiary assault mirrors the movement more generally but it also had specific personal implications. In her autobiography she joked about prison and her family, flippantly suggesting that this was hardly a 'big deal' for unconventional people like the Haigs: 'The truth is that it was almost the done thing in our family to go to prison'.[31] Her father had a similar sense of humour. In November 1913 he proposed the vote of thanks to C.F.G. Masterman at a huge Liberal gathering at Westminster's Central Hall. There had been a few interruptions from suffragettes. D.A. remarked what a wonderful evening it had been and added: 'When I go home I shall have the pleasure of telling my wife and daughter – both of whom are at present out of prison – what a treat they have missed.'[32]

Margaret's autobiography even suggests that prison for Florence Haig was a pastime: she went 'at such intervals as she could afford to spare from her own trade of portrait painting'.[33] One of Florence's great-uncles had been imprisoned for speaking in favour of men's suffrage during the turbulent years leading to the 1832 Reform Act. Her sister Eva went to prison for a month early in 1913.

Sybil's sisters were also incarcerated. Edith Haig's granddaughter has recalled that Edith was viewed 'as a great backslider' by the family as she had not been to prison. Margaret boasted that Aunt Janetta, widow of a Deputy Lieutenant and High Sheriff of Durham, 'went most regularly, never less than once a year'.[34] She steeled herself to break one of the lovely plate-glass windows displaying fashions at D.H. Evans. She carried her hammer in a brown paper bag and Florence Haig hid hers in an umbrella. They broke two windows apiece (Margaret's account of Janetta smashing window after window is entertaining but fanciful)[35]. After being let out on bail Aunt Janetta returned to the department store the next day to buy a new hat.

She was staying at Llanwern when Sybil and Margaret held a garden party to win over local clergy to the cause. A representative from the Church League for Women's Suffrage spoke (D.A. was a member). The intention was not to promote militancy, but Aunt Janetta insisted on greeting each clergyman with 'How do you do – I've *just* come out of prison'.[36]

Janetta and Sybil's sister Lottie contrived to be arrested on an occasion that became infamous: the attempt by more than 300 women who volunteered 'active service' in Westminster on 18 November 1910. The event was carefully orchestrated and all the women on the deputation were told to wear special badges. A four-page circular of instructions from Christabel Pankhurst spelt out the plan and explained what would happen to those arrested.[37] Ironically, given the outcome, it stressed that their quarrel was not with the police but with the government. In the event, the women's attempt to enter Parliament (divided into detachments) to present a memorial to the prime minister, which protested against the policy of 'shuffling and delay', resulted in prolonged physical attacks by the police. They were so brutal and humiliating (of 139 statements alleging violence, 29 included indecency) that on the Home Secretary Churchill's instructions the charges against the 115 women and four men were dropped the following day.[38] The confrontation lasted six hours and became known as Black Friday. Margaret had accompanied Lottie to Parliament Square though not as a volunteer. Shocked by the police aggression she witnessed, she found herself swearing aloud in public.

Another suffragette providing vital moral support that day was the novelist and former actress Elizabeth Robins. She drove round the area in a cab, collecting exhausted women and taking them to teashops. She called the journey from Caxton Hall to the Commons 'a via dolorosa' and saw enough to 'send me away sick and shuddering'.[39] Meanwhile Aunt Lottie had given several hearty whacks to a police horse. She refused to accept the mounted policeman's suggestion that she head home and was taken to Scotland Yard only to be dismissed with a caution the next day.

Margaret carefully placed herself in the crowd but not the front line because she had promised her husband that she would never go to prison. But although this promise had been made as part of a 'laughing bargain' in 1909, four years later when women were still denied the right to vote and the atmosphere much more charged, Margaret reconsidered her position.

Yet there was perhaps another reason why she was prepared to engage in militant action by 1913. In her autobiography she states that 'Cecilia and Eva Haig were both arrested' for their suffrage activities.[40] This brief statement about her older relatives (Florence's sisters) hides as much as it reveals. Cecilia was one of the women severely assaulted and trampled on in Parliament Square on Black Friday. Florence nursed her for just over a year but Cecilia died on the last day of 1911.

There is no absolute proof that the violence of that day, whether from police or onlookers, was directly responsible for any women's deaths. The journalist H.N. Brailsford (secretary of the Conciliation Committee) and Dr. Jessie Murray compiled a memorandum on the treatment of the women's deputation by the police and submitted it to the Home Office. Their request for a public enquiry was not granted. The testimony they gathered included evidence from the disabled May Billinghurst. She told how the police threw her out of her invalid tricycle which was then immobilised. She was left in the middle of a hostile crowd.

The WSPU claimed that two deaths before the end of the year – of Mrs Clarke (Mrs Pankhurst's sister) and Henria Williams – were attributable to Black Friday. In fact Mrs Clarke was not injured on Black Friday but did take part in window breaking, for which she was imprisoned for a month. She died of a brain haemorrhage shortly after being released. However, the authors of the memorandum argued from their evidence that the elderly Henria Williams (who died on New Year's Day 1911 of heart failure) 'had been used with great brutality'.[41] She did, though, have a pre-existing heart condition, so might possibly have had a heart attack at any time.[42]

The memorandum was completed before Cecilia's death, so her loss of life could not be considered there. But in *Votes for Women* in early 1912 Cecilia's death was attributed to 'the terrible treatment to which she was subjected on Black Friday', and it was stressed that she had been well beforehand.[43] Sylvia Pankhurst later argued that the day's injuries were responsible for her death and for that of Nurse Ellen Pitfield, who was wounded and subsequently died in 1912.[44] She stressed that Cecilia was 'a tall, strongly built, reserved woman, comfortably situated, who in ordinary circumstances might have gone through life without ever receiving an insult, much less a blow'.

On 14 January 1912 Annie Kenney planted a weeping cypress tree in memory of Cecilia in the arboretum at Eagle House, Batheaston. This was the home of the pro-suffrage Blathwayt family. Here was a place where trees were planted to commemorate prison sentences and hunger strikes and where a 'Suffragette Rest' was provided for those in need of recuperation. The plaque identifying Cecilia's tree stated that she died 'from injuries while on a Deputation to the prime minister'.[45]

It is what Margaret does *not* say that is significant. Her account of Black Friday makes no mention of her cousin Cecilia despite the fact that the Haigs were such a tight-knit family. Neither was her subsequent death then funeral at Highgate mentioned. Margaret did, however lay the blame for the disastrous day on Winston Churchill, stating that he had decided on a new policy of terrorising the women into giving up the fight.[46] She referred to the allegation that he had arranged for arrested women to be discharged, thus preventing the creation of martyrs, and that he had given orders to the police to treat the women as brutally as possible. It was 'understood' that he had drafted in police from the East End who were unused to dealing with suffragettes. The raid on Westminster was to be made 'such an intolerable, humiliating and unbearable thing that no woman who took part in it would ever face it again'. Margaret added that Churchill officially denied such motives and claimed that his orders had been misunderstood. Her anger was channelled through this attack. The family tragedy was not mentioned in print.

Black Friday marked a turning-point in suffragette tactics. No longer would there be raids on Parliament. Stone-throwing at property became the militants' new weapon, followed by incendiary activity. Robins saw it as engendering 'a new sense of sex solidarity'.[47] Margaret concluded that she could no longer be held to the promise that she had made to her husband in a somewhat different political climate.

Splitting hairs, she reasoned that she had promised not to go to prison rather than not to break the law. There was, she convinced herself, only a comparatively small risk of being caught and so, without saying a word to her husband or family, she began to take 'what quiet share I could' in such activities. This, of course, suggests that she was involved in rather more than the one infamous incident where she was found out.

The drama teacher and actress Edith Lester Jones of Cardiff (who ran elocution classes for suffragettes on Friday evenings in Newport) provided some fascinating oral testimony many years later. This magistrate's daughter described filling a letter box in the centre of Cardiff with an envelope containing treacle, ink and soot – the 'filthiest mixture' she could find. Margaret, she said, gave her 'magnificent support' during this period and the two women 'worked together quite a lot'.[48] Edith Lester Jones and a Miss Bach also attempted (in disguise at night) to burn down a house in Cyncoed, Cardiff. They broke in through the window – 'in the approved way with a stone in brown paper' – and lit a fuse then fled. When she undertook what she called her 'little bit of arson', Edith Lester Jones stayed 'of course' with 'Mrs Humphrey Mackworth'.

In late October 1912 the *Western Mail* reported 'an extraordinary outrage' by suffragettes in the Ilford area. Letter boxes had been tampered with and mail damaged. Matchboxes filled with cocoa or cotton wool were saturated with paraffin. A note made clear that it was 'hateful work' but that the government needed to be made aware that 'there can be no law or order until women get the right to vote'.[49] Arson attacks did not remain 'extraordinary' for long. Emily Wilding Davison had already set fire to three pillar boxes in Parliament Street in London the previous December, and in her defence explained that she was seeking to gain the attention of the private citizen. She had been sentenced to six months in prison.[50]

Close to 50,000 pillar boxes existed across the UK by the early twentieth century. From the spring of 1912 they were targeted. This activity soon gathered pace, attracting both support and opprobrium. Liquid tar, treacle, gum and gunpowder were used. One woman attacked the same post box in Lewisham ten times in four months, starting with ink and progressing to phials of phosphorous. The Postmaster-General Herbert Samuel (whose young nephew Hugh Franklin was a suffrage activist who attacked Churchill with a horsewhip) invited the public to help prevent such disturbances and offered rewards to those obtaining the arrest of an offender.

Wales had its share of sabotage. On one weekend in early March 1913 there were fourteen attacks on letter boxes in Cardiff alone. Golf links and race courses were attacked, telegraph wires cut as part of an accelerating 'Women's Civil War'.[51] When McKenna visited Cardiff in May (primarily to discuss church disestablishment) women could not get into his meeting in the Park Hall without prior permission. McKenna denounced 'the criminal and sensational activities of certain women who endeavoured to further a political cause by means of violence'.[52]

There were some hoaxes, attempts to discredit the movement by claiming that suffragettes were responsible for disorder. Wales had seventeen branches of the National League for Opposing Woman Suffage by 1913. Not far from Margaret's home, a lad employed in the grounds of Llangattock Rectory set fire to a shed and stables, and left a paper demanding votes for women.[53] He later confessed that he had tried to blame the suffragettes for his own actions. In a speech in Cardiff in February 1913, Mrs Pankhurst took full responsibility for the burning of Lloyd George's new house at Walton Heath. Her trial and subsequent prison sentence of three years and hunger strikes literally made the situation more inflammatory.

New legislation, the Prisoners Temporary Discharge for Ill-Health Act, appropriately nicknamed the Cat and Mouse Act, permitted prisoners to be released on licence if their health was endangered after hunger-striking. They were subsequently incarcerated again without further trial. Mrs Pankhurst was re-arrested nine times between late May 1913 and mid-June 1914 under this act. It intensified the drama of the suffrage story, particularly since she became extremely weak and at times was thought to be close to death. The Cat and Mouse Act had been devised by McKenna and rushed through Parliament. Mrs Pankhurst remarked how he would 'bring us to death's door as often as he can, and so hopes to make us permanent invalids'. She added, 'Well, we shall see.'[54]

The atmosphere was heightened further in June by the drama surrounding the death of Emily Wilding Davison at the Derby. Charles Mansell Moullin (vice-president of the Royal College of Surgeons and pro-suffrage husband of the London Welsh suffragette, Edith Mansell Moullin) sought in vain to save her life. It was rumoured that she had been a secretary at Llanwern Park. This seems unlikely, although she would have been known to Sybil and Margaret. A graduate, she had been a schoolteacher and private tutor before immersing herself in women's suffrage. She was imprisoned eight times between 1909 and 1912 and endured horrific forcible feeding. The attempt to link her with the Thomas family suggests how they were viewed by those nervous of suffrage militancy.

In that same month Margaret took the action that landed her in prison.[55] In her autobiography written twenty years later, she admitted that her branch had already performed 'various small acts of militancy', but nothing spectacular. So 'I decided that we had better try burning letters'. But she was not the first Newport suffragette to take militant action and receive punishment. In March 1912 Olive Fontaine (who became co-secretary of the Newport WSPU with Margaret later that year) was imprisoned in London for a month with hard labour for window-breaking. When she was released, the Newport WSPU held a meeting to welcome her home, at which 'the heroine of the occasion' told her audience that she was 'glad to be out of Holloway, but gladder still that she went'.[56]

Margaret's attack was not the first assault on Newport's letter boxes. There were several local newspaper reports in December 1912 of pillar box 'outrages' using uncorked bottles with fluid.[57] The following April, two were targeted in the Stow Hill area of Newport, not far from the WSPU office. A policeman noticed that one was emitting smoke and intervened before any damage was done. The glass tubes containing acid were labelled 'Votes for Women'.

It is possible that Margaret was behind these attacks too. If she had also been involved in incendiary activity in the spring, Housman's account of their dinner conversation would make more sense. Margaret had initially disapproved of such tactics, but the heightened atmosphere of 1913 polarised many opinions. She reasoned that attacking letter boxes did not run the risk of damaging life. Her action (described by Edith Lester Jones as merely doing 'something to upset the inside of a pillar box')[58] was no different from that of many other women. But the attention it received was remarkable.

Margaret's account of the background to the episode is interesting, not least because it raises some of the practical difficulties involved. She went all the way to the WSPU headquarters in London to get her ammunition. Suffragettes worked with sympathetic pharmacists in devising concoctions and one chemist was sentenced to five years' imprisonment for her collusion.[59] Margaret was given twelve long glass tubes with corks. Six contained phosphorous and the other six held a chemical compound. When mixed together they produced flames. She travelled home in a crowded third-class railway compartment with her incendiary materials in a flimsy covered basket on the seat beside her. To Margaret's alarm, at intervals the woman sitting next to her casually leant on the basket with her elbow .

Then there was the question of where to hide the tubes. Margaret decided to bury them at Oaklands in the vegetable garden under the blackcurrant bushes. A week or so later she took them to the WSPU shop in Stow Hill to demonstrate to members how simple an operation this was. According to her autobiography, they were not convinced, so she decided to set an example and take action herself. However, she found it far from easy.

On 25 June she placed two of the tubes in a foolscap envelope and took a tram for the five-mile journey to Risca Road, Newport: 'My heart was beating like a steam engine, my throat was dry'. She was so nervous that she drew attention by walking past her target several times (for half an hour according to one account) before plucking up the courage to drop the package, with the corks removed, into the letter box on the cemetery wall. She posted a handwritten postcard. The basket was buried again under the blackcurrants.

By now suffragettes were notorious throughout Wales. As the daughter of a Harlech domestic servant later explained: 'In those days the very name of Suffragette was something mysterious, even unpleasant. We'd say "Here comes a Suffragette" and run like blazes.'[60] A recent article in the Monmouthshire press had deplored an earlier 'senseless attack' on Newport letter boxes by 'these fanatical women' and ended with a plea that the public cooperate. Now they did so. Margaret had been observed by a window cleaner and several ladies. The Harrison sisters lived opposite the letter box. Although they could not see what was put into it, as one of them later explained in court (prompting laughter) 'She knew Mrs Mackworth was a Suffragette, and was suspicious'.

Within a few minutes, smoke could be seen coming from the letter box. A crowd gathered and, according to the *Argus*, 'some caustic comments' were made about the suffragettes and such outrages. Water from a nearby house was used to extinguish the smoke (some newspaper accounts mentioned flames). A postman rescued the letters.

Margaret's autobiography claims that nothing happened (apart from the spread of rumours) for a week or so, but this account does not fully record what followed. The next day, as she was on her way from Oaklands to a tea party in Llanwern village, Detective-Sergeant Caldecott and Police Constable King appeared and signalled for the car to stop. The *Western Mail* commented that she took this 'in good part in her usual light-hearted way'. In the first of a series of somewhat farcical actions reinforcing her social status, the Mackworths' chauffeur apparently drove them all to the police station (though in *This Was My World* Margaret claimed that she was driving). She was permitted to write notes, so she sent one asking her husband – who was at a puppy show – to provide bail and for Aunt Lottie to come to the station.

Margaret was locked in a cell with a wall covered in vomit. It smelt like a urinal. She remained there for four hours, the chief constable hoping that this would 'put the fear of God into me that I should never want to misbehave again'. Aunt Lottie offered to stand bail but, to her extreme annoyance, this was refused. It was said that when Lottie was angry you could almost see red sparks coming out of her 'terrific flashing eyes'. Humphrey arrived and he and Margaret paid £50 apiece. She then returned home.

The following day Margaret appeared before the Newport magistrates. According to the local paper, hundreds were turned away from the court. Aunt Lottie, in the spirit of the French Revolution, was resolutely knitting while waiting to be let into court. A worried Humphrey attended – this was a far cry from the society he must have envisaged on marrying the ex-debutante of Llanwern – and the secretary of Pontypool WSPU Clara Butler (daughter of a former High Sheriff and suffragist mother) was also present.

Margaret's solicitor John Moxon sought a fortnight's adjournment. He was a member of the Men's League for Women's Suffrage and had asked a question at the 1909 Llanwern reception for ex-Holloway prisoners. His request for adjournment was granted. The *Western Mail* described Margaret as 'one of the foremost leaders of the suffrage movement in the county of Monmouth'. The charge, made by the Postmaster-General, was the first of its kind in the town. Margaret was accused of unlawfully placing an explosive substance in a post office letter box. The press, including the *Suffragette* newspaper, described her in relation to her husband, father or father-in-law. Sybil was not mentioned.

Her parents were in the United States. D.A. was not pleased to hear what had happened but did send a telegram offering to try to get the eminent T.H. Healy KC (Mrs Pankhurst's barrister) to defend his daughter. But since Margaret 'did not particularly want to get off' she felt that this would have been a waste. Her mother was fully in support. By the time the case was heard on 11 July, her parents were home and able to attend court along with many others. The street outside was, according to the press, besieged by suffragettes from various parts of the country. Constables were placed all along the corridors and at each entrance. Eventually thirty or so watched the all-male bench (which consisted of six magistrates), lawyers and court officials at work.

Margaret pleaded 'Not Guilty' as the WSPU required, but 'made no special effort to pretend that I had not done the thing'. Lyndon Moore, the prosecutor (who actively supported the NUWSS) outlined the 'extremely clever and wicked plan', as well as expressing his regret that a lady of Mrs Mackworth's 'position, accomplishments and qualities' was charged with a crime. The contents of the tube had been prepared 'by a chemist of exceedingly great ability'. The chemical compound in one of the tubes was not described to the court lest it revealed vital information to eager ears. It was written down for the magistrates to read. In defence Moxon explained that Margaret was merely advancing the cause that was close to her heart, namely bettering the social position of the women of her country, and had acted from the best of motives. He attempted, not very convincingly, to distance her actions from those of the WSPU in London, claiming that this was an isolated case. He stressed that all reforms were preceded by some unrest, that there had been great provocation and that little damage had been done. He was right: just eight letters and five postcards had been damaged.

Margaret was found guilty and fined ten pounds plus ten pounds costs. The chairman of the bench added euphemistically that there was 'the usual alternative which I do not wish to mention'. Margaret refused to pay her fine or allow others to pay for her. Humphrey now reminded Margaret of their agreement that she would not go to prison. But she reasoned that letting down the suffrage cause would be worse than reneging on her promise. Her power of argument eventually persuaded a reluctant Humphrey that not only should she go ahead but that she should hunger strike too, especially since she had never promised not to do that. She was sentenced to a month in the county gaol at Usk.

Margaret arrived there in a highly unorthodox fashion, travelling in her father's car with the chief constable, her solicitor and the governor of the gaol. 'To Prison in a Motor' was how one newspaper headed an article on her court appearance.[61] Due to suffrage pressure the treatment of imprisoned suffragettes had improved. Margaret's cell was clean and light. She was permitted to wear her own clothes and have her own books. But she was deeply affected by the loneliness and the psychological effect of being 'Behind the Locked Door'[62].

It was, she later wrote, 'sheer taut misery'.[63] But she refused to see her solicitor when he arrived to try to persuade her to pay her fine.

Florence Haig scribbled her thoughts about inmates and prison conditions on squares of toilet paper and in a notebook when she was incarcerated.[64] Evelyn Sharp's observation of the treatment of non-political prisoners within Holloway Gaol was translated into short stories and a heightening of her social conscience. Communal hymn-singing in chapel was Margaret's only reference to other prisoners. Her hunger and thirst strike soon made her too weak to participate. The warders were kind and the doctor appeared horrified at the possibility of forcibly feeding his prisoner. The chaplain (the one person who seemed determined to punish her) stopped her reading library books because of the hunger strike, so she sat in her cell playing noughts and crosses on a slate.

After three days without food or water Margaret was feeling very feeble. She took a little water on the fourth night but still refused food and any medicine. The authorities were concerned about her health and released her on the sixth day under the terms of the Cat and Mouse Act. She was to return to gaol in eight days. She tore up her licence into little pieces in front of the warders and left with her mother and husband. She was weak and bruised, somewhat jaundiced and depressed. According to the press she remained at home in bed for some days cared for by hospital nurses. Her autobiography instead states: 'I went straight home and to bed for a day'. Llanwern villagers stress that she did not go home but stayed in a local cottage (probably Aunt Lottie's) to escape the press.

Whether this also meant that, like other 'mice', Margaret had plans to evade re-arrest we shall never know, since on the day that the licence expired (24 July) Margaret's fine was mysteriously paid. Now she did not need to return to prison. It has been assumed, but never proved, that her husband paid the money. On the same day an inaugural meeting of a branch meeting of the Church League for Women's Suffrage was held in a local hall. Sybil was one of the organisers. Margaret attended and, according to the press 'seemed to be quite recovered from the effects of her "hunger strike"'. When asked about the payment, she retorted that the fine had been paid contrary to her wishes and that she had not 'the faintest idea who paid it. I think it is an extraordinary law that will allow of a fine being paid without permission'. In response to a question about being re-arrested she answered, somewhat disingenuously, that she did not really know when the licence expired as she had torn it up as soon as she received it.

When newspapers reported that rather than return to prison she had chosen to pay the fine, Margaret countered with a letter reiterating that it had been paid 'entirely against my wishes'. This letter hinted that the Home Secretary might have arranged for it to be paid. Indeed, on the day that her fine was paid, Lady Sybil Smith, Evelyn Sharp and Emmeline Pethick-Lawrence were arrested after refusing to leave the House of Commons following a deputation to protest against the Cat and Mouse Act. After serving just four days of a fourteen-day sentence, they were suddenly and unexpectedly released unconditionally. Lady Sybil Smith was the daughter of the Countess of Antrim and the mother of seven children. The government had been bruised by the adverse publicity after a disguised Lady Constance Lytton had been badly treated in prison. It was now treading more warily. Sharp protested to McKenna against the alteration of her sentence.

Margaret had escaped lightly in every respect. Her crime was not great compared to the damage inflicted by some suffrage activity. Neither were its consequences. A tiny amount of mail had been destroyed, but a lot of energy was expended on bringing her to court and publicising the case. Many attackers of pillar boxes received three-month sentences. Unlike suffragettes in the limelight at the same time, for example Kitty Marion who received three years' penal servitude, or Annie Kenney who got an eighteen-month sentence, Margaret would not have been in prison for long even if she had returned there. As it was she spent just five nights in gaol and the means by which she arrived there were nothing like the indignities faced by many women. Her experience in the small gaol at Usk was a far cry from Holloway before spring 1910 when some rules were relaxed.[65]

Katharine Gatty (a member of the Irish Women's Franchise League with thirteen previous convictions) had smashed a pane at Abergavenny's post office the previous summer, then spent a month in Usk where she was twice forcibly fed after hunger striking. But Margaret escaped the horrendous pain and indignity of this punishment. After the introduction of the Cat and Mouse Act forcible feeding was not widely used.[66] Indeed, the evidence suggests that the authorities were, in the main, embarrassed by Mrs Mackworth's presence rather than determined to punish her. Her main complaint about conditions seems to have been that the mattress was very hard. Within a very short time she was lying out in the sun 'on the stock-scented terrace in our garden'.

Not surprisingly, concern was voiced about preferential treatment. The Newport and Monmouthshire branch of the 'Antis' was Wales's largest. And Margaret was known for her attacks on what she called their 'threadbare arguments'.[67] But they were not the only ones to complain. At a Newport Trades Council meeting the events in the police court were described as a 'farce'. James Davidson deplored the fact that a woman who had committed a crime subsequently went to lunch in the chief constable's office. But A.B. Moon praised Margaret for having the courage of her convictions, electing to go to prison rather than pay a fine that would have been 'a mere flea-bite' to a woman in her position.

Two councillors questioned the chief constable at a Watch Committee meeting. He made some lame excuses. Mrs Mackworth had been taken to his room after the sentence had been passed because the women's cells were being painted. As time was getting on, her parents had decided to send to the Westgate Hotel for some food and she had shared this. She had wished to go to gaol in a Black Maria but the chief constable had feared a suffrage demonstration, hence the private car. The prison governor accompanied them because he had been attending a meeting in Newport. The Watch Committee declared they were satisfied. Tip-toeing around the Thomases and Mackworths was not unusual.

The local press printed anonymous indignant letters with pointed pseudonyms such as 'Child of a Poor Man', 'Skilly', 'Equality and Justice' and 'Poor and Undistinguished'. They claimed that there was one law for the rich and another for the poor. One signed 'Citizen' asked why a court of justice had become a place of entertainment. Why had ladies been allowed in the well of the court and the chief constable's office become a tea room? This was hardly the treatment meted out to poor vagabonds convicted of sleeping rough. Class inequality came to the fore. 'Worker' declared that:

> the wives of the miners, by the sweat of whose brow the person now in Usk prison is enabled to live in luxury and devote her spare time to wanton and mischievous acts, would certainly see that she did not represent them in any movement which might be necessary to advance the welfare of themselves and the children committed to their cause.

'Fairplay' asked whether the prison had a drawing room in which militant suffragettes might be entertained. A martyrdom consisting of a nice lunch, an apology from everybody connected with the case and a ride in a motor car was, one cynic wrote, 'enough to cause a smile on the face of an owl'. However, Sybil told the press in mid-July that her daughter had not wished to take food before entering prison. She had only done so when told that if she did not eat, her fine would be paid immediately. Sybil did not specify who had said this.

Some used the incident as an opportunity to reinforce the value of domesticity. As one correspondent from Twickenham saw it:

> It is a pity that women, especially married women, cannot find sufficient domestic duties to keep them from such acts as these, and helping to lower the

opinion of the British woman in the eyes of other nations.

Another letter argued that only single women should have the vote, not married women. They had husbands to vote for them. If they wanted something to do they should help the poor and needy. Nevertheless, this lively discussion of who deserved the vote enabled ordinary citizens to debate the issues in print. One writer stressed that women like Mrs Fawcett were doing splendid work.

The day after Margaret began her sentence, Newport Suffrage Society advertised its forthcoming open-air meeting with the words 'Women's Suffrage does not mean spoiling other People's Property'.[68] After a slow start in Wales, NUWSS branches had flourished in the face of escalating militancy. Newport Suffrage Society (only formed in 1911) boasted several hundred members by the summer of 1912.

But just one day after Margaret's release on licence, a Newport WSPU fête and sale of work was held at Llanwern Park, hosted by Sybil. It raised fifty-five pounds. Margaret did not appear at her curio stall. In the evening there was a concert (violin solos, dancing and dramatic sketches) and a meeting. It was reported that Margaret was not well enough to attend but her 'bold and aggressive action' was applauded. Lady Isabel Margesson called her 'truly courageous'. Pontypool WSPU passed a vote applauding her hunger strike.

The National Eisteddfod was held in Abergavenny in the first week of August. There was concern, since suffragettes had targeted the Wrexham Eisteddfod of the previous year. There had followed an appalling over-reaction to the suffrage interruption of Lloyd George's speech in the north Wales village of Llanystumdwy. Now McKenna was one of the two presidents on the Thursday at Abergavenny. But his appearance in the pavilion was changed at the last minute (he spoke in the morning rather than the afternoon). All passed off peacefully. D.A. was due to preside the next day but did not, in the end, attend.

As for Humphrey, he was somewhat concerned about the incriminating evidence that remained under the blackcurrant bushes. He dug up the basket with the remaining unused tubes and threw it into an underground rainwater tank. But it opened and all ten tubes floated up for all to see. So, using the weapon he knew best, he shot them to smithereens with his rifle. Although clearly embarrassed by his wife's actions, he had to some extent colluded in her activities, and Margaret was aware that she was in a rather different position from some of her privileged contemporaries. Lady Sybil Smith's husband, for example, refused to talk to her about suffrage, let alone imprisonment. Neither did her erstwhile friends support her. Her mother took the 'high principled lunatic line'. She told Evelyn Sharp that 'the notoriety scorches me'.[69]

Margaret did not cease to be a committed suffragette. On 23 October she published an uncompromising article in the *Western Mail* on the same page as the editorial, denouncing the Cat and Mouse Act. The legislation had, she wrote, been rushed through 'a somewhat reluctant and shamefaced' House of Commons and was not in accordance with the best traditions of past statesmanship at times of unrest. It had introduced a radically new principle into British law, had greatly enhanced the powers of the Home Office and police yet patently failed in its bid to annihilate militancy. Forcible feeding had just been resumed, so the reasoning that the act would stop this abhorrent practice had, Margaret argued, been proved false. She even asked whether McKenna's plan all along might not have been to reintroduce this torture once a decent interval had elapsed.

She remained secretary of the Newport branch of the WSPU. Some idea of its many activities can be gained from the weekly reports she sent to the *Suffragette*, the new official organ of the WSPU, which had started in October 1912 with an initial circulation of about 17,000. Margaret's erstwhile ally Rachel Barrett was its assistant editor and in effect ran the paper as Christabel Pankhurst was in France. After moving from Newport to Cardiff to become the organiser for all of Wales, Barrett had helped Kenney with the national WSPU campaign. In the spring of 1913 Barrett had been arrested, along with other members of staff. She was subsequently imprisoned, went on hunger strike and became an elusive 'mouse', successfully evading the authorities. She and Kenney's sister Jessie defiantly produced what was now in effect an underground paper.[70]

Pontypool, Cardiff and Newport sent in regular reports. Margaret complained that her reports were often cut down. She also wrote occasional reviews for the paper, misremembering this later and claiming in her autobiography that they appeared in *Votes for Women*.[71] The *Suffragette* openly promoted militancy and the government sought, unsuccessfully, to suppress it.

Margaret's reports for the months after her imprisonment suggest a busy and lively branch. Indeed, throughout its existence Newport was one of the WSPU's most active branches in Wales, which only boasted a total of nine WSPU branches. Its success must have been helped by the fact that, unlike many branches which saw changes in key personnel, Margaret was its secretary throughout its existence (though she shared the post with Olive Fontaine for about six months from late 1912). Its autumn campaign in 1913 opened with a lantern lecture on the history of the militant movement. On Wednesday afternoons members and friends gathered for At Homes and evenings were devoted to public meetings, some of which Margaret chaired. She appealed for people to host meetings in nearby Risca, Crosskeys, Abercarn and Newbridge. There is no mention of events at Oaklands though Margaret continued to address meetings in the Newport area as well as speaking outside her home patch. In November she and the Cardiff-based Wales organiser Annie Williams spoke in Penarth, with Sybil chairing the meeting. That same month the office moved to a more central space at Western Mail Chambers, Newport. Prid, who had been the WSPU organiser for Bristol for the first half of 1913, addressed some open-air meetings in the Newport area.

The Newport branch held a Christmas sale, jumble sales, interviewed doctors and asked them to protest against forcible feeding. It ran *Café Chantants* at which members sang, danced and acted. It sold Christabel Pankhurst's *The Great Scourge, and How to End It* with its uncompromising articles on prostitution, venereal disease and the white slave trade. In line with other branches, members interrupted tea rooms and church services with speeches and sent copies of *The Great Scourge* to all local clergymen (Margaret contributed five shillings towards this). In April 1914 she was one of twenty suffragettes who went on a deputation to the Bishop of Llandaff to urge his support in their protest against the Cat and Mouse Act and forcible feeding. She spoke about the degradation of the system, equating forcible feeding with physical assault. The following month, when the House of Lords debated women's suffrage, the Bishop of Llandaff voted in its favour. Margaret also appealed in the *Suffragette* for suggestions to increase sales of the paper and to recruit new subscribers during 'Suffragette Week'. This celebrated the moment when the government had raided the paper but failed to silence it.

All this evidence of group activity comes, however, from suffrage sources rather than Margaret's autobiography, which ignores the individual suffrage stalwarts of Newport. By the time she came to write her account she might well have forgotten their names and, had she remembered them, she would not necessarily have included them in a book that was aimed at a wide readership. The result is, nevertheless, an account that does not convey much sense of the group activities of Newport WSPU.

On 7 August 1914, just after war had been declared, the *Suffragette* report for Newport thanked Mrs D.A. Thomas for lending her 'lovely grounds' for a WSPU fête. But not all of Sybil's activities that year were so pacific. Back in February she had been arrested in London. This was, according to Margaret, something that her mother had decided must be undertaken although her husband disapproved of such action.

Sybil organised a petition attacking the Cat and Mouse Act as cruel, against the best traditions of British law and 'subversive of constitutional liberties'.[72] It also denounced forcible feeding as an 'outrage on humanity'. Prid helped to obtain the signatures of 108 people (about a third of whom were men, including thirteen clergymen). The plan was to deliver the petition to Asquith and to hold a meeting in front of the entrance to the House of Commons. Sybil did not approve of the stone-throwing that had replaced parliamentary deputations. She had chosen instead a peaceful means of protest that nonetheless involved breaking the law since it was illegal to hold open-air meetings within a mile of Westminster. Such a tactic did not go down well with all the supporters of the petition. Twelve days before this protest the novelist Israel Zangwill, who had played a prominent part in the law-abiding Men's League and signed the petition in good faith, wrote an angry letter to Sybil denouncing her plan.

Undeterred, on 24 February Sybil and a small group held a meeting at the Hotel Cecil, then walked to Downing Street. Nevinson, Henry Harben and Miss Eaton took the petition to the prime minister but he would not meet them. The group moved on to Parliament Square and held their meeting by the statue of Richard the Lionheart. They delivered speeches, protesting against the government's denial of the right of petition and made 'a definite attempt to get into prison' (as Housman put it). Sybil tried to get onto the statue 'quite a dozen times' according to the police. She then walked into the centre of the road and began addressing the crowd. Margaret's cousin Katherine Haig (who lived in Cardiff) placed herself on the statue's plinth. Anticipating trouble, about 300 policemen intervened. Sybil, Haig, Housman, Harben, Nevinson and the radical journalist Francis Meynell were arrested and marched to Scotland

Yard. According to Nevinson they continued 'to pour out eloquence of the very best en route'.

The next day was Sybil's fifty-seventh birthday. She spent much of it in a cell at Bow Street, as did her partners in crime. Called one by one before the chief magistrate Sir John Dickinson, they were charged with 'Interfering with the police in the execution of their duty'. Sybil was the last to appear. The press called her a 'lady of distinguished appearance' in 'costly black and grey furs'. Margaret, who was in court with D.A., heard her mother carefully describe the group as 'a body of constitutional suffragists'. Sybil explained that, for some months, she had asked Asquith to receive them but he had constantly refused. She therefore justified her action by declaring that 'there was no other way as a woman but to go and do this. I went quite deliberately and intended to be taken up, for I knew that was the only way in which my views could be heard'.

Each of the defendants was ordered to be bound over to keep the peace and be of good behaviour for six months on the payment of £5 each (Meynell, who had winded a policeman was also fined £2). They all refused these terms, claiming that they had been doing their public duty, so were given one day's imprisonment, which simply amounted to being held in the cells until the court rose that afternoon. Nevinson was disappointed but he wittily acknowledged in his diary that 'you can't go to prison if the law keeps you out'. Sybil's refusal to be bound over was greeted with a loud round of applause. Margaret sent the protesters 'an enormous lunch'. D.A. declared that he was proud of his wife: 'she answered the magistrate very well indeed'. He presented her with a Greek Archimandrite gold cross studded with diamonds and emeralds. An inscription was added later commemorating both her birth on Ash Wednesday 1857 and the dramatic birthday on Ash Wednesday 1914.

The authorities had turned the tables. Conscious of the scandal that could be roused by imprisoning the wife of a former Liberal MP and immensely wealthy businessman, they had retreated. Nevinson's autobiography points out that 'owing to the great wealth and high position' of Mrs D.A. Thomas, the Home Office had been consulted. Tongue in cheek, he added that 'since we are all equal before the law, and it would never do to imprison a lady of her quality' they were all dismissed with 'a further lecture on the beauty of law and order'. Imprisoning voluble and influential journalists like Nevinson would also have been great publicity for the militants. As it was, he composed a vivid article for *Votes for Women* from his cell. The following month, Margaret wrote a long and favourable review of *Prisons and Prisoners*, in which Lady Constance Lytton recounted her horrendous treatment as a suffrage prisoner in disguise.[73]

The evening after Sybil appeared in court a public meeting was held at Kingsway Hall chaired by Mrs Pethick-Lawrence. Sybil sat on the platform with her fellow protesters and was received with great cheers. But not everybody was pleased. As a result of her arrest, the committee of the London Society for Women's Suffrage requested that Mrs Thomas resign her membership of the London Society for Women's Suffrage.[74] She had been a member since the 1890s and was a vice-president.[75]

Ironically, just under six months later on 4 August 1914, the day Britain declared war on Germany, Sybil

Thomas was involved in discussions with McKenna and the press baron Lord Riddell (who would later play a part in Margaret's life) about the terms under which suffragette prisoners were to be given an amnesty. For Margaret, the war would halt suffrage work, but once the conflict was over she would become a leader in the British campaign to enfranchise women over twenty-one.

CHAPTER FOUR

Survival: The *Lusitania*

It was not long before the First World War affected Margaret personally. Early in November 1914 her brother-in-law Major Francis Julian Audley Mackworth was killed in action. Humphrey became assistant superintendent of the Remount Service and was stationed in Bristol which meant that Margaret only saw him at weekends. His father's death that year saw Humphrey inherit the family title and Margaret become Lady Mackworth.

The war would turn the protester into a patriot, though at first Margaret adhered to her pre-war allegiances, even appearing as a voice of opposition to the military or at least as a bridge between them and the suffrage movement. Four days after the declaration of war, the Defence of the Realm Act was passed, giving the government emergency powers over many areas of everyday life. Worried about a rise in prostitution due to the large army presence, Colonel East, who commanded the Severn Defences, issued an order banning women (except for licensees, relatives, servants and lodgers) from Cardiff's public houses after 7pm. A curfew was also imposed between 7pm and 8am with the threat of a court martial for being caught in the streets. Such blatant gendered targeting smacked of the state regulation of vice and ensured a response from feminists.

Since the start of the year a number of suffrage supporters had come together in a new mixed-sex organisation called the United Suffragists (Sybil was a vice-president). It would remain committed to campaigning for the vote throughout the war, and was particularly concerned to combat sex discrimination and champion the interests of women affected adversely by wartime conditions. Ten women alleged to be prostitutes were charged with breaking the Cardiff curfew, remanded for two months and warned that a repetition of the offence would result in prison for six months with hard labour. Two more were apprehended. The United Suffragists responded.

Their deputation to protest to Colonel East consisted of Margaret, Mrs Woolf, proprietor of the Royal Hotel in the centre of Cardiff, the Rev. Herbert Davies and United Suffragists Evelyn Sharp, George Lansbury and Barbara Ayrton Gould. Margaret introduced the deputation. They expressed concern that power was being placed in the hands of the police to identify certain women as prostitutes. This and a large United Suffragist meeting in Cardiff had the desired result and a week later the order was withdrawn and all the women released.[1]

Yet within months Margaret and Sharp were taking radically different positions on the war and women's service. For Sharp, the conflict underlined the need for religious faith, steering her towards a pacifist position. Margaret, however, chose to undertake service to the state. Although not going so far as the militaristic *Women's Dreadnought* edited by Christabel Pankhurst, she would not protest again about wartime impositions. She was well aware of the deliberate fomenting of hate against Germans, and acknowledged many years later that some part of her understood that this meant 'believing many lies' but she argued that 'unreasonable hatred' had been justified in the circumstances.[2]

Margaret had experienced some melodramatic moments in the suffrage struggle but nothing could have prepared her for the drama of May 1915 when she almost lost her life. In March of that year her mother-in-law died, and soon after the Dowager Lady Mackworth's funeral she set off on a ten-day voyage to New York. She was joining her father who was already there on a seven-week business trip. It was not her first visit: a year earlier she had sailed to New York with Humphrey on the *Mauretania*. But the brief spring interlude in Manhattan in 1915 when Margaret mixed business and pleasure with D.A., who much admired American 'can do' attitudes, was later recalled as the most enjoyable of her many travels. The escape from wartime Britain was very welcome, and in retrospect the contrast with the horror of what happened on the return voyage must have made this period seem especially precious. For Margaret and D.A. had booked to travel home on the *Mauretania's* ill-fated sister ship, the *Lusitania*.

Incorporating the latest in steamship technology, this vast Cunard luxury liner, which had been built on Clydeside, left Liverpool on its Maiden Voyage in

September 1907.[3] In 1915 it remained the largest and fastest passenger ship in commercial service. But crossing the Atlantic was now acknowledged to be a dangerous activity. On 4 February Germany had declared that the sea around the British Isles constituted a war zone. Two weeks later it announced that enemy ships in the area were subject to being sunk without warning although efforts would be taken to avoid sinking neutral ships.

Rumours circulated in New York about German plans. Margaret explained later that 'it was freely stated and generally believed that a special effort would be made to sink the great Cunarder so as to inspire the world with terror'. On the morning of 1 May, the day the *Lusitania* began its voyage home from New York's Pier 54, American newspapers included a grim message with the notice of sailing. It came too late for steerage passengers who were already aboard. It was a reminder (dated 22 April) from the Imperial German Embassy in Washington that a state of war existed between Germany and her Allies and Great Britain and her Allies and that vessels flying the flag of Britain or her Allies were liable to destruction in those waters. It added that 'travellers sailing in the war zone on the ships of Great Britain or her Allies do so at their own risk'. Margaret and D.A. read this warning. Cunard meanwhile assured passengers that good care would be taken of them when they reached the danger zone.

Margaret later wrote that no British and scarcely any American passengers made last minute cancellations but that some penned farewell letters to be sent home on another vessel. The *Lusitania* was by no means full: with 1,257 passengers aboard (and a crew of 702 out of a possible 850), it was 841 short of its total passenger capacity. Nevertheless, partly due to price reductions, the passenger list was the fullest since the outbreak of war. After alarmingly fast motor car journeys around New Jersey, where Margaret and her father had been driven at speeds averaging sixty, and occasionally exceeding seventy miles per hour, D.A. had joked that he would feel safe on the *Lusitania*.[4] Margaret was convinced that most passengers were 'very fully conscious of the risk we were running'.

But were they? Unknown to its passengers, the *Lusitania* was carrying cargo that included munitions for the war effort. In the increasingly bellicose atmosphere of 1913 the liner had been fitted for war service. Mounts were concealed under the deck in readiness for guns and it was officially designated an Armed Merchant Cruiser. The guns were never fitted, but the vessel carried thousands of cases of small-arms ammunition: 4,200 cases of Remington rifle cartridges, 1,259 cases of empty fragmentation shells and eighteen cases of non-explosive fuses. Recent diving expeditions have photographed rifle ammunition in situ in the bow section of the ship.

There have been ongoing debates about whether the German torpedo, the first of two explosions that passengers heard, was sufficient to have caused the mighty *Lusitania* to sink. There remains controversy over what else the cargo might have contained. It has been suggested that additional, undeclared, contraband high explosives such as gun cotton might have been responsible for the second explosion.[5] The diary of the U-boat's captain shows that it only torpedoed the vessel once, and all the evidence suggests that the second detonation sounded very different from the first. The Germans sought retrospectively to justify their action by stressing that the liner was a legitimate military target armed with guns and cargo that included considerable 'war material'. It has even been claimed that Winston Churchill, First Lord of the Admiralty, engineered events to bring the Americans into the war.

Marine forensic investigations have led to alternative explanations. In 1993, an expedition to the wreck using remotely controlled cameras showed that the exposed area of the magazine was undamaged. Robert Ballard, who led this expedition, has argued that the second explosion was caused by a coal dust explosion in the bunkers. When the vessel was torpedoed the coal bunkers were almost empty. The first explosion flooded the bunkers, which contained large amounts of coal dust. This was ignited with fatal consequences. Another explanation, aided by modern marine forensic techniques, is that an explosion in the vessel's steam-generating plant was responsible.

An expedition in 2011 by Greg Bemis (who owns the wreck) sought to cut through the hull in the search for evidence of explosive damage. However, despite costly and sophisticated diving expertise and camera equipment, what was really demonstrated was the serious deterioration of the wreck over the past seven years. Attempts to test the possible causes of the second explosion through controlled laboratory experiments and computer modelling at the Lawrence Livermore National Laboratory in Northern California have also proved inconclusive. Radically different explanations of what caused the disaster have continued to emerge but the consequences for the ill-fated passengers remain irrefutable.

Margaret and her father had taken their places in first-class cabins on the *Lusitania*. They were due to dock in Liverpool a week later. The vessel had now made over a hundred transatlantic crossings. Although Margaret had not previously travelled on this famous liner, D.A. and Sybil had done so in May 1914. On what proved to be its final voyage, departure was delayed by two and a half hours as additional passengers were taken on from another vessel. Had they sailed on time it is conceivable that they might not have encountered a U-boat.

On 5 and 6 May the *U-20*, a German submarine, sank three vessels off the south coast of Ireland. A message was sent twice to the captain of the *Lusitania* warning that submarines were active. He closed watertight doors, posted double lookouts, ordered a blackout and had lifeboats ready to be launched. Passengers thought that if they were attacked it would be in the Irish Sea on the final night. But at 2.10pm on 7 May, off the south-west coast of Ireland and with the Old Head of Kinsale visible (a rocky promontory with a lighthouse), a torpedo was fired by the *U-20*. The *Lusitania* sank.

Margaret and D.A. had just left the elegant first-class dining-room. The vessel was travelling at eighteen knots. It was a sunny May afternoon. They had been about to take the lift in order to walk on D deck when they heard 'a dull, thud-like, not very loud but unmistakable explosion'. They rapidly left the lift: those who remained were soon trapped as the electrics failed. They drowned.

D.A. went to look out of a porthole but Margaret ran upstairs to collect her lifebelt from her cabin on B deck. She could feel the boat listing badly and it was difficult to keep upright. She grabbed the lifebelt and got one from her father's cabin then made her way up to the boat deck. She chose the starboard side to be as far away as possible from the sea. There seemed to be no emergency plan or procedure. She later compared the panicking steerage passengers to 'a swarm of bees who do not know where the queen has gone'. Margaret watched a 'terror-infested crowd' rush a lifeboat before it was ready and half of them fell out.

The starboard side was now at an alarming angle (a fifteen-degree list) so no more boats could be launched. Although the number of lifeboats had been increased since the *Titanic* disaster three years earlier (which must have been in the minds of all), it was very difficult to use them: some lacked oars and those on the port side could not be launched. Most people had by this time abandoned the ship. Margaret unhooked her skirt, donned her Boddy Belt (lifebelt) correctly[6] and prepared to jump. But it was too late, as water was now flooding the deck:

> We were not, as I had thought, sixty feet above the sea; we were already under the sea. I saw the water green just about up to my knees. I do not remember its coming up further; that must all have happened in a second. The ship sank and I was sucked right down with her.

D.A. claimed that it was a mere twelve and a half minutes from the moment of explosion to the ship disappearing. Most accounts suggest eighteen minutes but certainly no more than twenty. The cruiser assigned to guide the *Lusitania* into Liverpool had been recalled.

Margaret found herself deep down under the water in darkness. She was still holding her father's lifebelt. Later she told the press that she was in 'mounting terror' of being drowned by becoming entangled with some part of the ship. But although her wrist caught on a rope and left a lasting mark, she managed to free it. She grasped a piece of board just a few inches wide and several feet in length.

She came to the surface amidst what seemed to be literally a sea of people. They were crammed together with 'boats, hencoops, chairs, rafts, boards and goodness knows what else'. A man held on to the other end of her board. Many prayed or slowly chanted 'boat' in a 'curious, unemotional monotone'. Half-dazed, Margaret was beyond feeling acute fear. She later wrote that with death so close 'the sharp agony of fear is not there; the thing is too overwhelming and stunning for that'. There was a sense of surrender and of death as 'a benignant power'. She fleetingly wondered whether she could have reached heaven without knowing it.

A few boats were visible but it was impossible to swim more than a few strokes and Margaret was loath to abandon her board. It was intensely cold and the swell made her sick. It also caused people and debris to begin drifting apart. She thought of a possible invention: strapping a small bottle of chloroform to each lifebelt would help the drowning person to lose consciousness. Looking up at the sun high in the sky she wished she could do so. That was the last thing she remembered.

But after about two and three quarter hours in the water, just as it was growing dark, she was picked up by a rowing boat. She had only been located because a wicker deck chair had floated up under her, raising her a little. A mark in the water was detected and Margaret was discovered. She was presumed dead. She and a number of bodies were transferred to a small patrol steamer called the *Bluebell* that was patrolling the waters between Kinsale and Ballycotton. She was dumped on deck. Luckily a midshipman thought there was possibly 'some life in this woman' and attended to her.

Margaret regained consciousness at about 9.30pm. She was lying naked wrapped in blankets on a ship's deck in the dark. Shaking violently, her teeth were 'chattering like castanets' and she felt acute back pain. But she was in her early thirties and had a strong physique. She was given some lukewarm tea and three men helped to move her to the warmth of the captain's bunk in the cabin. There were a number of other lucky survivors there. Most had terrible tales to tell – 'there are no veils just after a shipwreck' Margaret later explained – but they were also almost delirious with the warmth and relief at being alive. A notable exception was the *Lusitania's* captain. Captain Turner was silent.

At about 11pm the steamer reached Queenstown (Cobh) Harbour. Up until this point Margaret was unaware of whether her father was alive. He had grabbed a lifebelt,[7] then got onto the last boat being launched, after making a terrified woman in front of him jump into the boat. As it drew away, the ship slowly sank and the lifeboat narrowly missed being hit by its funnel. Coincidentally, D.A.'s secretary, A.L. Rhys Evans, who had accompanied him on his travels (but was not mentioned in Margaret's autobiography),[8] was also in this boat. D.A.'s first words to him were apparently, 'Did you see anything of my daughter? She was just on the threshold of a brilliant career. Oh! Why was I not taken instead?' After rowing for two and a half hours a small steamer took the survivors on board. They reached Queenstown in the early evening. A Catholic priest gave D.A. dinner and brandy. It was his first alcoholic drink for fifteen years.

A steward from the *Lusitania* told Margaret that her father had been rescued and was on shore. D.A. stood on the quay for several hours, desperately searching for his daughter amongst the bodies brought ashore. Then the steward informed him that she had been rescued. Margaret borrowed a soldier's overcoat and carpet slippers from the steamer's captain. Covered in black and brown dirt and bruised from head to foot, she crawled onto the gangway and was reunited with her father. 'It was' he told the *Western Mail's* special correspondent, 'the most joyous moment I have ever experienced'.

They went to the Queen's Hotel which, ironically, was run by a German. Afraid of reprisals, he had shut himself in his wine cellar for the night. This dirty, shabby hotel was a far cry from the Waldorf Astoria in Manhattan, but it provided shelter. Margaret was given biscuits and fizzy lemon and stayed in a room with another survivor. Unable to sleep, she exchanged stories with her companion who had been perched on a floating piano in a packing case. By 5am reporters were demanding their story. Post Office staff remained on duty from Friday morning until late on Saturday night dealing with thousands of private telegrams and cables.[9] On the Sunday additional telegraphers and equipment were drafted in from Dublin to deal with the journalists' despatches. A hotel guest went to Cork to buy clothes and the all-important hairpins for the female survivors.

One further night was spent in the hotel then Margaret was well enough to insist they move to a cleaner place. She still had a high temperature and was taken by ambulance on a stretcher to the railway station then by train with her father to the comfort of Dublin's Shelbourne Hotel. They were accompanied by their erstwhile dining companions on the *Lusitania*, Dr Howard Fisher, an American doctor and his young sister-in-law Dorothy Conner, who had enrolled as a Red Cross nurse. They had been on their way to start a field hospital in Belgium. After swimming to a boat Fisher had watched an Italian surgeon operate on the leg of one of the *Lusitania's* crew using just a penknife.

Margaret spent a week in Dublin, too ill to leave bed. Sybil and Humphrey joined her in the Shelbourne but Margaret's retrospective accounts do not dwell on their fears and relief. D.A. took to his bed too after a few days. His secretary was left to deal with a mass of correspondence. Margaret, who had been diagnosed with bronchial pneumonia, spent a further two weeks in bed once she got home to Oaklands.

From 1915 Margaret had a new part-time home in London: Chelsea Court in Embankment Gardens overlooking the River Thames. She and Sybil's cousin Nina Jameson shared a flat in a substantial, recently-built red-brick mansion block looking south across the river to Battersea Park. They experienced a number of air raids: the first was less than a quarter of a mile away. Margaret tried, when possible, to keep out of London when there was a full moon since it guided Zeppelins. Tough on herself, she suffered for a time from what she called an 'unreasoning' terror of night raids. Eventually she became more accustomed to them. For about a year and a half after the disaster she would wake at about 2.30am with night sweats.

She was relieved to have been too dazed for much of her time in the water to remember the precise horrors that haunted many survivors. The company that produced the Boddy Belt now quoted her in their advertisements: 'Without your belt' she declared, 'I could not possibly have survived'. Margaret, her father and Evans had been extremely lucky. D.A. was greatly amused by a poster advertising the *Cardiff Evening Express*. It declared in huge letters: 'Great National Disaster. "D.A" Saved'. He obtained a copy and it remains in his family's possessions.

There were 764 survivors.[10] Less fortunate were some Monmouthshire compatriots. Nine members of the Royal Gwent Male Voice Singers had been touring the United States and Canada. They had taken part in a concert on board the *Lusitania* on the final evening of the voyage. Six survived but the conductor G. F. Davies of Newport and two other members perished. A Monmouth man who was returning to Wales to introduce his young Canadian bride to his mother and join the British army survived but as a widower.

There were some remarkable stories of near escapes. One woman who was in the water got drawn into the liner's funnel, but a rush of air forced her out again and she fell into a lifeboat. She and more than fifty other survivors arrived at Fishguard in Pembrokeshire from Rosslare. One was a Russian who still wore the lifebelt that had saved him.

In the weeks following the disaster, bodies were washed up on the Irish coast. 885 bodies were never recovered. There had been the loss of 1,198 lives. More than forty per cent of the crew perished. A larger than usual number of small children had been on board since families of Canadians serving in the forces had been travelling to Britain. Less than thirty per cent of the children survived.

Amongst the dead were some well-known figures including the theatre impresario Carl Frohman. It was said that as he went down with the vessel he was quoting from his greatest success, 'Peter Pan'. The New York fashion designer Carrie Kennedy and the multi-millionaire Alfred G. Vanderbilt perished along with writer and feminist Alice Moore Hubbard and her philosopher husband Elbert Hubbard. So too did the Irish art collector Sir Hugh Lane who, it was rumoured, had brought with him lead tubes filled with paintings by Rubens, Rembrandt and Monet.

News of the disaster provoked some anti-German rioting in Liverpool and London and businesses run by people of German origin were attacked. Propaganda flourished on both sides. 'Avenge the *Lusitania*' became a popular slogan on British recruitment posters. An American newspaper cartoon depicted little children in the sea holding out their hands and asking the Kaiser 'But why did you kill *us*?' The lives of 128 Americans had been lost, yet their country was not at war.

This death toll had a huge impact on public opinion in the United States. In her spy novel *The Messenger*, Elizabeth Robins (who was American-born) described the day after the *Lusitania's* sinking: 'the country [was] in a state of excitement such as the United States had not known since the assassination of Lincoln'. She added, 'The *Lusitania* dead recruited tens of thousands'.[11]

President Wilson made a formal protest to the Germans. Forty-four more lives were lost in August (including those of several Americans) when the British

White Star liner *Arabic* was torpedoed. Germany was forced to suspend all-out submarine warfare the following month. It was resumed in January 1917. In April of that year, the United States declared war on Germany. In the same year, Walter Schwieger, commander of the *U-20* that sank the *Lusitania*, ran into a British minefield when in charge of another U-boat and was killed.

The Board of Trade, headed by Lord Mersey, the Wreck Commissioner, had begun investigating the events in June 1915. They interviewed 36 witnesses, one of whom was D.A., who was also a member of the Advisory Committee of the Board of Trade. Asked about the demeanour of the officers and crew, he replied that the former behaved very well and the stewards 'and certainly the stewardesses, exceedingly well and heroically'. Margaret had told the press about one brave stewardess, who had accompanied a passenger back to her cabin in search of a lifebelt when the deck was almost vertical. D.A. also told the inquiry that the captain's command for 'Women and Children First' was not, he thought, obeyed by many of the crew. And although he was now less critical than earlier[12] about the panic when disaster struck, neither he nor Margaret could forget that the catastrophe was worse than it need have been.

In the wake of the *Titanic* disaster, Margaret had complained in the Monmouthshire press about the 'hideously inadequate' number of lifeboats available for its passengers.[13] She had connected that sinking to the fact that the vessel had followed a dangerous northerly course in the hope of saving a few hours. She had argued in 1912 that 'the passion for record-breaking and money-making' was 'an essentially masculine one' whereas for women 'the preservation of life will always be of far more importance'. Had there been adequate laws, lives might have been saved. Ergo giving the vote to women would help safety.

The *Lusitania* inquiry exonerated Cunard, the Royal Navy and Captain Turner (even though the Admiralty had tried to claim that he had been negligent). Blame was laid squarely on the German government. However, evidence had revealed leaky boats and a lack of clear instructions and lifebelts on deck. Years later Margaret claimed that the ship's authorities were so afraid of frightening the passengers that they did not even provide boat drill: 'If they had, many lives would have been saved'.[14]

It would be easy to presume from the *Lusitania* ordeal that Margaret would be terrified of water for the rest of her days. She did now have a fear of being shut in under water and train journeys to and from Wales became something of an ordeal as the route necessitated travelling through the Severn Tunnel. But neither she nor her father abandoned sea voyages and, ironically, D.A.'s vital work in conserving and distributing food supplies arose from the stranglehold of a submarine blockade. As for Margaret, both work and pleasure saw her return time and again to the sea.

In August 1922 she was aboard the *Adriatic* when a short circuit in the reserve coal bunker led to the deaths of five men. Three others were seriously wounded.[15] Instead of turning on an electric light, an engineer had lit a match. The fire was, however, contained. Margaret was far from being reduced to a nervous wreck. She even claimed that her experience in 1915 made her much less afraid of dying than she had been as a nervous child.[16]

She also became a proficient swimmer and took up diving. Her god-daughter stresses that from the time Margaret was rescued 'you couldn't keep her out of water'. She also suffered from a bad chest and bouts of bronchitis for the rest of her life. However, her application form for a place at St Leonards School shows that at the age of sixteen she was already prone to bad bronchial colds.[17]

Although Margaret turned an ordeal into something positive, it altered how people chose to see her. There is a fascination about those who have survived against the odds, even in wartime. When Octavia Wilberforce met Margaret she described her as 'a romantic figure, for she had been torpedoed in the *Lusitania* and such a miraculous escape seemed to mark her out for a special destiny'.[18] Virginia Woolf told Vanessa Bell a version of events which included Margaret swimming under water, saving herself and her father, and D.A. subsequently dying from the shock of the disaster.[19]

Margaret wrote several accounts of the disaster. On the eighth anniversary, the *Spectator* published her dramatic story up to the point where she reached land and her father. This was later reproduced in almost identical form as a chapter (simply called 'May 7th 1915') in her autobiography. Her brush with death made her think about warfare and what months in the trenches could do to a man's nerves. 'I still cannot understand' she wrote, 'how any of our soldiers remained sane'.

Years later, she wrote an essay on 'Dying and Killing'. Here she suggested that what made it possible for 'normally kindly German sailors to torpedo without a qualm ships carrying non-combatants was the knowledge that they themselves had volunteered for a service from which it was practically certain they would never return'.[20] Nearer the time of the tragedy she was unwilling to associate German sailors with any kindness. In 1921 she commented that her ordeal had made her realise 'what German brutality meant'.

Some of the *Lusitania's* crew members now joined up. Margaret too was determined to do what she could to help the war effort. Her opportunity came when Lloyd George headed a coalition government at the end of 1916.

CHAPTER FIVE

War Service

Less than a month after the *Lusitania* tragedy of May 1915 a 'Great Patriotic Meeting' was advertised to consider 'universal war service for men and women'. Mrs Pankhurst chaired the event at the London Palladium on 3 June.[1] Margaret (described as having been on the torpedoed liner) was billed to speak. In the event she was not sufficiently recovered to be able to attend, but Mrs Pankhurst read out a letter from her.

Margaret's language was uncompromising:

> I do not think that any survivor from the Lusitania can be otherwise than deeply interested in the suggestion of universal war service for men and women which you are considering today. Doubtless the outrages and horrors in Belgium should have brought home to one clearly enough the sort of fiends that we are fighting, but the thing one has witnessed with one's own eyes is somehow more real...

She commented on the number of small children who perished, adding that

> The brutality of people who could make war on these defenceless babies seems to me a thing we ought to give everything we have and are to fight and get rid of. Mad brutes of that type are very much too dangerous to live at large.

The meeting raised more than £2,000 for the WSPU's war fund. A resolution was passed supporting concerted efforts 'to ensure speedy and complete victory' and requesting that the government establish universal obligatory war service.[2]

The WSPU's paper the *Suffragette* had been resumed. At first Margaret thought it filled a useful gap and took the right line. The following month it began displaying the words 'For King. For Country. For Freedom' above its title. In October it was renamed *Britannia*. 'Lack of patriotism', it declared, 'is a disease like any other.'[3] But, unlike Sybil and Florence Haig who sent money to its Victory Fund, Margaret now seems to have distanced herself from further involvement with the paper.

Instead she devoted her time to women's war work. The significance of this has been underplayed in her autobiography, and consequently in other accounts of her life. *This Was My World* has a mere seventeen words describing her post in Wales.[4]

At first she helped with the placement of Belgian refugees in Monmouthshire, as did her parents and Aunt Hetty. By the end of 1915 almost eight hundred of these refugees were registered in the county. Margaret provided financial assistance for Belgian refugees at Adrian Court Lodge in Usk.[5]

She was also busy dealing with her father's affairs. D.A. had been propelled into the limelight by Lloyd George and was enjoying the power that politics had previously denied him. In the summer of 1915 when Lloyd George was Minister of Munitions, he had appealed to D.A. to visit America to establish arrangements for the purchase of munitions. D.A. admitted that it was a daunting prospect. He could not rid himself of memories of the *Lusitania* and told Lloyd George of his fears. But this simply resulted in the Minister explaining that he would not have asked him to make such a sacrifice in facing the same voyage so soon had it not been for the urgency of the American mission. He added that he could not think of an efficient substitute.[6] So D.A. agreed, doubtless encouraged too by the opportunity this offered in personal terms.[7]

Less than two months after his ordeal at sea, D.A. sailed from Liverpool on the *St Louis*. They were escorted through the danger zone by two British destroyers. A Scotland Yard detective accompanied the party which included Sybil (she had insisted on accompanying him this time). On arrival in New York, they were met by the British Ambassador. D.A. told Margaret in a letter that 'I go about constantly guarded by detectives'. The industrialist J.P. Morgan, the key figure in D.A.'s negotiations, had just been shot and seriously wounded by a German at his country house.

D.A. was away for five months. Lloyd George had engaged in protracted and, by his own admission, bitter battles with his fellow countryman in the past. As Gerard

Charmley has shown, the duel between the two men occupied twelve of the twenty-two years D.A. spent in the House of Commons.[8] But Lloyd George did recognise D.A.'s international reputation as a businessman, his negotiating skills and determination. He later declared that D.A. 'inspired the whole heart of America with the flames of liberty' and 'gave to America and the Allies a breathing space and a chance. That service of his cannot be over-estimated'.[9] In the New Year honours list of 1916 D.A. was given a peerage. He took the title of Rhondda of Llanwern, genuflecting to both his roots and his present home, and he adopted a motto 'Diligentia absque Timore' (Diligently without Fear), which deployed his initials.

Lloyd George became prime minister in December 1916. This paved the way for important opportunities for both Margaret and her father. D.A. became president of the Local Government Board. He quickly recognised the potential for creating in its place a Ministry of Health, and his ideas to combat infant mortality in particular began to absorb his energies. After six months in this post he was made Food Controller, starting at the Food Ministry in mid-June 1917 aged sixty-one. But, as Margaret put it, '[i]t killed him in just over a year'.[10]

By this time she had assumed more and more business control on D.A.'s behalf and had taken on official war work for the Ministry of National Service, initially in Wales and later in London. By January 1915 some two million men were serving in the armed forces. The consequent labour shortage at home led to recognition of the value of mobilising female labour for war service, enhanced by the need to expand the supply of munitions. By May, when Lloyd George became Minister of

Munitions, about 50,000 women had already registered their availability for employment. That August all women as well as men between sixteen and sixty-five were required to register their names, ages and occupations. Civilians working on essential jobs such as munitions had their wages and conditions of employment determined by the government.

Conscription for men began in May 1916. That year saw a concomitant sharp increase in female employment, and by early 1917 a million additional women had entered wage-earning occupations. In January the War Office decided to create a Women's Army Auxiliary Corps (WAAC) for non-combatant posts in France.[11] This was to be a crucial development for Margaret.

Meanwhile the National Service Department (NSD), with Neville Chamberlain as director-general, sought to enrol male volunteers who were too old for military service and 'probably women' for war work in essential industries. The implication that women were something of an afterthought was compounded by the department's announcement that a new section under 'woman control' for women volunteers would not enrol on exactly the same terms as men. To do so, it was claimed, would have caused 'great irritation and great annoyance' because they could not place many of those who would come forward but '[t]hat does not mean that women are not wanted'.[12] The press promptly reported that women were not wanted.[13] It was not a good start.

However, the section was to be headed by May Tennant, former chief woman inspector of factories. And this, as *The Times* declared, was the first important war appointment for a woman.[14] Seven centres – five in

England, one in Scotland and one in Wales – were established to deal with all this work. In February the first three women commissioners were named. Margaret was to be the commissioner of Women's National Service for Wales and Monmouthshire. The other two women (for London and Scotland) were released from service on the National Health Insurance Commission. Most of the new women commissioners were civil servants lent by their departments. John Rowland, in charge of the civil side of the NSD in Wales, had been a Welsh insurance commissioner. Margaret, by contrast, had no comparable experience. Although she would soon clash dramatically with Violet Douglas-Pennant, Margaret's appointment had been suggested by her. Douglas-Pennant was also an insurance commissioner and Chamberlain's first choice for Margaret's post. She had declined due to prior commitments.

On 17 March 1917, a meeting in London's Albert Hall inaugurated the women's section of the National Service scheme. It was attended by the Queen, despite the fact that there had been a recent bereavement in the Royal Family and that she did not usually 'do' public meetings. The Royal Box included Margaret's relative Lady Haig (her husband Sir Douglas Haig had been made a Field-Marshall in the New Year honours). Queues began at noon for the 3pm meeting. So many people arrived that additional speeches were delivered outdoors. It is not known for sure whether Margaret was in the hall but it is likely. Her mother sat on the platform. Sybil was active in voluntary work. Margaret had helped her to raise money for a national fund for Welsh troops, and part of Llanwern Park had been turned into a military hospital.

The meeting was a far cry from the pre-war suffrage protests and rousing rallies at the Albert Hall. There were, though, some reminders that, if present, Margaret might have found the atmosphere a little awkward. As the meeting began, a woman in the gallery shouted out that she was there on behalf of the Women's Suffrage Federation to express their strong opposition to National Service, which they equated with industrial compulsion.

One of the main platform speakers was Violet Markham, a Liberal and daughter of a managing director of a coal and iron company. Before the war she had addressed an Albert Hall audience as a prominent anti-suffragist.[15] Now she was May Tennant's deputy and one of Margaret's 'superiors'. Markham made a special plea for women as nurses. Chamberlain presided and various speakers outlined schemes for getting women to work on the land, for collecting waste wool and cotton for recycling and helping in areas such as infant welfare work and girls' clubs. The War Secretary Lord Derby emphasised that comparatively few women were now needed in France (about ten times the required number had just volunteered to go there in response to an appeal). Markham carefully defined their policy: this was not a general call for women to come forward. Appeals for volunteers to undertake work of a clearly defined nature would be made from time to time. They would be specifically targeted and women who were currently employed should remain in post unless or until required elsewhere.[16]

But before Margaret and the other commissioners could start work, internal government disagreements about their remit and, indeed, very existence, surfaced to threaten their position.[17] Chamberlain stressed that they would have 'much wider functions than the mere enrolment of women'. They would help to ascertain demand, make arrangements for substitution, settle disputes and 'keep the Department in touch with local conditions of the employment of women'. However, the Ministry of Labour clearly felt that they were likely to encroach on the work performed by local Employment Exchanges, most notably the jobs done by their female officers. The Ministry of Labour criticised a draft memo outlining the principal duties proposed and even suggested that matters such as permitting them to settle disputes between employers and volunteers about terms and conditions of service would be better dealt with by the male commissioners. Terms were still not settled in late March.

Tennant and Markham were incandescent. They believed that their authority and that of women government officials more generally was being undermined, remarking that '[w]e hardly think it is necessary to adduce arguments in support of the modern view... that it is desirable that women officials should deal with matters intimately affecting women workers'. As for handing over many of their responsibilities to men, that 'hardly calls for serious consideration from us'. Although she would later argue that setting up separate recruiting agencies distinct from Labour Exchanges was wrong, Markham now criticised the 'very difficult and unfriendly spirit'[18] shown by the Employment Department of the Ministry of Labour, and she and Tennant threatened to resign from their posts unless the women commissioners were given a mandate.

The scheme did go ahead – the Treasury formally ratified the appointments in April – but Margaret was not starting her first government post in the most propitious of circumstances. The story of this women's section of the NSD has been called 'a sorry tale for all those caught in its web'.[19] As Markham recognised, it faced an uphill battle and was developed too late to be accepted by other departments and work effectively.[20]

Margaret and her colleagues were charged with recruiting volunteer women to work in agriculture (under the Board of Agriculture's scheme for training and placing women on the land),[21] and had to organise Selection Boards for the WAAC. Their main function was arranging and writing appeals, receiving application forms and in some instances interviewing candidates. They were concerned with special appeals for state labour and did not deal with ordinary industrial employment. A report in 1918 on their work added that they also acted 'as the Intelligence officers of the Women's Section'.[22]

So what did Margaret do? She and her deputy Mary Jones of Rhiwbina were based at the Law Courts in Cardiff but they did get out and about as well. Food shortages and the effects of conscription meant that women were badly needed on the land even though Welsh farmers had their doubts about female labour.[23] Women's War Agricultural Committees had been created in 1915 and the Women's Land Army established by 1917. Now about 10,000 women were required to assist in emergency measures to increase the nation's food production. The women's section of the NSD sought assistance from more than 1,000 Women's War Agricultural Committees in England and Wales, and on 31 March a National Service rally was held in Cardiff.

Margaret was contacted the following month by the

south Wales representative of the Board of Agriculture.[24] He wanted her to organise meetings in large towns. She was happy to oblige, believing that there was an urgent need for action. She was concerned that young women had not been coming forward 'in anything like the numbers required' even though training centres were ready to receive them immediately. Headquarters advised her to keep costs down and to use local speakers. She arranged what proved to be 'extremely encouraging' meetings in Cowbridge and Bridgend. As a result farmers sought more information and new offers were made for training. Lady Plymouth, for example, arranged for a number of women to be trained for market gardening on her St Fagans estate. She organised and spoke at a number of open-air meetings. In Pembrokeshire, a morning meeting of farmers in Haverfordwest (already in town to sell their stock) was followed by an afternoon address attended by about a hundred farmers in the main square. Margaret met some of them later at the railway station where they made further enquiries about securing women workers.

The Board of Agriculture admitted that there were some difficulties in training women volunteers and was anxious that Margaret act only with very close cooperation with them. Such an approach encapsulated the difficulties she and colleagues faced, caught by bureaucratic and petty rivalries on every side. But their south Wales inspector was full of praise for the work she had undertaken and informed Markham, who duly reported back to Margaret, that it was 'cheering to hear that you are apparently making some impression upon the farmers'. She added that if Margaret could convert them and persuade them to have the women 'you will indeed be rendering true National Service'.

There was, however, ongoing unease about chains of command and the allocation of tasks. When Margaret discovered that officers of the Department of Employment had been instructed to deal with John Rowland rather than with her, she wrote to the Ministry of Labour to stress that all communications concerning women should be made directly to her. Sometimes both of them vied for the same work. This happened with the translation of Women's Land Army posters and leaflets into Welsh. Rowland was a Welsh speaker but Markham told him that they had felt it wise to accept Margaret's offer to organise this as it related so closely to her particular work.

Demand varied from month to month and the Board of Agriculture did not require new recruits in June. But in early July Margaret was once more making an urgent plea for female land workers. In a direct appeal in the press she accepted that it was difficult to realise that the State had as much right to a girl as to a boy – not the sort of comment she would have made a few years earlier – and added that, nevertheless, 'the daughters are needed now'.[25] In a heartfelt, if hackneyed, statement, she declared that '[e]very girl who goes on the land helps in the solution of the problem, which our enemies have set us, how to carry on in spite of submarines'.

Margaret's appeal was confident, dramatic and direct from its opening statement:

The State has something to say to each of her daughters to-day, and it is this: – I have new work in which I badly need your help. Is the service which

147

you are already giving me of greater urgency to me than that which I need you to do now? If so, stay where you are; if not, come into the new work.

She argued that the time had come when every girl must be asked to work full-time. The words 'duty' and 'service' were carefully reiterated. There was 'a definite and ascertained demand' for their contribution. They should leave non-essential employment and take up this vital work. Margaret conveyed the sense that a turning-point had been reached and, as a matter of urgency, those whose jobs were not essential to the workings of the State must now embrace this 'great opportunity of service'.

As well as needing workers on the land, WAAC clerks were wanted by the army in France. Margaret depicted young women both as potential dutiful daughters of the State and as the children of parents who were required to lend their offspring to their country. She ended by appealing to these parents, even adding that this sacrifice was 'so small in comparison to the one they made when their sons went to fight'.

Yet in an article for the monthly journal *Welsh Outlook* (also published in July) Margaret stressed that these 'Khaki girls' were 'to all intents and purposes soldiers'. Here she was being economical with the truth. The advent of women's auxiliary services meant that women wore military uniform for the first time (there was some unease about this), but this was a paramilitary organisation. In fact only male subjects were entitled to commissions from the Crown and the WAAC did not have military ranks. The WAAC corps had been formed out of necessity and the army was emphatic that women were servicing rather than serving.[26] The formal basis of the scheme was spelt out in Army Council Instruction No.1069 which stressed that no woman was to be employed unless a soldier was released for other purposes. Four women clerks were seen as the equivalent of three soldier clerks. Margaret sought, however, to turn the women's secondary status into something more heroic and palatable by suggesting that women enabled men to achieve great things for their country: 'every girl who joins the WAAC sets a soldier free for the actual fighting'. Yet women were not perceived as a valuable addition to the army but as a necessary adjunct.[27]

In her *Welsh Outlook* article, Margaret stressed the unprecedented opportunity provided by National Service for women.[28] She represented it as the first official large-scale demand made on women's services by the State. Drawing on Kitchener's recruiting slogan, she made clear that 'Your Country wants YOU' now really did apply to women. Not wanting to minimise the importance of munitions work, driving, shops and other civilian jobs, she described it as the 'Official Seal set on the doings of the last three years'.

On 13 July headquarters asked Margaret to make clear as soon as possible her suggestions for a recruiting campaign in Wales that would provide the War Office 'with an adequate number of all classes which it requires'. It anticipated an imminent demand for large numbers of clerical workers. Three days later she spoke at a large evening meeting at Cardiff's City Hall on behalf of Women's National Service.[29] The Lord Mayor presided. It was explained that women were required to work on the land but the main appeal was for work in France with the

WAAC. This work was not for 'flighty, frivolous girls who wanted to amuse themselves'. They wanted hard workers, 'girls who were stickers'. This, it was stressed, was the highest service that women could give. Margaret's speech played on a particular kind of patriotism. She alluded to rumours about the women's work in France (criticisms of alleged immorality would soon lead to an official enquiry), suggesting that 'happily these were now less prevalent than formerly, because they had South Wales girls working in France'. She made it clear that the authorities felt a strong sense of responsibility for the welfare of those who went to France. She understood the need to focus on respectability and to reassure parents that young single women who were away from home for the first time would be safe, especially since they had to sign on for a year or the duration of the war (whichever would prove to be the longest) and only had a fortnight's annual leave.

Acknowledging that girls were more influenced by their parents than were young men, she appealed again to the 'parents of South Wales to realise their great responsibilities and allow their daughters to go'. And she ended with an emotive appeal to national identity. 'As a Welshwoman' she was 'very anxious that Welsh women should act up to the best traditions in this hour of the nation's need'. The meeting cheered this.

Margaret had been surprised at the relatively small number of Welsh girls who had volunteered for work in France but, keen to boost morale, she suggested that those who had responded were 'the best, the most courageous and enterprising type'.[30] New recruits were to replace men in clerical work and undertake some other jobs such as domestic work and gardening. By April 1917, 4,710 had been accepted from the UK. Wales supplied 286 of these women, many of whom were clerical workers, though there were waitresses, cooks and a few working in transport. It was estimated that the boards should between them produce about 250 recruits weekly for the next few months, but the exact type of work available, like the ground rules for recruitment, varied.

Margaret and the other women commissioners faced a difficult task anticipating and responding to the shifting balance between supply and demand. Instructions from London were often not clear. In late April she was preparing for a joint selection and medical board in Cardiff to select candidates for clerical work. She was told that some domestic workers might be interviewed too, though the War Office might also change its mind. Advertisements were placed in half a dozen newspapers in early May urgently requesting clerical workers aged between twenty and forty for France.[31] Applicants selected for interview at the YMCA in Cardiff in mid-May received a letter signed by M.H. Mackworth (the draft version had crossed out the word 'Lady'). Some were rejected as unsuitable but 148 were summoned for interview, though subsequent rejections (for medical reasons and on grounds of unsuitability) as well as some dropping out meant that only about two-thirds of this number was finally accepted. Boards in Cardiff on 31 July and 1 and 2 of August yielded 83 for France out of 204 summoned for interview. Now medical orderlies and experienced drivers who could repair vehicles were needed. Responding to and regulating demand for different kinds of work was not easy. Housemaids and waitresses were in demand.

It was proving far more difficult to recruit domestic

workers than clerical staff, not least because of low rates of pay and prospects, but Margaret was told in no uncertain terms on 11 June that shorthand typists were not required for the next board though 'it is impossible to tell how long the present situation will last'.[32] When she asked about demand for Voluntary Aid Detachments in July, having frequently referred people to such work, she was told that, due to a very positive response, no more of these nursing posts should be advertised.

Margaret sent weekly updates about the number of applications to the London office. She was concerned that hostel accommodation be provided in Cardiff for those attending interviews from a distance. She suggested that those candidates whose enrolment was postponed should have their wages paid by the War Office. She also dealt with correspondence that ranged from details of what undergarments the girls needed for France to occasional special pleas on behalf of individuals.

There was some debate about rates of pay. Advertisements stated that shorthand typists could earn up to thirty shillings (wages were linked to speed in words per minute) for a forty-two hour week with a bonus at the end of the first year and overtime. But this was the top rate. In her *Welsh Outlook* article Margaret stated that the starting pay of 23s a week was good. Fourteen shillings a week was deducted for board and lodging from this, but she emphasised that uniforms were provided and there were minimal extra expenses.

However, most women commissioners were, privately at least, critical of the rates of pay imposed by the War Office and most regions felt that the starting rate was too low for a good clerk.[33] Much depended on the local 'going rate' for clerical work. In London and urban centres such as Leeds the pay was seen as an obstacle to recruitment, but the Scottish commissioner and Margaret argued that rates compared quite favourably locally. In Cardiff the usual rate for general clerks was 17/6d rising to a guinea (with occasional higher rates) and in other parts of Wales it was even lower. Margaret reported that, unlike some areas, there was no evidence of women being deterred by the low rate of pay. She acknowledged that wages were in fact low but did not feel that the young women were disadvantaged. She did, however, suggest that it might be prejudicial to recruiting were the rates for France (where there was a certain 'glamour' attached to the post) adopted for WAAC posts in England.

Ever alert to publicity, Margaret arranged for the first contingent of fifty 'lady clerks' bound for France (including twenty-two from Cardiff) to march from City Hall to the railway station. They were led by the military band from the Cardiff barracks. Margaret's picture appeared in the paper, showing her giving final instructions as they set off for an initial three weeks' training in London.[34] The streets were lined with people bidding them farewell, numbers probably boosted by the fact that a London film company had been engaged to record the event. The film was shown in all the big cinemas in Cardiff. The *Daily Mirror* patronisingly remarked that 'The Welsh maidens, look you, are volunteering, in considerable numbers for the Women's Army in France. Lady Mackworth, who is recruiting for Wales, says so'.[35]

In addition to writing for local newspapers in these months, Margaret and her deputy contacted women's organisations, the Cardiff Shop Assistants' Union and local authorities. They circulated several thousand chapels across Wales and all sixty-nine National Service Committees in south Wales, asking them to display their posters.[36] Pillar boxes, once targeted by Margaret and others in their arson campaign were now used to display posters advertising for women clerks in France. Local people were caught up in the recruitment drive. Mary Collin, who had chaired the Cardiff and District Women's Suffrage Society and was headmistress of Cardiff High School for Girls, held recruiting meetings in school.[37] Her two domestic servants joined the WAAC.

Margaret and her assistant toured north Wales in June.[38] They held a meeting in Caernarfon and met editors of local papers, representatives of Labour Exchanges and Mayors in seven other towns to gauge local needs and plan for the future. There was some resentment that the Welsh contingent did not liaise more with the commissioner for the north-west and it was noted that Lady Mackworth's advertisement in the Liverpool newspapers for north Wales was twice as big as the one for the north-west. A selection board was held in Liverpool in mid-June. Margaret was disappointed at the small number of candidates but pleased with the educational standard of the thirty recruits who finally made it to France. She did, however, recognise that many young women had already gone into munitions work. She had sensibly suggested that candidates should be interviewed in Wrexham as well as Liverpool but the War Office refused to oblige.

Margaret wrote monthly progress reports on all aspects of the commissioners' work and attended meetings held in London. She was present at one in late June[39] where it was agreed that closer cooperation was needed between the War Office and the NSD over the detailed administration of the boards. The women argued that 'much confusion and difficulty' had arisen through War Office failures in organisation. There had been delays in sending successful women abroad with a 'consequent irritation, unrest, and wastage of candidates'. Some had even given notice to their employers but not been summoned.

Mona Wilson, chief commissioner for England complained that, even after recruiting for the War Office for three months, instructions to commissioners remained vague and lacked uniformity, showing 'a lack of recognition of the proper relations' between the War Office and themselves.[40] The War Office protested that the women were not producing the requisite number of recruits but in practice they had difficulty even absorbing even the current supply. There had been unease about the division of labour from the outset and lack of clear directions exacerbated an already tense situation.

On 16 July Lord Derby presided at a conference at the War Office about the future of recruits for the WAAC. He announced that extensive recruiting arrangements were being suspended while the decision was being made about whether or not this work should in future be undertaken by the Employment Department. Ironically this took place at the same time as the big meeting in Cardiff City Hall at which Margaret made an impassioned speech. It explains why Markham, billed as its chief guest speaker, did not show up. And it points to the gap that existed between the infighting in London and the work in other areas where commissioners like Margaret had to respond to changing demands, sustain propaganda and produce results even though their jobs were, unknown to them, about to disappear.

Markham was in charge in the final weeks of the women's section since May Tennant's son was killed in a flying accident. Never one to mince her words, Markham complained bitterly at Chamberlain's lack of support and blamed problems on his breach with the Ministry of Labour. As early as 7 June she was anticipating 'the parting of the ways', arguing that Chamberlain had made a complete surrender to the War Office.[41] A few weeks later she described the NSD as living 'on the brink of a volcano'[42].

In August Chamberlain resigned. The women's section also ceased to exist and work was divided between other departments. The Employment Department of the Ministry of Labour took over the organisation of WAAC recruitment, and Land Army recruitment became the Board of Agriculture's responsibility. Markham later admitted that she had 'nearly touched the bottom of disgust and despair, so odious were the intrigues with which we had been surrounded, so useless the inefficiency with which a great piece of national work had been conducted'.[43] Margaret was one of the casualties of this unfortunate situation. Yet, organisation of recruits had proceeded against the odds. More than 14,000 women had been placed in positions through recruitment in England, Wales, Scotland and Ireland in six months, the majority in the Land Army and WAAC.

Margaret remained busy. Quite apart from business work[44] she was still involved in WAAC recruitment. For example, in early November at a meeting at Pontypridd Town Hall (where she was described as the ex-commissioner), she spelt out the need for women to work in France.[45] She depicted life there as 'happy and healthy' and 'like a big college', though there is no evidence that she had witnessed the situation personally. Every class of women, she argued, was needed for a variety of jobs, but no half-timers or shirkers were wanted. She also emphasised the need to punish the Germans.

She spoke too at a public meeting held in Newport Town Hall to stress the need for women recruits to the WAAC.[46] Her use of language is interesting. The audience was told that the army was a huge business as well as a fighting machine. Women might not fight but they could with instruction run the business. Currently about 150 were needed weekly from the UK (Wales had provided 627 women and girls in the last six weeks). Newport audiences more used to hearing Margaret emphasise the urgency of the vote, listened to her telling them this was 'direct and urgent work'. Another speaker was Lyndon Moore who had been the prosecutor in her court case. When the resolution supporting the initiative was carried, Margaret responded with the WSPU motto 'Deeds, not Words'.

Had she not been ill, she would doubtless have been present at the gathering in Cardiff on 23 January when newly-recruited WAACs from Bristol (many of whom were Welsh) marched through the city.[47] Helen Gwynne-Vaughan, the WAAC's Chief Controller Overseas, and Lord Treowen, director of Recruiting in Wales, were present. In the evening Sybil was one of the speakers at the City Hall and mentioned that her youngest sister had joined the

WAAC. She did not add that Lottie had done so by pretending that she was fifteen years younger than her actual age.

Rumours about immorality in WAAC camps became rife. It was even claimed that WAACs were being recruited for army brothels.[48] By the start of 1918 there were 22,479 serving members of the WAAC.[49] Less than 5,000 were stationed in France, but stories of widespread licentiousness were having an adverse effect on recruitment just as increased numbers of women were required there to replace men needed for the spring offensive expected by the Germans. An all-female commission investigated the situation. Eighteen camps and eleven hostels were visited and it concluded in March 1918 that the charges 'rest on no foundation in fact'.[50]

Recruitment to the WAAC picked up dramatically in the spring, stimulated not only by renewed confidence in the corps but also by changes in conditions in the labour market at home, with former munitions workers joining them.[51] Margaret participated in a week-long women's war service exhibition in Cardiff in April. Held in the large department store of James Howell and Company, it opened with a resolution from 'the women of south Wales' that every single man who could be replaced by a woman would be. This was sent to Sir Douglas Haig.[52]

Margaret's message was that Welsh women had recruited more successfully than any other region, but were now needed more than ever as they were 'passing through the greatest crisis in our country's history'. They were not only required in the WAAC (which in this month became Queen Mary's Army Auxiliary Corps – QMAAC) but also in their naval equivalent, the Women's Royal

Naval Service (WRNS) and in the Women's Royal Air Force (the WRAF, nicknamed the Penguins because they did not fly). Margaret once more appealed to parents, asking that those who had given sons readily would now give daughters to 'the service of the nation'. Sybil, who chaired the Advisory Committee of the National War Savings Committee and played a key role in the establishment and extension of the National Kitchens movement, spoke about the need to save food.

Two thousand attended on the opening day. There were lectures and demonstrations of work such as butter-making. The exhibition was a resounding success. By the end of the week almost 10,000 had visited, including many from the valleys. More than 1,000 had enrolled. The WAAC, WRNS and Land Army did particularly well, though few chose the air force. In June Margaret opened a similar week-long exhibition in Swansea's Albert Hall, accompanied by G.H. Roberts, the Minister of Labour.[53] His choice of words could have been better. He described their mission as the 'Wake up, England' appeal and suggested that far from there being a sex war or the evolution of a third sex, the sexes would be brought together into a 'great brotherhood of sacrifice'. Margaret outlined different types of work open to women, from making aeroplanes to agriculture, and made her now familiar appeal for those not already doing work of national importance to come forward. Amy Dillwyn, Swansea's eminent industrialist, writer and feminist, now in her seventies, made an appearance.

During this period Margaret was, however, based in London. Since February 1918 she had returned to work for the Ministry of National Service, in what her autobiography simply calls 'a big job'.[54] She accepted the post in January, but a minor operation forced her to delay the start of work by a few weeks. She divulged little about the work in *This Was My World* though acknowledged that she took it up enthusiastically. She temporarily set aside all her business commitments – something few could do without serious consequences – and 'devoted myself to the new job'.[55]

CHAPTER SIX

Responsibility and Reputation

1918 was a watershed year for Margaret. It brought her the vote, opportunity and tragedy. Her new job effectively ended her life in Wales and saw her committed to employment in London. She was now Chief Controller of women's recruitment in a new women's section that was part of the Ministry of National Service headed by Sir Auckland Geddes. Margaret's brief was to advise on women's recruitment policy for National Service. The ministry's headquarters were in the Windsor Hotel in Victoria Street. This street also became Margaret's business headquarters. Conveniently close was her parents' flat in Ashley Gardens. Public and private life also came together through her job: her personal assistant was Mrs Helen Archdale, soon to occupy a central role in Margaret's life.

Violet Markham approved of the direction in which women's recruitment was moving, though she wryly observed that the policy of the new women's section was

similar to what she and May Tennant had sought a year
earlier. Privately she acknowledged that 'Lady Mackworth
is a nice sensible woman', appreciating that at least she
was familiar with the situation.[1] She wrote to Margaret,
wishing her well in her 'important and onerous duties'
and advising her to keep on the right side of the very able
Miss Durham at the Department of Employment since she
might resent the shift in authority away from her
department.[2] With characteristic frankness Margaret
responded by admitting that her earlier experience of
inter-departmental rivalries had given her 'a most
wholesome fear', so she was 'looking forward to the work
with not a little trepidation'.[3]

The press reacted favourably to Margaret's
appointment. The *Queen* magazine viewed it as evidence
that the government now recognised the need to increase
the efficiency of female war worker recruitment. Readers
were advised that she had already proved to be 'a woman
of rare business capacity' who would doubtless tackle her
new responsibilities effectively.[4] The *Sketch* noted that she
was related to the Commander-in-Chief on the Western
Front. Although the WAAC was currently receiving bad
publicity, it was confident that with a Haig in charge of
women's recruitment, 'the right type of young woman' –
by which it meant 'the well-educated and refined girl of
the period' – would be attracted to the administrative side
of the corps.[5]

Margaret's position was not easy. Her tasks included
dealing with press rumours about the likelihood of female
conscription.[6] In addition to ongoing battles in getting
other departments to take women's perspectives seriously,
there was rivalry and distrust between women's groups

and corps. The decision that the Ministry of National Service be responsible for controlling recruitment of all women involved in work of national importance had been taken when there was a definite shortage of suitable women. Not long after this the shortage briefly became a surplus. Then shortages became apparent again in certain areas, notably clerical and domestic work. Such fluctuations exacerbated an already complicated situation.

Margaret encountered some resistance to her personal scheme for recruitment. Concerns surfaced in correspondence and in meetings held by Margaret and Colonel Consellis (who ran the women's section) with both the Ministry of Labour and various women's organisations.[7] A conference in April brought the three service corps on board. By carefully modifying her proposals, Margaret managed to placate the Joint Women's Voluntary Aid Detachment Committee, but the Women's Legion under Lady Londonderry still harboured serious reservations, fearing that the new regulations would 'seriously disturb' the present system of recruiting for the Legion and wanted the entire scheme deferred.[8] It was a valuable, though frustrating, lesson in trying to placate and persuade without appearing to compromise too much. Margaret later concluded that '[w]e were able to do useful scraps of work here and there, but not much more'.[9]

Markham shared Margaret's desire that the country's 'woman power' be utilised more fully and effectively, with greater centralised control. She drafted a Woman Power Memorandum calling for the establishment of a Woman Power Council to create some order out of the apparent chaos. This was sent to Margaret who was then asked by Lord Milner (Secretary of State for War) to comment on how it fitted in with her own plans. Close consultation ensued with, amongst others, Markham, Tennant, Philippa Strachey (of the Women's Service Bureau) and Mona Chalmers Watson. A redrafted memorandum followed.[10]

Margaret's department set up a committee to explore the possibility of giving ex-service women the same facilities as men for emigrating to the dominions. This resulted in the Society for Overseas Settlement of British Women.[11] Her influence was demonstrated in the August 1918 issue of *Overseas* (the journal of the Overseas Club and Patriotic League of Britons Overseas). This commemorated the fourth anniversary of the war with a special issue from the Ministry of Information providing propaganda for the Dominions. It contained a message from Sir Douglas Haig and articles by figures such as Bonar Law, Lord Northcliffe, Sir Auckland Geddes and Margaret.

On 20 June Major Evelyn Wrench, head of the Dominion section at the Ministry of Information, had written to request her contribution. He sought to flatter, suggesting that 'naturally no account of Great Britain's effort would be complete without including a message from you'. The result was 'The Women of Great Britain'. This article applauded the role played by women over the past four years in organisations ranging from the Territorial Nursing Service and Women's Emergency Corps to the Women's Legion and QMAAC. Unlike the somewhat patronising praise of women displayed in the other articles, Margaret's contribution simply declared that women had, like the men, done their duty. And it opened with a pointed remark:

> Nothing in the whole conduct of the War has been
> more striking than the readiness and the ability of
> the women in nearly all the belligerent nations to
> render invaluable service to their respective
> countries, and nothing has been stranger than the
> slowness of various Governments to realise the vast
> capacity of the resources upon which they might
> draw.[12]

Yet although this went out in her name and Margaret
endorsed its sentiments, due to her father's illness she did
not write the article herself though she approved it in
draft.[13]

By the time proofs arrived D.A. had died and Margaret
had replaced her title of Lady Mackworth with that of the
second Viscountess Rhondda. In August when the article
appeared, events were set in train that would have serious
repercussions for how Margaret's war record was to be
seen and remembered. That summer was an especially
bleak time for her. Ironically the trouble arose over the
job loss of another Welshwoman, the very person who had
initially recommended Margaret for the post of Welsh
commissioner: Violet Blanche Douglas-Pennant.

The two women appeared to have much in common.
Douglas-Pennant was the sixth daughter of a Welsh peer
of Scottish descent. Baron Penrhyn owned one of the
largest estates in north Wales and one of the world's
biggest slate quarries. Douglas-Pennant sat on many
public committees and performed philanthropic work in
London. She had been a health insurance commissioner
for south Wales for seven years, sat on the south Wales
Belgian Relief Committee, chaired a select committee on

nursing staff for the Scottish Women's Hospital Unit in
Serbia and helped to set up the WAAC.

Closer inspection reveals divergent influences.
Although Douglas-Pennant's father dominated north
Wales and Margaret's father was a leading industrialist in
south Wales, their outlooks were very different. D.A. was
a Welsh Liberal and liked to see himself as a forward-
looking employer. The Tory Baron Penrhyn is perhaps best
remembered today for the longest dispute in British
industrial relations, the three-year lock-out of his
quarrymen between 1900 and 1903. His sixth daughter
was seen as the most progressive member of the family.
Douglas-Pennant was fourteen years older than Margaret
and forty-nine when, on 13 May 1918, she was asked to
take charge of the WRAF as its second commandant. The
first commandant had left after only one month.

Although created in April 1918 at the same time as
the Royal Air Force, the establishment of the WRAF had
not been carefully planned. It soon had 14,000 in its
ranks (most had previously served on air stations in the
army, navy and British Legion) but only 75 officers
covering over 500 camps. It suffered from what Beryl
Escott has called 'a scrambled start'.[14] Douglas-Pennant
accepted the post provisionally, taking 'a month's look-
round' to assess the situation. She was not impressed by
what she saw. There was a lack of uniforms for new
recruits, no clear chain of command, what looked like
nepotism in appointments at headquarters, as well as a
serious lack of training and decent accommodation. She
was, she claimed, 'blocked at every turn'.[15]

When the month was up, she decided not to take the
job and admitted that she did not feel she was the right

person for it. She was persuaded to stay on by assurances of imminent improvements and a clarification of her position. Her appointment was confirmed on 18 June. She tried to improve matters. For example, she used her contacts at the London County Council to secure the out-of-term use of Avery Hill Training College at Eltham to train 450 officers. But staffing and other problems persisted. There were clashes over appointments. Senior staff used to being in command resented her appointment. She was faced with resignations and offered to resign herself. To placate her, a few senior officials were replaced but in August she was summarily dismissed.

Margaret's involvement arose because she had been asked by Geddes to compile a report on women's welfare in camps. Earlier rumours of immorality had resurfaced and on 5 August Sir Willoughby Dickinson had asked in the House of Commons that a committee be created to inquire into and advise on the 'general condition of affairs and the possibility of securing that the conditions under which the women are living and working shall be uniformly good'.[16] The Chancellor of the Exchequer was not convinced that this was necessary, but requested a report. Margaret had to summarise the situation. She completed her short report by 22 August, dealing with nine different organisations. She was especially critical of the WRAF because on 13 August Philippa Strachey, suffragist and director of the voluntary employment organisation the Women's Service Bureau, had told her that they were so worried about the state of affairs in the WRAF that they did not feel they could place any more recruits there.[17]

Margaret informed Geddes of the situation. He asked

her to see Lord Weir at the Air Ministry. Geddes also wrote to Weir on 19 August, stressing that the present arrangements for the WRAF were so bad that unless they improved he would have to embargo recruitment. Margaret and Strachey met Weir on 26 August and were told that he had already made up his mind to 'supersede' Douglas-Pennant. They concentrated in this meeting on the best means of improving organisation generally in the WRAF. Weir had received Margaret's report that morning and he remarked that she had dealt rather severely with the corps.

Two days later Douglas-Pennant was told by General Brancker (who had just taken over as head of the RAF's 'manning') that she must leave the very next morning. Margaret also saw Brancker. He suggested that she might become commandant. Fortunately she demurred. Her immediate response was that 'in view of the great disorganisation at the moment, I thought it was imperative to have a woman for that work from one of the women's corps, because she would get it in order more quickly'.[18] Douglas-Pennant later claimed that her dismissal was connected to Geddes wanting the post for his sister Mrs Chalmers Watson (he described this as 'fantastically untrue').

But it was by no means the end of the story. The events outlined above were examined in minute detail as part of a sustained attempt by Douglas-Pennant to clear her name. Although Margaret did not feature prominently in the public furore immediately after the loss of Douglas-Pennant's job, she was caught in the crossfire that ensued when Douglas-Pennant protested against her treatment. The adverse publicity was intensified over time so that

Margaret risked losing her reputation as an effective wartime administrator. As the fight for justice unfolded, so she was increasingly drawn into the saga. Her role in the dismissal was subjected to intense scrutiny.

There is no doubt that the manner in which Douglas-Pennant had been dismissed was unwarranted. After twice being persuaded to stay on and after only ten weeks in post, General Brancker told her to go because she was 'grossly unpopular'.[19] A letter sent to her from the Air Ministry a few days later admitted that she had worked 'most wholeheartedly and untiringly'.

Douglas-Pennant contacted senior political figures in a bid to secure an inquiry, arguing that her dismissal was part of an attempt by other senior WRAF officers to cover up gross immorality in the camps, most notably at the motor transport depot at Hurst Park. In October 1918 the prime minister appointed Cecil Harmsworth to enquire into her dismissal. Douglas-Pennant was also deeply concerned about rumours suggesting why she had been dismissed. Harmsworth interviewed a number of witnesses, including Margaret. He recommended a full judicial inquiry, but this did not materialise and the report of his investigation was never published. Questions were asked in Parliament.

In May 1919 a White Paper published Air Ministry correspondence relating to the termination of Douglas-Pennant's appointment. Although Margaret did not feature in this she did write a letter to *The Times* in June.[20] The White Paper and the newspaper had given the case publicity, focusing on Geddes and Dame Katherine Furse (Director of the WRNS) so Margaret felt it only right to point out her own role. She explained that she was responsible for advising Geddes on the Douglas-Pennant situation and '[i]n these circumstances I feel as much responsibility attaches to me as to anyone outside the Ministry directly concerned'.

The House of Lords subsequently voted for its own Select Committee. Supporters of Douglas-Pennant were critical as it placed the onus on her to account for her actions and prove why she had been dismissed. The five-man Select Committee, chaired by Lord Wrenbury, began hearing evidence in mid-October. Margaret cut short a visit to Canada to appear as the final witness on 11 November 1919.[21]

When questioned, Douglas-Pennant claimed that there was an intrigue against her and that Lady Rhondda was part of this. She sought to discredit Margaret's report (on the conditions for women employed on war work in camps) with its focus on the shortcomings of the WRAF. She was also very concerned to demonstrate that she had not been consulted about it. She had, she explained, only had a couple of meetings with Margaret and they had not discussed the WRAF. They had spoken about 'the war and the weather' over lunch and on the other occasion 'we talked a little about her difficulties, I think'. Douglas-Pennant was very concerned to suggest that she hardly knew Margaret. When it was pointed out that Lady Rhondda was a very well-known public woman, she replied dismissively that she had not had very many years' experience and when pressed about her being a prominent figure, answered that '[h]er father, of course, was so well known'.

During the Harmsworth investigation, Douglas-Pennant sought to discredit Margaret by suggesting that, previous to her National Service employment, she 'had never done any public work, excepting as a Militant Suffragette'.[22] In the House of Lords inquiry when asked whether Lady Rhondda was 'actuated by will or malice' towards her, she claimed that Margaret was 'made to believe, or induced to believe, or was misinformed – that she certainly tried to get rid of me without any justification'.

Margaret's recollection of these meetings was somewhat different. She remembered talking about the corps at the first meeting. The two women later discussed plans for a scheme about common selection boards for all the corps, including the WRAF. She had to answer detailed criticism about her report from Douglas-Pennant's lawyer. It had given the QMAAC and WRNS a clean bill of health but had stressed that '[t]he WRAF is still very disorganised, despite the fact that the corps has been in existence seven months'.

Her report pointed out that unless the 'guiding principle of control of women by women' was observed, inevitable 'chaos and disaster' would follow. An adequate supply of officers, especially senior officers, was imperative, yet the WRAF had practically no senior officers in place. There were large numbers of workers in camps throughout the country with no women officers in control. This, Margaret argued, had led to 'a state of disorganisation, inefficiency and lack of discipline amongst the workers'. Unless speedily remedied, the reputation of all the corps was threatened in the eyes of the general public. The report stated that the WRNS, only two months senior to the WRAF, had already managed to get its house in order. This was not an entirely valid comparison: the WRNS had gradually built up its numbers from scratch whereas the WRAF started with 14,000 women plus officers being transferred from the QMAAC and a further 2,000 from the WRNS.

Douglas-Pennant could hardly deny that there were major problems in the WRAF – she had, after all, baulked at the immensity of them after her first month in control – but she felt, not unreasonably, that Margaret's report did not reflect the improvements she had been busy implementing. These included initiating a system which had trained 480 officers, opening two large depot hostels and improving medical treatment for recruits.[23] Cross-examination sought to show that Margaret's report was inadequate and even inaccurate. The WRAF had been formed on 1 April and so was not seven months old when Margaret's report was written.

Margaret provided a robust defence though at times she sounded somewhat vague. Her report had been hastily compiled when she was still getting over the loss of her father. Although she had read the papers of the three women who resigned, she did not discuss the specific problems with Douglas-Pennant or corroborate the information she used as the basis for her recommendations. When pressed on her sources and whether Dame Katherine Furse might have influenced her – something she denied, although she had talked to her – she explained: 'I was living in a world in which that [information] was soaked into one day by day and hour by hour by all the people you met, and I have not the least idea what individual [sic] told me' (about the WRNS).

Douglas-Pennant also told the Select Committee that a few days after her dismissal she went to see Margaret as a matter of courtesy (having no idea that she had been implicated in her dismissal) and told her: 'An extraordinary thing has happened. I have been suddenly shot out of the force.' She reported that Margaret had expressed shock and surprise. She had apparently begged Douglas-Pennant to fight this, saying, 'Take it to Court'. In this version of the story, Douglas-Pennant confronted Margaret, saying that she had heard that she had gone to Lord Weir 'and demanded her head on a charger'.

Margaret in turn denied that she had ever mentioned recourse to the courts. 'I should not have dreamt of saying that', she declared. When Douglas-Pennant had mentioned that National Service ought to intervene, Margaret had told her that it would be 'totally impossible'. She acknowledged that she might have mentioned that if Douglas-Pennant felt she had been unjustly treated, she should try to get an inquiry but, being in an official position, she had said as little as possible.

Margaret's evidence ended the inquiry. The Select Committee took the unusual step of making an announcement immediately: all accusations of immorality against individuals were deemed to be without foundation.[24] The report was published in December. All Douglas-Pennant's allegations were refuted. No intrigue or concerted action was detected by any of the individuals she had named. Nobody had induced or compelled her removal or resignation by any improper means and 'Lady Rhondda was acting perfectly bona fide in discharge of her duty to Sir Auckland Geddes in giving him help in dealing with an unsatisfactory state of affairs'. Margaret's report had played no part in determining Weir's actions. In a damaging character statement the House of Lords suggested that Douglas-Pennant was:

... full of zeal and activity, much impressed with her own importance, very reckless in her imputations upon others... and one not at all likely to get the best out of those with whom she had to work, or over whom she had authority.

An editorial in *The Times* argued that the government had been completely justified in refusing to reopen her case.[25] The report, it claimed, was a 'very crushing document' about a woman obsessed by her grievance. She had brought outrageous allegations without any real proof. An important principle had been recognised: those in public service, especially in war time, were not indispensable. They could be removed if the minister deemed that this was right. It was only the 'blind zeal' of Douglas-Pennant's champions that had succeeded in inducing the House of Lords to grant the inquiry and, had she thought 'less of her injured dignity, she would have spared herself this overwhelming humiliation'. The Treasury decided that the legal costs of Lady Rhondda and five officers of the RAF and WRAF implicated in the inquiry (amounting to £5,392) should be paid, as they were all public servants at the time of the alleged events. Margaret was reimbursed £375.[26]

Douglas-Pennant and her doughty champions were, however, more determined than ever to press on. It was felt that the Select Committee had never got to the bottom of why she was sacked and that 'a grave injustice had been done to a valuable Public Servant'.[27] For many, this case was a symbol of what was rotten in the state. For those critical of Whitehall's workings here was a scandal that demonstrated its propensity for secrecy and cover-ups. 'Pure administration' was needed. One of the many pamphlets on the case explained that it was vital to press for justice for Douglas-Pennant and in the process to show 'that in public life we have no room for men who seek to hide up the truth'.[28] In the wake of the House of Lords inquiry, a committee was formed 'to sift the facts which had not been allowed to emerge at the Inquiry'.

This committee financed the publication of a hefty tome by Douglas-Pennant. *Under the Search-Light* was, like the minutes of the House of Lords Select Committee, more than 450 pages long. It was published in 1922, an especially demanding year for Margaret who was in the process of getting divorced and was embroiled in a petition to the House of Lords. Douglas-Pennant's publication was repetitive and uncompromising, arguing that she had not been accorded even basic justice. In the course of her many claims and grievances she reiterated the charges she had made earlier against Margaret. She dismissed Margaret's report as misleading and highly inaccurate, suggesting it was based on gossip, though she conceded that it did reflect conditions *before* she became commandant. She stated that Margaret was unable to take over as commandant herself, as her father had just died. She painted herself as a victim of Margaret's credulity and inexperience but also implied that she was scheming, claiming that the actions of both Lord Weir and Margaret throughout had been 'against every tradition of fair play and honourable dealing'.

Douglas-Pennant now put the spotlight on Margaret's meeting with Philippa Strachey. Thirty-one pages of the book form a chapter called 'Lady Rhondda's Secret Statement'. Here she suggested that Margaret had supplemented her report with 'a secret and apparently most serious statement', which she had received from Strachey whose sources were Mrs Beatty and Miss Andrew who had recently left the WRAF. What exactly was said was not known and had not been revealed at the Select Committee, but Douglas-Pennant was at pains to demonstrate that Geddes then wrote Weir a letter that had since disappeared. So far more was at stake than the official report alone.

'To this day', wrote Douglas-Pennant in her book, 'I have never been allowed to know of what I was accused.' She asked why the Select Committee did not investigate the nature of these charges and why Strachey was not subpoenaed to substantiate them.

The *Liverpool Post* suggested that, if true, Douglas-Pennant's dismissal 'must rank as one of the gravest official wrongs of modern times' and a number of people including Lady Rhondda 'must be regarded with suspicion'.[29] Public opinion was polarised. A public meeting in support of Douglas-Pennant back home in north Wales (at Bangor) was addressed by the Bishop of St Asaph, the principal of the University College of North Wales and the secretary of the Quarrymen's Union.[30]

Renewed attention was paid to the case in the summer of 1925 when the *Manchester Guardian* ran four detailed articles on the case.[31] They were by the renowned war correspondent and champion of radical causes, Henry W. Nevinson. A Leader explained that 'a lady of the highest character and distinguished public service' had been dismissed 'under every circumstance of indignity' and never told what she had been charged with. For six years she had sought in vain to obtain justice.[32]

Nevinson's articles told the whole story from Douglas-Pennant's perspective. A skilled and persuasive writer, he made the case read like a 'whodunnit'. He disliked the cover-up and the way in which several prime ministers had failed to sanction a full and open judicial inquiry. In the course of his revelations he emphasised the undisclosed communication accepted by Margaret. And he suggested that much was based on hearsay. It was like 'The House that Jack Built':

> General Brancker was acting under orders from Lord Weir, Secretary for Air, who was acting upon information supplied him by Lady Rhondda, who was acting upon information supplied her by Miss Philippa Strachey, who was acting upon information supplied her by Mrs Beatty and Miss Andrew, two of the 'munitions officers' who had resigned a fortnight after Miss Douglas-Pennant's appointment because she refused to appoint some of their unqualified friends to high office in the Corps Force.[33]

An extra element of scandal was introduced by statements apparently made to the Late Tyson Wilson MP (the ILP Whip) who had received a letter from Mrs Beatty. It was alleged that he had said that 'if the facts were known Miss Douglas-Pennant could never hold up her head again'.[34] He also apparently told a WRAF captain that she was 'a very bad woman, not only a bully and virago, but immoral' and that WRAF women had 'threatened to mutiny, as no decent woman could serve under her'.

Yet Nevinson had been reluctant to take on this

journalistic assignment.[35] His diary reveals that although he found Douglas-Pennant 'straight' and 'amiable', she did not quite satisfy him that Strachey's communication was something secret and separate from Lady Rhondda's report.[36] He privately admitted to contradictions and vagueness on both sides though he never talked to Margaret – whom he knew slightly – for her side of the story.

Despite the *Guardian's* championing of Douglas-Pennant, it was far from a straightforward case of left versus right. Indeed, one of the tragedies of the scandal was the way in which individuals took sides and became entrenched in their positions. The Labour MP Ellen Wilkinson took issue with Nevinson's claims and argued that Douglas-Pennant 'seems to have been the last person who should have been placed in charge of human beings'.[37] Elizabeth Robins told Nevinson that she had heard ill of Douglas-Pennant and that she was 'a superior bully of women under her'.[38] In December Evelyn Isitt (who worked for the *Manchester Guardian* and had written Margaret's article for the magazine *Overseas)* 'violently' defended Margaret. She told Nevinson that Margaret and Dame Katherine Furse had suffered as a result of his articles and that their only charge against Douglas-Pennant was 'incapacity and their only interest the welfare of the girls'.[39] The responsibility lay with Lord Weir alone and the manner of dismissal was the only wrong. When Nevinson next met Douglas-Pennant she suggested that Furse rather than Margaret was the real 'intriguer'.[40]

For the *Manchester Guardian*, issues of British justice and state security were at stake. It sought to uncover the secrecy surrounding the scandal and demanded reparation. A pamphlet from the Douglas-Pennant Committee then reproduced the newspaper's articles and drew attention to Margaret's role. She was 'the channel' through whom the charges were conveyed, so: 'Will she give the public the benefit of her information?' After all, she was 'a lady of great position and unblemished character. It would seem that she owes to herself no less than to the woman on whom she was the means of inflicting a deadly and unmerited injury such an act of elementary justice.'[41]

Douglas-Pennant and her supporters kept up the pressure. Furse remarked that 'Miss Douglas-Pennant would have no interest in life if she dropped her long defence'.[42] On Christmas Eve in 1929 the Attorney General declared (in reply to a question in the House of Commons) that there had never been grounds for suggesting that she was 'guilty of any kind of moral turpitude' and inefficiency. But July 1931 saw a new twist in the scandal when a meeting was held by the Douglas-Pennant Committee in Central Hall Westminster, for adults only. Here her lawyer announced to a hushed audience that 'at long last' the unstated charge was known and that 'she was accused of being immoral with women, in other words, of being a Sapphist'.[43] It was said that Lord Weir had been so shocked by the information that he had 'lost all sense of reason' and declared that she must be dismissed forthwith. Just three years after the publicity surrounding the infamous censorship case of Radclyffe Hall's lesbian novel *The Well of Loneliness*, the Labour MP W.J. Brown openly called it a charge of lesbianism.

In November 1933 a Douglas-Pennant League was

created 'for the Promotion of Honesty, Truth and Justice in Public Life and in the Administration of Public Affairs'.[44] At its inaugural meeting it was declared that she had been the victim of a campaign of 'vile scandalmongering'. Geddes, it was claimed, had practically compelled Weir to act as he did because of the information he received about shocking conditions in certain of the WRAF camps. The meeting was told that the names of the camps were now known and new evidence proved that the women employed in them were never under Douglas-Pennant's control. It was claimed that statements on oath from (unnamed) 'unimpeachable quarters now proved that Douglas-Pennant had been grossly defamed by Mrs Beatty. The allegations that she was 'a moral pervert of the worst description and a danger to the women under her charge' meant that 'there can be little doubt that Beatty's secret statements to Lady Rhondda were equally wicked and untrue'. The following year Douglas-Pennant told Nevinson that she had new evidence against Mrs Beatty, claiming that she had been promoting lesbianism amongst her girls and that she had been Brancker's mistress.[45] But Mrs Beatty could not defend herself: she was no longer alive. Douglas-Pennant lived on until 1945, obsessively seeking to clear her name until the end.

Over a period of sixteen years there were times when Margaret featured quite prominently in the exposures. Katherine Furse (who greatly admired the way Margaret had given evidence in 1919) felt sorry for Douglas-Pennant but could not forgive the way she had been personally attacked. She had told Markham the previous year that she believed that Douglas-Pennant had 'two personalities'.[46]

Douglas-Pennant had also confided in Markham, suggesting that Margaret was inexperienced and gullible, so effectively did the dirty work for others.[47] Nevertheless, public comments uncompromisingly implicated Margaret at a time when she was seeking to build up her public reputation.

Nobody emerged unscathed or with much credit from the whole sorry affair. Douglas-Pennant's dismissal seems to have been premature and was clearly handled badly. It became an opportunity for people to protest at the lack of open government as well as what was seen as a specific miscarriage of justice. But Douglas-Pennant turned her case into a personal crusade that at times treated and accused others in what was also a questionably cavalier fashion. The case goes a long way towards explaining why Margaret was so reticent in her autobiography about her stint in charge of women's recruiting at the Ministry of National Service. It merited just one paragraph. Revelations were still rife when she was writing her book.

Shirley Eoff has suggested that the charges and inquiries were 'significant as an indication of Margaret's tendency to rely heavily on the advice of others'.[48] It does seem as though she might have checked her sources more thoroughly before submitting her report. Eoff also refers to 'her developing showmanship', evident in the confident and witty manner in which she spoke out in the Select Committee (which does not accord with the inexperienced figure Douglas-Pennant tried to paint). But Margaret's dignified refusal to engage directly in the protracted and salacious mud-slinging was surely a wise move. On New Year's Eve 1925, Nevinson reviewed the past year in his diary. He described the '[t]errible' Douglas-Pennant case as 'a true briary bush'.[49] The Douglas-Pennant affair must have seemed to Margaret like a cloud that persistently hovered ominously close at a time when she already had numerous personal worries.

CHAPTER SEVEN

Being D.A.'s Daughter

Two-thirds of the way through Margaret's autobiography is a chapter entitled 'The Last Years'. This is no attempt to forecast her fate. It is the story of D.A.'s death and forms part of a section entitled 'My Father's World'. D.A. had been dead fifteen years by the time it was published but it is he – in life and in death – who, more than any other person, haunts this book. The Viscountess, who mixed with the artistic and social elite internationally readily acknowledged that the days spent with her father were 'amongst the most glamorous that I can remember' and that he exercised the greatest personal influence on her.[1] 'There was', she wrote, 'nothing in heaven or earth that we did not discuss together.'[2] This is a remarkable statement about a Victorian father who had been born in the middle of the nineteenth century.

D.A. cherished Margaret. After the sinking of the *Lusitania* he admitted that '[i]f I had lost her my life would have been blighted for ever, and everything would have become a blank for the future. She is more than a daughter to me; she is a real pal.'[3]

He died in July 1918 when he was at the peak of his fame and popularity. He had recently achieved a singular success in a post he had taken on reluctantly. It had been seen as a poisoned chalice. His triumph against the odds as Food Controller made a compelling story. Rationing was introduced just one month before D.A. became seriously ill but, as the *Evening Standard* put it, 'No Minister has achieved quite the same popularity as the Minister who ruthlessly cut down the people's food allowances'.[4] The fact that he seemed determined that all should be rationed was popular, demonstrating commitment to a collectivist approach from an acknowledged individualist and immensely successful businessman. D.A. belatedly won the accolades denied to him for many years. The story of his death at the height of his success was contrasted with the fact that he had never even been made an under-secretary of state during the twenty-three years that he had sat in Parliament as a younger and rather fitter politician. This survivor of the sinking of the *Lusitania* could now be seen to have sacrificed his life for the nation just like brave combatants.

For Margaret, D.A.'s death was an intense personal tragedy when she too was making her mark in national war work. Summer 1918 was disastrous for her. She lost the person she most cared for. The Douglas-Pennant scandal questioned her professional judgement, providing publicity when she least needed it. And, as we shall see, her marriage was all but over.

D.A. had suffered from heart problems since his youth and had survived six attacks of rheumatic fever. Margaret first knew that something was wrong during a country walk one March weekend in 1917 when he complained of a pain in his heart. A heart specialist diagnosed angina. Margaret had a private meeting with this specialist and was assured that D.A. could live until he was ninety if he slowed down and took care. She was well aware that this was impossible.

Not long after this, Lloyd George offered D.A. the job at the Food Ministry. Conscious that the official lives of food controllers in other countries had been both unpopular and short and that such a post would have a huge, possibly fatal effect on his personal health, D.A. was not enthusiastic. And he was especially keen to put into practice his plans for a Ministry of Health. Margaret spent a hot summer's evening walking up and down the lawn at Llanwern with her parents, considering the situation.[5] At first D.A. suggested that somebody else be appointed. Nobody suitable emerged. Conscious of the difficulty of refusing a post in the midst of war, he assumed office in June 1917.

He travelled huge distances, addressed numerous meetings and had to win over public opinion. But he always thrived on challenges and knew how to court the press. His strict adherence to setting an example with personal frugality in food consumption was not conducive to his wellbeing. He worked extremely long hours in a department that had grown from a staff of 400, when he took over, to 5,000 employees. He frequently woke at 3 or 4 am and would then start work.

A year after his health warning and just after his sixty-second birthday, D.A. went to Llanwern for Easter. He was unwell and took to his bed. Margaret sent a handwritten letter to Lloyd George a few days later explaining that although he was much better, the doctor had said he must remain in bed for a few days.[6] D.A. had asked her to assure the prime minister that the work of the Food Ministry would not suffer in any way. But he had contracted pleurisy and spent April and May in bed or in a chair in the garden. By June he was worse. Margaret, who had a heavy workload in London, travelled to Llanwern most weekends. D.A. tried to resign but his offer was refused. Although very weary, he insisted on dealing with the daily official bag from the Food Ministry.

He was promoted to the rank of Viscount on 3 June for his service as Food Controller and, as the prime minister explained, the King had agreed 'that the Remainder of your peerage should be settled upon your daughter'. The monarch assented to this 'in cases where the service rendered to the State is very conspicuous'. Lloyd George added that '[i]n my judgement there has been no case during the King's reign where it was better justified than in yours'.[7] Viscount Rhondda of Llanwern was delighted.

Sir Thomas Horder (the King's physician) was in charge of the patient and stayed at Llanwern during the final weeks. Although a house was rented by the sea at Southerndown in the Vale of Glamorgan, D.A. was not well enough to be taken there. Margaret arrived on 28 June and was still at Llanwern on 3 July when her father died.

D.A. was cremated at Golders Green in London then his ashes were brought to Llanwern on 6 July. Flags flew at half-mast on public buildings in Newport and business was suspended on the Cardiff Coal and Shipping

Exchange. The mourners, led by Sybil, Margaret and Humphrey, walked in procession for the three-quarters of a mile through the park drive along to St Mary's Church. The ceremony took place under the old yew tree. Numerous relatives attended as did Welsh dignitaries and political and industrial colleagues past and present. Margaret's old friend Prid sent one of the many wreaths which were conveyed to the church on several farm wagons. D.A.'s cousin, the Congregationalist Minister Arnold Thomas, gave the address. Somewhat dramatically, at the end of the service Margaret descended the ladder into the open grave, kissed the urn and left a posy of roses.[8]

Three days later she and Sybil attended, as did the Lloyd Georges, a memorial service at St Margaret's, Westminster. Lloyd George had told the dying D.A. that his efforts represented 'one of the most distinctive triumphs of the war'.[9] President Hoover sent a message via the US Food Administration in London.[10] Journalists gave fulsome praise for a politician who had always taken the press seriously. The *Daily Telegraph* declared: 'When history completes its record of the leaders who baffled Prussia's ambition for the mastery of the world a distinguished place will be given to Lord Rhondda'.[11] The *Merthyr Express* devoted almost three pages to his life. Its subtitle 'a National Misfortune' would have amused him.[12] The *Daily News* noted that he was 'fortunate above all in the equal comradeship both of wife and daughter'.[13]

Margaret, Sybil and Humphrey were the executors, trustees and chief beneficiaries of D.A.'s Will.[14] In 1935 in memory of D.A., Margaret and Sybil gave the National Trust 2,130 acres of the Sugar Loaf Mountain north of

Abergavenny, a well-known Monmouthshire beauty spot.[15] It was the second largest freehold gift that the trust had received.

But D.A.'s legacy was not just financial and titular. Margaret was keen to endorse projects related to her father's work.[16] She helped to consolidate his plans for a Ministry of Health.[17] A somewhat sycophantic article in the *Queen* told how her 'filial duty' benefited the country, and described her as 'a coadjutor' at one with her father 'in sympathetic understanding of his hopes and aims'. By education, training and companionship she had become 'a veritable second self'.[18]

Shortly before his death D.A. had established the Association of 'Win the War' Centres. The idea was to establish local advice centres dealing with the everyday problems of wartime. Official information was available about, for example, the economic use of food and fuel, the production and preservation of food and the collection and elimination of waste. The Association neatly fused the interests of the two ministries that employed D.A. and his daughter and Margaret now developed it further. The membership of its General Council demonstrates how she drew on the country's most influential figures to add to her father's legacy. It included Lloyd George, Bonar Law, H.A.L. Fisher and the Lord Mayor of London. Two centres were established by mid-July. More were planned, including a fuel economy exhibition designed to show people how to economise on light and coal rations – which was somewhat ironic, given the source of the Thomas/Rhondda wealth – but the end of the war effectively ended the scheme.[19]

Margaret and Sybil wanted a permanent record of

D.A.'s achievements. He had already played his own part in this in 1916 (when he had become Lord Rhondda and was awarded the Freedom of the City of Cardiff) by making a gift of statuary to Cardiff. Nearly 1,000 people had watched Lloyd George unveil the impressive monumental marble figures in the City Hall after years of planning.[20] And perhaps the decision to include Boadicea, along with the ten selected heroes who comprised the Welsh Historical Sculpture, showed D.A. genuflecting to his daughter. Margaret in turn did, as Dai Smith has put it, 'much to marmorealize' D.A.'s memory.[21]

Eight years later he was commemorated in Magor, Monmouthshire, close to where his grandfather had farmed. Margaret and Sybil (who was made a Dame Commander of the Order of the British Empire in 1920 for her voluntary war work) paid for a war memorial to be erected in the village square. It was dedicated to local men who had lost their lives in the war and to D.A., 'For He Too Died Serving the Nation as Food Controller'. He is depicted on one side in a circular bronze cameo portrait.

D.A. was portrayed in print in three publications with almost identical (and somewhat unimaginative) titles. The prolific writer the Rev. Vyrnwy Morgan wasted no time in penning a flattering, sycophantic picture. Wary of both nationalism and nonconformity, his D.A. was made to fit the author's conception of what Welsh politicians should espouse.[22] Further praise was heaped upon him in the memoir by David Evans, political correspondent for the *Western Mail*. This reproduced more than thirty detailed and glowing tributes, from the *South Wales Daily News* (which saw D.A.'s career as exemplifying 'the exceptional character of Welshmen') and *Bristol Times and Mirror* (claiming that he possessed 'the typical English qualities of courage and grit') to specialist papers such as *Oil News*.

Evans also wrote two chapters on D.A. for the official biography. Unsurprisingly, they showed the south Wales coal industry from the top down, giving for example, only D.A.'s perspectives on the Cambrian Combine dispute of 1910-11 and not mentioning the Tonypandy Riots of November 1910. *D.A.Thomas. Viscount Rhondda* (1921) by 'His Daughter and Others' was Margaret's first book and a way of handling her grief and respect for her father. She chose an unusual structure, a form of collective biography with twenty chapters, in twelve of which she unfolded D.A.'s life story. Interspersed were contributions from specialists focusing on specific aspects of the businessman and politician at work.[23]

Yet although the lack of a single authorial voice was refreshing, enabling experts to have their say, Margaret's approach did not easily lend itself to an overall assessment of D.A.'s achievements. The family involvement, the fact that it appeared only a few years after D.A.'s death, and the lack of an overview by a historian make it a somewhat fractured read and one which does not – perhaps could not at that point – explore the interplay and tensions between D.A.'s aspirations as industrialist and politician.[24]

In the preface Margaret explained that it was 'only after considerable hesitation and consultation'[25] that she and Sybil had decided that she should be responsible for her father's biography. She mentions that a contributor to the section on politics had to withdraw at the last moment. What she does not say is that the published book was far from the original plan for a life of D.A.

The journalist and author Harold Begbie had been

commissioned to write D.A.'s life. However, Margaret was not happy with the result. Begbie was an erstwhile Liberal social reformer who was fast becoming somewhat right-wing. In August 1919 Margaret told Sir William Beveridge (who had worked at the Food Ministry with D.A.):

> Everyone who has seen the proofs has been dissatisfied with the tone of the book and I think it probable that the book may not be published at all in its present form – certainly not until it has been drastically revised.
>
> Those most competent to judge feel it wouldn't do justice to my father's memory.[26]

Margaret was about to go to Canada on a combined holiday and business trip. She consulted Sir Thomas Horder (her father's physician) and decided that the book should be drastically sub-edited and that she would take control later in the year on her return.

She was keen to publish a chapter by Beveridge (he had suggested that he would try to place one somewhere else if not wanted for this volume) but, she told him that Begbie's chapter on food 'must I think be left out'.[27] Begbie did, however, contribute a chapter on D.A.'s political philosophy. Ramsay MacDonald, who saw D.A. as 'one of our greatest captains of industry and one of the ablest servants of the State at a time of critical danger' did not agree with this piece, arguing that D.A.'s individualism was rather more subtle than Begbie's interpretation allowed.[28]

So Margaret's first publication did not have an auspicious start. Working on it in Italy in January 1921, she admitted that it was moving 'dreadfully slowly'.[29] However, by this time she had launched *Time and Tide* and gained immeasurably in her understanding of literature and publication. When the matter of payment for contributors had been raised in August 1919 she had told Beveridge 'I am not sufficiently cognisant of what is the usual thing in the writing world to be able to judge of such matters'. She could not plead such ignorance for long.

Mary Agnes Hamilton helped Margaret to get the book into shape. A feminist, journalist and later a Labour MP, she was a contributor to *Time and Tide*. *D.A. Thomas* was published in October 1921 by Longmans, Green and Company. More than 300 pages long, it cost a guinea to buy. Margaret received £127 in royalties for the first six months of sales. On the whole it was well received. The *Contemporary Review* dubbed it 'the best biography that has been written for many a year' and a very relieved Margaret wrote to Robins, 'I am bursting with pride'.[30] The *Morning Post* called it a 'notable' book and *The Times* commented on her 'shrewd eye' for character and 'frank and keen humour'.[31]

Margaret's avoidance of hagiography impressed, though did not endear D.A. to all reviewers. The *Christian World* acknowledged that his gifts were great but called his morality 'pagan': 'not even his daughter can make of him quite an attractive personality'.[32] The reviewer for the *Times Literary Supplement* was not alone in thinking Margaret's contribution the best.[33] The experts, it was observed, wrote in a somewhat ponderous manner, but her writing was 'intimate and vivacious'. The *South Wales News* went further, declaring in somewhat hyperbolic language that it was a volume 'throbbing with human interest'.[34]

Margaret clearly had greater latitude than did her contributors. She was well aware that by acknowledging her father's foibles she was likely to be taken seriously, and that accounts of his various public achievements (largely the preserve of the selected contributors) could thereby be enhanced. It cannot, however, have been easy knowing what to disclose or keep private. In the first five chapters she followed biographical convention in outlining the earlier years of D.A.'s life. She added to the personal touch by including a selection of his letters to Sybil during the year of their engagement.

Considering the depth of her feelings for her father and the overwhelmingly reverential tone of most biographies to date – it was only three years since Lytton Strachey had broken the mould – Margaret's approach was brave. Maurice Hewlett noted that the subject had not been allowed to 'make a genial appearance before posterity. There need not have been roses *all* the way, but one likes to feel that there were some part of the way'.[35] Here was an account of an eminent Victorian that in its structure and in Margaret's chapters struck a distinctly modern note. This was all the more appropriate since D.A. had never run with the pack.

Margaret's assessment of D.A.'s social skills implied her own preferred approach to dealing with individuals. For example, she criticised his attitude to his 'superiors', arguing that '[h]is somewhat thorny pride made him unconciliatory and contradictious'.[36] But she admired the way he never patronised and how he valued intellect. She praised his capacity for hard work and application. D.A.'s vitality and his boyish delight in life are evident in Margaret's writing, whether scoring a victory over a political opponent in one of his newspaper 'pen-and-ink fights', securing a business deal or winning a prize for his Hereford cattle. The book ends with Margaret's declaration that he was the happiest man she had ever known.

The politician, journalist and lawyer Llewelyn Williams contributed two chapters on D.A.'s political life. He had his own agenda. He had set up the first Welsh branch of Cymru Fydd (which advocated self-government for Wales) in the early 1890s and in 1916 had broken with Lloyd George. His account points up D.A.'s achievements at the expense of Lloyd George. Kenneth O. Morgan argues that D.A.'s role in the demise of Cymru Fydd was more consistent than Williams suggested, especially when his views on the importance of industrial south Wales for the country's future are appreciated. Morgan also sees Margaret's rather generalised comments on D.A. and nationalism as simplifying his political beliefs and understanding of how Welsh Liberalism might and did develop over time. With the benefit of a hindsight not available to Margaret or Williams, Morgan contends that D.A. advanced and helped to modernise the national movement in Wales, not least by shifting attention to the urban, more heavily populated south.[37]

The three chapters on D.A. and the Ministry of Food were by insiders. Beveridge's substantial contribution was accompanied by short assessments from Professor Sir E.C.K. Gonner, the Ministry's Director of Statistics, and from the man who had worked most closely with D.A., the trade unionist and socialist Rt Hon J.R. Clynes, who had been chosen by him as Parliamentary Under-Secretary. They underscored D.A.'s achievements, drawing attention to his personal style of leadership, his transformation of the department's administration and image as well as his offensive against profiteering and the all-important system of compulsory food rationing.

The chapters do not suggest the wariness with which D.A.'s work was seen by many up until February 1918 when rationing finally took off. Margaret did quote Lloyd George retrospectively, admitting that it had looked for a time as though D.A. had failed. But at a time of acute shortages and lengthy food queues, others too had expressed doubts.

In December 1917 Sylvia Pankhurst had addressed miners' wives at Llwynypia Baths in the Rhondda where she had witnessed early morning food queues. The Home Office received an account of her speech in which she remarked that 'Lord Rhondda has bought up German firms, and is drawing high profits, although he is Food Controller. He doesn't go short of anything, neither does Lady Rhondda or Lady Mackworth'.[38] She urged people to worry the Food Controller and Food Committees as a tactic in articulating opposition to the war. In the same month the delay in the implementation of food rationing caused concern to other members of the Pankhurst family with very different views on the war. The Women's Party (formerly the WSPU) sent a deputation to D.A. to demand compulsory rations and was critical of the delay.[39]

Just before rationing was implemented, the *Daily Mail* had complained about D.A.'s appointment of an alderman as director of the National Kitchens scheme.[40] D.A. had supported women's suffrage and it had been understood that he believed in women's fitness to undertake responsible work. So why, the paper asked, could he not have entrusted such a post to a woman? Yet Margaret and her father were well aware of this newspaper's own record on suffrage. It was, after all, the *Mail* that had first coined the word 'suffragette' – as a term of derision. And once rationing was introduced on 25 February the harassed and weary Food Controller became the hero of the hour. This success story was understandably the focus of the volume to commemorate D.A.'s life.

There was, however, another story that Margaret could not tell publicly. When D.A. commented that his daughter Margaret 'knows more about my affairs than any living soul' he was speaking the truth.[41] Although she has always been thought of as an only child, this was not so. D.A. had two other children, and Margaret undertook financial responsibility for her half-sister and half-brother after her father died.

It is not clear when she first learned of their existence. Certainly her published writings make no reference to the fact and her desire to be discreet was enhanced by the need to prevent her mother from learning about the situation. Most probably, D.A. confided in Margaret during or in the aftermath of their ill-fated trip to America in 1915. He had gone on ahead, most likely to see his son Jonathan Samuel (John) who had been born the previous July, his little girl Rachel Janet (known as Janet) who was almost three and their mother. Samuel and Rachel had been the names of D.A.'s parents.

D.A.'s lover was not, however, American. She came from much closer to home. Evelyn Salusbury was the second daughter of Florence and the Rev. Charles

Salusbury, Rector of Tredunnoc, a village on the River Usk, close to Caerleon. Evelyn, known as Ebbe to her family, had been born in 1875 and was closer in age to Margaret – just eight years older – than she was to D.A. He was fifty-six when Evelyn's first child was born.

The Salusburys knew the Haig Thomas/Rhondda family well. One of Margaret's aunts was a Salusbury: Henrietta (Hetty) married Sybil's brother, Alexander in 1910. The Llanwern estate had been owned by the Salusbury family in the late eighteenth century. Mary Salusbury lived in The Cottage just beyond the gates of Llanwern Park. Earlier illustrious family members included William Salesbury (sic), principal translator of the New Testament into Welsh and Hester Thrale, Dr Johnson's learned friend. In her twenties Evelyn stayed several times at Aunt Janetta's home near Durham. And a family member recalls that one of Evelyn's two brothers once proposed to Margaret.

Evelyn became one of D.A.'s private secretaries at Llanwern. D.A. had built a single-storey estate office behind his study and she worked there. She contributed to Margaret's book on D.A., writing one of the Appendices. In this she recollected playing chess with him and bicycling trips. She stressed his zest for life and how he 'often made us feel quite ancient and blasé, though we were a good deal his juniors'.[42] She added that she tended his bees after he retired from Parliament in 1910 and concentrated on business.

Just before Christmas a year later a Mrs Evelyn Owen, aged thirty-six and fitting Evelyn's description, arrived in New York from Genoa. She gave her previous address as Glasgow where her married sister's family had property.

On 2 April 1912 her daughter was born in California. Janet was the name of one of Evelyn's sisters (Evelyn had apparently turned down a marriage proposal from the man who then married Janet Salusbury). The Register for St Leonards School, which Janet later attended, includes the 'Name, Designation, and Address of Parent or Guardian' of pupils. Janet's entry cites the late Edward Owen, a journalist residing in Anastasia, St Augustine, Florida.

D.A. had been developing business interests in the United States and Canada and made a number of trips there between 1913 and 1915. Evelyn seems to have moved around. She appears to have been back in the UK in Glasgow for a while in 1913 then sailed back to New York from Glasgow with her little daughter in late January 1914.[43] Her son was born in St Augustine that July. The family lived briefly in Monterey before moving to Canada, where they settled at Blackmore Hill, Victoria on Vancouver Island. The story circulated was that Evelyn had been asked to look after two very young children whose parents had died during the influenza epidemic at the end of the First World War. Not for many years were the children aware that this woman was their natural mother.

Margaret colluded with D.A. in keeping this family secret. When he was created Viscount Rhondda of Llanwern just before his death, the title was for him 'and the heirs male of his body *lawfully* begotten' (my emphasis) but in default of such an heir Margaret was granted the title *and* described as 'the only daughter' of David Alfred Baron Thomas. Recognition of D.A.'s other offspring makes clearer the enigmatic terms of his Will

198

made on 11 November 1916. Here he bequeathed to Margaret his account books, letters, papers, memoranda and manuscripts.[44] She was requested to examine them 'and in her discretion to destroy such of the same as she shall consider ought not to be preserved'. She was given 'sole and absolute power and discretion' to decide whether to show or disclose them to anybody. D.A. devised a way of including his lover in his Will without naming her. Five thousand pounds was to be held in trust to pay an annual income to those daughters of the Rev. Salusbury who remained unmarried. This proved to be an expensive arrangement: in the event Evelyn and three sisters remained single.

When D.A. died in 1918 Margaret had to break the news to his other family. The previous month Evelyn had sent her photographs of Janet and John. D.A. died on 3 July. Late at night on the 9th Evelyn wrote Margaret this short, poignant letter marked Private:

> I was thankful for yours which has just arrived – it was dreadful knowing nothing. I thought all along it was overwork – till an operation was mentioned, but even then it seemed nothing in the least critical – I can't realise it – it is a bitter blow. Now you and I are alone on this job, I long more than ever for our meeting when the war is over. Meanwhile – please let me know if there was any message or wish about 'them' – please tell me anything you can. I only hope 'they' will be some consolation and joy to you...

Euphemistic private exchanges continued between the two women, Evelyn signing herself 'With our best love' as Rachel J. Owen but addressing Margaret as Lady Mackworth.

In 1919 Margaret made plans to visit Canada as part of a business trip. Evelyn was due to make a brief visit to her homeland, but was keen for Margaret to see the children first: 'I *do so* want my handiwork "checked up" as it were, before I come away. You know the feeling – I should come away feeling more at rest, somehow, if you had seen them'. Her letters were brimming with plans for showing Vancouver Island to Margaret. The children were resourceful youngsters who enjoyed outdoor life.

Margaret felt it best to travel in a group and then to meet up later at a hotel on the island. Evelyn recognised that this was probably the wisest step and suggested that Margaret stay on, ostensibly 'to do urgent business'. She should 'naturally stay here with us as it is so lonely in an hotel by oneself'. Evelyn told Margaret that she hoped that this might be 'a sort of beginning to our being allies afterwards'.

At a time when illegitimacy was so frowned upon both women were concerned about detection, not least because the children bore a distinct likeness to their father, as photographs show. Margaret took after her mother rather than her father so did not bear a resemblance to them. Evelyn admitted that she hoped that her (Salusbury) sister would not join the party 'because relations can ask and press questions that others cannot so well, but if that is unavoidable – please draw a bright picture of how delighted I would be'. She requested an extra £200 since running expenses had increased alarmingly and her trip to Europe would incur the cost of leaving the children in school in Canada.

Margaret went to Canada in 1919 but it is not known whether she managed to spend time with her new family. There is naturally no reference to them in the decidedly jaunty account in her autobiography. The Douglas-Pennant case required that she appear before a Select Committee of the House of Lords that autumn. It necessitated cutting short her travels by three weeks and this might have wrecked her plans. The summons home would have provided another reason to curse the fact that she had ever got involved in Douglas-Pennant's destiny.

Margaret was involved with the family for the rest of her life. Evelyn, Janet and John left Canada in the early 1920s. They spent time in mainland Europe and Ireland but in 1922, after a brief spell in Devon, settled near Welshpool in mid-Wales. Margaret provided £1,000 annually for the children's education. When Janet went to St Leonards in 1925 it was to Bishopshall West. Prid was now the housemistress there.[45] Margaret was Janet's nominator and responsible for her fees. She remained there for six years. Janet was a very talented pupil and awarded school scholarships worth £20 per annum in both 1929 and 1930.[46]

In 1927 John went to Eton College but in this year relations deteriorated badly between Margaret and Evelyn. It has been suggested that Margaret wanted to adopt the children and that, not surprisingly, Evelyn demurred. Certainly there was a marked change in the tone of letters exchanged, some of which were handled by lawyers, and there is evidence of considerable disagreement between the two women about financial provision.

Margaret was facing economic pressure on all sides, and relations seem to have got more difficult as her own financial situation deteriorated. Evelyn, however, already in a precarious position and determined to secure the best possible future for her children, was unlikely to appreciate Margaret's perspectives, particularly given the public image of this society high flier and prominent business-woman. There was the added awkwardness of needing to preserve secrecy.

In July 1927 Evelyn sent Margaret the Eton entrance list adding: 'I sincerely hope that you are organizing for them financially – so that their careers will not be hampered for lack of funds. Judging from the "Programme" they were meant to have every advantage in reason; and it would be a pity if you failed to carry out "his wishes"'.

At the end of that year Evelyn sent her 'annual begging letter'. There had been a bad storm in October and Evelyn warned that an additional £500 might be needed for repairs. Eton was proving costly with many extras expected. Evelyn added: 'This was the enterprise that your father had most at heart of any – his sole chance of extending his personality – and he certainly would not have wished it to be stinted'.

Margaret must have found such a phrase distressing. As D.A.'s daughter she saw herself carrying on his beliefs and work. Just over a week later she sent a cheque for £500. She added that she was prepared to undertake house repairs as soon as conditions in the Welsh coalmining industry – and therefore dividends – improved. She was not convinced about Eton requiring so much money and she felt that attention was focused on John to the detriment of Janet.

By January 1929 communication was through Evelyn's lawyer who wrote to tell Margaret that very nearly half of her total income (of £2,500) was being spent on the children and there was insufficient income to 'be able to entertain in a suitable way the friends that the boy and girl have made in the neighbourhood'. A new hot water system and electricity would cost more than £1,000. It was pointed out that Margaret had spent a lot of money 'in other directions', restoring a castle[47] and investing heavily in *Time and Tide*. Evelyn felt that the claims of the two children were 'much more legitimate and pressing than these and other claims upon you which you recognize'. Troubled by this Margaret talked to Sir Thomas Horder (D.A.'s surgeon) who was one of the few people 'in the know'. He supported her.

Margaret offered to supply more income providing Evelyn undertook not to raise again the question of increasing payments. Not surprisingly, Evelyn refused such a condition and also stated that she was quite prepared to abandon the programme for the education of the children (which had been instigated by Margaret). She would take them overseas and live off the income from the settlement with the Public Trustee administering finances, a move which would effectively have eliminated Margaret from the lives of her half-sister and half-brother.

It was agreed that the house would be settled on the children. Money was paid for refurbishment, and in June Guest Keen and Nettlefold shares (800 ordinary shares of £1 each) were settled on the children for them to receive in their twenties. Margaret and Horder were the Trustees. An agreement of 1936 stated that money from the shares due to Janet when she was twenty-five should be paid to

Evelyn until then. Margaret seems to have been keen for a reconciliation, but early in 1932 Evelyn was writing that this was not feasible until the children were put in a sound financial position and Margaret honoured 'your father's legal responsibility to them by an adequate settlement'.

Unknown to Evelyn, in the year ending April 1932 Margaret's expenditure exceeded her income by more than £6,000 and she was under pressure from her accountant to make considerable savings. In addition, Evelyn also made it clear that she preferred to be free from 'the embarrassing interest of your somewhat overwhelming family'.

Relations between Margaret and the children were less painful. Margaret had been denied siblings as a child and was keen to maintain what was not only a link and commitment to her father but also the closest she would come to having a brother and sister even though she could not acknowledge this publicly.

Affectionate thank you letters followed Margaret's Easter and birthday gifts in the 1920s. In March 1930 when Janet was eighteen Margaret wrote to her (addressing her as Jan) at school to see if they could come to stay in the south of France in August and perhaps go on to Switzerland. She offered bathing, fishing and picnics and pointed out that it would cost nothing. It is not clear whether they went, though Janet drove Margaret's convertible Sunbeam to Agay for her three years later, travelling back across the Dordogne with her. Some years later Janet commented in a letter to Margaret: 'Why were we brought over here to make complications worse? If we had stayed in Canada things might have been all right for everyone'.

John did not leave Eton until 1933. Both children went to Cambridge University. John became a journalist aided by Margaret's connections. He worked briefly on the *North Yorkshire Post* and on the *Sheffield Telegraph*. He became a flying instructor and then a fighter pilot in wartime France. Tragically he was shot down over Douai and died in Cambrai Military Hospital in May 1940. He was aged twenty-five, had recently married and his son was born posthumously.

Janet's degree was in the Natural Sciences. A highly accomplished scientist, she worked in plant breeding and was dedicated to the preservation of the countryside. Her father would have been delighted to know that, like him, she built up a herd of pedigree cattle. She and her family saw Margaret increasingly frequently in her later years (Theodora Bosanquet knew the story).

Throughout all these years Margaret had to shoulder her worries privately and was determined to protect her father's secret. During the Rhondda Peerage Claim the question of D.A. and heirs must have caused some anxious moments for her. To make matters worse, his name was posthumously linked with the scandalous story of a statesman told in Arnold Bennett's 1926 novel *Lord Raingo*. In September 1918, not many months after D.A. died, Bennett had acquired explosive material for this novel. The eponymous Lord Raingo was a millionaire businessman and childhood friend of the prime minister, a fellow Lancastrian. During the war Raingo was made Minister of Records and received a peerage. He was unhappily married and had a mistress. He also had a weak heart (Doctor Heddle looked after him) and he died in office. His young mistress, who had a son, took her own life.

The Cassell publication was advertised in advance. The *Daily Express* described how Bennett had based the novel on the life of a real Cabinet Minister who held office during the later years of the war: 'He has cast an actual life which has only been known to a few persons into the mould of a novel'.[48] Posters advertising the serialisation of *Lord Raingo* in the *Evening Standard* stated that the year was 1918 and asked 'Who is Lord Raingo?'

There was a lot of speculation. The names of Lords Riddell and Beaverbook were mentioned in the press. But Leonard Woolf was unequivocal, writing in the *Nation*: 'The hero of the book is unmistakably the late Lord Rhondda.'[49] Arnold Bennett's journals reveal that on 22 and 27 January 1925 'Y' and 'B' (also referred to as 'M.B.' and, it would seem, Lord Beaverbrook) supplied him with details about a Lord X.[50]

Although the figure and fortunes of Lord Raingo as described in the eventual novel differed in a number of important respects from D.A.'s life, the information jotted down in Bennett's journals bears an uncanny resemblance to D.A. This describes (in disparaging terms) the son of a successful grocer who read mathematics at Cambridge then was a politician for over twenty years. He was not an effective public speaker and was constantly passed over by Lloyd George. He left politics, formed a coal-combine and became wealthy. He had married above himself, lived in a Queen Anne house, kept cattle and enjoyed publicity. Lloyd George eventually gave him office and a peerage but he died on the verge of a very great future.

Bennett's journal also mentions the mysterious woman who committed suicide. 'Y' had apparently been told by

'X' that this woman was his only companion and 'Y' had been charged to hand over £25,000 bonds to her if 'X' died. In the event she predeceased him. But Bennett noted that 'Y' was not sure whether she had been his mistress.

So the broad outline of D.A.'s life story, albeit with some sweeping and inaccurate assumptions, seems to have given Bennett the bare bones for his depiction of Raingo. The story of the mistress looked promising for fiction.[51] Nevertheless, the fact that D.A.'s name was posthumously linked, albeit via fiction, with such a scandal suggests that rumours, however far off the mark, circulated about his private life.[52]

Lord Beaverbrook read the draft manuscript to vet it for what Bennett called 'political correctness' (in 1925 that meant accuracy).[53] The story of the mistress made several peers nervous. One was Lord Birkenhead, an immensely wealthy Lancastrian who had enjoyed a meteoric rise in government circles and had a young mistress: Mona Dunn, daughter of a close friend of Beaverbrook's. She died aged twenty-six. Birkenhead boldly deflected attention from himself by attacking in the *Daily Mail* what he saw as irresponsible writers who were too free with their pens. He took Bennett to task for basing his character on a real statesman.[54] According to A.J.P.Taylor, Beaverbrook assured Birkenhead that 'the situation appeared to him drawn from the life of Lord Rhondda'.[55]

Bennett responded to Birkenhead (they got on well in person if not in print) by denying that there was one neat model for Raingo. Birkenhead then implied in the paper that the subject was no longer alive and so unable to defend himself. By such a suggestion he thus increased the likelihood that Lord Raingo should be read as Lord Rhondda. Bennett, who enjoyed the publicity all of this gave him, denied having had the slightest acquaintance with the deceased statesman (which was likely) but none of this proved how much basis in truth there might or might not have been in his story.

Sybil seems to have been kept unaware of these allegations. Margaret, who was much closer to London society, literature and politics is unlikely to have been so fortunate. She had already had serious problems with Birkenhead over her own claim to sit in the House of Lords.[56] Her prime concern was, however, lest her mother suspect the truth about a situation that was definitely not fiction. Evelyn (now called Salusbury once more) and the Haigs would meet in the summer months in Radnorshire. In August 1935 and 1936 Sybil's diary recorded going from Pen Ithon to tea with 'Evie Salusbury' and enjoying herself. On the second occasion she met Canadian and Californian women there.

There was an awkward moment when Margaret rented a house in the Scilly Isles for a holiday. Sybil's diary recorded visiting her there in September 1935. One day she sailed round Tresco with Professor Winifred Cullis and Theodora. Margaret did not accompany them since, as Sybil's diary explains, 'John and Janet Owen were coming to St Mary's'. Sybil saw the children and her curiosity was aroused.

On returning home she wrote to Margaret. She recounted how, pre-war, D.A. had visited the Salusburys and on his return, as they were dressing for dinner, mentioned that there was a secret that he shared with at least some of that family. He had not elaborated. Sybil later thought that she had stumbled upon the truth. When visiting Canada she had talked to a Canadian girl whose elder sister had been in school with Evelyn. Sybil innocently mentioned the girls' aunt (a Mrs Owen) as she had been told that Evelyn had been travelling with her. The girl denied all knowledge of such an aunt or, indeed, of Evelyn.

Ironically, Sybil later deduced that D.A. had simply been kindly helping Evelyn to get a job. She thought that she now knew D.A.'s secret. When she had witnessed the children in the Scilly Isles she had been struck by their resemblance to the Thomas family. So she erroneously presumed that this meant that her nephew Peter Haig-Thomas (the son of D.A.'s brother John Howard and Sybil's sister Rose) was the father of the children.

A draft reply exists of Margaret's reply to Sybil. Not surprisingly, there are a number of crossings out for this was a very difficult letter to compose. Margaret clearly felt that it was kinder to allow her mother to maintain the fiction. So in her reply she acknowledges that it is a mystery. Carefully choosing her words so that she does not tell an outright lie, she writes, 'As a matter of fact I think your explanation fits the case.' She mentions that 'John has rather a look of Uncle J. the more you mention though he is much better looking and hasn't got a wandering eye'. She admits that 'I've always had an affection for the pair of them which I suppose is natural enough'. She adds that the children were not at fault: 'on the contrary it's bad luck'.

We do not know whether or not Margaret ever sent a version of this letter but in early October she was at Llanwern and mother and daughter discussed the situation. Sybil wrote in her diary that '[s]he thought I was quite right in my idea of supposition' and so seems to have settled for this explanation. Later that month Evelyn's brother Van and his wife stayed at Llanwern and her sister Betty Salusbury came over too. Sybil also stayed with Alexander and Hetty (née Salusbury) and was godmother to Evelyn's niece Sylvia.

Margaret continued to provide financial support for D.A.'s children, though her own rapidly dwindling fortune made the situation increasingly embarrassing for everybody. She died in 1958 and Evelyn seven years later. Margaret left £20,000 in her Will to her half-sister and an equal amount on trust for her late half-brother's son when he reached the age of twenty five (though they were not named as such). The residue of property after bequests had been made was for Janet who was also an executrix. However, Margaret's Will had been drawn up when her finances were healthier than at the time she died. Bequests exceeded the money available. But Margaret had at least managed to keep secret the story of D.A.'s other daughter and son.

CHAPTER EIGHT

'Quite a different place': Reconstructing the Public and the Private

In October 1917 Margaret told a journalist that:

> I think the war, awful as it has been, did a
> wonderful thing for women. It brought about a
> revolution for them which one may well imagine
> centuries might have otherwise been needed to
> encompass. But now women have seen what they
> can do; they have learned to have confidence in
> themselves to undertake the most amazing and
> difficult tasks.

Society had not yet grasped the full implications of this
revolution. 'But', she added, 'we *do* know the world will
never be quite the same again'.[1]

Margaret was involved in administering the transition
from war to peace and the plans for giving women a say in
the running of post-war society. Exactly four months after
her comments were published, the Representation of the

211

People Act was passed (on 6 February 1918). Six million women over thirty were enfranchised. Approximately two million more women who qualified in terms of age were excluded by residential criteria.[2] At the end of the year she was able to vote for the first time. She made it clear, however, that the vote had not been granted as a reward for women's 'magnificent war work' but because the government and the country knew that denying it would have spelt a renewal of militancy.[3] But she also discovered that there was a serious gap between what women felt they could and should now do and what society was prepared to endorse.

Margaret gained vital experience in investigating women's opportunities in the latter stages of the war. She was the sole female member of a committee examining methods of employing administrative staff in the Ministry of Munitions and suggesting possible economies and improvements. This Staff Investigation Committee held thirty meetings between late April and mid-November. Margaret attended only half of them, but this period coincided with her father's illness and subsequent death. Her most valuable contribution was in any case through the women's panel.[4] This was her idea and she convened and chaired it.

The main report stressed the need for better training and coordination of duties, along with less duplication of tasks. The women's panel produced a separate report which was in broad agreement but had its own specific observations and recommendations. It emphasised the amount of work that was devolved to women. In addition to providing almost all the ministry's clerical staff, their work included chemical and mathematical research, statistics and accountancy. Margaret the businesswoman was interested in this evidence of women's business acumen. The panel noted that although women's salaries in administration and technical work compared well with pay outside the ministry, there was some dissatisfaction at higher levels where they received half (sometimes two-fifths) of the salaries men received for doing similar work. Although lack of prior experience needed to be taken into account, the panel was concerned about the evident disparity.

The panel commented on the haphazard nature of recruitment of temporary female staff in the civil service and suggested that methods of selecting and grading women administrators should be overhauled and a female staff officer appointed. Despite consideration of the special conditions of wartime, they argued that the minimum forty-eight hour week had been excessive and had probably resulted in a loss of efficiency. They were also critical of the lack of clear promotion within clerical grades.

Margaret was also appointed to a new Women's Advisory Committee as part of the Ministry of Reconstruction established in July 1917. Headed by Dr Addison (his successor was Sir Auckland Geddes), the new ministry was to provide the means and mechanisms for the transition to peace. By the beginning of 1918, some 87 committees were dealing with aspects of reconstruction. Although the ministry existed for less than two years, it displayed a buoyant approach and ambitious intentions in post-war social and economic planning.[5]

Chaired by Lady Emmott, the Advisory Committee's nine other members included Maud Pember Reeves from the Ministry of Food, Mabel Tuke of Bedford College and Madeline Symons of the National Federation of Women Workers. However, due to illness Margaret only attended two meetings between the Advisory Committee's inaugural meeting on 21 October and mid-February 1918.[6] One of its tasks was to investigate the effect of women's employment in war work on domestic service and its prospects.[7] Margaret was one of seven who signed its majority report though several expressed written caveats. Dr Marion Phillips supplied her own minority report urging a minimum wage and maximum hours.

Such disagreements were hardly surprising. The domestic service question neatly encapsulated debates over class, gender and skill in post-war Britain. For many it suggested the stability and deference of a Victorian world that was fast disappearing. For others its low pay, lack of status and training and long hours made it rife for reform. The Women's Advisory Committee included Lady Birchenough, who made reference to her own household, suggesting that those in houses with staff would resent outside interference, and Lilian Harris of the Women's Cooperative Guild, who argued that counteracting the living-in system and providing adequate wages should be paramount.

Margaret was interested in a precise regulation of hours of service that made provision for meals and leisure. She also participated in a discussion on training, and advocated advanced training with a maintenance allowance. The majority report, which was issued in March 1919, stressed the lack of adequate affordable training. It urged a wide system of training facilities and local centres and clubs run by joint committees of workers and employers that might eventually enable domestic service to be unionised.[8]

All this was a rehearsal for the Ministry of Labour's substantial enquiry in 1923 into the shortage in the supply of domestic servants. The wartime economy had absorbed many former domestic servants: in addition, clerical work and other jobs offered greater freedom and higher wages. Decline in demand was especially marked in middle-class homes affected by the trend for smaller families, houses and, gradually, labour-saving devices. Even though many women remained in service in hotels, hospitals and other institutions as well as private homes, there was concern about the perceived shortage of labour.

Margaret attended some of the sessions (and was praised by the *Manchester Guardian* for being one of the few people who had taken the trouble to do this).[9] She approved of the enquiry and was especially scornful when the popular press attacked it. When the Duke of Rutland told *The Times* that '[t]here is only one possible solution of the servant question, and that is to leave it alone', she defended the 'scrupulous fairness' the enquiry showed to all sides.[10] She labelled foolish those who objected to the probing of the subject and argued that neither employers nor servants should be blamed: the shortage was a result of new social conditions. Margaret liked its balanced and clear recommendations.[11] She led a debate organised by the Women's Freedom League in which she went further than the report, advocating more grants to the Central Committee for Women's Training and Employment which helped to find work for unemployed women. This was conceded by the government later that month. She not only stressed the skilled nature of housework, but also supported domestic training for boys.[12]

A month after the report was published, she founded the Women's [Political and] Industrial League (WIL) and became its president.[13] It sought equal training and employment opportunities, representation and treatment in industry (though that word industry was interpreted very widely). At an unsettling time of rapid change and adjustment, it was concerned about the dismissal of large numbers of women who had been employed in vital war work. Although all non-commissioned ex-service men were given free unemployment insurance policies, at first this was not the case for women ex-war workers.

Margaret told the press that WIL's intervention was needed urgently: there must be no return to pre-war conditions which largely designated women's labour as unskilled with low pay and prospects. The only remedy was to organise women on a large scale. Women, she declared, were joining from across the country: they included tailoresses, shop workers, engineering operatives and factory workers. A feature on Women in Public Life in the *Queen* waxed poetic in praise of the courageous young Margaret (she was thirty-six). But it also sounded a warning note: 'The mantle of Elijah' had 'fallen upon an Elisha full of enthusiasm, and we know it will be worn quite nobly, whatever the personal cost of its wearing might be'.[14]

Margaret presented to the prime minister a WIL Memorial seeking urgent reassurance and commitment.[15] Careful not to antagonise, it acknowledged the claims of discharged soldiers and sailors and praised the skilled men who had trained women in war work. It emphasised the importance of women in trades such as engineering, and the obstacles now threatening them. Artificial restrictions on women's employment in industry needed removing as a matter of justice and in the interests of national industrial efficiency. It sought improved working conditions but acknowledged that women had no separate interest from men. They merely wanted conditions conducive to working efficiently.

Lloyd George's response was that that when pledges to trade unions had been fulfilled, women would find ample scope for employment. He made remarkably positive (and, as time would show, unrealistic) promises about equal opportunities, declaring that there would be no discrimination against women in the new industries and that pre-war occupations would be kept open. As a supporter of 'equal pay for equal output', he declared that 'to permit women to be the catspaw for reducing the level of wages is unthinkable'. There would also be new opportunities for training and education in schools and universities. He took issue with WIL's complaint that women were not being consulted on important questions of reconstruction, but sympathised with the claims for more effective representation on committees.

Yet, although Margaret and WIL won praise in the mainstream press for extracting such commitment from the prime minister, putting promises into practice was quite another matter. The non-party WIL represented a cross-section of suffrage and industrial experience and included many talks from the trade unionist Julia Varley, but it was far removed from directly and solely representing the interests of women workers.[16]

Margaret stressed the importance of women joining

trade unions. However, although seeking the common interests of the whole – with women 'labourers, operatives, supervisors, works managers, and directors' working together as members – may have seemed an exciting and novel way forward for some, such an association did not suit the class and trade unionist consciousness of many, and appeared idealistic to others.[17] And her claim that while individual trade unions were concerned with the needs of a particular industry, the WIL would deal with 'the common interests of the whole'[18] could be seen as encroaching on the territory of the trade union movement. Moreover, the interests of industrial women workers were specifically covered by the Standing Joint Committee of Industrial Women's Organisations formed in 1916 with strong Labour, Cooperative and trade union credentials.

And despite Lloyd George's pledge, there was evidence that, as Margaret put it in mid-February 1919, women were being discharged 'in a wholesale manner' in government departments and their rights totally disregarded. Despite the large numbers of female dilutees (unskilled or semi-skilled workers who had replaced skilled men), sex discrimination was rife in favour of male dilutees. More than half a million women workers received unemployment allowances though Margaret reckoned that there were probably a further million industrial women currently out of work. She accepted that a period of adjustment was inevitable, but was nonetheless concerned that a grave and increasingly costly national problem was being badly handled. She emphasised that productive work was crucial for all for the sake of the future.[19] Yet her indignation provoked letters to the press questioning whether many women needed employment. A Hampstead woman asked whether childless widows with war pensions or wives of those in government offices should be working. She called the dole 'a curse to the country'.[20] Others saw domestic service as the answer for women rather than new and costly opportunities. Margaret declared that the Ministry of Labour seemed to recognise only three forms of work for women: tailoring, laundry and domestic work. The Ministry must have 'been asleep during the war'.[21]

WIL held protest meetings when civil servants and other workers were dismissed, issued reports and questionnaires, organised lectures and generally did what it could to publicise the situation and remind the government of its erstwhile promises. In July 1919 it organised a deputation to the War Cabinet Office from industrial, commercial and professional women representing eleven different trade unions and associations to discuss women's representation at the forthcoming International Labour Conference in Washington DC. Once again it was led by Margaret who was becoming a familiar figure in deputations and in emulating her father in penning indignant letters to the press.[22] In 1921 alone she spent £317 of her own money on WIL.

The reconstruction years saw her follow D.A. in another respect. At the Local Government Board he had been responsible for Poor Law Administration and eager to develop plans for a Ministry of Health. Twenty-one different departments had charge of the nation's health. A shake-up of the system was overdue. D.A. was especially concerned about the appallingly high rates of infant mortality. It was he who established National Baby

Week (Margaret was later vice-chairman of its council. It boasted over a million members by 1921)[23]. D.A.'s interest in infant deaths was hardly surprising: he had been one of just five survivors out of his mother's seventeen children. Spearheaded by Addison (a medical doctor), plans for integrating and centralising insurance and medical committees as well as ending the Poor Law had been developing since 1914 and D.A. eagerly took them forward.

But after six months he was moved to food control. Some of the impetus for reform was lost.[24] As Kenneth O. Morgan has shown, there was procrastination and a watering down of the original Rhondda-Addison plans.[25] Addison became the first Minister of Health in mid-1919 but only after delays in the development of the Ministry of Health Bill.

Margaret was, from the start, enthusiastic about the potential for the bill. In November 1918 when it was first introduced, she described the establishment of a separate health ministry into which the Local Government Board and other bodies were subsumed as 'the biggest thing that can be done for the nation' (though she would not be a fan of the National Health Service developed by the Labour Party after the Second World War).

Influenced by the influenza epidemic – as many people were now dying monthly from this as had perished in the Great War – she stressed the importance of research. Her main message was, however, that women should be properly represented in a health ministry. For it to be successful, she warned, wives and mothers must be consulted, since

> Our standard of health must of necessity depend on
> the amount of knowledge of it which the individual
> woman in the home possesses. It is impossible to
> over-estimate the importance of women to such a
> measure.[26]

Her views were aired the following February at a large
meeting advocating a health ministry at London's Kingsway
Hall. Sir Kingsley Wood presided, and the prime minister
sent a message of support. Here Addison alluded to the
need for an advisory council 'formed of men, experienced
and capable, to give advice and criticism'. Margaret's
speech endorsed the importance of keeping in touch with
public opinion. But, she added (to cheers from the
audience), it was vital to make use of women. In addition
to an advisory council of expert men and women, she
wished to see a council composed of ordinary wives and
mothers learning, advising and acting as a link between
the ministry 'and the homes of the country'.[27] Addison
expressed his willingness to act on her suggestion and
make use of the services of women.

Never one to take such promises for granted, Margaret
convened a Watching Council. Its brief was to consider
the measures necessary to strengthen women's position in
the proposed ministry. It included Sybil, Mrs Chalmers
Watson MD and Lady Selbourne. WIL and more than forty
women's organisations were affiliated. Just over a week
after the Kingsway Hall meeting Margaret addressed the
Royal Institute of Public Health on 'Women in the
Ministry of Health'. Her message here and in speeches in
Manchester, Sheffield and Newcastle was that the 'the
vast mass of the health of the country lay in the hands of

women to make or to mar'. The 'unintelligent' way of scattering a few token women on committees was outdated. Maternity and infant welfare were especially important in the building of a healthy nation. To be effective women had to be placed where they could have direct access to the Minister.

Opening a maternity hostel in Harrow soon after this, Margaret stressed that the care of the young should form one of the principal objectives of the new ministry. And she explained how her father had seen it as a means of saving life and giving children a good start.[28] The women's amendments to the Ministry of Health Bill had just been tabled. One was for an all-female Women's General Consultative Council, with direct access to the Minister and representation for all health services that were largely run by women. A second was to avoid sex discrimination in ministry appointments, which should themselves be fairly divided between the sexes and a third made provision for one of the chief secretaries to be female.

On 19 March the Standing Committee on the Ministry of Health Bill met.[29] Sir Samuel Hoare proposed that one of the advisory councils should be called the Women's Consultative Council with an exclusively female membership. Earlier that day he had received a communication from Margaret on behalf of 500,000 women demanding a fair opportunity to express their views. Many women now had the vote but it would not be until December that the first woman MP would sit in Parliament. So the point about women's opinions being heard was especially pertinent. Addison, whose record on women's rights was not seen as sound, expressed his opposition to the amendment. Some of the councils, he argued, would have highly technical issues to deal with, such as finance, building operations and housing, so it would be impossible for them to have a substantial number of women. The amendment was defeated by 22 to 14 votes.

Margaret and many others were furious.[30] Robins penned an angry letter to *The Times* declaring that 'Health is the great universal concern of women'.[31] Quite apart from their care of children, she asked any man to consider 'from the time he opened his eyes on the world till he closes them in death, who will have had most to do with his health?' She had recently expended much energy in the development of the New Sussex Hospital in Brighton, run by women for women, and Margaret had donated £500 to it. Robins had persuaded her to become its honorary treasurer. In a letter advertising the hospital and appealing for funds Margaret had argued that there was 'no graver, more compelling *national service* [my emphasis] than caring for the health of the mothers of the future.'[32]

Yet the association in Robins' letter of women with instinctive caring and Margaret's somewhat categorical statement to the *Pall Mall Gazette* that women were 'fitted by nature to care for the health of the race' did, as they were both well aware, run the danger of slotting women into gendered and narrow definitions of what was or was not appropriate for them.[33] Both became better known for espousing equal rights and criticising those, sometimes called New Feminists, whose primary emphasis was on women's special and different qualities from men.

Some prominent women rejected the idea of an all-female council. Margaret Llewelyn Davies and Dr Marion

Phillips, vice chair and secretary of the Standing Joint Committee of Industrial Women's Organisations, believed that a consultative council of the public rather than one composed of women was the way forward. The National Council of Women also criticised Margaret's proposals, arguing that separatism was no solution and that all health issues 'must be dealt with as the business both of women and men'.[34] She believed, however, that only a women's committee would ensure that Whitehall was fully in touch with women's demands.[35]

Eventually, in February 1920 – under the new Health Act – the Consultative Council on General Health Questions held its first meeting. Its brief was to identify inadequate provision for safeguarding the nation's health and suggest remedies. Women formed a majority of the members and included the trade union organiser Gertrude Tuckwell. The deputy chairman was Arthur Greenwood, later Minister of Health. Margaret was chosen to chair this council.[36] In this capacity she participated in a conference on international health in Brussels. One delegate remarked on the 'vision and wonderful grasp of international questions' that she displayed there.[37]

Two years later, *Welsh Outlook* speculated on possible female candidates for Parliamentary leadership and suggested Margaret.[38] And when in 1923 the Women's Freedom League mooted an 'ideal women's cabinet', Margaret was their choice for the Minister of Health.[39] She would not live to see a woman in charge of health, though in 1929 Margaret Bondfield became the first female cabinet minister.[40]

Margaret was, however, one of the first female justices of the peace. The Sex Disqualification (Removal) Act was passed on Christmas Eve 1919 followed by the Lord Chancellor's announcement of seven women magistrates, including Margaret Lloyd George. In July 1920 the Lord Chancellor's list ensured that female justices were appointed across England and Wales. In Wales, a dozen female borough and thirty-one county magistrates were announced, and by 1923 there were more than a hundred women JPs. Margaret was one of the first four for the county of Monmouth. She was sworn in at a court adjoining Usk gaol where she had been incarcerated seven years earlier. The law breaker had become a law enforcer.

Many of the early women JPs were already prominent public figures, either through their families or in their own right.[41] Some were active in local or national politics and many were already committed to the women's movement. Although within thirty years nearly a quarter of the magistrates of England and Wales would be women, they were not always welcomed. When Elizabeth Dashwood (better known as the writer E.M. Delafield) was appointed in Devon, a fellow magistrate resigned in protest.

Margaret did not attend regularly. Absenteeism was nothing new: D.A. had been a Glamorgan JP from 1881 but had moved at the end of the following year and had not continued to sit. It might be claimed that Margaret's aims were grander than local government. However, her compatriot Winifred Coombe Tennant of Neath, who was also a pioneer Welsh county magistrate took her new position seriously. She also managed to stand as a Liberal Parliamentary candidate, be active at a national level in feminist and Liberal politics, advise Lloyd George and become the first British woman delegate to the League of Nations Assembly in Geneva. She was selected as chairman of the bench in April 1922, helped to galvanise other women JPs in Glamorgan and was active in the Magistrates' Association.[42] But Margaret's career and the end of her marriage saw her residing in England rather than Wales post-war, and she already had many other commitments.

Reconstructing life in London was less of a break than it would have been for many people. Margaret had attended school there, was used to staying in Ashley Gardens and more recently had established herself in Chelsea. She had spent less and less time at Oaklands as the war progressed. The reference to her 'attitude of instinctive nationalism' in her autobiography was to pride in Britain in the First World War.[43]

D.A. had a direct link to the Rhondda Valleys that prompted his title. It went beyond the wealth they generated. Margaret did not. She liked the name, though it must have been a bit of a trial for her since she had some difficulty enunciating the letter 'r'. Most of the people she knew mispronounced Rhondda, not recognising that 'dd' is a single letter in the Welsh alphabet and pronounced like a 'th'. In her autobiography she described Rhondda as 'a beautiful Welsh word'.[44] George Bernard Shaw had just written to tell 'Dearest Rhondda' that this was '*such a lovely* name' that he would address her thus in future.[45] But that is what it became for her: a name and a title rather than a familiar place. Just as the awkward tag 'South Wales and Monmouthshire' signalled a linkage with Wales rather than England yet also denoted a difference, so too was Margaret, like her county, in an ambivalent borderland position.

She did, however, see her home county as part of Wales. When an article in *Time and Tide* mentioned Newport in connection with the bombing of Welsh urban centres during the Second World War, several readers protested that it was not in Wales. Margaret hastily defended Monmouthshire's Welsh origins.[46] She cited Welsh place-names and explained that the county was 'taken from Wales' by Henry VIII but had a population that was still largely Welsh.

She recognised statutory obligations both as a landowner and from familial loyalty. In 1921 she attended a lunch in the partially restored hall of Pencoed Castle for the Magor Farmers' Association's agricultural show.[47] That same year she gave £41 to charities in Magor, ten guineas to the Royal Gwent Hospital in Newport and Humphrey's Llangibby Hunt received £50. She would write 'St David's Day' as the date for letters she wrote on 1 March, and was president or a patron of numerous Welsh organisations such as the Rhondda Welsh Male Glee Singers and South Wales and Monmouthshire Women's Electrical Association.

In London, particularly during the years when Lloyd George was prime minister, Margaret was sought after as part of the *crachach*, the Welsh elite who could grace dinner tables and provide vital funding for native causes. She attended Downing Street for a committee meeting arranged by Margaret Lloyd George for organising the Welsh stall at the British and Foreign Sailors' Society Bazaar.[48] She appealed for funds for the Portmadoc Players to perform in London and praised their performance in Hammersmith in her paper, adding that Wales contained some of the finest material in the world for the creation of a national theatre.[49] At their matinee Lloyd George and Margaret occupied boxes. They both attended events hosted by the influential London-Welsh Honourable Society of Cymmrodorion. On St. David's Day in 1917 the Welsh 'Great and Good' held an auction at Covent Garden for Welsh troops, raising £550 in two hours. Megan Lloyd George was the auctioneer and the rostrum was decorated with leeks. Margaret, Sybil, Lady Mond and Ivor Novello provided items for auction. Such contacts could be vital for Margaret's own fundraising. The anonymous benefactor who first offered £100 for the Oxford Women's Colleges Fund (for which Margaret was treasurer) was Lady Mond.

As a guest of honour at a luncheon held by the Welsh Circle at the Lyceum Club in 1922, Margaret declared that 'We Welsh are too modest' and that, although Scottish achievements were constantly broadcast, nothing was ever said about the Welsh. Press descriptions of her outside Britain tended to pick up on her Welsh identity but they used worn clichés. In an article that managed to refer to her as both Welsh and English within one paragraph, the *New York Times* claimed that she displayed the business acumen of 'the canny Welsh'. Its sister paper the *New York Tribune* accounted for her 'odd mixture of practicality and a brooding romanticism' by explaining that her mother was Scottish and her father Welsh.

Unlike Gwendoline and Margaret Davies, also heirs to Rhondda colliery fortunes as the granddaughters of David Davies of Llandinam, Margaret's travels did not ultimately translate into art and the arts within Wales.[50] Although more generous to Welsh institutions than has previously been recognised, Margaret's fortune was primarily dedicated to *Time and Tide*. From the 1920s she reconstructed herself as a figure centred on London society whose country residence was in south east England.

Yet *Time and Tide* included more coverage of Wales than was common in other London-based publications of the time. Its events lists included the annual National Eisteddfod Proclamation Day. On 9 August 1933 sheep dog trials at the Royal Welsh Show in Aberystwyth was one of just two events announced in the week's list. Commenting on a government report on the Welsh language, an editorial stated that 'survival of the Cymric in speech, song and literature is surely desirable'.[51]

In November 1937 Margaret made a statement about what her paper stood for. Singling out peace and democracy she declared that she wished to see an England, a Scotland and a Wales which were real democracies. She even stated that 'there is a strong case to be made out for each of the three countries' being in a position to manage its own internal affairs.[52] Despite this, before 1945 her paper and publications frequently referred to England when Britain would have been a more accurate term.[53]

The First World War had drawn a personal as well as public line. The breaking down of customs and conventions had left Margaret, as she put it, 'in quite a different place' and 'curiously free' as she and Humphrey spent less and less time together.[54] Peace signalled a need to confront what she had known for some time: the need to reconstruct her own life. This meant facing the breakdown of her marriage.

Margaret divorced Humphrey on the grounds of his

desertion and misconduct. Divorce was very expensive and primarily associated with the privileged, despite some current widening of the social groups involved. It was shaming and both grounds and consequences were different for men and women. Betty Archdale (Helen Archdale's daughter) who came to know Margaret very well when she was growing up, later claimed that a lot of Margaret's friends ostracised her as a result of her divorce,[55] though this is unlikely to have been the case within her feminist and literary circles.

Wartime marriages, the strain of separation, and the glimpse of independence the period from 1914 to 1918 had provided for women, as well as the horrendous psychological effects suffered by many combatants, put a huge strain on couples when peace returned. In 1920 there were nearly four and a half times more divorces than there had been ten years earlier. In December 1922 when she obtained her decree nisi, Margaret wrote a review of Alfred Sutro's play 'The Laughing Lady' for *Time and Tide* (using the pseudonym of Anne Doubleday). She remarked that the device of having the heroine return to her somewhat boring ex-husband when she had just escaped from him seemed too like Victorian morality. Somewhat mischievously she added that '[o]f course divorces are all the rage just now'.[56]

Suffrage had, to some extent, saved Margaret's marriage pre-war by supplying much-needed excitement and purpose. Her first review had been a damning critique in 1912 of H.G. Wells' book *Marriage*. Despite Wells' 'firm determination' to appear advanced on the woman question, Margaret, like other feminists, denounced his opinions as one-sided and antediluvian.[57]

In the mid-1930s she wrote two articles on marriage.

Here she deplored the position of the 'kept' wife, a dependant who was 'not a full human being' and the presumption that a husband and wife should be regarded as one, the 'twin halves of a Philippine nut'.[58] In her view married people should remain separate individuals, retaining their own keep and status. She even suggested an early concept of Wages for Housewives, arguing that any wife who wished should be able to go to court while still living with her husband, and if she could prove that she did all the house management and/or housework she should be entitled to a proportion of her husband's income – up to seventy-five per cent – to spend on the house and at least ten per cent more for her own private use.[59] The fact that two people were married should be their own private affair and they should, if they wished, retain separate social lives. Yet such a view was far from conventional in the Monmouthshire of the early 1920s. Whereas wartime gave Margaret the freedom to be her own person, assume responsibility in the workplace and enjoy the liberty of living in Chelsea, the resumption of peace posed difficulties for her and for Humphrey.

Margaret had become a wealthy woman in her own right with her own title. She now had a career as a businesswoman and wanted to dedicate herself to *Time and Tide* as well as furthering the legal rights of women. In 1921 she spent £454 on her Oaklands home in Monmouthshire. In the same year Chelsea Court cost a hefty £3,751.

The Mackworths had no children. In her autobiography Margaret stated that she had 'wanted children more consciously than many women do'.[60] In 1927 Holtby had an intimate discussion one evening about Margaret's 'desire for a child' and 'how she had tried and failed to have one'.[61] But Margaret speculated in *This Was My World* that even if she had had five or six children, it was unlikely that she would have felt fulfilled without a public life. She and Humphrey had always been incompatible – she described them as 'rather an oddly assorted couple' – and their marriage primarily a social match.[62] In the 1920s Holtby was told by an old friend of Margaret's that 'all her friends prophesied disaster from the start' when she had married Humphrey.[63]

In the autumn of 1921, after returning from a holiday in France, Margaret wrote to Humphrey. His reply addressed her as 'Dearest' but this was a weary, bitter letter. He complained of 'awful trouble with the servants'. He had just dismissed the cook and gardener and consequently the two maids gave notice: 'Never mind, I will get some more somehow or let the house & go away'. He then told her how he strongly objected to her Kent cottage[64] and asked:

> What right have you to leave alone [sic] so much as a married woman, you expect me to do just whatever you please, and not to complain, you never consult me about any thing. As I have told you before I am tired of it all & have been for years.
> Yr. loving husband
> Humphrey

Humphrey produced an ultimatum: unless Margaret lived ten months of the year in Monmouthshire they should divorce.[65] She contacted her brother-in-law John and he was supportive, admitting that he had known for some time that all was not well. So far as he knew Humphrey had 'no thought of any other marriage, but I think he is very lonely'. He hoped that they could both make some sacrifices. But Margaret could not contemplate what she later described as 'an uncomfortable life-sentence.'[66]

At first Humphrey tried to resist the drastic step of divorce. He told Margaret in November that he had seen two independent doctors, 'who both tell me that some worry which I am experiencing is causing grave danger not only to my health but to my life'. He added, pointedly: '*You* know the only worry I have'. Alarmed, Margaret consulted Sir Thomas Horder, who had been such a help when D.A. was dying. He reassured her. He doubted these claims, adding that 'most people don't trouble to distinguish between outraged pride, pique & emotions of a similar kind, and wounded affection', and that it was not difficult to obtain medical opinions of the sort Humphrey mentioned. Horder regretted that Humphrey did not seem to have 'the sense or generosity' to arrange a mutual modus vivendi, adding that '[i]f he loved you in the way that alone matters he would not stand out for what is in your case an impossible concession: the forcing of your nature into a groove of devastating narrowness'.

Faced with an impasse, Margaret and Humphrey decided that the complicated plans for dissolving marriage needed to be instigated. Margaret would sue for divorce on the grounds of Humphrey's statutory desertion and adultery and he would not contest this.[67]

On 24 November 1921, Margaret received a letter from Humphrey stating that:

It is idle not to realise that the present position is impossible. We cannot go on as we are. I have thought the whole thing over most seriously, and have come to the conclusion that it is better we should definitely separate, and that I should not live with you any more.[68]

Her reply six days later asked whether he really meant

that the past thirteen years are to go for nothing and that all we have to admit is failure? I can hardly think that this can be so, and, if possible, I want to try to prevent a separation.

She asked him to reconsider 'and to resume your life with me again'.

In practice this was far from what Margaret desired. However, as a woman wanting a divorce from her husband she needed to prove both adultery and desertion, since infidelity by a husband was (unlike a wife's unfaithfulness) not considered sufficient grounds for divorce. These letters were designed to provide the court with evidence for the latter. They showed publicly that Margaret had sought to repair the marriage and demonstrated that they were not in agreement, even though their actions were in fact collusive and jointly planned. In his reply on 6 December, Humphrey said he was afraid that:

We must admit that our married life has been a failure. The reasons why you know as well as I do. That being so, it is useless to ask me to re-consider my decision which is final and was only taken by me after fully weighing everything.

Mr Justice Horridge then granted Margaret a decree of restitution of conjugal rights against her husband.

Just before Christmas in 1921 Margaret admitted to Robins: 'I'm rather dreading the new year – my husband and I have split and it's going to get into the papers'.[69] She did not wish to apportion blame. Yet fault and blame lay at the heart of divorce at this time. Margaret told Robins that it was 'both our faults – or perhaps neither' adding poignantly 'we simply never fitted – though we tried to pretend we did for thirteen years'.[70] It was, she told Robins, a 'beastly' process they had to go through to effect the legal change.

Soon after this the two women discussed the situation over lunch. 'He's a nice man', she told Robins, 'But he does nothing.'.[71] Robins, who had had known real tragedy in her own personal life – her estranged actor husband had committed suicide – also knew that it was difficult to find a time when Margaret was *not* busy doing something.

On 1 May 1922 Margaret, accompanied by her mother, appeared at the Law Courts in London. Her address was given as 15 Chelsea Court. Her petition for divorce stated that the marriage 'was one of affection and remained one of affection' for many years and that until 1920 'we remained the best of friends'. It was explained that Margaret had written regularly in the autumn when abroad and received no reply and when she offered to go to Oaklands, Humphrey said he would be away.

The timing was especially difficult for Margaret who was very much in the public eye. 1922 was a year of legal wrangles for her. She was engaged in a tough and public legal battle to sit in the House of Lords. This generated publicity and controversy in the press. Divorce cases helped to sell daily and Sunday newspapers. That same year the first divorce trial in the Russell v Russell case involved so much sexual scandal and suggestive reportage that George V complained to the Lord Chancellor (John Russell's mother was Lady Ampthill, Lady of the Bedchamber).[72] Margaret's divorce was widely reported too. After her court appearance in May, a newspaper placard had announced 'Lady Rhondda's Wrecked Happiness' in huge letters.[73]

Margaret purchased the lease on her London flat that year and on 21 December the Divorce Court granted her decree nisi. A professional co-respondent had been hired for the night as was the custom in divorce cases at the time. In court the visitors' book of the Midland Grand Hotel St Pancras was produced. Margaret was asked whether she recognised any signatures for 5 July 1922. She identified her husband's handwriting. Beneath it was the name Margaret. When asked if she had stayed at the hotel on that night she answered in the negative. Hotel employees were then called to attest that they had seen Humphrey accompanied by 'a lady'. The court was told that they had stayed one night and the chambermaid confirmed that she had seen them in bed together in the morning. No defence was made and at last the sordid farce was played out.

Margaret sailed on the *Balmoral Castle* with her mother and friends that Christmas.[74] Commenting on this in a letter to Holtby, Vera Brittain remarked that the party included 'an unattached male' (the Hon. Charles Rhys, eldest son of Baron Dynevor). 'I wonder' Brittain wrote, 'how long she will be away and if she will return re-married'.[75] The following September Humphrey and Dorothy Llewellin were married in London. She was twenty-eight, from Caerleon and, appropriately, the daughter of a Colonel who was a solicitor and secretary of the Llangibby Hunt.[76] They had no children.

Margaret and Humphrey's timing was unfortunate. Later in the same year as the decree absolute was granted, new divorce legislation was passed. It would have simplified (to some degree) and speeded up their case. The Private Members' Bill that resulted in the Matrimonial Causes Act received the Royal Assent on 10 July 1923. It had been sponsored by the National Union of Societies for Equal Citizenship (NUSEC), formerly the suffrage NUWSS.

From now on, adultery by either husband or wife could be the sole grounds for divorce. Three days after the law was passed the Leader in *Time and Tide* addressed the issue of equal divorce. This heartfelt account described the situation prior to the new legislation and suggests the legal charade that Margaret and Humphrey had undergone:

Supposing that a husband, having been unfaithful, agreed to allow his wife to divorce him. There were two ways open to them. Either he had to allow her to plead for divorce on the grounds of cruelty and misconduct, a course to which naturally enough he was usually opposed; or he had to refuse to return to her and she had to plead on the grounds of desertion and misconduct, in which case she had to write a letter begging him to return, which was read in court, and had to be couched in language which the court considered sounded genuine. If questioned she had to swear that she wanted him back, although every person connected with the case was fully aware that his return was the last thing she wanted, and that she was perjuring herself in the witness box. The net result was that it took a woman twice as long to divorce her husband as it did a man to divorce his wife, and the publicity was also doubled. The whole thing was a humiliating and objectionable farce.[77]

Margaret's life had changed dramatically over the past eighteen months. In January 1922 a fascinated Robins had remarked in her diary that Helen Archdale 'has come to live at Chelsea Court with R.!!'[78] The next day Robins visited their shared country retreat, Chart Cottage just outside the village of Seal near Sevenoaks in Kent. So who was Helen Archdale?

Helen Alexander Russel was seven years younger than Margaret and had been born in Roxburghshire, Scotland.[79] She was a feminist who, like Margaret, had parents who believed in women's rights. Her mother Helen de Lacy Evans had been one of five pioneer woman medical students at Edinburgh University. Her father was a journalist on the *Scotsman,* and had actively supported women's medical training. Like Margaret, she had been a pupil at St Leonards, though she left seven years before Margaret started there. She then attended St. Andrews University before meeting in Egypt, during a spell of invalidism that affected a number of clever young women, the Anglo-Irish Captain (later Lieutenant-Colonel) Theodore Montgomery Archdale. There followed a period of conformity that Helen later characterised as being 'up against a wall of "not dones"'.[80] She spent some years as an army wife in India before returning home in 1908 with sons Nicholas and Alexander and one-year-old Betty.

Helen joined the WSPU and was deeply impressed by a meeting with Mrs Pankhurst. A year later she was arrested, along with Adela Pankhurst and others for rushing the barricades outside the Kinnaird Hall Dundee where Winston Churchill was speaking. Sentenced to ten days in prison, they became early hunger-strikers but were released after serving four days. Helen became a WSPU organiser in Scarborough and then Sheffield.

In 1911 Adela, who suffered from ill health, was boarding with the family in Sheffield.[81] Over the next few years Helen helped to take care of her. Helen's husband (who had never approved of his wife's suffrage activities) was still in India. Helen had, in the meantime, moved to London where she spent two months in Holloway after participating in the mass window-breaking of late 1911. She became the WSPU prisoners' secretary and worked on the *Suffragette*, then *Britannia*. Here she gained compositing and editing skills that would stand her in good stead after the war.

Helen's children had some distinguished governesses. Jennie Kenney (sister of the more famous Annie with whom Margaret had worked) taught the children in Battersea and later in Milan. Adela Pankhurst was their governess in Berne, Switzerland before emigrating to Australia in 1913. Helen was in frequent communication with Adela's mother Mrs Pankhurst, who admitted to her that '[r]ecent years would have been more difficult for me but for your goodness'.

When war broke out, Helen's husband was posted to France. Before this she had become the manager of the Ensbury Growers Ltd.[82] This farm and gardens near Bournemouth enabled women to lease land on market-garden leases for smallholding activities such as poultry-rearing, orchards and intensive culture on a cooperative basis. The outbreak of war saw the scheme adapted so that women could be trained to work on the land in place of men. It was still in existence in May 1915. Later Helen became Lady Clerk at the WAAC headquarters under Mrs Chalmers Watson whom she had known in school.

It was in 1918 that Helen became Margaret's assistant at the Ministry of National Service, dealing with correspondence, card indexing and contacting and classifying details of women available for naval, military and air service. She earned an annual £150. But just before the war ended her husband was drowned. The *Leinster*, the Dublin mail boat on which he was travelling to Holyhead (after visiting his mother) was torpedoed. Ironically, the *Irish Times* linked the incident to the *Lusitania*, hoping that these two tragedies would mark the first and last such wartime incidents off the Irish coast.[83]

Helen received £300 annually as an army widow. She became Margaret's personal secretary (which included working for the Ministry of Health Watching Council and the WIL). The children were now boarding at Bedales and soon Margaret was paying their school fees. The youngest child Betty (Helen Elizabeth) – who became a successful barrister, captained the first English women's cricket team to tour Australia and later earned renown as an educator in Australia – transferred to St Leonards in September 1920 and stayed there for six years. Margaret was her nominator. Betty and Janet Owen were at St Leonards together for a year and a term though in different houses.

Betty later explained that her mother and Margaret both 'thought on the same lines and spoke the same language. They were liberals with a small l. They quickly became close friends.'[84] Helen was tall and of generous proportions. After attending the Josephine Butler centenary meeting at Westminster Hall in 1928, Nevinson's diary notes, somewhat unflatteringly, that he sat next to 'the enormous mountain of Mrs Archdale'.[85]

When Helen moved to Chelsea Court she rented number 12, the flat below Margaret's.[86] Her three children were now teenagers, though rarely there: in term-time they boarded and holidays were largely spent in Kent. Helen may have formally occupied her own space but the exclamation marks that accompanied Elizabeth Robins' remark about her living at Chelsea Court 'with R.!!' suggests how others viewed the arrangement.

Margaret's flat reflected the sophistication of the 1920s.[87] Echoing Llanwern but with a modern twist, it had a Chinese theme: a black lacquer ceiling and black-and-gold wallpaper depicting Chinese scenes, with plain orange curtains as well as Chinese lacquer cabinets. There were recessed wall lights and three big windows looked onto the river. In the entrance hall was a large Welsh dresser displaying brightly-coloured china. Flowers were in abundance.

During the years of reconstruction Margaret had made the transition from war administrator to a leading advocate of women's equality. She had also effected a major change in her private life. Humphrey had been a country gentleman. Margaret had become, as Betty

Archdale later recalled, 'a city dweller, a politician, and an intellectual'. Although the break-up of her marriage 'hurt Margaret enormously', according to Betty, she 'found the personal help she needed in mother'. Unusually for a mother of three, Helen admitted that she found motherhood 'greatly overrated, greatly sentimentalised'.[88]

The two women were committed to an Equality First perspective. They also formed a partnership through their commitment to an exciting new venture in business and journalism: *Time and Tide*. But before assessing this paper's significance for Margaret's friendship with Helen, for women and for British journalism, we need to examine Margaret's role as an immensely powerful and wealthy industrialist in these same years.

CHAPTER NINE

'The Queen of Commerce'[1]

In 1919 the chairman at the Annual General Meeting of Celtic Collieries Ltd addressed the gathering as 'Lady Rhondda and Gentlemen'.[2] It was a tag that was becoming only too familiar to Margaret. Yet although Welsh women workers played a much smaller part in the formal economy than their English counterparts during the industrial revolution, there had already been some notable examples of female entrepreneurs in south Wales. Lucy Thomas (c1781-1847) of Waunwyllt gained the title of the 'Mother of the Welsh Steam Coal Trade' after the first shipment of Welsh steam coal to London. She managed her late husband's colliery, opened up drift mines and helped promote the steam coal trade that would give Wales and Margaret's family such prominence.[3]

The Victorian Amy Dillwyn was another Welshwoman who became, against the odds, a business success.[4] In 1892 when her father died with debts of over £10,000, she had to leave the family home at Hendrefoilan,

Swansea. She had inherited his ailing Llansamlet Spelter Works. She took over its management, paid off her father's creditors and invested in the works. From her office at Albion Chambers in Swansea, she declared: 'Altogether I am becoming a man of business.' She turned the firm into one of the largest producers of zinc in the UK with annual profits of about £10,000, and effected a successful merger with a German metallurgical company.

A brave and independent woman, in 1905 Dillwyn went on a business trip to inspect zinc ore in the mines of Algeria. The adjective 'formidable', with its hint of unease, has been readily applied to women like Dillwyn, though her many achievements are increasingly being recognised.[5] Like Margaret, Dillwyn was the offspring of progressive, Liberal parents and became not only an international businesswoman but also a journalist and suffragist and published six novels.

The best known exemplar was Lady Charlotte Guest. Margaret was well aware of the multifaceted achievements of this phenomenal achiever.[6] She was originally from Lincolnshire but lived in south Wales from 1833 when she married John Guest, who ran the vast Dowlais Iron Company (not far from D.A.'s childhood home). Guest was the first MP for Merthyr Tydfil and a Whig. As a member for Merthyr Boroughs, D.A. was one of his political heirs.[7] Margaret sat on the Board of Directors of GKN (that developed out of the Dowlais Iron Company) for thirteen years. She also knew Charlotte Guest's suffragette grand-daughter Mildred Mansel.

Although Guest's aristocratic family had disapproved of her association with trade, her intelligence and catholic interests – combined with an unusually enlightened ironmaster husband – saw her become conversant with the demands of an ironworks that literally surrounded the family home and provided their wealth. Expanding demand for bar iron for building railway tracks from the Rhondda to Russia made Dowlais the largest ironworks in the world.

As Sir John Guest's health failed, so his wife became more involved in the daily running of the works, helping to negotiate contracts, deal with compensation claims, accounts, manage the workforce and even translate (from French into English) a pamphlet on the advantages of using hot air in the manufacture of iron. She had ten children and during this same period learned middle Welsh and undertook a pioneering translation of the medieval tales known as *The Mabinogion*. Her diary shows her establishing schools and her interest in the works. She recorded the weekly make of finished iron and the fact that 'it is now more congenial to me to calculate the advantage of half per cent commission on a cargo of iron than to go to the finest ball in the world'. Like Margaret, she radiated determination across a range of interests and commitments.

When her husband died in November 1852, Charlotte Guest became sole active trustee. A second marriage several years later marked a break with Wales and commitment to a new joint venture collecting ceramics across Europe. Charlotte Guest was only formally at the helm for a few years, but Margaret was involved in business within and beyond Wales for rather longer.

So how had this come about? Not long after Margaret married, D.A. decided to take on a business associate: 'something between a highly confidential secretary and a right-hand man'.[8] When he discussed with Sybil the problems of ensuring both loyalty and ability, she suggested 'Why not try Margaret?' D.A. did just that. Unusually for his time, he did not make a rigid demarcation between home and work, and had long discussed business with his wife and daughter. Margaret recalled that when Sybil was away and she was about eleven or twelve, he had 'poured out a stream of description of some deal he was engaged on at the time' as she sat 'palpitating with pride' at being treated as a grown-up yet terrified of saying the wrong thing as she understood so little.[9]

Sybil's proposal was a radical one and D.A. took a bold and progressive step in implementing it. Lady Charlotte Guest may have written 'I always feel here in my proper sphere' when she described walking round the works. But despite her careful inversion of the language of prescriptive literature that described woman's place, there was a gulf between her and the overwhelmingly male workforce of Dowlais. This went way beyond her class and status as an employer. Her gender ensured that acceptance by the oligarchy of fellow employers was equally problematic for her.

Margaret had hesitated before accepting her post. But she did not take long to decide that household management could be consigned to Saturdays. The very generous salary of £1,000 per annum made her one of the country's best-paid women and more than doubled the Mackworths' income (in 1916 D.A. told the *Western Mail* that he was committed to equal work for equal pay for women[10]). Prid helped to convince Margaret that she would be doing more for feminism than years of militant suffrage activity.

Each weekday she caught the 9.05am train to the resolutely masculine environment of Cardiff Docks. In the 1890s Cardiff had become the world's largest coal exporting port. D.A.'s headquarters, Cambrian Buildings, was in Mount Stuart Square, close to the Coal Exchange where the world's first million-pound deal had been made in 1907. The only other females in the building were two telephonists on the top floor. Margaret worked on the first floor, next to her father's wood-panelled office. In effect she served a valuable informal apprenticeship. She learned how the business worked by attending all his interviews and conferences, finding the negotiation of deals infinitely more interesting than the 'interminable and somewhat irrelevant conversation' of the drawing room. She began filing confidential business papers and taking down, then drafting confidential letters and memoranda. She soon managed to persuade her father to let her sign the letters she wrote for him. He was so fussy about how letters were phrased that it was easier not to involve him: 'To draft a business letter for him to sign was sheer pain and grief.'[11]

In 1915 when Margaret joined her father in New York she revelled in a combination of business and pleasure in a country that was not yet at war. As well as watching him negotiate business deals, for the first time Margaret felt 'almost a social success'.[12] She gained immeasurably in confidence, bolstered by being in a less formal society than at home and from the assurance that radiated from her father. They went to the theatre most evenings and visited country clubs. Margaret even gave a talk about British perspectives on women's suffrage in response to a request to speak. She was 'bombarded with eager questions'.[13] She and D.A. appreciated the apparent openness and enthusiasm of Americans and the esteem accorded to business and success.

They held discussions in Manhattan about establishing a barge goods transport service on the Mississippi, one of several schemes that did not work out due to the war. Margaret later recalled talks about Pennsylvanian coal mines. D.A. gained partial control over a small West Virginian mine. His ideal was for a British-American combine for the shipment of American coal to Europe (supplies were much cheaper than at home). He also envisaged controlling Sales Agencies and docking and storage facilities in Mediterranean ports and South America. Here again the war thwarted his ambitions.

During D.A.'s long overseas trip later that year, Margaret was given Power of Attorney and control of his private affairs. This, she stressed, 'meant complete control; once he was away one heard, beyond an occasional letter, very little of him'.[14] Nevertheless, when D.A. did write, his letters were full of advice as to how he thought business was best conducted. Thus, after Margaret had refused to guarantee an overdraft for a client, he wrote to her from New York, approving her decision:

> I make a standing rule not to guarantee any account in which I am not personally and largely interested, and I want you to hold fast to this rule under all circumstances. I quite appreciate your difficulty in saying "No". That is one of my peculiar weaknesses also. The best way is to make up your mind beforehand definitely.[15]

D.A. wrote from Ottawa that he wished to purchase property and land adjoining his Estate. This was the 4,000 acres belonging to the Perry-Herrick family and included the manor and castle of Pencoed, a large Tudor residence built from the stone of a Norman Castle, as well as rich farming land extending down to the moors by the River Severn. Margaret cabled that she needed a free hand to carry through this property deal worth well over £100,000. D.A. characteristically granted this. She negotiated the deal and her father only learned of the successful outcome when his ship docked in Liverpool a couple of months later. It was rumoured that D.A., now the second largest landowner in Monmouthshire, wished to build a country seat there either for himself or, more likely, for his daughter and son-in-law. Margaret inherited the Perry-Herrick estate when her father died. A house was built just north of the castle. Between 1919 and 1921 she spent thousands of pounds on restoring the ruined mansion, but the work was never completed. The focus of Margaret's life was now London-based.

Margaret and her father also participated in discussions about Canadian ventures. There were plans (that he was never able to complete) for railways across Northern Canada. D.A. had purchased the Peace River Development Corporation in northern Alberta including some land, stores and boats and was keen to explore the potential of oil resources in western and north-western Canada. He did not live to see the outcome, but on 14 August 1919 Margaret, Humphrey, Sybil, Uncle Edric Haig and his new young wife Nellie, Humphrey's brother John and his wife set off on an expedition to Alberta for Margaret to assess her father's purchases and possibly add to them.[16] Margaret's most intrepid journey had coal as its coveted prize, though there was also an important personal dimension involving D.A.'s other family.

Margaret and her relatives were accompanied by the Canadian V. Lloyd Owen (who had originally arranged the sale) and another businessman who was keen for Margaret to purchase coal measures he owned in an extremely remote region. They travelled by train to the small, but strategically placed, Peace River Crossing. This was the only town within a radius of several thousand miles. The journey took thirty hours as the train travelled along a bumpy track at just fifteen miles an hour. From Peace River Crossing they embarked on a huge steamer (almost 162 feet long) now owned by Margaret.[17] It was called the *D.A. Thomas*. It had originally been intended to transport oil and coal deposits from Peace County. Once a fortnight during summer months it plied the Peace River, transporting both passengers and freight. It was the last boat of the season and they were plagued by mosquitoes. Margaret played bridge with the ship's cook every afternoon. Despite passing uninhabited wilderness, the vessel was well equipped with electricity, hot and cold running water in each of the thirty state rooms and silver service dining.

From Vermilion, a shanty town inhabited by traders, missionaries and native Indians, they spent five days on another family possession, a gasoline boat called the *Lady Mackworth*. Margaret's namesake conveyed them to Hudson Hope in the foothills of the Rockies. The men slept on the dining-room floor. A barge was attached to the boat's side for the ladies to sleep under an awning. Their bedding was frequently soaked by waves. Despite having nearly drowned four years earlier, Margaret seems to have taken this in her stride. The day after arriving at Hudson's Hope, she, her uncle and aunt and the two businessmen set off on horseback in search of the coal measures. Margaret nicknamed their owner the Cinema Beauty. A tall, slim, self-centred man with a perfect tan and 'eyes just the right blue', he wore a panama hat and white trousers as though he were on the Riviera. At lunch he sat on some strawberry jam which rather spoilt the effect.

They passed through gloomy woods then set up camp. The next day they carried on by foot, crossing a river in a canoe carved out of the trunk of a birch tree. A night was spent at the house of a trapper with the wonderful name of Carbon River Jones. They had to wash in the icy Peace River. It was now autumn and increasingly cold. It was also difficult negotiating the undergrowth and took eleven hours to walk about eleven miles. They ate bear meat and arctic trout cooked on a camp fire. Eventually, according to Margaret's tale of endurance and survival, just three of them braved the final mile: Carbon River Jones, the Cinema Beauty and herself. It took them through deep moss. But this pilgrims' progress went awry as they encountered a final obstacle. A raging torrent twenty feet below them (they had expected a dried-up rivulet) meant that nature won and the coal was neither glimpsed nor bought by Margaret. But the Canadian quest confirmed her powers of endurance and bravery, not least in crossing the Atlantic again.

Margaret also began, even before the war, to take responsibility for the newspapers, journals and printing firms that her father owned or partly controlled. It was a valuable training for her later career. D.A. had gradually obtained control of a number of previously independent papers.[18] They included the South Wales Printing and Publishing Company (Margaret later chaired its board). In the industrial heartland he obtained the *Pontypridd Observer* and *Merthyr Express*. A shrewd operator, he was also the largest single shareholder (with fifty shares) of the Labour *Merthyr Pioneer*[19] and owned the Aberdare-based colliers' weekly paper, *Tarian y Gweithiwr*. This was not D.A.'s only Welsh-language paper. He acquired *Y Tyst* and the Liberal *Baner ac Amserau Cymru*.

The heart of D.A.'s business empire might have been in south-east Wales (acquisitions included the *South Wales Journal of Commerce*) but he ensured that his – and his daughter's – influence over public opinion extended across the country. He purchased the *North Wales Times* and controlled the *Cambrian News* in Aberystwyth. Its editor, John Gibson (who died in 1915) advocated women's rights. In 1931 the paper offered to pay a correspondent who would provide regular reports on Margaret's Six Point Group.[20]

D.A. even contemplated purchasing the *Pall Mall Gazette*, telling the journalist David Evans that '[a] newspaper in London is a source of political power and I am prepared to spend some money on it'.[21] In the event it was his daughter who would do this, albeit in her own way.

Within Wales the newspaper that exercised the greatest influence was the Cardiff-based *Western Mail*. Here D.A. gained financial but not political control. Indeed, he and the paper (which viewed itself as 'independent Conservative') locked horns on a number of occasions, especially during industrial disputes. In February 1916 Lord Riddell, chairman of the board, resigned and his 1,586 ordinary shares of £10 each were purchased by D.A. but transferred nominally to David Watkin Thomas, the company's general manager. He undertook to vote in respect of the shares as D.A. wished.[22] This was not done publicly. Two other members of the board, William Davies and Hughes Morgan, also held shares for D.A. under the same terms as trustees. In effect the Thomas family soon had fifty-one per cent of the shares (3,672 out of the 7,200 ordinary shares). The covert nature of this transaction was, Margaret later argued in court, because her father was well-known as a Liberal, and it was felt that it might damage the paper were it known that the paper's controlling interests were in Liberal hands. Part of the agreement was that the paper would be left to pursue its own policy.

At this point the fortunes of the *Western Mail* were starting to recover from the impact of the war. Net profits for 1917 were just under £13,000 and circulation was up. The board of directors was not happy with the balance of ownership. The deaths of both David Watkin Thomas and D.A. emboldened them to take action. In December 1918, without notifying Margaret or D.A.'s other executors, they held an Extraordinary General Meeting. Here they agreed to increase its capital and regain control from the Rhondda Estate by creating a further 5,000 ordinary shares of £10 each. Robert Webber, a member of the board, asked Margaret to sell her shares to him in March 1919. She refused. She also took legal action to stop the issuing of the new shares.

It was too late. In March 1920 Margaret, Sybil and

Humphrey (D.A.'s Executors) brought a case against the Western Mail Limited and the company directors, arguing that the issue of the new capital was a contravention of the company's Articles of Association concerning the transfer of shares. They sued William Davies and Hughes Morgan for breach of trust. Margaret gave evidence. She asserted that the paper had not looked after her interests and had tried to emasculate the Rhondda position by reducing the real value of her shareholding. She also argued that as she was the majority shareholder she could not see how the duties of her trustees (who were directors of the company) towards her could conflict with their duty to other shareholders.

The Times' report of Rhondda v The Western Mail Limited was carefully headed: 'The Control of a Newspaper'. The three-day court case resulted in the company paying all costs. Margaret met the directors privately. She gave an assurance that her holding would not affect the political policy of the paper. Allegations against the board and individuals were withdrawn. The shares of the Rhondda Estate were to be re-registered in the names the Estate chose – either their own names or those of nominees. Importantly, the new capital created on the death of D.A. was to be cancelled or issued in proportion to holdings. The board (now described by the *Western Mail* as the strongest newspaper board in the country) was extended to include Margaret and Henry Seymour Berry. They both became directors for life.

Berry and Margaret's fortunes (in both senses) were closely allied. This Merthyr-born businessman had been D.A.'s protégé. Berry's father had been his election agent in 1900 and from 1915 his son acted for him in many business undertakings when D.A. was involved in government. He, along with Lord Merthyr and D.A. were the first three Freemen of Merthyr Tydfil. During the lock-out that followed the General Strike in 1926, Berry was made Lord Buckland of Bwlch.

Since the summer of 1915 when Margaret's father was abroad she had been sitting on boards on D.A.'s behalf, 'acting really as a kind of unofficial liaison officer to report to him how things were going and to give the Board his views on any line of policy'.[23] At this point she was spending half of the week in Cardiff and the other half in London. She was determined to persevere in public life and in the boardroom. She was convinced that the extraordinary circumstances of wartime afforded her an opportunity: at present even the most conservative of directors were prepared to accept the presence of a woman. She was greatly helped by Berry, who was part of a remarkable upwardly mobile family: the hundred pounds he lent his two brothers helped them to become phenomenally successful newspaper barons as Lord Camrose and Sir Gomer Berry. Margaret penned an approving portrait of these brothers for *Time and Tide*. She saw the Whitehall flat they shared as a symbol of the way they acted in concert: 'They are scarcely individuals. They are a family organism'.[24] Seymour Berry helped to teach her the value of working with others.

It would not be easy for Margaret to emulate D.A.'s business record or indeed his relentless energy, scheming and 'missionary zeal', captured in Dai Smith's account of how D.A. envisioned 'The World of South Wales'.[25] In 1901 D.A. had resigned as managing director of Cambrian Collieries Ltd. His only business connected to the mining industry for the next five years was his partnership in Thomas & Davey, the Cambrian's sales agents (Margaret would later chair this company). But in 1906, aged fifty, he rejoined the Cambrian Board. He forged ahead, acquiring a controlling interest in the Glamorgan Colliery at Llwynypia. This laid the basis for what became known as the Cambrian Combine, centred on the Rhondda. Long cherished, it formed part of what Smith calls D.A.'s 'vaulting ambition'.[26] In 1896 he had published a pamphlet on the state of the coal trade in which he had envisaged the effects of companies combining to control and to regulate the steam coal trade.[27]

By 1910 Cambrian Collieries Ltd controlled the Cambrian Collieries at Clydach Vale and crucially the Glamorgan Coal Co Ltd, Naval Colliery Co Ltd (Penygraig) and Britannic Merthyr Coal Co Ltd (Gilfach Goch). The four companies centred on the Rhondda retained separate identities and traded under their own names, but a system of collective production was developed with the purchasing of materials as well as control over prices being centralised. They operated technically as a single unit under one supervising management. The holding company Consolidated Cambrian Trust became Consolidated Cambrian Ltd in 1913. It was during 1913-14 that coal production reached its apogee. The company was now registered with a nominal capital of £2 million to acquire all the share capital of the four collieries. This development represented what the *Western Mail* called D.A.'s 'extraordinary genius for organisation' and ensured his enterprise 'a foremost place among the great industrial combines of the Kingdom'.[28] This vertically integrated

organisation was a massive achievement and legacy for
D.A.'s daughter. As Martin Daunton has observed, D.A.
'viewed the entire coalfield as a single gigantic interest
with common economic needs'.[29]

Whatever touched D.A.'s core business as coal owner
seemed to be brought within his ambit so that he obtained
control over distributing as well as producing coal. He was
involved in the formation of an insurance company that
acquired much of the insurance business for his own
undertakings, and he became a partner in a Cardiff
stockbroking firm. He sat on the board of the Port Talbot
Railway and Docks Company, and from 1914 was a vice-
chairman of Ebbw Vale Steel and Iron Company. He
centralised the agencies for the sale of the coals produced
at the collieries he controlled and created distributive
organisations, such as shipping, in the countries where he
traded. In 1906 he had set up Lysberg Ltd. to break the
monopoly exercised by Cardiff merchants over the
importation of pit props from south-west France which
kept prices artificially high. The following year he took
over the sales agency L.Guéret Ltd to develop European
bases.

David Evans saw 1916 as '[t]he *annus mirabilis* of his
coal-owning achievements'.[30] In this year he made a
number of valuable new colliery deals such as acquiring a
controlling interest in the flourishing Ferndale Collieries
of D.Davis and Sons Ltd and, further west, the anthracite
Gwaun-Cae-Gurwen Colliery. He was now the most
powerful coal owner in south Wales and controlled a
dozen collieries and their sales agencies. And he made
some canny business deals arising out of war such as the
acquisition from the Board of Trade of shares in the

German-owned Sanatogen Company Ltd (now called Genatosan Ltd). Margaret would chair this company with Berry as deputy chairman.

On taking up political office at the end of 1916, D.A. resigned his directorships. Margaret, along with Berry, assumed greater control as politics then ill health engulfed him. As early as 1917 her annual services to various companies were valued by a businessman at £10,000.[31] And in this year a magazine described her as 'the best known and most capable woman of business in the Kingdom'.[32]

By the time he died in July 1918, Margaret had gained considerable business experience. D.A.'s estate was valued at £883,645. Margaret and Sybil were left £100,000 each in trust and appointed partners in his companies. Margaret later inherited Sybil's share and the Llanwern Estate. Margaret's cousin Peter Haig-Thomas – the son of D.A.'s brother and Sybil's sister (and the same age as Margaret) – became managing director of half a dozen of D.A.'s Welsh colliery companies and a director of two others. However, a year later he was on the board of just D.Davis and Sons and the Welsh Navigation Steam Company.[33]

In the same year Emily Talbot of Margam and Penrice died. She too was the daughter of a Welsh MP and owned collieries as well as land. Her father the longstanding Member of Parliament, C.R.M. Talbot had died in 1890. She had inherited everything (her elder brother had died in a riding accident) and became Britain's richest heiress. Now Margaret was one of the country's wealthiest women, though unlike Miss Talbot, who had been a generous benefactress but not actively engaged in business, Margaret was an ambitious businesswoman. This meant that she had a number of obstacles to face and devised strategies to overcome them. How well did she fare?

In addition to the world of business management being overwhelmingly male, plenty of talented women were thwarted due to their families lacking the money to educate or place them in positions where they might have developed business acumen. Many others found that it was their brothers (regardless of their age) who were the automatic beneficiaries when it came to inheritance. Here Margaret was fortunate as her parents' only child and the offspring of a couple who appreciated women's potential.

She wrote in the 1930s:

> I have no illusions. I know perfectly well that, being a woman, if I had not happened to have a famous – and rich – father, devoid of the usual inhibitions about using female material if it happened to come handy, I should never have been heard of outside my locality at all.[34]

This disclaimer does not quite ring true. Quite apart from the fact that her mother and, to a lesser extent, her husband were also tolerant of her ambitions, Margaret's intelligence and personality suggest that she would have made some sort of name for herself one way or another, regardless of her father's legacy and support. Nevertheless, her broad point was valid. She had a head start: attending a school that took girls seriously, enjoying a valuable unofficial apprenticeship while her father was alive and inheriting a fortune on his death. In 1919 a memorandum on 'Equal

Pay for Similar Duties' by the National Union of Clerks paid Margaret a compliment. It described her as D.A.'s former 'right hand man' in his business affairs and added that she was 'and is, far superior to the many existent guinea-pig directors'.[35]

Yet there was a price to pay. D.A. died at the height of his fame and success. The man described as 'The Napoleon of the world's coal trade'[36] was a very hard act to follow. He had been pre-eminent among the new native plutocracy of Wales. Kenneth O. Morgan has described his Cambrian Combine as a 'huge oligopoly... that dominated the Welsh economy almost as comprehensively as did the empires of Rockefeller or Carnegie in the United States'.[37] His commercial interests penetrated the leading world markets. Acknowledged as a cultured, versatile and well-connected man, who had the ear and admiration of the prime minister as well as the trade unionist, even though both had experienced serious differences and difficulties with him, this Oxford-educated millionaire was a force to be reckoned with and always ploughed his own furrow. Reviewing the year 1918, the *Colliery Guardian* wrote of July that 'The outstanding item this month, so far as the coal trade is concerned, was the death of Viscount Rhondda'.[38] Margaret was inevitably cast into D.A.'s shadow.

Although sons frequently followed their fathers into business, many spent at least a period learning the job, if not literally at the coal face, then at least working on site. Quite apart from the fact that D.A.'s main business was one of the most masculine-dominated of all British industries the breadth of his concerns would have made it difficult for anybody to acquire real knowledge and understanding of his portfolio. Women were not yet members of the stock exchange and were excluded from gentlemen's clubs. What Margaret called professional 'gossip' (a gendered expression that would doubtless have been described by its male participants in more elevated terms) has always been vital and she was well aware of being denied access. As she put it: 'Though one is in the life, one is not, one cannot yet be, altogether of it.'[39]

Moreover, as she recognised, boys from well-off, successful families were socialised into expectations of leadership and a need for confidence was instilled into them. Girls, in contrast, were prepared for a domestic life. Margaret was aware that as a girl 'if one failed at anything it did not really matter'.[40] Ambition was 'held up to her as a vice – to a boy it is held up as virtue'. Admittedly this was written retrospectively as the feminist looked back on her formative years but the autobiographies of numerous women achievers bear testimony to the sense that being a Victorian daughter from a privileged background spelt the sublimation of ambition beyond carefully circumscribed boundaries. When her father took the highly unusual step of bringing his daughter into the business world, Margaret found that it was one thing to be tolerated as her father's representative – after his death it was quite another to be taken seriously in her own right.

The situation was compounded by her desire to do what she felt D.A. would have wished, regardless of whether changing economic circumstances made this the wisest move. However, her most cherished undertaking was the independent creation of the *Time and Tide* publishing venture. It appealed to her more than heavy industry, fused her business skills and literary interests, and, crucially, provided a platform from which to advocate women's equality. It absorbed vital time, money and energy. It also kept her physically removed from Cardiff which, despite the importance of London and international markets, had been the hub of D.A.'s business empire.

Women's involvement in business was helped when the country was at war. They were very visible in the workplace, albeit in non-managerial positions. In such extraordinary circumstances, there was greater latitude. In 1917 Lady Boot, wife of Sir Jesse Boot of Nottingham, was appointed a director of Boots Cash Chemists Ltd. She had for some years been responsible for the development of the toiletry and gift side of the business as well as influential in design and fittings for the shops.[41]

Yet the coming of peace in late 1918 brought with it an unrealistic assumption by many that 'normal service' would be resumed. Margaret's own war service had helped her credibility and confidence despite the shadow of the Douglas-Pennant case and she had gained at last the right to vote. But none of this ensured that she would be accepted as an equal by fellow members of boards. Even in the United States of the 1970s, Katharine Graham, the immensely powerful head of the *Washington Post* faced difficulties and stereotyping as a highly successful businesswoman. She found that she was 'always being depicted as the difficult woman, while whoever left the company was the victim of my female whims. I was still a curiosity, a woman in a man's world'.[42]

In order to be taken seriously, Margaret adopted various strategies from the outset. Although Seymour Berry's belief in her abilities clearly helped, she felt that it would be expedient in meetings to minimise members' awareness of having a female presence in their midst. She therefore chose to make verbal interventions sparingly. Urgent or pressing matters would be listened to regardless of gender but anything trivial she knew would be associated with her as 'Woman'.

At a time when men routinely smoked in meetings, she did not want to object and thus prompt resentment. So she began smoking Balkan Sobranie cigarettes as soon as she entered a boardroom. As for swearing, she watched her own language and, calculating that since the men would feel decidedly uncomfortable if they swore in front of a woman, she let them apologise if they happened to swear. She wore sensible suits and shoes, seeking to blend in rather than stand out.

In 1918 Margaret sat on the board of thirty-one companies and chaired seven (she always insisted on calling herself chairman, not chairwoman). They ranged from the Cambrian Artificial Limb Company to the South Wales Printing and Publishing Company and the Rhondda Engineering and Mining Company. The following year this had risen to thirty-three (chairing seven and as deputy-chairman of a further two).[43] At the start of the 31st AGM of North's Navigation Collieries held at the Great Western Hotel at Paddington that year Berry paid tribute to D.A., his predecessor as chairman. He added that Lady Rhondda 'was very closely associated with him [D.A] in all his undertakings, and her presence on this board and on many others is a source of strength to her colleagues... she well merits the reputation she has made for herself in the business-world'.[44] The venue, handy for travellers by train from south Wales, became a familiar one for Margaret.

She had also acquired substantial interests in the Graigola Merthyr Company Ltd founded by Thomas Cory and Frank Ash Yeo. The largest manufacturer of patent fuel in south Wales, it included French interests. Sir David R. Llewellyn (who had twenty-three directorships by 1923) secured the deal for just under two million pounds in late 1918. He chaired the board, Margaret was its deputy and Berry was also a director. By 1923 she was chairing eleven companies and was deputy chairman of three.[45] During the inter-war period she chaired thirteen different boards, was a director of at least forty-eight companies and a shareholder in many others.

Between them Berry, Llewellyn and Margaret controlled much of the south Wales coalfield, systematically developing the policy established by D.A. and acquiring shares in a large number and range of companies that effectively gave them enormous power. Margaret had served a valuable informal apprenticeship with the prime shaper of the modern south Wales coalfield and had ready cash. Berry had valuable business skills and connections. It is worth noting, though, that it is his name not Margaret's that tends to be mentioned in books on business history, even though at the time both received much attention from the press. Llewellyn, known as D.R, was a colliery manager's son with technical expertise. He had worked as a mining surveyor in the United States as well as in the south Wales coalfield where he introduced mechanised coal cutters. The pattern in the early 1920s was for one of these three to chair a company while the other two sat on the board (and sometimes an additional Berry or Llewellyn brother). For example, Llewellyn and Margaret were directors of the Imperial Navigation Coal Co based in Port Talbot, with pits in the Cymmer area. Its chairman and managing director was Seymour Berry. Llewellyn chaired the Troedyrhiw Coal Co with Berry and Margaret on the board.

This was an ambitious trio. They emanated from south Wales which remained at the heart of their enterprises but their perspectives and dealings extended way beyond Wales. Close in age (Margaret was in her late thirties in 1920 and the two men in their early forties), they represented a younger generation eager to consolidate their business interests and wealth in spectacular fashion.

In his book on capitalist combination in the coal industry, published in 1924, D. J. Williams used a vivid image to describe the insidious effect of what he called the Berry-Llewellyn-Rhondda group. Their interests, he wrote, 'extend like red threads through the mesh of capitalism in south Wales and, as in a tangled skein, it is impossible to say where they begin and where they end'.[46] Their monopolistic position was all the more worrying in his view because the companies retained formal independence (rather than being one registered company), and thus effectively obscured the real power they wielded. This labyrinth meant that workmen did not know their employers and both the destination and distribution of profits were unclear, affording 'infinite possibilities' for obscuring the general financial position'.[47]

Their most prestigious acquisition was the family firm of John Lysaght Ltd in September 1919 for five million pounds. This was a significant galvanising and sheet steel business that owned Scunthorpe steel works and works in Bristol, London and Wolverhampton as well as rolling mills at Newport. They employed about 8,000 people and were shippers from Avonmouth to branches being developed in Australia and across the globe. This deal was described by *The Times* as 'one of the biggest and most important transactions for some years'.[48]

In January 1920 Lysaght's merged with GKN, although the companies continued to operate under their existing names, and Margaret and D.R. remained directors with Berry chairing the company. The following year GKN acquired nearly all the share capital of the Gwaun-Cae-Gurwen Colliery Company (Margaret sat on its board), one of Wales's largest anthracite mines with 1,500 employees. Although suffering from the incursion of American coal into French and Mediterranean markets, the demand for anthracite had picked up post-war. In 1929 the company was sold to the Amalgamated Anthracite Collieries chaired by Lord Melchett, formerly Sir Alfred Mond.

GKN also acquired a controlling interest in L. Guéret Ltd on whose board Margaret sat. They were one of the largest shippers of coal in south Wales and sales agents with large interests in major French and Italian coal distributing companies. Margaret's relationship with GKN developed further in late 1923 when they made a successful takeover bid for D. Davis and Sons Ltd and Consolidated Cambrian Ltd. Margaret now sat on GKN's board and attended its AGMs in Birmingham. Berry became chairman in 1927 but the following May was killed in a riding accident. Faced with a tough economic climate, in a controversial move that many saw as an attempt to get rid of both financial problems and militant colliers, the individual companies that comprised the Consolidated Cambrian went into voluntary liquidation in

1928 only to be re-acquired by GKN the following year from the receiver.[49]

In 1930 GKN brought together its coal holdings in a new, large subsidiary company called Welsh Associated Collieries controlling 32,000 men. But production and exports continued to fall, and in March 1935 protracted negotiations with the Powell-Duffryn group resulted in them taking over the assets and liabilities of GKN's coal holdings and forming Powell Duffryn Associated Collieries Ltd, the largest coal producing company in Britain with more than one hundred mines.[50] Margaret resigned from the board the following year and was paid £2,000 compensation.[51] In this same year Merthyr Tydfil, which her father had represented in Parliament, recorded 60.6% of its insured population as out of work. It became known as '[t]he town that died'. Dowlais had been Charlotte Guest's home, the site of the world's largest ironworks and the original launch pad for what became GKN. The closure of the works produced an unemployed rate of 80%.

Margaret also sat on the board of shipping companies such as the Globe and Hazelwood Shipping Companies and Guéret's Anglo-Brazilian Coaling Company.[52] One of the first companies on which she held a seat was Lysberg Ltd, which had expanded from being pitwood importing agents into coal-shipping, coal-selling and ship owning. She chaired Lysberg Ltd post-war and the Plisson-Lysberg Insurance Company which had been created to manage the insurance of D.A.'s undertakings. Margaret was also a director of R. Marten and Co Ltd, a London-based shipping company formed in 1914 with D.A. as a partner. But it had financial problems. She provided guarantees for the company's large overdraft three times within six months from late 1918. It then went into voluntary liquidation for three years and was wound up in 1922.[53]

When she chaired the AGM of the British Fire Insurance Co Ltd at Cannon Street in April 1920, Margaret was received with cheers. The private company formed in 1908 had gone public the previous year. Two of the Berry brothers and D.R. were on the board. It provided insurance for homes, personal accident and sickness as well as private and commercial vehicles. Margaret predicted very promising prospects as a result of reorganisation and an increase in capital, but three years later the company was taken over by London & Lancashire Insurance.[54]

Coal was still all-important when Margaret inherited her father's business interests. Wales had, since the 1870s, become the leader in dry steam coal. The use of steam power at sea had spelt success for collieries such as North's Navigation. The fact that steam coal left no smoke plume on the horizon had made it the choice of the British Admiralty and this smokeless fuel was popular in domestic use. But in many respects Margaret could not have taken over the reins of her father's business at a worse time. The artificial prosperity induced by war and its immediate aftermath camouflaged the longer-term trend of a decline in demand from pre-war export levels as well as relative inefficiency and excess capacity. Profits came from the export of coal and this trade was now under threat. 'Never in the history of the coal trade', declared the *Colliery Guardian* in January 1919, 'have the conditions been so difficult as in the year just ended'.[55]

The emergence of alternative sources of power, such as

the use of oil for steam coal in shipping, would adversely affect most of the collieries with which Margaret was associated. She had diversified into steel but the development of continuous strip-mill production in the United States meant that, for the time being at least, Wales and England were once again lagging behind foreign competitors. Geological conditions in the south Wales coalfield tended to make mechanisation difficult and as late as 1938 only twenty-six per cent of coal was cut mechanically there compared to the British average of fifty-nine per cent.[56]

South Wales was renowned for the militancy of its miners and there was a history of troubled labour relations (in which D.A. had been embroiled). At the AGM of D. Davis and Sons in March 1922 Margaret and fellow board members were told how the strike of October to November in 1920, along with government restriction on the exporting of British coal, had meant that the Americans had encroached on some of their more important markets in France, Italy and South America.[57] Exports of coal to France from south Wales halved between 1914 and 1921. The ending of the operation of the Coal Mines (Emergency) Act spelt a cessation of the subsidies that had bolstered trade.

The three-month national stoppage that began in April 1921 meant a further loss of export markets, and although a strike the following year in the United States lasted even longer and helped boost the demand for coal on the continent, this was only short-lived. Two years later the same board was being told that '[t]he menace of American coal competition may be in its infancy, but its growth is not only inevitable, but will become accelerated unless something is done immediately to counteract it'.[58] Coal companies wished there could be a return to the eight-hour day. For some outside these boardrooms, for example E.D. Lewis, son of a Rhondda miner and author of a book on the Rhondda valleys, the way in which large combines gobbled up smaller concerns was itself a menace which helped to explain the sudden decay of the coal industry.[59]

At Consolidated Cambrian's AGM in March 1922, Margaret and the board were told that for the first time there would be no dividend on ordinary shares.[60] The following year this was repeated in worsening conditions. Those at the AGM for D. Davis and Sons Ltd that year heard that it 'was one of the most critical in the annals of the south Wales coal trade'.[61] In addition to the 'calamitous' coal strike, local conditions such as coal trimmers at the docks resisting night shifts, were 'throttling the revival in its cradle'.[62] For the first half of 1922 Margaret's income after paying super tax was just over £9,000, but it was already being exceeded by expenditure and would shrink to less than a third of this amount before the end of the decade.

The French and Belgian occupation of the Ruhr in 1923, after Germany had defaulted on its payments of compensation to the allies for war damages, halted most coal production there and temporarily helped Britain. But the Dawes Plan, effective from the autumn of 1924, led to the resumption of coal production in the Weimar Republic. The large mines of Germany, with modern production techniques, proved to be very effective and Polish mines were now undercutting British prices. Germany's payment of coal reparations to Belgium, France and Italy exacerbated the situation, as would import restrictions in France and Spain in 1927.

The Return to the Gold Standard in April 1925 caused further difficulties for the mining industry and unemployment rates soon rocketed. Between the summer of 1925 and April 1926 the average price of coal for export fell by two shillings a ton. Then, 3 May 1926 saw the start of the General Strike two days after more than a million miners were locked out of their pits pending acceptance of severe wage cuts and an extra hour on the working day. Margaret allowed her business premises at 92 Victoria Street to be used by the government's Supply and Transport organisation that deployed the Volunteers or Blacklegs (depending on one's political perspectives) who drove motor cars, buses and taxis during the strike.[63] After nine days the General Council of the Trades Union Congress surrendered unconditionally. The miners remained out for months.

In April 1927 the *Daily Herald,* committed to promoting the interests of Labour rather than Capital, produced an elaborate diagram (put together by the Transport and General Workers Union) illustrating the inter-connected, monopolistic nature of the press and heavy industry.[64] It drew particular attention to five individuals: the Berry brothers, T.J. Callaghan (who sat with Margaret on several boards and was chairman of Cambrian Collieries, a director of Graigola Merthyr and of GKN) and Viscountess Rhondda. This handful comprised 'the suns around which the planets move'. Together these employers were linked up for 'silent, unseen, but effective action' that was more powerful and insidious than proposed anti-union legislation.

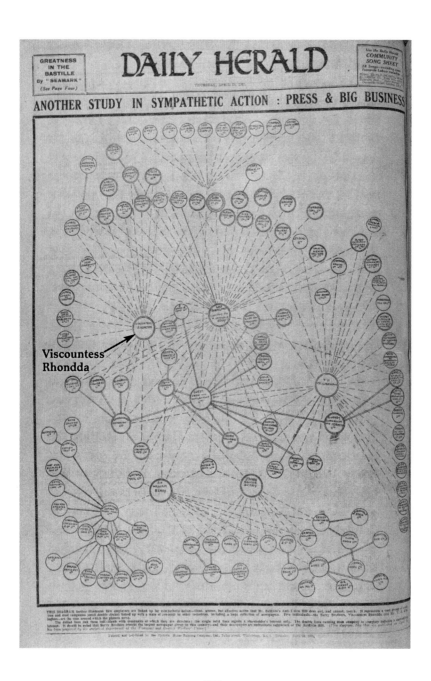

Nevertheless, the events of 1926, along with the Wall Street Crash and its global consequences, had a significant impact on Margaret's financial position. With the demands of *Time and Tide* her expenditure already exceeded income, but whereas in the financial year 1925 to 1926 it was only by £273, by April 1927 it had shot up to £3,544. At the end of 1927 Margaret told a relative that '[p]ractically every colliery is up to its eyes in debt to the Banks and the Banks must for their protection now insist on some solution. Very possibly the situation will end in the closing down of something like half of the pits with the highest working costs.'

In 1924 Margaret had been a director of more than a dozen Welsh coal companies (as well as numerous international coaling companies). By 1930 she still sat on the board of two-thirds of these but most of the former (including the Cambrian collieries) then became part of Welsh Associated Collieries Ltd and Margaret did not sit on its board. By 1933 she was a director of just two coal companies: Graigola Merthyr (where she was deputy chairman) and North's Navigation. Within four years they had gone.[65] In 1926 she had been a director of twenty-six different companies. She sat on the boards of half that number by 1929.[66]

Meanwhile the Rhondda Valleys, at the heart of D.A.'s industrial creation, had become synonymous with images of depression. With consistently high unemployment rates (prolonged unemployment was higher than in any other part of Britain), the Rhondda was investigated by many as an area characterised by health problems, decay, distress and depopulation. By the eve of the Second World War its coal production had plummeted to a third of its

1913 level. Dependence on the coal industry (in 1921 more than sixty-six per cent of its males over twelve had worked in coal mining) and a lack of alternative jobs for men, let along women, exacerbated the situation.

Margaret's promotion of women's employment opportunities was demonstrated through WIL, which campaigned for women workers' rights. With heavy industry dominating the part of Wales where her businesses were concentrated, issues of employment and unemployment largely concerned male rather than female workers. She does not seem to have voiced much specific concern about the women in Welsh mining families whose lives were dependent on the collieries she helped to control. Despite her title, her association with industrial Wales in these years was overwhelmingly through her directorships. In December 1923 she added her voice (in *The Times*) to a plea for shop assistants to be given three consecutive days off over the Christmas holiday. A letter a few days later from a Rhondda man writing in the *Daily News* pointedly suggested that Lady Rhondda lead a movement for the payment of statutory holidays including a fortnight each summer for miners. They received no pay when not working.[67]

Welsh miners' wives were, however, discussed in an unattributed article in *Time and Tide* on 'The Threatened Coal Strike' in September 1920.[68] Although the miners of south Wales had been (somewhat patronisingly) praised by the paper in June for settling down to steady effort and solid production, thus making them 'fully entitled to occasional political extravagance', readers were now warned of the dangers of a strike. The price of domestic coal would increase, the country would be paralysed and the effects long lasting. Women, it was argued, had an equal right with men to decide a matter that affected all: 'It is intolerable that miners' wives and mothers should have to stand by and see their irresponsible sixteen-year-old sons vote on an issue so vital – boys with no experience, no outlook, who regard the strike as a holiday.' Here was a very different perspective from that of the women and young men who would express solidarity with their menfolk over the coming months and years.

Time and Tide appeared on 7 May 1926 in a typed truncated form, one of two Strike editions. The paper supported the government in refusing to negotiate 'whilst the pistol of the General Strike was held to its head'. In a letter to *The Times* during that long hot summer of the 1926 lock-out in south Wales Margaret conceded that reduced wages bore heavily on many households. Her point was that those with young children were the ones most likely to suffer and that allowances paid by the state for children – in effect Eleanor Rathbone's scheme for family allowances – had been largely ignored by the miners yet would make a vital difference to them.[69]

Time and Tide reported on strikes by women for equal pay and employment opportunities as well as dismissals but when it came to personal advocacy, Margaret's prime focus was on opportunities for educated middle and upper class girls to enter business. She wasted no opportunity to address the socialisation of the latter and the importance of gender equality. Parents must resist turning their daughters into 'hothouse flowers' she told the press: girls and boys should be brought up alike to develop character and brains and be seen as an individual.[70]

In articles and speeches Margaret stressed that young women in comfortable circumstances should enter a business or profession. Her father had told Cardiff Business Club in 1916 that 'enforced idleness is repugnant to all right thinking women... women who have no families requiring their attention should be encouraged to engage in occupation [sic] which they are in many cases as well qualified or even better qualified than men to perform'.[71]

Yet Margaret's statements tended to ignore the fact that most women lacked the progressive parental and economic support that she had enjoyed. She told the National Council of Women at Southport in 1926 that 'one of the stupidest things' attempted by women was 'to work hard all day and then perform all household duties when they get home'. Women must stick to one job.[72] If, however, her comments are set alongside those of some of her fellow public speakers on the subject, the need for uncompromising words becomes more apparent. In a lecture at the Institute of Hygiene Dr James Fenton told his audience in the year of the General Strike that a permanent strike by all business women would be a boon. He was not alone in arguing that women competing with men in business interfered with the wealth and happiness of the race.[73]

At the first international conference on women in science, industry and commerce Margaret declared that she would like to see fathers engage their daughters in their businesses as they did with sons. She unashamedly approved of nepotism in this instance: 'on the whole it was the natural and the best way of carrying on a business' and 'You cannot have a better friend at your back than a father'.[74] The business world, she told *Good Housekeeping*, operated by precedent. Miss Jones might be eminently suited for the post of branch manager but was not promoted because there was no precedent for this.[75] The presence of an employer's daughter on the board would make a vital difference. Margaret knew of five instances where businessmen had employed their daughters, and each case was producing good results: 'the future of women in business largely depends upon the action of business men who have daughters'. Such claims raised as many questions as solutions but, as a living illustration of her point, it was not easy to challenge her.

Margaret believed that her father had enjoyed a distinct advantage as a businessman with a university degree (his position was relatively rare before 1914). She promoted opportunities for university-educated women to enter business, and established a business and university women's committee with Professor Caroline Spurgeon of Bedford College, London. Members included managing directors of various businesses as well as the heads of women's colleges. Part of an international initiative, this developed out of the conference held by the International Federation of University Women held in Oslo in 1924 to discuss the place of university women in the world's work. Margaret spoke there about the control of industry from the woman's viewpoint and was described in the press as 'the Directress of the Cambrian collieries'.[76]

She contributed a section on 'Business and Commerce' to a book on careers for girls, advocating commerce as a career and citing examples of other women pioneers such as Lady Wolverton who was a director at Glyn, Mills, Currie and Co from 1888.[77] Margaret told the *Ladies Field* that it was probably best for the aspiring businesswoman to begin as a shorthand typist in an establishment where no prejudice existed against women. She could make herself useful and 'in time may become a power'. Such statements show just how far removed she was from the world of the typing pool.

Yet there was, close to hand, one example of an erstwhile typist who vied with Margaret as an inspirational entrepreneur. Aged nineteen, Beatrice Gordon Holmes earned a pound a week typing. She became Britain's first woman stockbroker, earning £5,000 annually. Her autobiography plays on the rags to riches theme, yet her father was a throat and ear specialist and the household of eight included a maid and nurse. Nevertheless, unlike Margaret, she did not enjoy parental support.

Beatrice Gordon Holmes's first post had lasted for less than two weeks. Sacked for incompetence, she acquired basic business skills working for eight years as a typist for a Danish firm exporting eggs. In 1904 she became a founding member of the committee of the Association of Women Clerks and Secretaries. Like Margaret (whom she knew) she found freedom and confidence through the WSPU and, in a memorable statement, explained that the women's suffrage movement 'gave us pride of sex, helped to stop the everlasting apology within us for being women, taught us to value ourselves and our abilities'.[78] She worked for eight years with William Thorold's financial issuing house.

The war gave her work opportunities as it did for many other women. The head of her firm and its male employees joined up, leaving her in charge. In 1921 she and the company secretary began their own company and in 1928 Holmes and Turner took over Thorold's. Within a year they had 140 employees. By 1936 they had not only survived while others collapsed but were ranked the leading Outside House and two years later helped to form the Association of Stock and Share Dealers. In that same year Gordon Holmes set up the National Federation of Business and Professional Women's Clubs of Great Britain and Northern Ireland which she chaired.

Margaret and Lady Astor MP petitioned International Rotary to allow them to develop a Women's Rotary in England but were turned down. Undeterred, Margaret then helped to establish and became the first president of the Provisional Club run along similar lines (with representatives from different trades and professions and fortnightly lunches). Newspapers made much of the fact that she was the first woman to attend the annual luncheon held by the British and Latin-American Chamber of Commerce in December 1926.[79] That July Margaret had become first (and to date) sole female president of the Institute of Directors. She had been a member of their Council since 1923.

She had been proposed by Sir John Cockburn KCMG, ex-premier of South Australia and a former member of the executive of the Men's League for Women's Suffrage and ex-president of the Men's International Alliance for Woman Suffrage.[80] He stressed that Margaret had proved herself in business affairs adding, more controversially, that women were more equable and businesslike than men, less speculative and so less prone to spectacular failures. She was unanimously accepted. The following year she was re-elected. The list of members suggests that she may well have been the only female member, though a few individuals supplied initials rather than first names. In this year only one member (with extensive interests in rubber plantations) was a director of more companies than Margaret. She remained president for a decade, longer than any previous president. When she died in 1958 the Institute had more than 600 women members.

Margaret helped to set up and was president of the Efficiency Club, a support group for increasing cooperation among business and professional women. It demonstrates, as had the women's suffrage movement, that networking is far from a modern concept. Members included women working in advertising, dentistry, health and business. Lectures covered topics such as coal dredging, staff control, gas manufacturing and how to conduct an interview. The club also sought to get women admitted to British Chambers of Commerce. Fittingly, Margaret was one of the first five women members of the London Chamber of Commerce. By 1927 they had 110 members.

Some of these successful women were now earning considerable sums: Edith Beezley an insurance director commanded £10,000 annually. Brewing headed the list of occupations for women directors (23) and there were 22 women directors of educational companies. Only two women were members of boards of colliery companies or coal distributing companies. The small number in heavy industry tended to be involved through their husbands, as in the case of Viscountess Pirrie, who became president of the board of the vast Belfast shipbuilding and engineering business Harland and Wolff when her husband died. This had been Lord Pirrie's wish. He had discussed business problems with her and credited her for many of the design features of the world's biggest steamship the White Star liner *Oceanic*. She became the first woman to receive the freedom of Belfast, its first woman magistrate, an honorary life member of the Belfast Chamber of Commerce and a member of the Shipwright's Company of London.[81]

Most women directors were connected with just one company. In only a couple of instances were women in the majority on the board. One was the Mumbles Railway and Pier Company in Swansea which was chaired by the Hon Mrs Olga Violet Daniell (who later also chaired Swansea and Mumbles Railways Ltd).[82] But although the number of women directors was increasing, there were still just a few hundred out of a total of 27,000 in the UK. An investigation as recently as 2011 showed women occupying a mere fourteen per cent of seats on British boards.[83]

Margaret was thus in an exceptional position. She was described as 'Britain's biggest Business Woman' and, somewhat less ambiguously, as 'the leading business woman of the western hemisphere'.[84] She claimed from the start that she found it exhilarating being a non-executive director. She relished 'the feeling of tackling interesting problems, concentrating on them, getting things done' though how she then used her experience and, particularly her money, with her own newspaper did not impress everybody.

Time and Tide brought together a number of Margaret's business interests. It was her answer to the belief in combining forces that had been so powerful for her father. It showed what women acting together could do and sealed her reputation as a company woman. From the start it included financial and investment information and advice and had a financial editor. In 1923 Margaret instigated a weekly series on 'Women and Their Money', designed to help employed women, war widows and others to gain information about matters such as taxation and trusts. She soon admitted, though, that some of the experts, such as stockbrokers and bankers, who penned these articles over the following two months were somewhat patronising.[85]

During the First World War, women began replacing men as commercial travellers and Margaret became the first woman president of the South West branch of the UK Commercial Travellers' Association. When she resigned her presidency at the end of 1917 she gave 500 guineas to its benevolent and orphans fund.[86] She was also active in the Women's Advertising Club of London and a great believer in the power of advertising. Addressing a lunch held by the National Magazine Company during the twentieth convention of the Associated Advertising Clubs of the World in 1924, she stressed that 'advertising was the breath of life' for traders.[87] In 1931 the Incorporated Society of British Advertisers held a luncheon in her honour. She saw advertising as creating 'courage, hope, and the atmosphere that could get them out of world crisis'.[88]

Although *Time and Tide* only carried a few advertisements each week in its early days, from its first number in 1920 there were weekly advertisements for the British Fire Insurance Company which Margaret chaired. The inveterate publicist also ensured that the paper displayed regular advertisements for John Lysaght's wire netting firm Orb as well as for Sanatogen, Genasprin (for colds and neuralgia) and Formamint (a sore throat tablet), products of Genatosan Ltd, which she also chaired. There were some whole page advertisements for the Salutaris Water Company based in Fulham. This produced drinks such as tonic water and ginger ale. Margaret sat on its board. This advertisement, published by the Time and Tide Publishing Company Ltd, was printed by the South Wales Printing and Publishing Company which Margaret also chaired.

Her business interests were further demonstrated in *Time and Tide's* reports of companies with which she was associated. Some of its readers must have been bemused by detailed accounts of, for example, the Gwaun-Cae-Gurwen Colliery Company. Four whole pages of the issue of 22 April 1921 were devoted to the AGMs of Welsh mining companies on whose boards Margaret sat. Meanwhile wives of eminent Welsh business colleagues were persuaded to help promote some of her other interests. Thus Lady Berry participated in a musical At Home to raise funds for the SPG.

Margaret was keen that business people were seen as influential in all walks of life. She was one of the first members and one of only three women to sit on the council of the British Institute of Philosophical Studies. Other members included eminent thinkers such as Bertrand Russell, Harold Laski and Julian Huxley. It sought, somewhat ambitiously, to apply the principles of philosophy to political, industrial and social life. She also supported the Industrial Institute which examined fundamental problems in industrial development and was one of two women on the council of the Bribery and Secret Commissions Prevention League, a powerful watchdog that influenced public opinion and publicised breaches of anti-corruption legislation in government and commerce.

Straddling the worlds of business and literature, Margaret felt that business people had an unjustifiably bad press. She sought to remedy this by pointing up attractions that were distinct from monetary gain. There was, she claimed, 'as much romance in shipping coal to South America as there was ten centuries ago in taking oil and spices on camel-back to Samarkand'.[89] She criticised writers such as Shaw who sneered at businessmen and efficiency.[90] Margaret approved of the directness of business people, contrasting their lack of affectation and posing with some of the Bloomsbury literary types. Efficiency was an important word in her vocabulary. Business people, she believed, 'get things done'.[91]

Yet, for all the praise she carefully heaped on the business world, Margaret admitted in the early 1930s that she was not really fitted for it.[92] She had embraced it as an escape from the world of the drawing room, seeing business as its antithesis and something she could share with her beloved father. By the time she inherited his business empire she was too far involved to retreat. Reflecting back, she claimed that, had she been a man, she would probably not have made business her chief occupation. Politics, the law or writing might have instead come first. From 1920 when she made writing by others her business, Margaret's interest, commitment and money were channelled into a venture that she shaped from the start and engrossed her as no other business had done. It resulted in Britain's most distinctive inter-war weekly.

1. Margaret's home Llanwern House (South Front)

2. Margaret's parents Sybil and David Thomas

3. Young Margaret reading

4. Sybil's miniature painting of Margaret with the *Lusitania* (left) and Usk Gaol (right) in the background

5. St Leonards School, 1901 Margaret is in the back row, fourth from the left. Gundreda is the first on the left in this row and Prid is fourth from the right. Miss Sandys wears a jacket and tie

6. Solomon J. Solomon's portrait of Margaret

7. Margaret driving Aunt Lottie in the Humber c1906

8. Margaret and Humphrey Mackworth's wedding in 1908

9. Pen Ithon Hall, Radnorshire

10. Lloyd George visits Llanwern in 1909.
Margaret sits in the front on the left

11. Newport WSPU Banner

12. Margaret (on left) Miss Lawton and Aunt Lottie
parading the streets of Newport in 1913 with a sandwich
board advertising a forthcoming suffrage meeting

Le Lusitania s'enfonce !

D'après The Sphere   L'At. d'Art Phot.
                                      216

13. A drawing in the *Sphere* depicts the scene
after the sinking of the *Lusitania*

14. Margaret the Welsh Commissioner (front, on right)
with WAAC clerks about to leave for France in June 1917,
on the steps of the Law Courts at Cardiff

15. Evelyn Salusbury (at the back)
with other Salusbury relatives.
John and Janet sit in front on right

16. The Young D.A.

17. The Young John Owen

18. Stonepitts, Kent

19. Helen Archdale (on left) at the *Time and Tide* office

Vol. 1.   No. 9. [REGISTERED AT THE G.P.O. AS A NEWSPAPER.]   **FRIDAY, JULY 9, 1920.**   WEEKLY. **Price 4d.** BY POST 4½d.

CONTENTS.

All MSS. and correspondence should be addressed to the Editor, at 88, Fleet Street, London, E.C.4.

It is frequently stated that the NEW ELECTORATE needs educating in political matters, since Power without knowledge is a very dangerous thing. A number of Political Associations are showing themselves most ready to do all that lies within their power to save the country from such a danger by educating the new voters as quickly as possible —some have even been formed for this purpose alone. To say that the love of imparting knowledge for its own sake is the one guiding motive of these various associations would be, however, to do them more than justice—rather would they agree with the gentleman who desired education not in order to arrive at facts, but in order that he might learn how to twist his facts correctly to his favourite pattern. That knowledge should accompany power is a general proposition which no one will be inclined to deny. We would all, an' we could, " Make knowledge circle with the winds." When, however,

we come to consider the actual case of the new voter, it is doubtful whether a profound knowledge of political theory is what he most urgently needs just now. The truth of the matter is that there is a good deal of superficial nonsense talked about the ignorance of the average elector. No doubt he or she is ignorant, but it is well to remember that if profound and accurate knowledge of every political question is to be the test there is scarcely a man or woman in the country fit to cast a vote. A regrettable state of affairs undoubtedly, and one to be remedied as soon as may be, but do not let us delude ourselves into supposing that a course of six political lectures is going to set the whole matter right. It is a profounder evil than that; at best we must leave Mr. Fisher to deal with it, and hope for some results in a few generations or so; at worst, we can but wait for a radical alteration in the whole human mind and character, a matter of a few million years more or less.

Meanwhile, and theories apart, we do most of us know without much teaching what we actually want. It did not take a course of instruction in the THEORY OF POLITICS to teach the Agricultural Labourer of 1884 that what he needed was shorter hours and better wages, though it took him a generation or more to learn the very A.B.C. of his newly-acquired power in such a way as to begin to achieve that result. It does not take a profound study of Professor Dicey's " Study of the Law of the Constitution " to tell the newly-enfranchised woman worker of to-day that what she wants is equal pay and opportunity with her male colleagues. Her difficulty, like that of the agricultural labourer, lies not in finding out her needs, but in discovering how to satisfy them. Power without knowledge may be a dangerous thing, but let no one delude himself in supposing that the mere possession of a vote necessarily gives power. The vote may, in fact, be compared to an instrument which only the skilled user can make effective.

Leaders of the old political parties have recently admitted that the Press and Publicity department of Labour is now much superior to that possessed by the older organisations : the new scheme of TRADE UNION CO-ORDINATION will probably lead them to concede at the same time that the general structure of Labour as a political force would be difficult to excel. The striking scheme outlined by the co-ordination committee of the specially-convened Trade Union Congress last December provides for a General Council of the Trades Unions, elected by Congress each year, in place of the Parliamentary Committee of the Congress, and for the establishment of administrative departments, with the

20. A front page of *Time and Tide* in the first year

21. Margaret shakes hands with Alice Paul in 1925 at London's American Women's Club. Emmeline Pethick-Lawrence stands on her right and Elizabeth Robins on her left

22. Margaret with Winifred Holtby and George Bernard Shaw at the Malvern Festival 1935

23. Churt Halewell, Surrey
in the 1940s

24. The Drawing Room,
Churt Halewell

25. Margaret in the garden at Churt Halewell

26. Theodora Bosanquet in 1930

27. Sidney George Strube plays on the popular Pear's soap
advertisements to indicate the difficulty of securing a seat
for women in the House of Lords

28. Alice Burton's painting of Viscountess Rhondda,
now in the House of Lords

29. The elderly Margaret on the steps of the *Time and Tide* office

30. The Llanwern Memorial to the Thomas/Rhondda family

CHAPTER TEN

Time and Tide: The First Two Decades

In May 1920 *Time and Tide* began life in Fleet Street, that London landmark poised between the City and the West End and synonymous with the production of national newspapers. By taking premises at 88 Fleet Street, it boldly asserted its position at the centre of the newspaper business. 'The Street of Adventure' was also an insistently masculine world as the writings of the war correspondent Philip Gibbs demonstrate.[1] *Time and Tide* was a newcomer with attitude, a weekly publication that occupied the second floor of a tall, narrow building overlooking Wren's St Bride's Church. It may have had sight of the past but it was committed to a fresh way of looking at the present and future.

For its origins we need to look back to Margaret's youth. Her first venture into journalism was called *Spring Tide*. She produced this short-lived magazine when she was fifteen. A voracious reader with 'the literary digestion of a shark', she also wrote stories.[2] One featured green-

eyed Beryl who got shipwrecked, though the survivor of
the *Lusitania* disaster could not remember her fate: 'I
think I just got tired of her in mid-ocean'.[3] But what really
interested Margaret, even as a teenager, was running a
magazine. The future businesswoman charged sixpence
per issue for *Spring Tide* though contributors (mostly Haig
cousins) got free copies. Advertisements were a penny a
line.

This magazine, renamed *The Shooting Star* was no
handwritten experiment. It was printed and sought a
professional touch. Its editor Margaret issued somewhat
bossy injunctions. A bout of measles saw the May, June,
July and August numbers of 1899 rolled into one issue.
Margaret complained that:

I have received very few letters this time. I don't
know why: I wish people would write oftener; it is
so easy to write a letter (it need not be a very long
one) and the ones who say they have no time for
writing anything else could easily find time to send
at least a short letter. Also, I wish that more
outsiders (I mean people who are not contributors,
but just happen to read the magazine) would write
and say what they think about everything; they
would not be prejudiced. As I have started saying
what I want people to do, I may as well add that it
would be very nice if everyone sent in their MS. of
their own free will, without my having to go touting
round for it; it is pure laziness on their part when
they do not, and it would save a lot of trouble if they
did.[4]

In the 1870s, the young Amy Levy (later a poet and novelist) had resorted to fining contributors who failed to produce articles in time for her *Poplar Club Journal*. 'Citizen Amy' estimated that targeting pocket money would do the trick.[5] One of Margaret's contributors, who wisely refrained from giving his or her name, was told that hiding behind the name 'A. Greenhorn' was 'almost superfluous; who but a greenhorn could have written such a foolish and vacillating article?'[6] And although the editor hoped to increase circulation from a guaranteed dozen, this does not seem to have happened. A bumper issue for Christmas (for which non-contributors would have to pay a shilling) promising pictures, poems, stories and articles – only inserted if they 'are specially good' – never materialised since orders for twenty copies were not received before October.

Margaret's departure to school in Scotland also helped to end the venture, perhaps to the relief of her long-suffering cousins. Yet there was some residual loyalty. *Time and Tide's* weekly competition (which inherited its predecessor's forthright tone when remarking on the quality of entries) was supported by Haig relatives. For example, Hester Haig won a couple of prizes in *Time and Tide's* competitions in 1923, cousins sent in letters and later David Haig-Thomas wrote occasional features.

Unlike Margaret's youthful efforts, *Time and Tide* enjoyed longevity. The title implied waiting for no man and the importance of time and the times as well as changing the tide of public opinion. Margaret and her directors were aware of their unique position and the need to seize the moment. Several had worked in women's war service and seen at first hand the potential for women's leadership and responsibility. Timing was of the essence.

The first decade of *Time and Tide* coincided with a series of firsts for British women. At last many had a vote in national elections. The paper constantly drew attention to other advances such as women MPs, jurors and magistrates, long overdue recognition such as granting women degrees at Oxford University, and the inadequacies of legislation such as the Sex Disqualification (Removal) Act.

The first editorial commented that '[w]omen have newly come into the larger world'. It drew attention to the need for an independent press.[7] To extend the aquatic analogy, the paper signalled a watershed in the lives of those newly enfranchised. Those behind *Time and Tide* wanted to ensure that post-war society would secure lasting equal opportunities that would be extended to all and move beyond enfranchisement. They would monitor carefully 'the ebb and flow of the tide'.[8]

The title drew on Margaret's earlier venture *Spring Tide*. Its masthead included a drawing of the tidal River Thames below the Houses of Parliament, Big Ben signifying its interest in Westminster politics. Margaret had a riverine residence on Chelsea's Embankment. When Robins (who had good reason to be wary of rivers)[9] first visited Chelsea Court she felt very conscious of the Thames below.

There was a familial connection too. The title genuflected to the ancient Haig motto:

> Tyde what may what ere betide
> Haig shall be Haig of Bemersyde.[10]

Margaret also liked the fact that the name suggested 'big, natural forces, strength and power' yet 'commits us to nothing'. And it was easy to request at a bookstall.[11]

Establishing *Time and Tide* was a bold venture for Margaret even though she was already a newspaper director and, two months before starting it, had been involved in the court case against the *Western Mail*. Like many journalists of her generation, she had no formal training. Yet she had written regular press features in her suffrage days and gained experience in the latter part of the war as a board member of the feminist newspaper *Common Cause*.[12] Letters from Margaret to Robins in 1919 suggest increasing frustration with its editorial policy (it had originally been an organ of the NUWSS) and annoyance that a short story Margaret had solicited from Robins had been 'cut down tremendously without asking my permission', making nonsense of it.[13]

Having her own review had captured Margaret's imagination from an early age though she was not the first Welsh woman to establish and edit an independent magazine for women.[14] Sarah Jane Rees (Cranogwen) had been editing *Y Frythones* (*The Female Cambro-Briton*) at the time that Margaret was born, but there is no indication that she was familiar with this Welsh-language tradition. Margaret had been impressed by the launching of the *New Statesman* in 1913 and the prospect that it might 'mould the opinion' not of the masses but of what she called 'the keystone people', the vanguard who in turn would influence and guide the many.[15]

At an At Home organised by *Time and Tide* in November 1927 Margaret developed further her vision for the weekly review (rather than daily newspaper) as *the* opinion-paper and a vital means of raising the level of debate about what modern culture and democracy might mean for women and men. She prophesied a future 'when no educated household will be found without a Weekly Review on its table'.[16] These were the papers charged with 'the highest office' in journalism. It was a lofty aim but Margaret was keen to give an upbeat message to the readers gathered at the Hyde Park Hotel, primarily loyal subscribers of at least five years' standing. She was used to thinking 'big'.

Margaret's venture was, however, distinctive from well-established reviews such as the *Spectator* and the *Economist*. It also differed from the newer literary reviews though some of its contributors wrote for 'Little Magazines' such as the monthly *London Mercury* which began in 1919.[17] T.S. Eliot started the literary quarterly *The Criterion* in 1922. He too sought a select, enlightened audience.[18] But his review (with backing from Lady Rothermere) was more elitist than *Time and Tide* and although not the organ of a political party, it was predictable in its opposition to the progressive views espoused by the influential *Nation*, another weighty weekly. *Time and Tide* eschewed a party political perspective but its initial mission was avowedly political in the sense that society was viewed through the lens of equal rights feminism.

By linking her fortunes with the weekly review and focusing on the intelligentsia – attempting to secure as readers 'only educated, intelligent and mentally-alive persons'[19] – Margaret was aiming at an audience distinct from that envisaged by the promoters of magazines such as *Woman* (edited in the 1890s by Arnold Bennett) or the

Edwardian *Ladies' Home Paper* which, as the name suggests, focused on the feminine and domestic. It was also markedly different from the short-lived Harmsworth experiment the *Daily Mirror* in its initial guise as a newspaper 'by gentlewomen for gentlewomen'. The growth of an educated public, and especially professional women, suggested that a market existed for something different. Despite fashion advertisements from stores such as Debenham & Freebody (the paper needed commercial advertising and advertisers recognised a useful market),[20] its content was never frivolous. Ellen Wilkinson put it well: '*Time and Tide* tells us what women think and not what they wear'.[21]

The *Freewoman* offered a different kind of model. It was a weekly review attempting to redefine feminism. Started by the ex-suffragette Dora Marsden in 1911, it too envisaged a select readership, declaring that 'we are not proposing writing for women whose highest journalistic needs are realised by [charging] a penny'.[22] But its concentration on women's sexuality, anti-statism and a controversial individualist approach to feminism narrowed its appeal.[23] Its fate was sealed with a sales ban by W.H. Smith. It was succeeded by the short-lived *New Freewoman* in July 1913 dedicated to modernist literature with a feminist slant. The feminism disappeared when it turned into the literary review the *Egoist* the following year. This and its immediate predecessor were financed by a woman, Harriet Shaw Weaver. But Margaret's paper proudly appointed an all-woman board and, unlike most feminist papers, *Time and Tide* was keen to appeal not just to the converted but also to win over the uncommitted.[24] As Michelle Tusan has argued, '[i]n many ways the paper represented the best hope for a widely circulating, influential women's advocacy publication'.[25]

Margaret's plans began to take shape in the autumn of 1918 when the end of the war was imminent. She told Chalmers Watson that she had always wanted to found a paper that would realise her dream 'to change customs and to influence ideas'.[26] Octavia Wilberforce later recalled how there were endless talks 'and many plans laid' as Margaret developed her ideas for producing 'an independent, unbiased periodical which would be directed by a picked body of distinguished women who had gained some recognition in the public eye, and would give confidence especially to women readers'.[27] Margaret was 'full of ideas about the position and potential power of women in the world' which she discussed with Wilberforce and Robins.[28]

Before establishing her paper Margaret sought to expose the unfair treatment of women by the mainstream press. She argued that their attitude towards women's work was 'conducive to their return to dependent and even sweated conditions'.[29] A deputation of women, including Robins, protested to national newspapers owners about their coverage – or lack of it – in their papers. In February 1920 Margaret asked Robins to join the board of directors for her new paper. She accepted. Margaret was keen for Robins to interest her friends and introduce future contributors, as she knew many influential people in the arts both in Britain and in her native America where her sister-in-law was president of the American Women's Trade Union League.

Margaret wanted the board to include Mrs Berry, wife of the *Sunday Times* proprietor, but her husband thought the venture a big risk. He also advised Margaret against going ahead. But early the following year the Welsh industrialist connection was cemented by Lady Llewellyn becoming a *Time and Tide* director. She brought with her a welcome investment of £1,000.

The team of women met on 4 March 1920. Margaret described it as 'A New Combine', a term that conjures up her father's creation: the mighty Cambrian Combine in south Wales. Chalmers Watson was chairman from the outset until her death in 1936, when Margaret took over. Dame Helen Gwynne-Vaughan, head of the Department of Botany at Birkbeck College and about to make her name as a mycologist, was a board member. Margaret had worked with both women during the war. The other original members were Christine Maguire of the Association of Women Clerks and Secretaries (who resigned after six months), Mrs H.B. Irving (the actress Dorothea Baird) and Robins. So far as was known, noted Helen Archdale proudly, 'there is no other similar review of general events in the whole world entirely controlled, edited and staffed by women'.[30]

The prospectus was agreed at the first meeting. A Time and Tide Publishing Company Limited was established with £20,000 capital. But although nominally owned by the company it was leased to Margaret, and from the start she controlled ninety per cent of the company's shares and subsidised the paper.[31]

The prospectus promised to deal with 'all interesting topics of the day in Politics, Industry and Art'. It would throw new light 'on subjects of great moment' in the lives of people at home and internationally.[32] Its fairness and willingness to print readers' letters and tolerate different viewpoints was widely appreciated. From 1928 each issue declared 'Independent Non-Party' under its title. It sought to represent the views of 'an intelligent onlooker rather than those of a partisan'.

According to her diary, Robins persuaded the board to delay the publication of the first issue until the end of April. In late March after another meeting she wrote: 'I am appalled at the childishness of the preparations.'[33] When copyright was not secured for a serial to which Robins was contributing, she admitted privately that she was filled with 'foreboding for the paper'.[34] Robins was unfamiliar with running a business but was in her late fifties and used to sitting on committees. She had been a famous actor-manager and was a very experienced literary figure. The board may have represented powerful women in the public post war world but most of its first members were not prominent in the arts or journalism. Robins told Margaret 'a *little* of what I feel' and does not seem to have offended her. A few days later she dined with Margaret, Prid and Helen and urged a delay of a further fortnight which was accepted.

A spate of board meetings followed accompanied by formal dinners. Robins noted that there was an 'exhausting discussion' at the board dinner[35] two days after the first number appeared. The review of the week (the paper's opening feature) on 14 May discussed the Liberal Party, thus conveying the intention to take current affairs seriously. Priding itself on breaking the mould with a non-party political, independent, pro-women (yet not exclusively female) and wide-ranging focus, it advertised itself as 'The Journal that gives a new aspect of current affairs'.[36] The Leader carefully stated that although this was a paper run by women at a time of unprecedented opportunities for them, it was concerned 'neither specially with men nor specially with women, but with human beings'. The paper retained the convention of having all letters addressed to 'Sir'.

Margaret and her team were conscious of the dangers of *Time and Tide* being dismissed as a women's magazine, and anyway sought to affect and change public opinion and ways of behaving across society. Their review uniquely bridged a gap between those papers which ignored the woman's point of view (they were only too happy to name and shame) and those which paid no attention to men's perspectives.[37] It carefully steered a course addressing the hopes and the disappointments of women already committed to equal rights at the same time as winning and maintaining readers without such an agenda.

It cost 4d (fifteen shillings for an annual subscription). This was increased to sixpence from 1928 to bring it into line with other weekly reviews in size and price. The first twenty-four page issue included messages of goodwill from eminent figures including Lloyd George (Margaret Lloyd George added her support the following week), Lady Baden-Powell and Dame Clara Butt.

The first issue asked in an editorial 'When will the authorities seriously turn their attention to Housing?' The focus of the Leader was the paper itself. Margaret had sent an earlier draft of the former to Robins for approval. Although she would soon gain a formidable reputation, her deference to the older writer was marked at this stage. She admired Robins' writing style, had read a number of her novels and praised her newspaper articles and short stories. She asked Robins to 'please deal firmly' with the Leader, admitting that she was not satisfied and that it seemed muddled and to lack a clear line. She had already worked on it for a week. Anticipating possible criticism, Margaret also wondered whether she had stressed women too much at the end.[38]

Mrs H.A.L. Fisher contributed an article on the Bastardy Bill, and there was a feature on the letters of Henry James. The concern with international affairs was signalled by the first of a series called 'The World Over'. A Fanny Burney novel was discussed by the essayist and poet Alice Meynell, and there was a 'playlet' by Margaret Macnamara (active in the Women's Institute). Both had been requested by Robins. Rebecca West (who would write extensively for the paper) did a theatre review and Christopher St John (Christabel Marshall) covered music. The journalist and poet Gerald Gould, who had been active in support of women's suffrage was the one named male contributor. There were articles too on gardening and lawn tennis. Book reviews, financial advice and 'In the Tideway', with items of special interest to women, followed over the next few weeks. Eleanor Farjeon wrote a pseudonymous weekly column of verse on the week's events.

Margaret, Wilberforce and Robins had discussed having a children's page but it never materialised (only in 1933 did a children's Christmas section begin as part of an annual Christmas issue).[39] There was, however, from week two, a ten-part serial by Robins and J. Woolley-Paddock (Wilberforce) of a children's story 'Prudence and Peter'. Published later in book form, this adventure story-cum-recipe book focused on twins, a boy and a girl. Both enjoyed cooking. This was an early example of non-sexist children's literature.

Robins was the first subject of 'Personalities and Powers' which became a feature on famous figures at home and abroad. Her friend Lady Florence Bell wrote her profile, though the original plan had been for Robins to get her old sparring-partner George Bernard Shaw to write about Lady Bonham Carter. Robins did not persuade Shaw but the *Newsagent and Booksellers Review* nevertheless described the list of contributors to the first issue as 'remarkable'. The *Bystander* declared it 'formidably armed'.[40]

In a wartime radio broadcast about *Time and Tide* Margaret recalled some of the difficulties facing her paper in its early days. She explained that a paper was

> like a live thing, it has to grow. And it has also to get accepted. That is part of its growth. Until it has grown it cannot be accepted – but until it has been accepted it cannot really grow.[41]

It needed 'the best thinkers of the day'. Whether she had quite such lofty ambitions back in 1920 is a moot point but she also pointed out that it took her 'extra long' to get accepted because she was a woman and that 'quite a few people' took the line that it could not be a really good weekly because it was edited by a woman.

What had the paper achieved by 1930 and had Robins' harsh judgement been premature? Some early features did not last. The personal sketches were popular but their quality uneven. Some were sycophantic while others were not very original or stimulating, so the feature was dropped. More worrying was the editorial position. Although Helen Archdale is always mentioned as the first editor (even in *This Was My World*) the original choice was Vera Laughton.[42] Described by Margaret as 'young and keen', she edited the paper for the first few issues. She and Helen did not see eye to eye and just one month after the paper began, she announced her resignation. She was persuaded to 'bide for a while'[43] but by late July Margaret was describing Laughton's contribution as 'dreadful'. She was sacked.[44] In effect Helen became editor from August though Laughton officially left on 1 October.

Circulation rose steadily in the first three years (especially with subscribers) though there were some worrying moments. It dipped during the first summer. Eoff estimates nevertheless that the paper was selling between 12-15,000 copies in the early 1920s, a very respectable figure for a new enterprise.[45] The *New Statesman*, for example, was attracting about 10,000 readers and only the oldest weekly review, the *Spectator* enjoyed a net circulation in excess of 16,000 copies.

The reviews advertised each others' issues. *Time and Tide* applauded the principles of 'independent oases where, in a world over-ridden by press trusts, the truth may be heard and spoken'.[46] When *Outlook* failed in mid-1928, *Time and Tide* was quick to point out where it had gone wrong: seeking to increase circulation it had fatally tried to become both a review and an illustrated fashion paper.[47] It recognised that independents were 'living precariously on the verge of bankruptcy because though the public – their public – wants them, reads them, and is influenced by them, it will not buy them'.[48]

The number of copies sold did not, of course, reflect

the numbers read. *Time and Tide* was available in doctors' waiting rooms and clubs. In 1928 it was estimated that if they counted all who read it, then circulation would probably be between about 60,000-70,000 weekly. From the outset Women Citizens' Associations, schools, women's colleges, women police officers, branches of the National Council of Women, MPs, peers, ex-officers in the women's services and many other groups were circularised.

Judged by its finances, *Time and Tide* was not a viable proposition. Without Margaret's money it would not have survived long. The expenditure needed for such a venture had been seriously underestimated. Margaret's business adviser in Cardiff had envisaged losses of about £3,500 for the first few years, based on his successful experience with other papers.[49] But he had not worked with a 'High Class Woman's Weekly' before. The losses quickly doubled, exacerbated by increases in paper and printing costs. Margaret told Robins in July 1920 that 'I simply can't afford such a heavy loss' but 'I'd almost rather do anything than stop just when we are finding our feet'.[50]

Margaret's immediate solution was to make a more definite appeal to women, to 'be more frankly feminist than we have yet been'. Although she had her doubts whether Gwynne-Vaughan would agree, her instinct at this point was for a paper that would be a rallying point for women.[51]

But her health was suffering from overwork and on her doctor's orders she had to take things more easily for a while. Between June and the end of September she cut down her contributions and input and removed herself to a Sussex cottage by the sea. This also allowed her some space to work on her father's biography and provided Helen with the opportunity to take more responsibility. Finances, though, did not improve. In 1921 the certified loss amounted to £9,970 9sh 8d. Margaret's private accounts show her making a loan of £5,500 to the paper in the same year. She would continue to subsidise it heavily.

Although the board broadly shared a commitment to further the rights of women, there remained much to divide them. Margaret's politics would shift dramatically over time but she was consistent in that whatever her perspective, she was not afraid of airing her views. She told Robins that her mother regretted 'what I think she regards as my Bolshevist tendencies'. This probably says more about Sybil and her daughter's perception of her mother than it reveals about Margaret but her outlook in the early 1920s was relatively progressive.[52]

Mrs Irving felt that the paper should be more supportive of Labour but Gwynne-Vaughan and Chalmers Watson (with the casting vote as chairman) were Conservatives. They worried that *Time and Tide* was perceived as pro-Labour and expressed particular concern about the paper's view of the British government's handling of the situation in Ireland. Margaret (who was delighted when the Irish Free State was created) was troubled by the rifts within the board and wrote to Robins begging her to attend meetings in order to help keep it intact. She offered to hold meetings at times conducive to the Sussex-based Robins, even suggesting that Wilberforce could be her substitute if she could not attend in person. In mid-January 1921 Margaret stressed that Robins' attendance would 'make a good deal of difference (perhaps all the difference)' as '[w]e have reached a crisis and shall have to make important decisions'.[53] She had already made some concessions and admitted that she was prepared to split the board rather than compromise further.

The board became more united due to an external threat. In June 1921 J.C. Squire of the *London Mercury* wanted to take over the *Woman's Leader* (formerly *Common Cause*) but with *Time and Tide* amalgamated with it.[54] The implication was that Philippa Strachey would edit the new paper with feminism the sole focus. NUSEC would have a big say in determining policy. All of this was inimical to Margaret's thinking even though it would cut costs and boost circulation. She especially resented the implicit threat that if they did not merge they would be destroyed. She held her ground. Her board supported her.

There were, though, personality clashes. Although Margaret wrote enthusiastically to Robins about Rebecca West's contributions to the paper in the autumn of 1921, Robins disliked West, largely because of her relationship with H.G. Wells. To Robins' chagrin West now joined the *Time and Tide* board. Robins felt that she was wasting her time at the meetings and was also critical of the choice of news items for the 'Tideway' column. She resigned in 1923 despite Margaret's entreaties.[55] Cicely Hamilton joined the board but was concerned how members might respond to her pacifism. Hamilton's memoirs stress comradeship and lively (rather than bitter) divisions, admitting, in print at least, to being 'in happy disagreement' with some members.[56]

In 1926, however, *Time and Tide's* editorial problems

came to a head. An action plan was drawn up. The 'Terms of Arrangement' of 24 June 1926 opened with the stark statement: '*Time and Tide* to be tried for one year more from October 1926'. The plan was to try to reduce costs by rationing money spent on contributors to an average of £42 per week spread over three months (Margaret was responsible for £12 of this and Helen for the rest). The size of the paper was to be slightly reduced in the summer and more economical publicity was proposed with increased book reviews (at the expense of film, finance and sport). In the first full year of publication there were about two hundred book reviews. By the end of the decade the annual number was closer to seven hundred.[57]

The new scheme included an extra page on politics and 'a stronger flavour of feminism'. It proposed a literary editor who would earn four guineas a week. This salary would come out of Helen's average weekly earnings of £30 as editor. She was responsible for office routine, but other questions were to be settled in consultation between the editor and owner. No criticism of staff was to be made by Margaret except in the presence of the editor or through her. The right to veto a writer or article that she particularly objected to remained Margaret's prerogative.

Helen had been resisting such changes for a year. She told Winifred Cullis that she accepted the terms in June only on 'the clear understanding that my experience had led me to think they were not workable'. In mid-July Margaret wrote her a formal letter giving her three months' notice. As we shall see, this would have a far-reaching effect on Margaret's personal and professional life.

Margaret had been working on the paper three days a

week but now took over as editor. Helen gave Cullis a terse account of events: the rescue plan had proved 'in practice, unworkable, and I was blamed and sacked'. In a draft letter that is unlikely to have been sent, Margaret admitted that she should have taken this step eighteen months earlier. She had earlier outlined what she saw as the ideal editor: 'someone who shares all our feminist views, is a practical politician (again in a feminist sense) and cares more for feminism than any other ideal and has knowledge of life's affairs'. That, she had told Robins in 1920, was as important as having someone who could write.[58] She now assumed the mantle herself.

From 1928 when women over twenty-one were enfranchised, there was a shift in the focus of *Time and Tide*. Its 'Literary Turn' from 1928 to 1935 saw it draw more widely on a younger generation of modern women novelists.[59] Modern literary critics have evaluated its contribution to a cultural politics of modernism.[60] Apart from the chairman and vice-chairman (Margaret), none of the original board members remained by 1928. The composition now reflected more directly the need to address different aspects of the paper. For example, Marion Jean Lyon the advertising manager for *Punch* was now a director. The paper's position as '[a]n independent, non-party weekly review' was spelt out more clearly. Margaret personally represented the continuity between past and present, but one of her strengths was her willingness to recognise new talent.

E.M. Delafield (Elizabeth Dashwood, born De La Pasture – hence the pen name) joined the board in 1927. She had links with Margaret's past, having grown up in Llandogo, Monmouthshire and worked for the Ministry of

National Service. She had been writing for *Time and Tide* since 1922 but it was her serial (starting in December 1929) which really caught the popular imagination. *Time and Tide* had wisely commissioned Delafield to write 'The Diary of a Provincial Lady'. The first instalment arrived with a note saying 'I don't think much of this. If you agree, put it into the WPB.'[61] Fortunately Margaret did not concur. This had been preceded by two excerpts from what proved to be a seminal book: Virginia Woolf's *A Room of One's Own*.[62]

In May 1929 *Time and Tide* signalled its change of direction by leaving Fleet Street and, as the paper proclaimed, moved to 'a house of its own'.[63] It took over two handsome four-storeyed early Victorian houses at 32 and 34 Bloomsbury Street. The former was the paper's engine house. This was an appropriate location for a paper at the cutting edge of developments in literature and increasingly popular with publishers. A proud Margaret told Robins, 'We sit in the pocket of the British Museum'.[64] Her first-floor office had a window that looked onto its dome. Just inside the door was a large table and a former employee remembers how she would lay out for Margaret each day 'every single paper you ever heard of, from *Reynold's Newspaper* to the *News of the World*'.

Time and Tide increased in size to thirty-two pages. This and a canny advertising campaign with more focus on professional women as consumers produced dividends. In 1931 it reported that the last two years had produced more revenue from this source than from subscriptions and sales combined.[65] It appeared – particularly through its expansion of book reviews – to be taking on the Sunday newspapers that were encroaching on territory previously occupied by weeklies. Jane Dowson and Catherine Clay have commented on the quality of its reviews of poetry and fiction as well as the original contributions of figures such as Stella Benson, Ezra Pound, T.S. Eliot, Sylvia Townsend Warner, Katherine Mansfield and many others.[66] The paper secured the English rights to D.H. Lawrence's last poems before they appeared in book form. In March 1933 the first literary editor Robert Ellis Roberts was appointed. Just before this, anxious that standards should not slip, Margaret sought Winifred Holtby's opinion: was the paper showing signs of carelessness anywhere?[67]

Much of the responsibility for the new direction of the paper emanated from Holtby, who became the board's youngest member when she joined it in 1926. Looking back on the paper after it reached its twenty-first birthday, Margaret recalled how Holtby used to come to the office two or three days a week.

In 1923 Holtby had spent hours working on an article on 'The Crime of Chivalry'. It was turned down by the paper whereas, by her own admission, the 'badly written, badly typed, absurd'[68] piece she dashed off for the *Daily Mail* was accepted. The following year Margaret was impressed by an article on education submitted by the twenty-five year old. She rapidly commissioned three Leaders and arranged for Holtby to 'write whenever I think that anything looks interesting in the education world' (she was at this point teaching English).[69] From then until her premature death in the mid-1930s, she wrote Leaders, editorial notes, home news, political features and much more, including book and theatre reviews. They were signed, unsigned and under the pseudonyms of Corbin H. Wood and GREC. Margaret's memorial essay to her in 1935 suggested that the paper owed its continued existence to her input.[70]

Part of the plan to increase the paper's visibility involved securing a contribution from George Bernard Shaw. Holtby told her friend Jean McWilliam in 1926 that *Time and Tide* was 'an adventurous little paper. We're going to aim high, and try to put salt on the tails of all the best men and women writers – from Shaw downwards.'[71] He had made occasional small contributions since October 1920 but in February 1929, following George V's serious illness, he penned a sketch called 'The King and His Doctors' for a bumper issue. Four times the usual number of copies was printed but the paper still sold out within an hour. Looking back in 1941 Margaret declared that this issue put *Time and Tide* on the map.[72] Shaw was generous with his articles, even occasionally offering unsolicited pieces. When one appeared an hour before going to press in June 1940 Margaret promptly dropped the week's Diary section to include it.[73]

Yet there was some slippage in Margaret's account. She wrote that she did not know Shaw at all well in the late twenties and that it took a great effort to write to him. She explained that she would not have dreamt of or dared to make such a request were it not an exceptional occasion. Yet she had chaired a SPG meeting at which he had spoken in 1925 and he chaired her 'Leisured Woman' debate.[74] Charlotte and Bernard Shaw met Margaret socially at home and in Europe, and he and Margaret had already written a number of long, affectionate and amusing letters to each other.[75] Nevertheless, Shaw's articles really did boost sales and visibility.

The year 1929 also saw the inauguration of 'Notes on the Way', a weekly feature by the Irish writer and *Observer* drama critic St John Ervine, whose provocative opinions ensured lively responses from the letters column. It was opened up in 1932 to guest contributors starting with Rebecca West and including E.M. Forster, J.B. Priestley, Malcolm Muggeridge (who also wrote book Leaders pre-war) and many others. It was described in 1938 by the poet and expert on India, Edward Thompson (father of the historian E.P. Thompson) as 'the greatest opportunity in current journalism', since nowhere else was there freedom from editorial censorship.[76]

The greater visibility of men's contributions – Margaret now sought a better balance between male and female writers – along with more emphasis on culture, led the feminist writer Dale Spender to suggest in 1984 that *Time and Tide* gradually lost its way.[77] Eoff conceded in 1991 that the paper's 'pure feminism' gradually become diluted but stressed that it 'did not abandon the causes that feminists of different persuasions held dear', remaining true to its initial commitment to equality and social justice while adapting to changing circumstances.[78] Clay has also emphasised that women remained firmly at the heart of *Time and Tide* as it consolidated its position as a leading review.[79]

Clay suggested (in 2007) that Holtby cleverly reversed Margaret's new editorial policy, broadening the paper's appeal by advertising rather than concealing its feminist standpoint. Analysing the text of an unattributed article of February 1928, she argued that this reflected Holtby's assertion that 'the feminist issue is an issue of general interest'.[80] But although Margaret would in time shift the paper in very different directions, in this month she was leading the final push for equal suffrage (as the next chapter shows) and anyway, as she later explained, she and Holtby had made a 'joint decision' to 'change the slant of the paper a bit, give it a broader base'.[81] Margaret's imprint on the article can be seen, as well as Holtby's, for example, in its reference to the Berry Brothers, and the views expressed in the article are not inconsistent with Margaret's thinking.

Margaret and Holtby can be seen as colluding here rather than one subverting the other's policy. While Margaret was only too aware of the financial imperative to broaden the base of her paper, her reasoning did not at this stage diverge from Holtby's. More recently Clay has shown Margaret, Holtby and other directors working together to enable the paper's survival by appearing to be more mainstream yet at the same time subverting this and actually furthering, sometimes by stealth, a commitment to feminism.[82]

In November 1930 Margaret told the American feminist Doris Stevens that she was 'clearing out' of 'feminist things altogether so far as I can. But five additional words provide an important qualification: 'except in so far as they come into T&T'. The purpose was to devote her energies to the paper. Margaret explained that: 'If I can make the paper go in a big way (as is beginning to seem possible) I shall have done as big a thing *for feminism* [my emphasis] as I am capable of '.[83]

From May 1931 the review *Foreign Affairs,* whose editor was Norman Angell, was incorporated into *Time and Tide* as a monthly supplement on world politics. This arrangement, with Angell editing the supplement, lasted for almost a decade. It reflected Margaret's increasing concern about international issues generally (rather than international feminism), especially threats to world peace. When accused in July 1936 of jumping to the crack of the prime minister's whip, Margaret's response was: 'What we stand and have consistently stood for is a policy of peace'. She added that at present Baldwin was the most likely to lead them to peace.[84]

From February 1935 the paper sported a bold, tomato-red cover. There were bumper double issues with substantial literary supplements. By 1937 there were 1,300 book reviews by 97 reviewers.[85] Delafield edited a volume of thirty-six short stories from the paper in 1932 showcasing many of the best-known women and men writers of the day. With a foreword by John Galsworthy, this was seen as useful propaganda for garnering further subscriptions.[86] But the paper's supplements, whether on economic issues or Spain and the Spanish Civil War addressed interests beyond the strong literary focus. One on universities included articles by Harold Laski (on academic freedom), G.D.H. Cole and a Chinese scholar addressing the future of the university.

In July 1934 there was an eleven-page supplement on Wales.[87] Contributors included Jack Jones. His literary and economic prospects had already been helped by writing *Time and Tide* articles on Welsh miners' tastes in literature. There was a provocative piece by the London Welshman Glyn Roberts called 'I Show You Wales'. He was so determined not to reproduce the usual stereotypes of Welsh history, politics and greatness that its lampooning produced indignant responses from Labour's Edith Picton-Turbervill and 'Wales Minor', who unequivocally asserted that Welsh people were modern and passionate realists. The latter was an entrant to a competition asking for a response to Roberts' article. Such an exercise suggests that Margaret may have deliberately commissioned his article in order to provoke a reaction. What is remarkable, given the paper's history, is that no correspondents took issue against Roberts' representation of a Wales that seemed to be peopled almost entirely by Welsh men.

Muriel Mellown has noted that *Time and Tide* was one of the first periodicals in the UK to publish the work of black writers such as the African-American poet Countee Cullen.[88] Walter Lippmann of the *Herald Tribune* began a monthly supplement on 'The American View' in 1931. Seven years later, in the heated atmosphere of 1938, the paper produced a sixteen-page supplement on the persecution of the Jews, including a letter from Sigmund Freud to Margaret.[89]

Time and Tide summarised its current concerns in October 1931 as the General Election approached. Its five demands demonstrate just how far the paper had moved from its early days when women MPs were such a novelty and the paper was urging an expansion in their numbers. Its priority now was a world conference to control currency and tariffs (the National Government had come off the Gold Standard the previous month). It also urged a reduction in armaments. Its ultimate objective was world cooperation with a settlement of political and economic problems as the first step. Equality of opportunities (legal, economic, political and educational) for all 'regardless of class, race or sex' was now fourth in its list of five objectives.[90]

Michelle Tusan places *Time and Tide* within the tradition of the advocacy press, arguing that Margaret's insistence on equal rights feminism alienated the paper from advocates of newer feminist critiques and meant that once the vote was achieved much of its impetus was inevitably lost.[91] However, even in its first number it claimed that it was not specifically concerned with women or men but with 'human beings', and after 1928 that commitment to humanity took it on to a new stage. Martin Pugh suggests that its feminist agenda did not outlive the 1920s.[92] An advertisement for the paper in 1943 lists twenty-eight recent contributors. Two-thirds of those *chosen* for this list were men.[93] Margaret also claimed that two-thirds to three-quarters of its political writers had always been men, though most wrote anonymously.[94]

But although content and focus suggest a shift in comparison to what had come before in the paper, when set alongside other contemporary weeklies and dailies, it is evident that the paper and editor were inevitably deeply influenced by its feminist origins. And despite a shift in the gender of its contributors (which would be even more marked in later years), in the 1930s it remained largely staffed by women.[95] Part of Margaret's success was that her review addressed women and men (rather than men and women) as equals and at the centre of politics, literature and art.

Margaret understood that in a period when the vote was no longer a rallying cry and when new forms of media were developing, the paper had to appeal more widely and become more mainstream in order to survive. In November 1923 *Time and Tide* signalled that it was far from averse to new forms of media, declaring that a radio set in people's homes would help to 'break the back of newspapers which consistently try to dope the public'. It was scornful of the way that the *Daily Mail* had managed to reduce a historic speech by the South African statesman Jan Smuts to just half a column.[96]

Yet the growing popularity of radio – the BBC had ten million listeners by 1927 – challenged the reviews, as did the popular press. With newspapers increasingly concentrated in the hands of a few, it was vital for the reviews to demonstrate their distinctiveness and collective strengths. The 'them' and 'us' by 1931 was not so much gendered as positing the important weekly reviews versus the press giants. Even here, though, the situation was complicated, for Margaret's old business associates the Berry Brothers were part of the newspaper oligarchy. They had purchased Rothermere's vast Amalgamated Press which sold over twenty million copies of papers weekly by the 1930s. St John Ervine told Brittain that Margaret would not print his critique of a paper owned by her friend Lord Camrose (formerly William Berry).[97] Having known the brothers 'since they enjoyed ices' Margaret had difficulty seeing them as press barons.[98]

She stressed in an editorial (of May 1931) that the weekly reviews and one or two newspapers espoused different standards from other papers: 'Their object is to tell the truth as far as they know it, to arouse criticism, to challenge opinion'. They took it for granted that readers wanted 'to face reality', see both sides of a question and show critical appreciation. *Time and Tide* joined the other leading London reviews (the *Week-End Review*, *Spectator* and *New Statesman*) in protesting against the *Daily*

Express when it attacked the League of Nations. These reviews presented themselves as the upholders of the 'decency of the press'.[99] *Time and Tide* was also at pains to stress that its independence did not mean that it lacked views. It took what it saw as principled positions free from party influence and bias. Margaret believed that the press should not be treated with kid gloves: 'I am all for attacks on the Press' she wrote. 'It is one of the organs of democracy and as such is a perfectly legitimate target.'[100]

Her survival strategy worked but at a huge cost. By 1930 Margaret's expenditure exceeded income by £11,914 and in 1931 this reached a staggering £15,837. Yet even those close to her seem to have been unaware of the burden she was carrying. Her Cardiff accountant had been warning her that so severe was her personal loss that urgent steps needed to be taken. In 1931 she reached an understanding with him that the next three years were to be 'devoted to economy of expenditure on the one hand and the curtailment of Time and Tide loss on the other'. The plan involved personal retrenchment and reorganising the paper so that its loss would be reduced to 'nil, or practically nil' by 1934. In December 1933 Margaret told Holtby that it looked as though the paper had covered its expenses. She added 'Imagine!!! At last!!!'[101]

'Imagine' was unfortunately the right term. Although Margaret had increased advertisements from clothing stores in particular and managed to cut her deficit to £6,950 over the financial year of 1933-4, a letter from her accountant in May 1934 shows that the paper made a loss of £7,170 over the same period. Despite the plan, over the three years Margaret's expenditure had exceeded her income by £17,332. She was taken to task and told that the encroachment into her capital had 'assumed most serious proportions and must be arrested'. And she was warned that she could not 'without the gravest financial danger, continue to provide, out of your own resources only, the losses still being incurred by *Time and Tide*'.

Yet, despite ongoing losses, the paper survived. Margaret put on a brave face to the outside world. But some of her team found it difficult. Dorea Stanhope, an ex-debutante and a niece of the Earl of Chesterfield, had been engaged as a favour to a friend in 1933. Margaret admitted to an American woman colleague that she had done this 'very reluctantly' as 'that type of young woman is usually hopeless'.[102] Stanhope had, however, proved to be 'quite brilliant' and within two years was an assistant general manager, writing, for example, all the motoring notes (she drove an open-top green car and wore leather gauntlets). She adored Margaret yet found it a 'terribly disheartening job'. Echoing some of Robins' earlier misgivings, she complained in a letter to Margaret that:

> The Board takes no interest whatever in production costs, advertising schemes, circulation drives or anything connected with the business side. There is the feeling that any effort in connection with SAVING expenses is treated with mild amusement by the editorial. It is too much weight to carry by myself. My ambition is to make money not watch it pouring away.

Margaret underlined all of this. Stanhope summed up a dilemma familiar to those devoted to the creative arts who venture into commerce by adding: 'You want a perfect production; I want a sound commercial proposition. We can't have both.' Yet the irony here was that she was not corresponding with an ivory towers idealist but with one of the country's most prominent businesswomen who, Stanhope protested, didn't 'really care whether you make money or not but I *do*'. The tragedy was that Margaret did care and needed to care, though the survival of her paper mattered even more to her.

In order to make that money Stanhope began an investment service with Patrick Thompson who ran the paper's investment and finance section. Concerned that the paper was no longer being put first, Margaret confronted Thompson who, deeply offended, immediately left *Time and Tide*. Her correspondence shows her to have been distressed by the loss of a personal friend.[103] But *Time and Tide* came first.

How was 'the Ed' (as Margaret was known in the office) perceived by other employees in these years? The loyal Holtby found her consistently supportive and multi-talented. In the boardroom, Holtby wrote, Margaret's 'vitality and resource can light up a committee as though a lamp had been brought into the room'.[104] Her editorial direction was 'a constant stimulus' and her 'alert, critical, receptive mind' was open to new ideas. It was, in short, well worth earning her praise. Brittain, however, had reservations about Margaret as editor. She believed that she exploited Holtby, overworking a woman who was seriously ill. Brittain (who had been writing a lot for the paper) and Margaret fell out in the autumn of 1931 when Holtby suffered her first major collapse.

The fact that Holtby had a fatal illness – Bright's Disease (renal sclerosis) – does not seem to have been fully understood by Margaret, or perhaps she did not wish to contemplate such a dreadful thought. Brittain told Holtby in no uncertain terms that Mrs Holtby and Margaret seemed to treat her illness as though it were the kind of thing she could shake off if she wished.[105] Margaret's reliance on the talented young writer increased after she suffered her own health problems at Llanwern in March 1931. An injection for a cold resulted in an anaphylactic shock and Margaret's pulse stopped for the best part of an hour. She and the doctor feared that she was dying. She recovered but remained in poor health for some time. A year later she was editing the paper from a London nursing home and a specialist was concerned about her nervous system. She began to spend more time recuperating abroad, which in turn increased the pressure on the competent, ever-willing and, as it turned out, terminally ill, Holtby.[106]

Writing from the American University Women's Centre in Paris in August 1931, Margaret told Holtby that the younger woman was overworking and living on her 'capital of nervous energy and vitality'. She should slow down. But she added that Holtby was one of *Time and Tide's* 'main props' and asked her to do four things for her. Her requests ranged widely. She even wrote from Mallorca asking Holtby to take Norman Angell to lunch 'and flatter him up a bit' since he was 'susceptible to the personal touch'.[107]

Assistant editors such as Margaret West (formerly on the administrative staff of the London School of Economics, then from 1933 manager of the Hogarth Press) and the novelist Phoebe Fenwick Gaye also wrote Leaders. But there was great reliance on Holtby. Abroad for five months from the autumn of 1933 Margaret told her (from Greece) that the paper seemed to be going from strength to strength and that perhaps it had needed to be taken out of the editor's hands for a bit and placed in the charge of herself and Gaye, whom she described as 'two bits of creative youth'.[108] Gaye had, however, only recently taken over as assistant editor, so the pressure on the conscientious and experienced Holtby was immense. She threw herself into her work. It 'filled her thoughts and dominated her sky', wrote Brittain.[109]

Letters from readers, some famous, some not, showed appreciation of Margaret as an editor. The Oxford-based publisher Basil Blackwell wrote in to stress that his family and friends regarded *Time and Tide* as the best-edited weekly.[110] Rebecca West emphasised the constantly high standards expected of contributors: 'The best one could write for *Time and Tide* has never been good enough for the paper; or for the editor and owner, who has made it what it is, after the image of her own integrity'.[111] This was after she had written for the paper for twenty-one years. Delafield also valued Margaret's support: 'I shall maintain to my dying day, that you have a special Editorial Instinct that warns you when a contributor is rather flagging, so that you *immediately* write and revive them.'[112] Shaw called Margaret '[a]n editor in a thousand'.[113]

Inevitably there were office politics. Theodora Bosanquet became literary editor in 1934. A former employee in the editorial department has recalled that she was not popular there. They called her (though not to her face) 'Old Bosey'. Yet Margaret's staff, including her personal secretary Edna Burns, remained with the paper for many years. In the mid-1950s the office manager had worked there for thirty years, the chief proof reader for twenty-six and the book advertisement manager for nineteen. One assistant editor in later years has recalled 'a comfortable bookish jumble in lovely big rooms'. And even though Dorea Stanhope saw the paper as 'an awfully big worry' and admitted that she often felt inclined to 'kick myself for being a fool and not trying for a job on a nice quiet little "daily"!', there was a sense of breaking new ground combined with a solidarity that she knew would not be easy to find elsewhere.

There was, claimed the long-term sub-editor of later years a '*Time and Tide* type'. Margaret believed that their aim was 'to work for the creation and maintenance of something we know to be more important than we are'.[114] She described the editor of a weekly review as merely 'one of a group of equals', a 'good literary-kitchen chef' whose readers were equally capable but too busy to do their own catering.[115] This flattered readers but contributors who dined with Margaret at The Ivy (far from its kitchens) or employees could be in awe of her despite her wish that they were not.

Although Margaret's determination was well known, she and her paper had a reputation for tolerance and fairness. She compared the weekly review to a salon 'in which writers and thinkers are free to think aloud, and to argue in full view of the other guests'.[116] Concerned to reflect current debates, she gave space to opinions that did not match her own, such as Wyndham Lewis's six articles on German National Socialism and Hitlerism in 1931. Such controversial views ensured a hefty postbag of indignant letters. Margaret also stoutly defended the paper's independence of party politics, stressing in 1936 that what it consistently stood for was 'a policy of peace'.[117]

Its progressive stance in the arts was confirmed in 1933 when her printers (De La Rue) refused to handle the sexually explicit Sean O'Casey story 'I Wanna Woman'. Margaret argued that this was not pornography but 'beautiful and moving literature' that was also 'profoundly moral'.[118] She saw the episode as an illustration that the laws on obscenity were outdated. When eminent figures such as Yeats, Desmond McCarthy, Harold Laski and Naomi Mitchison responded with indignant letters attacking censorship, Margaret was reminded that *Time and Tide* was serving a useful function. Sylvia Townsend Warner commented that 'literature is more pernicious than liquor' in English law.[119] The next year Sean O'Casey was a guest editor for 'Notes on the Way'.

Virginia Woolf appreciated Margaret's judgement and influence and admitted that she was concerned about the reception of *Three Guineas*, but 'if someone like yourself feels that there is some scattered truth flying about in it then perhaps it won't be, as I so often feel writing to be, a mere bonfire of words'.[120] This was not just flattery. Woolf confided in her diary that Margaret's description of being 'profoundly excited and moved' by what she had read was '[a] good omen' as it showed that it would be discussed and might make 'more splash among the inkpots than I had thought'.[121]

Woolf's fiction did not greatly appeal to Margaret personally. She admitted to Holtby that 'I can't get what you people see in her – she never makes me catch my breath as Plato does or Shaw'.[122] But, good editor that she was, Margaret recognised the need for her paper to reflect modern taste and originality. She was, though, impressed by *Three Guineas* and told Woolf that she had doubled her donation to the Fawcett Library (which became the Women's Library) as a result of reading it. She felt that it could not have been written two years earlier and that it had 'come at exactly the right moment'.[123] She read it through from cover to cover twice. *Time and Tide* pronounced it a 'revolutionary bomb of a book',[124] the 'finest example of what England can produce in literature'.

William Berry may have had doubts about Margaret's ambitions in 1920 but by the 1940s when the paper's circulation had reached 40,000 copies he readily admitted in a book on British newspapers and their controllers that she 'has made the paper respected for the vigour and breadth of its views'.[125] The *Manchester Guardian* applauded its progressive stance and argued that Margaret had made it 'one of the freshest and most distinguished of the "weeklies"'.[126] More recently Mellown called *Time and Tide* 'one of the great literary and political reviews in the history of British periodical literature'. Its story was 'largely the story of Margaret Haig, Viscountess Rhondda'.[127]

But it was never easy operating in a world where some still had reservations about female editors. One of the reasons why Margaret had been impressed by *Three Guineas* was because Woolf's analysis chimed with her own sense of being an outsider. The book discussed the creation of a Society of Outsiders for the daughters of educated men. This would help to prevent war and ensure freedom but through perspectives and means that differed from those of the privileged Insiders with their access to networks of influence. Margaret signed a letter to Woolf as 'a very grateful Outsider'[128]. Woolf replied by return of post, saying that this proved the book's argument: 'as a woman shut out from so many of the newspaper sanctuaries you have to fight to enter; and thus don't think, as those within naturally do, how to shut others out'.[129]

Margaret elaborated on this, telling Woolf in June 1938 that:

No woman who tried to run a Weekly Review could remain unaware of how much she was an Outsider. It's not only that to run that kind of paper one *must* know something of the inside gossip that is going on & almost all the official gossip centres are closed to women (It's like trying to make something without the tools). It is also that the presumption amongst the average general public is that that kind of paper can't be run by women & all advertisers belong to the general public. Also the general public is convinced that what women have to say on public affairs cannot have any real weight, so that if one uses many women's names one's circulation & – again – one's advertising is affected.[130]

She even admitted that 'I go through the paper every week taking out women's names & references to matters especially concerning women because if I left them in it would soon kill the paper'. Yet Margaret added this important rider: 'But it's maddening'.[131]

Margaret's survival strategy and growing concern about the world crisis and primacy of maintaining peace necessarily altered the focus of her thinking and her paper. She sensed 'a fresh outbreak of the women's movement' in the mid-1930s, but, as she explained in correspondence with Robins, the urgent and crucial question was now 'whether Europe explodes before we have got a real grip'. If that happened then she was convinced that it would spell 'the end of feminism *and* Western civilisation for generations to come'.[132]

In October 1937 Monica Whately of the SPG, which Margaret had founded and chaired, wrote to the paper expressing her disappointment that this foremost British weekly had failed to give even the briefest mention of the work of the Eighteenth Assembly of the League of Nations on the status of women.[133] The key international women's organisations representing forty million women had sent representatives to Geneva. The omission was remarkable given the fact that in 1930 Margaret had been instrumental in setting up an equal rights body dedicated to putting pressure on the League of Nations.[134]

Margaret's response was revealing. She agreed that such events were important and deserved notice. Yet, using an excuse which she would not have tolerated from others in the early days of the paper when feminist priorities were clear, she argued that a weekly review rather than a daily paper could not report everything it would wish to cover. Whateley had drawn attention to the fact that the paper's 'Events of the Week' had included the arrival of Mussolini in Munich. Margaret was on surer ground here and unapologetic: 'In the present state of world tension it was – in Europe – the most momentous event of the week in which it took place'.

Whateley might have questioned Margaret's choice of events but History would vindicate the editor. As for how to go about achieving gender equality, Margaret now subscribed to integration rather than autonomy, urging that rather than acting as a class apart, women should use the powers they had won to work together with men in the world, side by side, for the common good.

It is worth noticing too that whereas such a claim would have generated a stream of indignant letters in the early 1920s, only two letters appeared in response to Margaret's statement (though it is possible that more mail on the subject was received but not printed). Readers continued to pen spirited responses to many other issues, and the number of letters trebled a year later during the Munich crisis. It was not only that Margaret and *Time and Tide's* priorities had shifted. So too had readers' reactions in a world that had changed dramatically from the days of 1920. Yet Margaret persisted in working for equal legal rights for women through her protracted struggle for their right to sit in the House of Lords.[135]

Remarkably, given all the demands that she faced and the paper's constantly precarious financial state, *Time and Tide* adapted and survived. It fought against the tide in its first decade, relentlessly seeking fairness for women. It became a leading and advanced literary space for women and men. Then, reflecting the deepening international crisis, it broadened its focus accordingly. In 1934 Margaret participated (via a radio broadcast) in the vast annual New York conference hosted by the *Herald Tribune* on 'current problems'. She was one of three speakers in the session on the changing status of women but her message was that '[t]he one thing that matters more than all the rest is international relations'.[136] In the same year a Leader in *Time and Tide* with the subtitle 'Equality First' was actually about German ambitions and their determination to assert them with or without the consent of the rest of Europe.[137] Somehow, though, *Time and Tide* retained a reputation for independence, gender equality and innovation. By the early 1940s in the midst of world war this review (shorn of its distinctive red cover) was selling more copies than ever.

CHAPTER ELEVEN

A Woman-Centred World

Time and Tide created a social as well as a working world. Margaret was at its heart. There were board dinners, for which directors dressed up. Contributors lunched with her at The Ivy, and later at Le Caprice, where she held court at the corner table. Luncheons were held too at the smart, subterranean Boulestin in the Strand. Holtby recalled attending a contributors' lunch there in 1926 with Margaret, Brittain, Margaret West, Rose Macaulay, Sylvia Townsend Warner, Lillian Baylis and Delafield.[1]

Grand new London hotels such as the Dorchester provided suitable venues for receptions and parties. Delafield's 'Provincial Lady' gaily describes 'hundreds of millions' invading the Hyde Park Hotel for a party for *Time and Tide* readers.[2] The fifth birthday dinner was held here. Speakers included the Lord Chief Justice, a Chinese Minister and Lord Riddell. A sketch of an overseas reception held by the paper at the Bloomsbury office in 1937 reveals many of the leading thinkers and artistic figures of the day amongst the guests (and, incidentally, suggests the presence of more men than women).

Although Margaret had some sympathy for the temperance movement,[3] unlike her father she did not abstain from liquor, and she hosted many cocktail parties. Naomi Mitchinson recalled attending her 'gorgeous parties' and 'driving back from one of them, cautiously since there had been a fair consumption of alcohol, but feeling splendid, as though the whole world was opening up and everything would work out, not only for myself, but for women in general'.[4]

In the 1920s Margaret and Helen lived at Chelsea Court during the week. Comments on Margaret's lifestyle could be barbed. She was unusual in that she brought together worlds that did not always mix easily: Bohemian Chelsea met big business. The intelligentsia could be wary of trade and titles. This urbane titled lady defied easy categorisation. She worked hard for a living and her salon looked to the future rather than the past. One London journalist declared that in Lady Rhondda's drawing room were seen 'more women writers to the square inch than anywhere else'.[5]

Early in her career Margaret's business style was praised in a Wesleyan magazine: 'She dresses quietly but well and her working-room is far more sparsely furnished, far less luxurious, than is the chief's sanctum in any five offices out of six in the city'.[6] Yet increasingly there were hints of a possibly fatal excess. Critics, though, seem to have been willing enough to share in the lifestyle. Malcolm Muggeridge recalled her homes as 'so luxurious that they were almost uncomfortable – the cream too rich to eat, the peaches too soft and large to bite into, the beds too downy to fall asleep in'.[7]

Margaret did enjoy rich foods such as cream from the Welsh countryside. She liked seafood too and *marron glacé*. At her first lunch at Chelsea Court Holtby was dismayed to be presented with lobster.[8] It was the one dish she could not stomach. Yet so anxious was she to get articles in *Time and Tide* that she ate the food and even had seconds. She then fled to Sloane Square tube station where she promptly threw up. But Holtby, who spent more time at Chelsea Court than many, thought Margaret's style elegant rather than extravagant or vulgar. She told her friend Jean McWilliam that the flat was full of 'lovely things – old brass, with great bunches of lilac, and Chinese lacquer cabinets – but unostentatious'.[9]

Literary parody of Lady Rhondda's world played on the helplessness of the ruling class when it came to household matters. Delafield's fictional Viscountess is called Anne (Margaret's theatre reviews used the Anne Doubleday pseudonym) and is first encountered in the south of France, where she is swimming and diving. She takes the diarist to her sumptuous Ashley Gardens flat in London. The housekeeper is out, and when her visitor asks for a glass of water Anne does not even know where to locate this, so offers what has been left in the jug after dinner.[10]

Margaret's friend Ellen Wilkinson, who became the first female Labour Member of Parliament, was also the first woman MP to publish a novel. Set at the time of the General Strike and subsequent Lock-Out, *Clash* appeared in 1929. Semi-autobiographical, it drew upon what Wilkinson had observed when travelling the country addressing meetings for the Trades Union Congress in 1926. The novel addressed the potential clash between her heroine's very different worlds: the impoverished coalfield communities of south Yorkshire and London's Bloomsbury. As a working-class woman representing Middlesbrough East and also inhabiting Westminster, Wilkinson understood well the divisions of geography, class and gender.

Margaret appears in the novel thinly disguised as Mary Maud Meadowes. Fat, fifty and rather tall, with curly hair and a sweet smile, 'her handsome face had hardly a line'.[11] She has been to prison as a suffragette, derives half her income from coal mines and has a home in Gordon Square (*Time and Tide* moved to Bloomsbury in the year that the novel appeared). The paper is not mentioned, though Mary Maud is described as 'a wealthy bachelor woman, an intimate of an exclusive Bloomsbury circle who bestowed fame on themselves by writing reviews of each other's books'.[12] Wilkinson's need to represent Mary Maud as part of the idle rich (as opposed to the industrious poor) means that she becomes little more than emblematic. She seeks satisfaction through philanthropy via the arts then helps the young labour organiser and book's heroine Joan Craig by providing funds for mining families during the political flashpoint of 1926. In the process Wilkinson makes her character a generous but impressionable woman, whose heart is in the right place, but who does not really think critically.

Wilkinson suggests the trappings of wealth. Mary Maud wears a mink coat and has a car that seats eight easily. In the early twenties Margaret enjoyed luxury cars. Mary Maud has a 'French dragon called Suzanne'.[13] For forty-six years Margaret's mother Sybil employed a French lady's maid named Suzanne. Wilkinson gives Mary Maud a conscience but exposes her more directly to the source of her wealth than was the case with Margaret at the time of the General Strike.

In 1930 when Holtby wanted Margaret to meet a group of Labour women, Margaret asked if she could come to their party then added 'or would they smell capitalist coal-owners and cheap labour for the mines?'[14] Margaret was well aware of how she and her ilk were perceived. The lessening of her involvement in heavy industry and increasing authority as an editor post-1926 reduced some contradictions and tensions.

It is not known how Margaret responded to her portrayal in Wilkinson's novel. What we can say is that the friendship between the two women flourished for some years after this, suggesting that Margaret had not been unduly offended. She would probably have warmed to some of the descriptions of Mary Maud who, as Maroula Joannou observes, voiced many of the novel's feminist perspectives.[15] Mary Maud was, we are told, 'one of those rare persons able to give silent sympathy and ask no questions'.[16] Brittain echoed this, calling Margaret 'a perfect listener'.[17] Wilkinson also tells us that Mary Maud 'had a genius for friendships'.[18] Many would have recognised Margaret here. Those who knew her have stressed how loyal she was to friends. Her generosity was legendary. She lent her Chelsea flat to Octavia Wilberforce for a summer and frequently gave or lent money to friends and relatives.

Sybil's diaries show Margaret visiting her mother every month. Friends came too. In January 1935 the *Time and Tide* director Winifred Cullis[19] was at Llanwern and returned at Easter. Other Llanwern house guests included

Cicely Hamilton and Dorea Stanhope. Occasional *Time and Tide* board meetings were held there. In May 1933 Holtby told her mother that she was off to Llanwern: 'It is a board weekend – Rather strenuous. We have a lot of work to do.'[20]

Newspapers announced 'Brainy Women on Holiday' when Cullis and Margaret went on holiday together to Norway in the summer of 1924.[21] They had spent Easter walking in the Pyrenees with Helen. It was Cullis who presented Margaret with her portrait in March 1933 at a dinner in her honour held at London's Rembrandt Hotel. A group of Margaret's friends had commissioned Alice Burton (who also visited Llanwern) to do this painting 'as a token of their regard and of their admiration for her splendid and disinterested work in so many different directions'.[22]

Margaret headed committees for many causes and individuals. In the early 1920s, for example, she chaired a function for the principal lady inspector of factories, Dame Adelaide Anderson, who was retiring after twenty-seven years. Three hundred guests attended and Margaret presented her with a cheque for £1,000. She sat on committees to help Sadler's Wells become an 'Old Vic' of north London and for a lunch to celebrate the jubilee of women in medicine, and was president of numerous societies and clubs, ranging from the Women Sanitary Inspectors and Health Visitors' Association to the St Bride Operatic Society for City Workers.

There were many appeals for financial support. As an heiress, Margaret was perceived to be immensely rich even when much of that wealth had diminished. When the writer and editor Glyn Jones wanted to launch an English-language periodical in Wales to be called *The Broad Arrow*, he sought wealthy sponsors such as Richard Hughes and the American Randolph Hearst and admitted that he 'tried to milk the Rhondda woman'. But 'there was nothing doing'.[23] He had told Margaret that Wales had no magazine like the *Spectator* or *Time and Tide*. Yet she saw her paper as encompassing Wales and his disparaging comments about *Welsh Outlook* (a 'poor creature' that would publish 'anything with good grammar')[24] would hardly have endeared him to her since she had written for it. But even had Margaret been well-disposed towards this venture there remained a gulf between how others saw her and her finances and her actual financial position, as well as between the money she spent on the paper and on maintaining her lifestyle and the amount available.

Margaret featured frequently in the Society columns of newspapers and magazines. Holidays abroad and travel in luxury liners were duly noted in the press. In February 1921 she was reported to be flying home from Paris in a Handley Page aeroplane after staying in Monte Carlo and Menton.[25] A racehorse called Lady Rhondda ran at Lincoln and Catterick racecourses in the same year.[26] The strong pound compared with continental currencies encouraged European travel for those who could afford it. Paul Fussell has observed that wars have resulted in travel by sea being remarkably good value for their victors. In the early twenties half of the world's ships were British.[27]

In 1927, Margaret told Robins that she had been 'lounging and bathing and then up at Geneva for ten days or so'.[28] Over the next five years she returned a number of times to Agay on the French Riviera. She enjoyed sunbathing and swimming off the nearby rocks at L'Estérel (the 'Calanque' of La Baumette). She could relax abroad and she shed more than inhibitions. One letter to Holtby tells how she has taken to bathing off the rocks each evening in the nude: 'very pleasant tho' perhaps a bit indecent (in the morning of course I bathe all correct in gown) but the Coast this year is going naked very fast & somehow modesty seems to be leaving one quite a lot'.[29] Recent illness had resulted in her losing two stone and boosting her confidence.

She also enjoyed skiing. She wrote to Holtby from the Grand Hotel in Stockholm in April 1930, telling her that she had more or less decided to come out there every year for a fortnight of skiing.[30] A year later she was skiing in Bergen. Margaret's travels took her far and wide. In the spring of 1927 she accompanied her mother on a trip to India and Australia. Returning from Bombay, their ship the *Nadera* stopped at Gibraltar where Emmeline Pankhurst came on board. That Christmas Margaret spent in South Africa with her old friend Prid, and she made the same trip two years later. In 1932 there was a voyage to Australia. It all bolstered the image of the hedonistic Viscountess.

Yet Margaret played *and* worked hard. Virginia Woolf noted after dining with Margaret in 1933 that 'she lives for *Time and Tide*'.[31] And work and play were often connected. The Geneva part of the 1927 trip, for example, was linked to her advocacy of equal rights for women and the League of Nations. She also attended European conferences of the International Federation of University Women and gave talks at the American Women's Club in Paris. She worked on articles, books and feminist causes on her travels and found some of this quite demanding as she had to type her own material and was not, as her correspondence with Brittain demonstrates, a proficient typist.

The following year the American Doris Stevens was one of a number of women who stayed with Margaret at Agay's Villa des Roches Rouges. The *Manchester Guardian* suggested that Lady Rhondda had initiated a new vogue in getting business colleagues and friends to holiday together (*Time and Tide* board directors Cullis, Cicely Hamilton and Holtby were amongst those who accompanied Margaret on this trip to the Riviera).[32] Yet with the deteriorating economic situation at home, it was hardly surprising that it was the luxurious 'lounging' of Margaret's lifestyle rather than fostering a sense of corporate identity that many emphasised.

Brittain noted in her diary in October 1932 that St John Ervine and the writer and journalist Leonora Eyles believed Margaret no longer edited *Time and Tide* properly 'because she goes off to the South of France or Norway or Madeira, doesn't even come back when there's a political crisis, leaves the paper "marking time" just when it should be giving a lead to its readers' and indulged in long 'schoolgirl holidays' annually.[33] Brittain thought Margaret should 'be the real editor instead of the rich leisured woman who runs a paper as a hobby', and told Ervine that 'someone who hadn't had to work their way up from the bottom but came in on top without any tradition of work probably didn't really know what work was'.

Margaret would have been deeply hurt had she read these remarks. Quite apart from her business training, work for *Time and Tide* was of paramount importance to her. And it was she who had publicly defined and denounced the very term leisured woman.[34] Moreover, the previous September, when Brittain and her husband George Catlin were holidaying at Saint Raphael, Margaret had entertained them at Agay's Hotel De La Baumette where she and her party were staying.[35] Brittain's comments were, though, made for private consumption and need to be understood in the light of her recent quarrel with Margaret about overworking Holtby.[36] Such remarks also ignore the fact that Margaret had been ill that year. Brittain knew that Margaret had been in a nursing home in early March and had undergone a rest cure in Alsace (with Cicely Hamilton). In June she had noticed that Margaret 'looked pale and was obviously thinner; prolonged illness has changed her a good deal'.[37]

In addition to Margaret's social life in London and on the continent, she and Helen spent time in the English countryside. Weekends (from Friday afternoons if possible until Monday mornings) were spent in Kent, not very far from where Margaret had lived as a tiny child. For four years she rented the picturesque timber-framed Chart Cottage in Watery Lane, Seal Chart. Larger than its name suggests, it comprises three small adjoining cottages – the oldest part dating from the mid-fourteenth century – with a garden laid out in 1911 by the renowned landscape designer and writer Gertrude Jekyll.[38] In 1925 the owner refused to renew the lease but luckily a wonderful alternative was available just a few hundred yards away: Stonepitts.

The oldest part of this handsome mansion dates back to the fifteenth century.[39] Built of red brick and stone with stone and oak mullioned windows and a massive old oak entrance door and hall, it underwent considerable alterations at the start of the eighteenth century. Margaret and Helen found it an atmospheric, spacious building with its low oak beams and panelled walls. There were seven bedrooms. It lies in a commanding position with views across the valley, the pretty village of Seal close by and Sevenoaks just a few miles away. Kemsing railway station was handy, and there was the luxury of a detached garage.

Until recently the surrounding land had been used for growing hops, and there remained four oast houses that Margaret and Helen briefly considered converting into guest houses. The gardens were enclosed within high, red-brick walls and included a tennis court, rose gardens, rock gardens and a kitchen garden, as well as a gigantic lime tree. After what Helen called the 'pleasant enjoyment' of the Chart Cottage garden, they decided to commission the elderly Jekyll to redesign the gardens in collaboration with G.L. Kennedy.[40] It was Helen who dealt with these arrangements. She supplied Jekyll (who never visited herself) with detailed information, sketches and photographs – one letter runs to fifteen pages – and it paid off. The garden was developed on different levels with attractive terrace walls and abundant blue and pink flowers and they made a number of alterations to outbuildings.

The two women entertained a stream of visitors in their cream-and-brown drawing room. Helen's daughter Betty recalled Rebecca West and Delafield there and how 'everyone wrote, read and talked as they liked. The result was some marvellous conversation and really gracious living'.[41]

Holtby spent her first weekend at Stonepitts in October

1925. She slept in an L-shaped bedroom with a huge peat fire. At first she found Margaret in her count(r)y mode 'stiffer and more gauche than I have ever seen her' but she slowly melted and became a charming hostess.[42] St John Ervine and his wife were also house guests. He 'talked till dinner, at dinner, and after, except when we listened to wireless [sic] on earphones from a crystal set' (this was a dramatisation of Hardy's *Tess of the D'Urbervilles*). On Sunday afternoon there was a tea party – 'everyone in tweeds, woollen jumpers and pearls' – enlivened by Margaret's neighbour, the famous stage actor Henry Ainley (who would help young Alec Archdale to become an actor). Holtby told Brittain: 'I never knew a woman draw people to talk so much'.[43]

Margaret's personal papers include an agreement drawn up between her and Helen about Stonepitts. It is a rough draft, in pencil, undated and may not have become a formal legal document. It can be seen as the product of two wary and cautious individuals with differing demands on their lives and finances who had already suffered in their personal relationships and wanted to ensure that they enjoyed some security in the future. It is also evidence of the fissures in their relationship.

There were three clauses. The first stipulated that neither should be forced to leave 'unless we separate by mutual consent'. Secondly, 'If we ever should separate (or give up Stonepitts)' Margaret would pay back to Helen any money she had spent improving the home, garden or field. It was also stated that nothing in the agreement should prevent either from leaving 'if we chose to do so taking with us all our own furniture and ceasing to be liable for the upkeep of the place', providing reasonable notice was given. Should Margaret's affairs make it necessary, she should not be prevented from selling the house.

It did not turn out well. Margaret's relationship with Helen resulted in considerable unhappiness. *Time and Tide* was a catalyst. Clearly Helen felt that she had been made a scapegoat and resented the way she had been dismissed as editor. But there were fundamental personal difficulties too. Helen had become a committed Christian Scientist, a faith Margaret did not share, and her sons were never close to Margaret. Over time the women's views on international feminism and politics more generally also diverged.

As early as 10 November 1926, Margaret illustrated how they were drawing apart. She did this in a heartrending letter that provides a glimpse of the vulnerable, sensitive woman unfamiliar to those who did not know her well. She was under considerable strain at this time, facing financial pressure as an industrialist and newspaper proprietor and working extremely hard on several fronts. She had recently taken over as *Tide and Tide's* editor, was the newly-appointed president of the Institute of Directors and active at home and abroad in equal rights. On top of all this, she was continuing to keep hidden her father's secret life and her relationship with his former mistress was about to turn sour.

Margaret's three-page handwritten letter survives in family papers. She never chose to destroy it. It begins by posing a fundamental question: 'I wonder if you too are realising how near the end we are getting?' She then reflected on their time together:

I don't know whether you ever ask yourself why we live together; if you ever go back to the time when we first came together. We began it for the only reason that can make living together possible, because we were very fond of one another.

She admitted that

I have paid heavily for believing that your love, that seemed a real thing, was real – when in fact it can only have been a passing surface schwärm [passion], much as I've seen you several times. I gave all I had to give and for years now I have been struggling not to see, what you were making only abundantly clear, that the only value I had in your eyes was as some one who could give the children treats. And even though that was my one role of value you shut me always and persistently outside the family circle and taught the children to do the same – one was allowed as a hanger-on – because one was useful – but no more. When I tried to tell you I cared, you sneered. I imagine you despised me because I was too ready to give – but you see you had been ready enough at first and I couldn't believe for a long while that you had changed.

Margaret's lifelong fear and fate was cupboard love: that people only really wanted to know her because she was wealthy. She cared for the children of those she loved but worried that, as with young John and Janet, she was not being permitted to spend the time she wanted with them. Referring to Helen's post as editor, Margaret argued that she should have taken the step of dismissing her much sooner. She accused her of behaving 'abominably' when the actual break came and asked her whether she had any idea of how it felt 'to see the friend one cares for doing things that are despicable'. There was more. Deeply wounded, Margaret claimed that Helen's egotism was so tremendous that 'at the least touch on it you lose all sense of kindness, and decency and proportion'. She did concede, though, that 'there are such fine things about you' and a generosity. But

> I imagine the end cannot be very far off now. To live together is possible only when people love each other. These last few weeks with the queer calm we are keeping on the surface, can't last.

She accused Helen of being, despite outward appearances, like a block of ice. She referred to a 'ghastly' visit they had made to Llanwern in the summer which had suggested to Margaret that the end was inevitable. She would be glad, she wrote, when it came since the present was not bearable. Helen had no right to live with her since she was so bitter and angry: '[i]t's horrible; oh Helen I trusted you – and sometimes now, it seems as if you were rotten right through.'

This intimate letter reads as though Margaret is working out her feelings as she writes: the moderate language of its opening lines gets replaced by more emotional outpouring as she finds a voice to express how she really feels. It is signed M.R. and there are numerous crossings-out. It ends by saying 'Maybe when the end does come I will send you this letter'. We cannot know for sure but evidence suggests that Margaret may not have done so. She worked with words, and perhaps writing out her raw emotions provided the catharsis she needed.

Over a year later Margaret was still elaborating on Helen's faults as she saw them. A pencil note explains how Helen could be 'disagreeable out of the blue'. This meant, Margaret wrote, that 'one cannot hurt her or be natural or feel safe with her'. The positive partnership in work and life that these two women had once enjoyed had been irrefutably fractured. Holtby told Brittain in April 1927 that Margaret was keeping the change of editorship 'as quiet as possible'.[44]

Salvation came in the form of international feminism. Helen went to see her daughter in university in Canada then became the international secretary of the SPG. In May 1928 she set off on a world tour acting as an ambassador for the society, visiting feminist organisations and studying the international position of women, particularly in relation to the rights of married women to retain their nationality. As a result of the Sixth Pan-American Union of all American Republics conference at Havana that year, an Inter-American Commission of women was charged with preparing material for what would become a study of the civic and political equality of women on the whole continent. As part of this research Helen was spending 'long, very hot, but very happy hours' in the Library of Congress in Washington studying the laws of the twenty-one Republics.[45]

But Stonepitts was still Helen's home. A letter Margaret wrote to her (from Chelsea Court) in October 1929 dealt with alterations to the house and pointed out that '[w]e do quite often see money matters differently'.

Margaret was reluctant to commit herself to doing much, both because the future there seemed uncertain and because 'I very much dislike spending a lot of money when I am already living beyond my income as I am these bad years'. The letter was, nevertheless, signed 'All love from Margaret' and in that same year Helen chaired the Women Peers Committee which worked hard to persuade society that Margaret and other peeresses should sit in the House of Lords. The following January Helen, her son Alec and Prid were all her guests at a PEN (Poets, Essayists and Novelists) Club dinner.

Margaret left Chelsea Court in 1930 and moved to 72 North Gate, Regents Park. In October Helen explained to a Dutch colleague that Stonepitts was shared by Lady Rhondda and herself at weekends 'but we do not necessarily go together in fact it is rarely that we coincide'.[46] The following spring Helen finally moved out of Stonepitts. They had sought, unsuccessfully, to let it for the summer of 1931, and then decided to sell the house.[47] Helen hinted that they hoped to return when the economic situation improved (she did not specify whether she meant British or more personal circumstances) but there was no going back. Instead Helen chaired the organisation Equal Rights International and moved to Geneva, which she enjoyed. 'In some ways', she reflected in 1950, 'those four years count to me as the happiest of my life'.[48] She returned to England in 1934 and continued to live close to Seal in rented houses. A few years later Margaret moved to Surrey.

Helen is conspicuous by her absence from Margaret's autobiography. Resentment seems to have persisted on both sides. In April 1939 Helen told Doris Stevens that she had lunched with Margaret, adding bitterly that '[y]ears do not improve her looks or her clothes or choice of clothes'.[49] Helen spent two years in Australia in the late 1940s where her daughter Betty was making a name for herself in education. She also stayed with her son Nick who now lived on Canada's Peace River which Margaret had visited in 1919.

Helen died in England at the end of 1949. Margaret remained in close contact with Betty although she lived in Australia. Betty stayed with her when she came to her mother's funeral. According to the Australian Nancy Lord (who worked for *Time and Tide*), Margaret had to be persuaded to attend the funeral and claimed that 'she hadn't cared about the woman'.[50] Lord had noticed how Margaret 'always spoke very much against Helen Archdale so you knew there had been some serious quarrel'.

In the forties Helen wrote her autobiography 'An Interfering Female'. It places great emphasis on women's suffrage and her later international work as an equalitarian feminist. It is noticeably reticent about naming people, is vague about dates and is remarkable for what it omits. Helen's intimate friendship with Margaret could not be deduced from this account. Although she is mentioned fleetingly in connection with the WAAC, SPG and peeresses' claim, as well as quoting briefly from her 'Leisured Woman' pamphlet, Helen's account of *Time and Tide* rewrites the script in a revealing way. She notes that Margaret proposed starting a paper to 'give the woman's point of view in world affairs'. This, she adds 'sounded marvellous and off we went... Lady Rhondda herself was in bad health for some years and it was not until 1927 [sic] that she took over completely the editorship'.[51]

Margaret retained other close female friendships. In 1922 a curious Robins had noted in her diary that Margaret wanted her to attend the House of Lords committee where her bid to take her seat was being considered. 'Will I come and support her – where is Archdale?' Robins commented, adding 'I don't ask but wonder'.[52] At the beginning of that year Margaret had holidayed in France with Mary Agnes Hamilton.[53] They were joined by Helen after three weeks and then Margaret and Helen spent a couple of weeks in the Balearic Islands. The year 1922 was one of personal and public crisis for Margaret as she grappled with divorce proceedings and the thwarted bid for the Lords. And it was to her oldest friend Prid that she turned for a holiday companion when the pressure mounted. Robins' 1922 diary records with amusement (and an exclamation mark) that 'I'm to find a lovely quiet US retreat for her and Pridden!'[54]

She obliged, directing them to Stonington Manor in south-eastern Connecticut. The well-travelled Margaret declared this old-fashioned and comfortable New England country hotel by the sea 'the most perfect spot'. It was tucked away behind trees and half a mile from the road. They sailed on the *Adriatic* from Liverpool in early August. Margaret's name was not on the passenger list so few of the two hundred first-class passengers were aware of her identity. Stonington was a welcome retreat from the publicity back home. Margaret did not, though, entirely succeed in escaping the press. She had been spotted by a journalist she knew and had given two interviews but hoped that nobody would 'come bothering down here'.

This was not to be. The feminist Alice Paul had wanted Margaret to visit Washington. When she stressed that she was on holiday and would not be going there, Paul sent an official of the National Woman's Party (NWP) to her hotel to interview her for the New York press. Many years later this young woman recalled the occasion.[55] Rebecca Hourwich, already experienced in suffrage and now NWP national organiser, was told by the head waiter that Lady Rhondda had been delayed and that she should have tea without her. She would join her as soon as she could.

In retrospect Hourwich interpreted Margaret's action as a deliberate snub to herself, to Paul and to the NWP for sending a 'whipper-snapper' (she was twenty-five) rather than a *New York Times* reporter. Unlike the *Liverpool Post and Mercury* which declared that 'There is no more accessible woman in public life' and noticed the twinkle in Margaret's eyes,[56] she was not impressed. The situation was not helped by the fact that Hourwich was by now very hungry but could not afford tea in this expensive hotel since she had brought only ten dollars with her.

By the time Margaret appeared, Hourwich was predisposed to be critical. In an unfortunate mixing of personal and physical features she later described her as 'brusque, self-centred, rather heavy and stocky, utterly humourless'. Margaret was, she claimed, unlike American feminists in that she made 'utterly no concession to fashion. Her hair was pulled back, her suit was well tailored, but dull, and no one would ever have given her a second glance'. Nothing about her 'suggested her commanding position, consuming ambition, dynamic energy, or imaginative initiative'. But Hourwich got her story and it was syndicated. The influential *Christian Science Monitor* gave it two full columns on their front page. She did a professional job, printing Margaret's views on the priorities of British equalitarian feminists and Lloyd George's failure to address the inadequacies of the 1919 Sex Disqualification (Removal) Act. She even suggested that Margaret had 'effectually disposed of the old theory that only men know anything about business.'[57]

Clearly, Margaret could appear intimidating. She was the first titled lady that Hourwich had met. Unfortunately, if she sensed that somebody was afraid of her, Margaret's respect for them tended to be lessened. The interview also shows how Margaret could never be 'off-duty' even in a faraway retreat. But, like many in the public eye, she sought, even as she shunned, publicity. She told Robins how the manager of her inn had helped her to keep reporters sufficiently in check 'to prevent them being a serious nuisance'. But, she added that 'incidentally it's been rather satisfactory to get the chance of advertising the Six Point Group and *Time and Tide* which I've done heavily'.[58] And, according to Hourwich, Margaret was keen to publicise her bid for the House of Lords. She could not resist the opportunity for publicity, yet wanted it on her own terms.[59]

Margaret was judged by female and male reporters on how she looked. Margaret Mary McBride writing in the *New York Evening Mail* called her 'a handsome, well-built viscountess' who looked as though she could never get tired. Here was a woman 'of the splendidly English type'. Margaret's eyes, hair colour and 'clear white skin' were described and readers told that 'she seems to possess immeasurable reserve force and nerves like steel'. She wasted neither words nor movements. Interrogating a famous journalist and businesswoman was a challenge:

McBride observed that, before you knew where you were, you were being interviewed rather than her.

Other American papers called Margaret 'a vivacious young woman' with the rosy cheeks of a seventeen year-old. She was almost forty. Time and again her youthfulness was commented upon. This was partly because she did not look her age. She had been described the previous year in the British press as 'a tall, well-made, jolly big girl'. Holtby noticed how 'she gets to look about eighteen' at weekends[60] and when Winifred Coombe Tennant met the thirty-five year old Margaret on the London train she described her as 'a young, forceful, capable and attractive woman'.[61] Newspaper accounts of this fresh-faced woman were contrasted with her achievements. One article described her as 'a young woman, almost I might say a girl' who was 'business-like in manner, yet most genial and pleasant in every way'. Despite the 'charming smile and quiet voice', her replies to questions were 'confidently given, her grasp of questions so quick' and her remarks 'full of experience, knowledge and the sweetness of the expert'.

Newspapers on both sides of the Atlantic used Margaret's appearance as reassurance that the masculine world of business had not adversely affected femininity. The *New York Tribune* noted that Margaret was the British Empire's leading businesswoman yet she possessed 'a quite old-fashioned femininity', was softly spoken, charitable in her opinions and 'refreshingly wholesome' in appearance. Unlike her Stonington interviewer, this reporter approved of her appearance, praising her black brocade dinner gown and Japanese silk wrap.

At home the *Evening News* took issue with any

suggestion that she was 'masterful'. This was rather 'the domination of mind, because even when Lady Rhondda is most determined she betrays a certain shyness that is pleasantly feminine'. A number of papers commented that she blushed easily. 'You had expected to find a keen-faced woman breathing energy from every pore, suggestive of a certain amount of hard determination',[62] wrote one journalist. Readers were, however, reassured that she 'does not convey any impression of the uncomfortable volcano type'. She suggested 'a girl... devoted to country life and sports' rather than an international businesswoman.

Clichés and contrasts abounded, some unintentionally amusing: 'She is not a monster, not even a steam engine' declared the politician Harold Begbie. He added, '[O]n the contrary, I can think of no woman a man in misery might more desire to nurse him, so gentle is her voice, so restful her manner, so calm and kind the expression in her eyes'. He wondered how she could be in the front ranks of business yet retain 'what makes a woman attractive'. But when he suggested that women might help to develop a more sympathetic body of employers, Margaret responded with 'I don't think sympathy is a question of sex, do you?' It is not clear how Begbie reacted when, a little later, she rejected his draft biography of D.A.

Margaret's appearance was, however, used by some journalists to suggest the antithesis of femininity. A Los Angeles paper described her as 'tall, athletic, with the stride of a comely man'. She wore 'sternly utilitarian well-cut clothes, short skirts, low heels' and no hat. The *Boston Sunday Post* noted that her face assumed 'almost masculine lines' when talking about suffrage. Another American paper remarked that her handclasp was 'quick and firm'. The *Daily Mail* commented on her boundless energy as she walked down to ground level from her office 'whistling at the top of her voice like a jolly errand boy' and *The Daily Mirror* depicted her 'whistling merrily' as she left work.

In the 1920s issues of sexual identity were addressed both directly and through more circuitous means. In a post-war society where so many men's lives had been lost and bodies and nerves broken and with women increasingly visible in civic life, many kinds of adjustments were needed. There was a reaction against the sentimentality associated with the Victorian period. Advice literature on marriage, family life and sexuality reflected both relief and nervousness about change, along with an expanding market for experts. Those mature women who were single, had undergone the scandal of a divorce or were widowed young did not fit easily into the pervasive mainstream culture.[63] Helen Archdale once asked 'Why should "spinsterhood" be grey?' It was a question that many women would have endorsed.[64] Some were only too happy to be perceived as artistic Bohemians but were well aware that their numbers and largely metropolitan locations were small and that a climate of censorship and careful boundaries of acceptable behaviour remained.

There was also renewed interest in the work of the male sex theorists of the 1890s on the sexual identity of men and women and their classification. The very titles of these pre-war publications had helped to ensure that studies such as Havelock Ellis's 1897 work *Sexual Inversion,* the first monograph in English on homosexuality, were not permitted to circulate widely or were banned as obscene. By 1910

Ellis had produced six volumes of his *Studies in the Psychology of Sex in Relation to Society*. The truly remarkable relationship that Margaret enjoyed with her father is demonstrated by their frank discussions together before the First World War of Ellis's ideas.[65] Margaret had been able to borrow his work through the Cavendish Bentinck Library (which became the Fawcett then Women's Library). But when D.A. attempted to purchase a volume he was at first refused. Booksellers were anxious not to contravene laws on obscene publications and a signed certificate was required from a doctor or lawyer endorsing a potential reader's suitability for consuming such material.

Margaret felt that Ellis 'opened up a whole new world of thought'.[66] She retained, however, some reservations about his ideas, though she did not specify what they were. Modern historians differ in their interpretations of whether or not Ellis reinforced negative stereotypes of female homosexuality. Although it can be argued that the new 'science' of labelling by sexologists permitted women to 'name themselves and their feelings', Margaret was not alone in being uncomfortable with being identified thus, especially since what had previously been seen as acceptable close bonds between female friends were interpreted differently after the war.[67]

The early 1920s saw a number of challenging ideas become more available in Britain – most notably Sigmund Freud's work in the English language – for those in a position to consume such material. It is, however, easy to underestimate just how privileged was Margaret's access to progressive thinking, attitudes and texts that were not shared by or available to many in the provinces or beyond an intellectual elite.

Margaret read Freud and even briefly met him in the 1930s. In 1920 she discussed his work with the student doctor Octavia Wilberforce. She criticised Wilberforce's assumption that doctors were the experts who must always know best, protesting 'how entirely I disagree with the theory that sex or psychology lie any more within the medical man's province than they do within any one else's or than any other matter of universal human experience does'.[68] She took the young woman to task for wanting Freud's ideas suppressed because she disliked them. That was tantamount to admitting that she was afraid of his views, protested Margaret, and as bad as those in the past who would not admit to religious doubt. Committed to freedom of speech, Margaret argued that 'you'll never get sex into its right proportion if you put a veil round it and say "Please don't look"'. Those openly addressing theories about sex like Freud, August Forel and Ellis were, she believed, in the long run helping to put the subject into proportion. And this was preferable to 'sweeping it under the carpet'.

However, this did not mean that Margaret agreed with Freudian psychoanalytical theories. What she admired was the way in which Freud was breaking new ground. Characteristically apologising to Wilberforce a week later for having expressed herself in a somewhat adversarial fashion, she admitted, 'I never did believe in Freud's sex theories.' And she remained critical of those who placed sex at the centre of explanations for human behaviour.[69] Looking back on the 1920s she suggested later that it was 'an oddly strained and excited' time with a feverish and confused elevation of sex, illustrated by the popularity of D.H. Lawrence's writings.[70]

Yet she happily published Lawrence in her paper, and although she argued that the Victorians 'were never so mad as to suppose that they could live by sex alone',[71] she readily admitted that their attitude towards sex had been 'impossible' and 'out of focus'. She was neither prudish nor censorious, and once advised Holtby that she should not always remain a virgin and need not marry.[72] But she would also have endorsed Holtby's critical comment in *Women and a Changing Civilisation* that Freudian psychology had 'sanctioned the extreme veneration of sex'.[73] She was a late Victorian herself and admitted to being puzzled by 'that perpetual, unsatisfied sex-hunger' which seemed to be so marked a feature of the younger generation of writers and readers.[74]

In addition to worries about mannish women, there was also concern (evident in fiction) about hyper-femininity and what were perceived as inappropriate passionate female friendships, especially in all-female institutions such as girls' schools. Relationships in general were being put under the microscope by the 1920s. In addition to the work of the sexologists and new psychologists, legal developments were drawing attention to relationships between women, with consequent infamous publicity in the popular press. Opponents of the Criminal Law Amendment Bill of 1921 sought, unsuccessfully, to insert a clause which would have extended the criminalisation of male homosexuality (in existence since 1885) to 'Acts of Indecency by Females'.[75]

There was considerable adverse publicity surrounding the 1928 censorship case of Radclyffe Hall's novel, *The Well of Loneliness* about a woman called Stephen who falls in love with another woman. Laura Doan has argued that for the first time it provided the public with 'one clear and identifiable image – not just a word – of the "lesbian" and over the next few decades a stereotypical lesbian would emerge'.[76] Just three years later charges of lesbianism were being made against Douglas-Pennant.

An editorial in *Time and Tide* in November 1928 suggested that the novel was neither 'very wholesome nor particularly good literature'.[77] It criticised the sentimental handling of its theme and a certain morbidity, but admired the courage shown in writing it and defended the need for freedom of expression and adults making up their own minds. In the novel Stephen and Puddle live in a flat on the Chelsea Embankment looking onto the river and across to Battersea Park.[78]

Margaret did not wish to discuss publicly the nature of her partnerships with Humphrey, Helen and Theodora. She valued and respected privacy. She was wary of sexual identities being prescribed by others and as a divorced woman who chose to share her life with an ex-suffragette and then in the 1930s lived with another *Time and Tide* feminist, she was well-aware of how damaging popular images could be. When her god-daughter suggested to her that a member of the *Time and Tide* staff might be a lesbian, Margaret's response was: 'That is a *slimey* thing to say. You might as well say the same of Theodora and me.' With the term connoting erotic relationships there was concern about labelling and portraying a personal lifestyle as deviant and unacceptable.[79]

Eoff has suggested that Margaret's friendship with Holtby was probably 'the deepest and most intense' of all her relationships.[80] The existence of so much documented evidence about them – some of it refracted through

Brittain's judgemental eye – encourages this. But now that we know more about Helen from Margaret's personal correspondence, it may be argued that theirs had been a more intense relationship, whereas her years with Theodora signified 'the deepest' and most enduring partnership.

The friendship between Margaret and Holtby (fifteen years younger) nevertheless ran deep. Although printed extracts from their correspondence omit endearments, Margaret's letters to 'Dearest Winifred' were signed 'Much love Margaret' and 'Much love dear thing'. In contrast, when Margaret wrote to 'Miss Brittain' she signed herself with the customary 'Rhondda' in 1928, progressed to 'Dear Vera' but reverted to 'Margaret Rhondda' the following year. Only in October 1935 did she say to Brittain, '[W]on't you call me Margaret? It seems more right and natural somehow?'

Seeking to unravel Margaret's attachment to Holtby and vice versa is complicated by several factors. Dominating Margaret's later recollections of her and modern interpretations is her premature death. Margaret felt guilty that she had not sufficiently encouraged her as a novelist. Not a lover of fiction herself, she had been severe in her criticism, admitting in one letter 'No it's no good – I don't believe I shall *ever* like a novel of yours! And I shall to my dying day remain convinced that you ought never to attempt them.'[81] She then told Holtby that she regretted having sent the letter. By the time *South Riding* appeared, it was too late for its creator to reap the benefits as she had died the previous year. In 1937 Margaret wrote, 'I doubt if we can today estimate how great a piece of work *South Riding* is'.[82]

Those of great talent who die young, whether popular and kind as Holtby seems to have been or even difficult and self-centred, get placed on a pedestal which makes it difficult to criticise them. Premature death also arrests the natural course of a friendship. What we shall never know for certain is how close they might have remained had Holtby not died in 1935. Margaret's later views suggest that there might, at the very least, have been problems had Holtby's politics remained relatively consistent. Moreover our understanding of her life is invariably affected by *our* awareness of the end of her story. Neither Margaret nor Holtby could know exactly how this tragic script would end.

The Vera Brittain factor is important. As Marion Shaw has shown, Holtby has suffered over time from being in her shadow, enhanced by Brittain's retrospective and careful fashioning of her for posterity in *Testament of Friendship*.[83] Holtby and Brittain's strong – and markedly different – feelings about Margaret come through in their correspondence with each other, as do their efforts (all in vain) to persuade the other of the validity of their respective views. Although in March 1933 Brittain had only glanced through Margaret's autobiography, she was keen to tell Holtby that she thought it a 'slight' book and that Violet Scott James had written a scathing review of it.[84] The latter's review was in part critical but also praised its 'imaginative and penetrative passages'.[85] The following month Brittain read the book properly. She told Holtby that she was

> ... *loving* it, and thinking what a really charming and honest and honourable person emerged from it, and

puzzling over *why* I'd never liked her and she'd never liked me when we have almost everything in common except, perhaps, my faculty as an artist and her business experience.[86]

Yet Holtby's response conveniently ignored Brittain's statement about disliking Margaret, remarking instead:

I'm *so* glad you like Lady Rhondda's book. She really *is* like that – 'charming and honest and honourable' – and I feel that she too some day will learn to understand you.[87]

As a wife and mother, Brittain continued to be utterly committed to her writing. She was based in London while her husband worked at Cornell University. In 1929 Holtby told her that Margaret approved of this attitude to marriage and 'seems to have come to like you *very much*'.[88] Yet, was Margaret aware that such conversations were being relayed to Brittain and how might Brittain have felt about her private life being dissected by Holtby and Lady Rhondda?

Holtby's comment was probably anyway wishful thinking. There is little written evidence to demonstrate that Margaret actively disliked Brittain pre-war but the latter's hostile feelings and sense of persecution are documented. The two women fell out in November 1931 when Brittain felt, not unreasonably, that Margaret was overworking her friend. The following year Brittain admitted that she had long felt uncomfortable in Margaret's presence.[89] Her diary describes her as 'stiff and constrained'.[90]

Rivalry was exacerbated by the autobiographies of both women appearing in 1933. Margaret nevertheless told Brittain that she found *Testament of Youth* 'extraordinarily interesting'.[91] It had arrived by the 9pm post and she had sat up late reading it and resumed the next morning. The part about the war would, she thought, stand 'as a picture of what those years were like'.

Brittain had written regularly for *Time and Tide* in the 1920s, but her contributions did not last. After Holtby's death, Brittain described Margaret as a constant taker.[92] Brittain no longer needed to moderate her sentiments in order to placate Holtby, but a polite truce existed for a time as both women sought to preserve Holtby's reputation and do justice to her. Margaret was helpful and supportive about the idea of Brittain writing Holtby's biography. In March 1936 relations seemed cordial enough. Margaret was considering publishing some of the correspondence with Holtby. She assured Brittain of her discretion and thanked her for expressing 'extraordinarily generous' comments about her own writing.[93] Margaret had a spell in a Hampstead nursing home (for a rest cure) and Brittain sent her a basket of flowers.[94] At this stage they were united in their need to keep Mrs Holtby on side. A letter signed 'Yours ever Margaret' told Brittain how she could not get a passage 'past the old lady – indeed she appears to be rather doubtful as to whether the fact that W was happy ought to appear in print'. She also told Brittain that the two of them *'mustn't* finish meeting'.[95]

Understandably, the publication of Brittain's *Testament of Friendship* soured relations. Margaret attended the launch on New Year's Day 1940. Brittain's representation of Margaret was not flattering. She described Holtby as having spent 'a great deal of time serving many persons much older than herself, who felt – as senior people so often feel – that youth can easily afford to squander its generous vitality, and who would not or could not realise that her time in the world was to be shorter than theirs'.[96] Ever polite, Margaret told Brittain, 'What a tremendous lot of work you have put into it, and how it brings back old memories – I should think it will have a very big sale', though she did not say she had enjoyed the book.[97] She reviewed it in *Time and Tide* and was diplomatic, suggesting that no two people ever see the third from the same angle.

Brittain had never accepted Margaret's friendship with Winifred. After her death she described Margaret as 'really W's evil genius' and that she 'gave little worth having in return for all that she took'.[98] She also claimed that Margaret 'had to suppress exasperated jealousy' after Holtby had been taken ill and made it clear that she intended to continue living in Brittain's household and not to 'move to Lady R., who wanted her'.[99] Yet it seems unlikely that, apart from the possibility of a brief period of convalescence, Holtby would ever have moved to Margaret's. She had anyway told Brittain, 'I couldn't live with Margaret, much as I love her'.[100]

So what was the basis of this friendship between Margaret and Holtby? They shared more than their commitment to *Time and Tide* and the SPG. Neither woman was the product of London or the Home Counties. Although some accounts suggest otherwise, Holtby was from a prosperous background. Indeed, recordings of both women reveal neither Welsh nor Yorkshire accents. Gill Fildes's description of Holtby's normal speaking voice as being 'at the extreme end of Oxford and B.B.C. English', applies equally to Margaret's tones.[101] Both had been to boarding school and Somerville College and were, in different ways, connected to the WAAC in the latter part of the war. They came from political families, had lost their fathers and had crucially been brought up to believe in women's equality and their own ability. Although their views on socialism and peace diverged, both were energetic and committed equalitarian feminists subscribing to Holtby's belief that '[i]f only you could see all adult men and women as human beings together, the rest would come quite simply'.[102]

Their personalities were different but this helped them to value each other. Holtby was horrified when Margaret suggested she become literary editor because she had difficulty refusing anyone. But although Margaret was a businesswoman she called Holtby her 'senior in spiritual wisdom and insight'[103] and valued her enthusiasm and her financial investment in the paper. When Holtby first travelled by air (with Margaret from Paris in 1931) a nasty storm could not dispel her excitement: 'even when sick, I rather loved it'.[104] Her adamant appreciation of people and experiences and rich fund of ideas led Margaret to compare her to 'a tree in spring, budding all over'.[105]

Holtby saw the best in a situation, although others in her position would have thought they had been dealt a rotten hand. Margaret, for whom luxury was the norm, relished her zest for life. 'Oh, Margaret,' Holtby wrote, 'why haven't we seventy lives? One is no use.'[106] When she died Margaret wrote that she was 'the most utterly unselfish person I have ever known'. Here at last had been somebody who Margaret saw as not wanting anything from her, instead giving lavishly and constantly.[107]

She helped Margaret to 'lighten up'. Her satirical sense of humour was infectious. When Margaret attended a house party at the Malvern Festival that included J.B. Priestley, Lilian Baylis, Dame Laura Knight and the poet and dramatist John Drinkwater, she wrote to tell Holtby that she could not abide Drinkwater. She added 'but I rather like people I can't abide, there's the amusement of deciding whether to be polite or not – so far I have been – but I wouldn't take odds on it lasting myself'.[108]

Margaret liked the way that Holtby encouraged *her* to write. One letter asked her 'ARE YOU WRITING YOUR BOOK? If not, then be ashamed of yourself! If you are, then accept my love and blessing.'[109] Margaret also took her advice not to cut out 'all the emotion' from her autobiography.[110] She felt that Holtby had 'done far more for me than I ever have for you'.[111] But Holtby did not see it that way. She was very proud of becoming *Time and Tide's* youngest director aged twenty-nine and was inspired by Margaret's encouragement, telling her: 'You strike sparks out of me'.[112] Holtby's collection of short stories *Truth Is Not Sober* (1934) is dedicated to Margaret:

To The Leader, With Homage
To The Editor, With Gratitude
To The Friend, With Love

In 1923, not long after first meeting Margaret, Holtby described her presiding at a garden fête at Lord Leverhulme's Hampstead home to raise funds for two of her causes: the SPG and the National Women Citizens'

Association. She was, Holtby told her close friend Jean McWilliam, 'large, in black, outspoken and capable, like a Cabinet Minister (which she ought to be) and a successful managing director (which she is)'. She also discerned that Margaret was, in more intimate conversation, 'desperately shy'.[113]

Marion Shaw suggests that Holtby was inspired by Margaret's feminism and suffrage record. Although Brittain felt that her friend never outgrew a sense of 'affectionate reverence' towards Margaret, Holtby knew how to tease her. Holtby's *Mandoa, Mandoa!* describes a fashionable Oxford Street party where the election results are announced. Margaret and Holtby had attended such a gathering on the top floor of the department store Selfridges in 1931. The novel includes a guest described as a 'minute viscountess smothered in purple orchids'.[114]

And in 1930 Holtby began a three-act comedy called 'Efficiency First'.[115] Set slightly in the future, it features Sarah Terrens – known to her staff as The Terror – a Yorkshire woman from a poor family who has been so dedicated and single-minded that she has created a vast business empire called Efficiency First Ltd with nearly 9,000 employees. Despite the difference in background, Margaret, who had set up the Efficiency Club in London, is easily recognisable. Sarah is described as a 'big, gay, self-confident handsome woman' in her forties. She is first encountered in flying kit and runs, in addition to her press and a host of companies such as Dynamic Dairies and the Silent Rubber Roadway Company, an air transport service. She has 'electrified the countryside' and revolutionised her native village with modern schemes. She engages the best chefs and enjoys diving off the Scottish coast. When a textile businessman says he finds it difficult to speak plainly in front of ladies, she has no compunction in telling him, 'I'm not a lady. I'm a businesswoman.'

Brittain loved this play: its plot was 'so amusing' and the dialogue 'so delicious' that she was disappointed it was never performed or published. In *Testament of Friendship* she added that 'judging by the uncompromising realism of her dialogue, the able heroine, Sarah Terrans, appears to have been first cousin to Lady Rhondda'.[116] She quotes Sarah's remark that '[t]hey think I'm a hard, grasping, aggressive disagreeable woman'. But what Brittain does not say is that rather than Holtby poking fun at Margaret, she is instead drawing attention in a humorous way to how others perceived women in business. It is the '[t]hey think' that is revealing. Sarah's own financial adviser states that '[i]t's not natural' for a woman to build up a big business. Her staff manager sees Sarah's press as existing simply to promote her boss: 'if she hadn't a press of her own, how could she tell the public what to think about her?' Sarah *is* absurdly acquisitive and ruthless, reducing everybody and everything – even her secret husband – to their potential use in gaining a business advantage. But she is presented as the obverse of the Leisured Woman model, and Margaret would surely have greatly enjoyed the words that Holtby gave Sarah to describe how many men saw marriage: 'sole monopoly at sale prices'.

Holidays helped to make Holtby feel fitter and gave Margaret the privacy she rarely enjoyed in London. People-watching from a café-cum-cocktail bar in Saint-Lunaire while Margaret drank grog and Holtby sipped hot chocolate was a welcome escape, though both women also worked on this Breton holiday. Margaret was, in many ways, a confidante for the younger Holtby. It is surely no coincidence that their friendship developed when Brittain became engaged to George Catlin. Despite the remarkable way in which Holtby sustained her friendship with Brittain and remained within the household, the marriage invariably meant a shift in their intense relationship. Over the following years Holtby's commitment to *Time and Tide*, increasing health problems and Margaret's estrangement from Helen, brought her and Margaret closer together.

Brittain commented with amusement on the stories that circulated about her own unusual domestic arrangements vis-à-vis herself, her husband and Holtby. She was more concerned though about rumours of Holtby's lesbianism. In *Testament of Friendship* she dismissed 'scandalmongers who invented for her a lurid series of homosexual relationships, usually associated with Lady Rhondda or myself'.[117] She handled this by elevating the significance of Holtby's friendship with Harry Pearson.[118] Brittain was keen to assert her own heterosexuality and that of her close friend. In contrast Holtby's study *Women and a Changing Civilisation* is more equivocal, suggesting that it was not known whether the 'normal' sexual relationship was homosexual, bisexual or heterosexual, though society was judgemental and prone to 'theorise and penalise with ferocious confidence'.[119] Holtby also maintained that '[t]o love other women deeply is not pathological. To be unable to control one's passions is.'[120]

Clay has explored webs of friendship forged by women through their mutual commitment to professional writing and an investment in what she calls 'the possibility of shared erotic interests'.[121] Her chapter on the friendship between Margaret and Holtby examines their correspondence in 1933. After a period of ill health, Margaret had embarked on an extended Mediterranean cruise with Theodora Bosanquet, president of the International Federation of University Women. The two women left in September on the *Orentes*, accompanied by nineteen boxes of luggage and four dozen books.

Margaret wrote to Holtby from Mallorca, the first port of call. Her letters were a mixture of suggestions about how her employee should proceed with the paper in her absence and descriptions of places such as Palma 'a *delicious* little town'.[122] Margaret was relaxed and proudly recounted diving from a high board.

They spent three weeks in Greece. The women found modern Athens rather dull and noisy but the Acropolis was 'pure joy'.[123] They travelled to Delphi, stayed in the ancient capital of Nauplia in the Peloponnesus peninsula and visited Epidaurus. From Rhodes they journeyed to the King David Hotel in Jerusalem. Margaret was unwell so they stayed a month in Palestine, followed by a visit to Cairo, which did not much appeal. Nevertheless, in mid-November Margaret was writing, 'I've never in my life had so many ideas all fresh and bubbling... Emotionally I feel happy and at rest as I haven't for years.'[124] The travellers arrived home in the second week of January 1934.

Margaret had been so moved by Delphi that she who traded in words found it '[s]omething one can't find words for, or explain even to oneself'.[125] She was not alone here. When the writer Evelyn Sharp reached Delphi on a cruise just four years later she called it '[o]ne of the supreme days of my life'. She wrote in her diary: 'No, I can't describe it. Even 200 cruisers and various clumps of information dealt out by excellent Professors could not take away the feeling of standing where the Delphic Oracle once drew all Greece to consult here.'[126]

Margaret's correspondence suggests to Clay that her friendship with Holtby might be 'constructed as romance' and part of the 'sapphic imaginary'.[127] From Delphi, Margaret told Holtby that '[s]omehow or other you just *must* come and spend a holiday there with me, dear woman. I can't bear that you shouldn't see it and I just want to be there when you do.'[128] Clay sees this representing Margaret's sexual desire for her. But it can also be interpreted as the holidaymaker's wish to share a sublime experience with a close friend who could not be there. Delphi, Clay argues, becomes 'a receptacle for intense desires', made most explicit by Margaret sending Holtby a piece of maidenhair from the spring at Delphi.[129] Yet this 'overt expression of lesbian eroticism' was also sent to Margaret's mother and Aunt Lottie.

Unfortunately, we only have Margaret's edited edition of Holtby's replies (included after her death in *Time and Tide*). They are largely concerned with the paper, public life and literature, although Holtby did write, 'There's lots of news, though nothing as lovely as your views of Delphi, which are almost too beautiful...'[130]

Clay also notes Margaret's comments about her clothes – or lack of them – on this holiday. At Formentor Margaret describes sunbathing in a pair of shorts and what we would call a bikini top made of striped pink and white silk. Able to laugh at herself, she compares it to peppermint rock and 'looking like mutton dressed in the frilliest of lamb cutlets'.[131] She adds that this exposes more of her than anything she can wear in public (in her room she wears nothing) and compares herself to the 'rather easily shocked' and *very* fully clothed' German gentleman in the room next door. For Clay this represented an attempt to engage Holtby 'in an erotic exchange' and literally a striptease.[132]

Another way of reading this is to see Margaret shedding her inhibitions along with her clothes in the Mallorcan sunshine. For once Lady Rhondda, always in the limelight at home, really was relaxed and happy. She was also aware of how much Holtby was fascinated by clothes and fashion. So she described her costumes as a way of entertaining the woman who was left in London working. In Jerusalem Margaret purchased 'the most thrilling pair of dinner pyjamas'.[133] On another cruise a couple of years later she told Holtby about her 'new coffee coloured trousers' which were 'a great success' but not appreciated by all.[134] Holtby, like Margaret, enjoyed the sun, sand and swimming. Ill in a nursing home in 1931, Holtby thought of 'striped umbrellas above a sun-baked plage, and swimming. Oh, Swimming! Do you know, I believe that is the greatest asset of physical pleasure I have ever learned?'[135]

The five-month cruise was in fact a turning-point for relations between Theodora and Margaret. They decided to set up home together on their return. Aware that tongues might wag and conscious of Helen's position, Margaret concocted an elaborate scheme that involved the ever helpful Holtby. From Athens she wrote, 'We aren't proposing to broadcast our plan just yet,' but she had contacted her agent to look for a large house or flat. If somewhere suitable materialised before their return, 'I shall say to everyone that Harrison has found me a home that is perfect but is too big for me so I've persuaded T. to take a couple of rooms in it'.[136]

They intended to write home in December and say that Theodora was going to 'do some research work for me on a book we are planning to write together' so they would be 'sharing homes for a bit till we get it done'. They had, Margaret wrote, discussed the possibility of a publication about the different means of influencing public opinion but she admitted that they doubted whether there was really time for such a venture. It would, however, 'make a good excuse to make the move not seem particularly surprising'.

The book was never written but Theodora joined Margaret at 1b Bay Tree Lodge, Frognal. Margaret had moved from Regents Park to this first-floor flat in a house close to Hampstead Heath in 1931 and stayed there for ten years. She had hated living on her own and after the bitter ending of her relationship with Helen Archdale, it was Theodora who offered a more stable and companionate future, grounded in a number of shared interests, which included improving educational and legal rights for women. And it is to Margaret's work for the equal rights of women in the inter-war years, at home and internationally, that we now turn.

CHAPTER TWELVE

Pointing the Way:
the Six Point Group and Equal Rights

We have recently passed the first great toll-bar on
the road which leads to equality, but it is a far cry
yet to the end of the road, and our present position
is not yet altogether a satisfactory one from the
point of view of the country as a whole. We have,
as a fact, achieved a half-way position, and that is
never a position which makes for stability.

Time and Tide 21 January 1921.

In this rallying cry, entitled 'At the Half-Way House',
Margaret argued that it was 'chiefly to women that we
must look for the motive power to complete the work
which their grandmothers began'. By suggesting that they
were moving in the right direction yet still had some way
to travel on the long road to equality, she was placing a
special responsibility onto newly enfranchised women
(who now constituted over a third of the electorate) to
complete the task that others had started for them.

The six points of the SPG were also explained in the paper's article. They covered legislation on child assault, protection for widowed mothers with young children and improved rights for the unmarried mother and child. Equal rights for men and women were demanded in the guardianship of married parents, teachers' pay and opportunities in the civil service.

Just as the Chartists had published their six-point People's Charter in 1838 announcing their concept of parliamentary democracy (they had considered including women's suffrage alongside men's but rejected it as too idealistic), so now a new charter made gender equality paramount. It demanded legislation in areas that had not been covered in the Sex Disqualification (Removal) Act of 1919 and so a transformation in the reality of daily life in twentieth-century Britain. At the same time '[t]he spirit of immediacy which characterised the suffragettes was kept alive'[1] by the SPG.

This 'social betterment' programme had been outlined in *Time and Tide* on 19 November when it was pointed out that although women's and men's aims and requirements might not differ greatly, women's position within the national economy necessarily affected them adversely. Letters of support had followed. The six points, explained Margaret in her 'Halfway House' article, were 'simple, easily understandable, and ripe for immediate legislation'. They were seen as attainable and could, unlike the Chartist programme, be adjusted over time. As one reform was conceded, so another demand would take its place.

Margaret understood that women's demands were 'as varied as the ships on the sea',[2] and that it was therefore important to select key reforms. The SPG list revolved around carefully chosen and pressing issues that had already been considered and debated publicly. Individuals such as Elizabeth Wolstenholme Elmy and groups such as the Women's Emancipation Union had waged campaigns back in late Victorian Britain. Private members' bills had attempted, ultimately unsuccessfully, to deal with some rights. Now energies needed to be concentrated on getting the government of the day to initiate legislation in order to turn demands into law: 'Everyone has grown tired of talking. We all want to get something done', declared Margaret.[3]

The SPG was formally inaugurated on 17 February 1921, less than a year after *Time and Tide* began. It was a London-based and emphatically non-party pressure group, with monthly meetings at its headquarters on the top floor of 92 Victoria Street. Margaret was its chairman and moving spirit and spent £137 of her own money on the group in 1921 alone. Founder executive committee members included Robins, Cicely Hamilton and Cullis. Lady Camrose (formerly Berry) became an organising secretary. There was group as well as individual membership and two dozen organisations including the BFUW and the National Union of Women Teachers joined. From the summer of 1921 the SPG was affiliated to the Consultative Committee of Women's Organisations (CCWO) whose president was Lady Astor. This umbrella body brought together a plethora of societies including NUSEC with its strong welfare agenda. Astor's aim was, as Cheryl Law has explained, 'to maximise the movement's parliamentary profile and influence and co-ordinate the work of women in relation to Parliament'.[4]

The SPG wasted no time in targeting one of its six points. In October 1920 an article in *Time and Tide* had declared that there was one 'most serious blot upon our civilisation which needs the attention of every *responsible* citizen.'[5] This was the frequency of child assault cases linked to the toll the war had taken on many men's lives, and light sentencing. Margaret and the SPG also demanded a feminisation of public and professional posts to accompany legal reform. They stressed that claims of assault needed to be handled sensitively. Women police and doctors were deemed essential, as were juries representing both men and women.[6]

Just over a week after the SPG was formed, the Bishop of London's Criminal Law Amendment Bill was introduced into the House of Lords. It sought to raise the age of consent in cases of indecent assault from thirteen to sixteen and to eliminate the possibility of assailants claiming in defence that they *believed* a girl to be old enough to consent legally. The SPG tried to put pressure on MPs but, as with many private members' bills, it was wrecked at the last minute. Margaret submitted a resolution to the CCWO that the government introduce its own similar bill. The SPG produced a pamphlet on the subject and hosted a luncheon at the Hyde Park Hotel where Margaret presided. Speakers included the Bishop of London (who had been pressing for reform for seven years), the actress Lena Ashwell and playwright Clemence Dane.

The following February, the government introduced its own bill. Margaret addressed small groups as well as a mass meeting at venues such as the Queen's Hall. The SPG also took a platform at Hyde Park where Brittain and

Holtby addressed anybody who cared to listen. They had to learn quickly how to overcome embarrassment at speaking publicly – and in the open air – about assault and prostitution, not easy for well-brought up young ladies.[7] The legislation was passed in the summer. Although the SPG would have liked the age of consent to be eighteen, sixteen was seen as a good result.

There remained, however, concern about the shortcomings of the 1919 Sex Disqualification (Removal) Act. This was not surprising. The legislation had been carefully drafted by Lloyd George's government to satisfy the post-war appetite for reform but not to go so far as the Labour Party's Women's Emancipation Bill which had included the vote for all women under thirty. The latter got through the House of Commons against the government's wishes only to be sabotaged by the Sex Disqualification (Removal) Bill. It bypassed a wider franchise but addressed professional and public legal inequalities.[8] Margaret compared the act to a leaky saucepan.[9]

She chaired a huge SPG meeting at Westminster's Central Hall on 1 November 1922. Brittain called this the group's 'most spectacular moment'. Speakers included Lady Frances Balfour, the Liberal candidate Frank Briant and Rebecca West, whom Brittain compared to 'an intrepid young thoroughbred'.[10] The legislation stated that '[a] person shall not be disqualified by sex or marriage from the exercise of any public function'. Yet, Margaret explained, it had not given women equality of opportunity and treatment in the civil service. Women teachers lost their jobs when they married: Glasgow and St Pancras Corporations and eighty-seven Education Committees had dismissed or recommended the dismissal of married women employees. It had failed to prevent the Senate of Cambridge University voting in December 1920 against allowing women to become members of the university. Women police were being dismissed (the Geddes report had recommended the abolition of female police patrols) and, as Margaret knew only too well, hereditary peeresses had been refused a seat in the House of Lords.[11]

In July 1923 representatives from twenty-six women's organisations formed a deputation to the home secretary (on behalf of the prime minister) to point out the failure of the 1919 Act. Then and later, feminist organisations that might not always see eye to eye came together, since what united them – and what might be ranged against them – was perceived as more significant than their differences of emphasis.[12]

At the deputation Margaret represented the SPG and spoke about the House of Lords.[13] She also explained how the government might easily change the way the act operated without the need for legislation. Orders in Council could deal with equality of opportunity in the civil service. The Home Office could increase the number of women police. If the government set a good example by not dismissing civil servants on marriage, then local authorities would probably do the same. The government should also refuse to give grants to a university that would not admit women. This last suggestion did not go down well with Mr Bridgeman, the Home Secretary, a Cambridge man who had voted 'with great pleasure' against a proposal to put pressure on his university.

In November 1923 Margaret wrote to the prime minister to remind him of the urgent need to address the

1919 legislation. The subsequent announcement of a general election meant that instead of receiving a further deputation, Stanley Baldwin responded in writing on each of the six points.[14] More sympathy was evinced towards the better protection of children than for women's equal rights. Equal pay for men and women teachers was deemed especially problematic and expensive.

Margaret was not generally in favour of private members' bills. They had difficulty progressing and she preferred an approach that boldly demanded a share of the vote. One that did, however, succeed was the 1923 Bastardy Bill, though the SPG felt this was because it was inadequate and that the laws relating to illegitimacy remained antediluvian because the child was not put first. Legislation failed to reflect the fact that children had two parents – illegitimacy tended to be seen as a woman's question – and, it was argued in *Time and Tide*, children should not be penalised for their parents not marrying.[15]

At the beginning of the year *Time and Tide* published supplements addressing each of the six points, with detailed articles by both SPG members and those with a specialised interest in the subject. For example, Rebecca West wrote on equal pay for teachers, Eleanor Rowland Wembridge explained the situation in the United States and Agnes Dawson represented the views of the National Union of Women Teachers. Margaret's contribution was on equal pay and opportunity for men and women in the civil service.[16] The goal was recruitment on the same terms as men (a promise had been made that civil service examinations would from 1924 be open to men and women alike) along with equal promotion and pay and a ban on penalties for women marrying.

Soon after it started, *Time and Tide* had devoted a page to the dismissal of married women civil servants and the need for Whitehall to 'fight its feudal instincts'.[17] In 1923 Margaret spoke at a deputation organised by the Association of Women Clerks and Secretaries to press the claims of those employed in the Ministry of Pensions.[18] In the same year, letters were sent by the SPG to each member of the London County Council protesting against the recommendation that women teachers be sacked on marriage and deploring resignation from this vocational 'calling' on grounds other than incompetence or unsuitability.[19] Yet the teachers and female school cleaners were systematically dismissed.[20] In the same year fifty-eight married women teachers in the Rhondda who had been sacked by their council and appealed lost their case.

The SPG set up a social committee whose members included Margaret's mother. It organised events such as a *Thé Dansant*. Upmarket venues – there was a concert at Claridge's and an At Home at Margaret's flat – demonstrate that the SPG was the province of privileged metropolitan ladies. It also addressed Women's Institute branches and Margaret wrote about the SPG in the Women's Institute magazine.[21]

The SPG's Parliamentary committee of supportive MPs included Philip and Ethel Snowden (she was a vice-president of the SPG). This committee was necessarily overwhelmingly male since, despite fielding thirty-three women candidates in the 1922 election, only two women MPs were returned. They were the Tory Lady Astor, who had in December 1919 been the first woman to sit in the House of Commons and the second woman member, the Liberal Mrs Wintringham. *Time and Tide* anticipated that the Coalition would parade women candidates before the public 'as proof of its breadth of mind then banish them to divisions where they can be quietly defeated!'[22] Coombe Tennant (who stood unsuccessfully for the Forest of Dean in 1922) kept a copy of this article in her cuttings book.[23]

Women's organisations, most notably NUSEC, the Women's Freedom League and the SPG, promoted candidates who supported women's emancipation. Through *Time and Tide* the SPG devised a way of naming and shaming those whose record was not good. It cut across party allegiances, publishing (from 1922) Black and White Lists before elections. The former exposed opponents of women's causes while the White list praised their advocates.[24] A Drab List covered those who did not live up to their promises. Dennis Herbert, Conservative MP for Watford, was 'outed' for his consistently bad voting and debating record. His hostile attitude towards the Criminal Law Amendment Bill and the Matrimonial Causes Bill was challenged at a meeting in Watford. Flourishing copies of Hansard, Margaret nimbly answered his taunts (which included an attack on *Time and Tide*). Her fighting speech converted the audience. It was a resounding SPG victory.[25]

The Black List contained some familiar pre-war 'Antis'. Lord Curzon, who had been president of the National League for Opposing Woman Suffrage, now made it clear that he would not give 'the slightest consideration to any resolution which they [the SPG] might put forward'. Since they attacked his policies during elections, even where he did agree with their views, he would 'endeavour to make it clear that your Organisation is opposed to me'. He was also convinced that the SPG was not representative of women voters and had no special right to speak for women as a whole.[26]

Those who made the White Lists, for example, Lady Astor, Margaret Wintringham, Frank Briant, Captain Wedgwood Benn and Isaac Foot, were treated to an annual luncheon at the Hyde Park Hotel. It was potentially good publicity but the press concentration on the 'exceedingly smart frocks' worn by the SPG (Margaret in brown velour and Robins elegantly attired in a short black coat with gold braiding) must have been disappointing.[27] *Time and Tide* complained that the only daily paper to provide serious coverage of the SPG was the *Manchester Guardian*.[28] It was uphill work attracting attention to any women's groups in the mainstream press and although SPG members were determined and focused, the group lacked the numbers and influence of NUSEC.

NUSEC encompassed 180 societies across Britain by 1922. Its president Eleanor Rathbone stressed the similarities between its policies and those of the SPG, and what the new group owed to NUSEC. Downplaying Margaret's misgivings about NUSEC she pointed out that Lady Rhondda had sat on their executive committee and that when she formed the SPG she 'did us the compliment' of adopting 'our plan of concentrating on six reforms'.[29] Margaret would not have put it that way but as Eoff has noted, equality and social reform were for her 'inextricably intertwined'.[30] Margaret subsumed social reform under the umbrella of equal rights and minimised difference. Whereas in 1918 the winning of the limited vote had caused Coombe Tennant (of the NUWSS/NUSEC) to write, 'Babes and mothers rejoice, for the day of your deliverance is at hand,'[31] Margaret did not approach issues through a familial prism privileging women's needs as mothers.

Although the two organisations could and did come together when it was thought necessary in order to press for legislative change – as for example with the Criminal Law Amendment Bill in 1921 – by the mid-1920s differences of perspective between them were becoming more apparent. The focus of the Guardianship of Infants Bill was one demonstration of this. Margaret chaired yet another mass meeting in March 1924. Here she called upon the new Labour government to fulfil its pledges to amend the Sex Disqualification (Removal) Act, give pensions to widows and carry through the bill giving equal guardianship.

What emerged was a government bill (replacing one introduced by Mrs Wintringham) but one that did not make the mother joint guardian with the father. Margaret complained that it watered down earlier proposals and failed to understand the mother's claim to equal guardianship with the father in the home. It did establish equal parental rights to children once a dispute went to court but not until that point. The SPG, Women's Freedom League and National Union of Women Teachers all opposed it. NUSEC, however, was keen to improve the position of mothers and anxious that legislation should pass so, after initial criticism, it backed the bill. Margaret addressed audiences in Trafalgar Square in July and November attacking this 'changeling bill' which, she argued, would put back the chance of real equal guardianship for twenty years.[32] A heated exchange in *Time and Tide* with NUSEC's president and parliamentary secretary saw Margaret draw on her stock of analogies with eating, arguing that the government had dropped the heart of the bill and dished up mere trimmings:

> If I ask for roast beef and am provided by one cook with roast beef, horse radish and Yorkshire pudding and by a second with horse radish and Yorkshire pudding but no beef – I feel justified in feeling I have something different.[33]

Despite such protests the act was passed in July 1925 and it was not until 1973 that legislation would be passed that granted women full guardianship rights.[34]

1926 was one of those years when simmering troubles came to a head for Margaret both politically and personally. In addition to the impact of the General Strike and a protracted lock-out in the south Wales coalfield, she had also to deal with *Time and Tide's* editorial crisis. Reporting in March on NUSEC's annual conference the paper commented on a 'big cleavage of opinion', claiming that within this large organisation (especially amongst the leadership) there was now 'a considerable number of people to whom feminism is by no means of the first importance'.[35] Rathbone objected. She also complained that *Time and Tide* saw equality and feminism as synonymous.

Margaret did not demur.[36] Reflecting the pre-war WSPU impatience with the NUWSS, the SPG had, as early as 1923, set out its stall very differently from NUSEC's, suggesting that women should be not only 'making themselves apparent' but also, prepared to be so unpleasant 'to the powers that be that they decide to give them what they ask'.[37] With the number of women MPs (temporarily) raised to eight by the beginning of the following year and the first Labour government, there had been greater hopes for success. Yet discussion of the latest private member's franchise bill[38] – there were eight of these between 1919 and 1928 – produced a new obstacle: the possibility of an age limit of twenty-five for women voters. This was especially worrying since some NUSEC supporters were less inclined than Margaret and the SPG to hold out for twenty-one.

Despite prime minister MacDonald's assurances, the Labour government did not adopt the bill. His Conservative successor Baldwin made promises but proved to be a master of prevarication. So by 1926 women's groups were increasingly impatient. There were also new outlets pressing for change such as the National Women Citizens' Association. Its many branches cut across party, educating newly enfranchised women in citizenship and local politics. Margaret was its national president between 1921and 1924.

In 1926 Margaret immersed herself and the paper in a new campaign for equal franchise. During that year the SPG dropped two of its six points. Equal guardianship had been dealt with, albeit in what was described as a 'pseudo-equality measure' and widows got their pensions (even though the SPG felt that the legislation was primarily concerned with the State providing for fatherless children).[39] These demands were replaced by equal political rights as the first point followed by equal occupational rights. Both points set them on a collision course with the 'New Feminists', whose priority was social reform, though there were internal differences of opinion and later secession. Believing equal franchise to be within reach, Margaret saw it as the SPG's immediate goal, not least because it was an essential prerequisite to achieving other points.

When Rathbone suggested that there was a close association between *Time and Tide* and the SPG and blamed the paper for 'the derelictions' of the latter, Margaret's response was somewhat disingenuous. She stated that *Time and Tide* had no connection, personal or political, with the SPG, other than the fact that she and one or two directors of the paper were also members of the SPG Executive.[40] Yet, not only was *Time and Tide* the main disseminator of information about the group's forthcoming meetings as well as reports on its activities, but in her Introduction to the *Time and Tide* supplements on each of the original six points in 1923 Robins had stated clearly that the group had enjoyed a material advantage from the outset. It had, she proclaimed, '[a] participating newspaper behind it'.[41] Once Margaret became editor links seemed even more apparent.

Margaret was especially busy in 1926. She became president of the Institute of Directors and was juggling with a range of not necessarily compatible issues. Nevertheless she saved much of her energy for demanding women's full enfranchisement. On 6 August 1926 Holtby, whose views were very similar to Margaret's, told *Time and Tide* where she stood. In a memorable statement she identified herself as an 'Old Feminist' who actually desired 'an end of the whole business, the demands for equality, the suggestion of sex warfare, the very name of feminist'. 'But' she added, 'while the inequality exists – I have to be a feminist and an Old Feminist with the motto Equality First.'

In order to invigorate the bid for equal franchise Margaret contacted Emmeline Pankhurst. She was now running the English Tea-shop of Good Hope in Juan-les-Pins. Margaret offered to bring her home to England from France to work for the SPG at a guaranteed salary of £400 per annum for three years. It was not the first financial overture that she had received. Not long after the war Margaret and some former suffragettes, including Lady Constance Lytton, Kitty Marshall and Dr Flora Murray, had raised funds to help both Emmeline and Christabel Pankhurst. Less than a third of their anticipated £10,000 had materialised, though some money had been sent to Mrs Pankhurst (who was lecturing in America and Canada) and a house had been purchased in Devon.

The new plan also backfired. In an uncompromising reply suggesting how far removed she now was from the sentiments of the SPG, Mrs Pankhurst told Margaret that the current world crisis was an inauspicious time for re-opening the franchise question. In her view women 'have already enough voting powers, if effectively employed, to secure the various ends to which the vote is a means'.[42]

Yet despite this rebuff Pankhurst returned to England in time for Christmas 1925. Unable to contemplate anything that seemed like charity, she came on her own terms. But although she did not work for Margaret and the SPG, she was fêted by them. A dinner followed by a reception at the Hyde Park Hotel on 2 March 1926 celebrated her return. About 250 attended, and Margaret presided. She told guests that although the young people of today could be envied, it had been worthwhile to live through the old days. Now they had to think about the future. The name of Pankhurst reminded them that they did not yet have full victory. Margaret asked what Mrs Pankhurst might do for them in the future, suggesting she might stand for Parliament. This was where she belonged.

Lady Astor had rushed over from the House of Commons. She was described in the press as 'looking very young and earnest' in her severe black suit and hat (in contrast to all the ladies in evening gowns). She now made a startling intervention, declaring, as though it were in her gift, that she would resign her seat tomorrow if Mrs Pankhurst 'saw her way to take it'.[43] The former suffragette leader was equally dramatic: 'If you want me there, if you think I can serve, if you think I can help, then, hard as the work is, I will go there if I am sent.' As the *Christian Science Monitor* observed, she sounded like a missionary accepting a dangerous post in a far-flung outpost. She added that if she were to go to Parliament she must fight for her own seat.

Astor's speech was remarkable since less than four months earlier she had written in no uncertain terms to Margaret telling her that she did not think it advisable to enlist Mrs Pankhurst's help. She had been sure then that the government was soon going to grant the vote and that Pankhurst's intervention might even do more harm than good.[44] Perhaps Mrs Pankhurst's legendary charisma, allied with concern about Tory procrastination, accounted for Astor's change of heart.

Pankhurst joined the Conservative Party later that year and in March 1927 launched a campaign to stand for the safe Labour seat of Whitechapel and St George's Stepney. She declared that she had been ready to die for the vote but was now prepared to die for the Empire.[45] Before this, however, she did participate in an event that reprised the drama and spectacle of the suffrage heyday.

This was a mass demonstration held on 3 July 1926. It was organised through an Equal Rights Demonstration Committee chaired by Margaret. They were using an old tactic but one that had not been seen since the outbreak of war: 'dimly, delicately, faintly, it recalled to men's nostrils the odour of militant days'.[46] About 3,500 marchers made their way from the Embankment to Hyde Park. There fifteen platforms had been erected and at 4pm speeches commenced. Mrs Pankhurst addressed the crowd, as did Margaret (from the SPG platform). Each platform put forward two resolutions: for votes to be granted immediately to women over twenty-one on the same terms as men and for a voice, seat and vote for peeresses in their own right in the House of Lords.

Forty women's organisations had come together for this event. There were speeches from elderly stalwarts such as the Women's Freedom League's Mrs Despard, as well as more modern figures like Lady Astor. There were some new specialist groups in evidence, for example women magistrates, and groups of young women under thirty, such as the Guild of Girl Citizens. Another modern touch was displayed when Mrs Elliot Lyn flew over the marchers in an aeroplane. Sybil attended, as did members of the Newport and District Women Citizens' Association. Readers of *Time and Tide* were told that this event marked 'the end of a period of lassitude' and 'the beginning of a fresh period of enthusiasm and courage'. They were reminded that 'This generation of women has a duty, a duty to its time, a duty of posterity, which it and it alone can accomplish'.[47]

Margaret's Equal Rights Demonstration Committee became the Equal Political Rights Campaign Committee (EPRCC) in July. Margaret was still in the chair. It spearheaded pressure for political reform through coordinating the activities of twenty-two societies. NUSEC, however, withdrew from affiliation. Margaret used the SPG platform to support it, for example at a meeting at Chelsea Town Hall in December. The EPRCC energised local women's groups and generally kept up pressure and publicity.[48] By February 1927 it was expressing indignation at the omission of enfranchisement from the King's Speech.

A deputation to Baldwin representing fifty-six women's societies was introduced by Lady Astor. Margaret spoke. All the prime minister would promise was a statement before Easter. In April it was announced that an equal franchise bill would be introduced in the following parliamentary session.

Margaret chaired about twenty EPRCC committee meetings in 1927. Her excellent connections helped. Attending a meeting of one of their sub-committees, she offered to get some well-known signatures for a letter to the press.[49] From April its propaganda included open air meetings in Hyde Park, Hampstead, Clapham Common, Regent's Park and Brockley Cross, poster parades with umbrellas in theatre land and lobbying MPs. Letters were sent to Conservative Party branches urging them to support the equal franchise resolution at the party's annual conference in Cardiff in October. The imaginative propaganda of the pre-war years was being deployed once more. Some of the more ambitious schemes had to be abandoned or modified: cinema managers were unwilling to exhibit slides advertising a mass rally in Trafalgar Square and Margaret's plan for a river procession of illuminated barges as well as a torchlight procession fell foul of several authorities. Thirty thousand handbills were printed.

The Trafalgar Square rally on 16 June had forty speakers and three platforms on the central plinth, one of which Margaret chaired. She called on the government to pass a simple equal franchise measure and to give peeresses in their own right a seat in the House of Lords. Her statement that this would probably be the last great suffrage demonstration caught the imagination of the press. Banners flew as in the old days. One of the stone lions sported a placard declaring 'Gentlemen prefer blondes, but blondes prefer the vote'. The hymn 'Jerusalem' (Blake's poem had been set to music by Sir Hubert Parry for the suffrage demonstration at the Albert Hall in 1918) and the 'Women's Marseillaise' could be heard from afar. So too could 'We Want Votes' sung to the tune of 'Three Blind Mice'.

The following February marked ten years since the partial victory of 1918. When the King opened Parliament, EPRCC activists drove a dozen cars (including Margaret's) round Whitehall displaying placards demanding votes for women over twenty-one on the same terms as men. Young Suffragists not only delivered a petition to the prime minister but also attempted to present a letter to the king at Buckingham Palace.[50] In March the Equal Franchise Bill was finally introduced and victory was in sight. It got a massive majority of 387 to 10 on its second reading, was easily carried in the House of Lords, receiving the Royal Assent on 2 July 1928 and ending many decades of campaigning.

The editorial in *Time and Tide* four days later was not triumphant. It cautioned that although a vital and overdue law had been passed, there were still struggles ahead:

> The vote is won but the fight is not over – neither the fight for equality nor the fight, with ourselves, to achieve the point of view of the equal, which is perhaps the hardest of all.[51]

But it also provided a spirited vindication of the militant methods that Margaret and many others had espoused pre-war. It drew upon the words of Henry Nevinson (who in turn borrowed his language from Robert Browning). Nevinson, who had resigned his post at the *Daily News* because of its problematic stance on suffrage, had declared that victory would belong to the militants. *Time and Tide* explained that:

> the vote was not won by sweet reasonableness, it was won by self-sacrifice and courage, and – above all – by that most difficult of all forms of courage, the courage to appear violent, unreasonable, ugly.

Four years earlier Margaret and Helen had proudly attended a dinner held for ex-prisoner MPs at the House of Commons. Nineteen men had recently returned to Parliament who had been imprisoned on religious or political grounds. Margaret met there male pro-suffrage activists Frederick Pethick-Lawrence, John Scurr and George Lansbury, along with conscientious objectors, Irish protestors and anti-vaccinationists. The small group of ex-prisoner women included Emmeline Pethick-Lawrence,

Barbara Ayrton Gould (who eventually became a Labour MP) and Evelyn Sharp.

Margaret spoke for this group, arguing that whatever had been the guests' reasons for incarceration, it 'must mean a dedication to the work of altering the prison system'. Unlike Sharp, who had written factual and fictional pieces about the treatment of non-political women prisoners,[52] this was not a subject in which Margaret had previously expressed interest. But she was applauded for suggesting that the treatment of prisoners needed tackling and that reform must be based on an understanding of the prisoners' point of view.[53] Such a speech suggests how her views had broadened to encompass social issues that she had not tackled pre-war, when her political activity had been concentrated on one specific goal.

Time and Tide's glorification of militancy and attribution of success to Mrs Pankhurst's wing of suffrage occluded the protracted work of the moderates and was not a version of suffrage history that appealed to Rathbone and NUSEC members.[54] Just how differently they chose to recall events was demonstrated that same year when Ray Strachey's constitutionalist history of the British women's movement, *The Cause* was published. Although Strachey's text covered almost 400 pages, half of Margaret's pointed review for *Time and Tide*[55] was devoted to the book's Appendix which reproduced Florence Nightingale's *Cassandra*. Strachey's own words were judged 'very readable' but Margaret was at pains to emphasise what had been omitted. Slightly mischievously, she suggested that Strachey maybe had to explain to herself even more than to readers why she had never joined the militants and so was 'hazy' about where credit was due, attributing motives and emotions that were inaccurate.

In October 1928 the EPRCC organised a Victory-and-After Luncheon attended by 180 at the Hotel Cecil. Margaret chaired the event. As its title suggested, it was not merely a celebration. Margaret's words made this clear. She was careful to describe the vote as merely one concrete symbol of equality and not an end in itself. She paid tribute to the pioneers of sixty years, adding:

> I wonder how many more generations are going to use up their lives before we can put the whole thing behind us, and forget that there was ever any difference of status, freedom, or opportunity based on the difference in sex.[56]

Speakers included the American Doris Stevens (who was staying at Chelsea Court), Emmeline Pethick-Lawrence, H.N. Brailsford and Dame Millicent Fawcett. In the evening there was a reception at Caxton Hall where Margaret once again presided. Almost three hundred tickets were sold for this. Cicely Hamilton's popular suffrage play 'How the Vote Was Won' was performed by the Actresses' Franchise League with some of its original cast. The 'Old Guard' spoke, as did younger new voters.

It was an election year in 1929 and 4,750,000 potential women voters added to the electorate. This was the first time that all adult women could vote and the EPRCC now regrouped as the Equal Rights General Election Campaign Committee (ERGECC). It drew up an Election Address and distributed it round the country. Its feminist programme advocated equality in economic status and moral standards as well as in the political arena. And it included equal rights in the League of Nations. Unsurprisingly the SPG and Women Peers Committee were affiliated but so too were groups such as the Bolton and Hereford branches of the Women Citizens' Association.

The ERGECC had a busy time targeting women MPs to explain their policies. They and NUSEC also organised deputations to the leaders of the three main political parties. Only Lloyd George permitted them to make separate representations. Margaret chaired the deputation to him where he announced a Royal Commission to investigate the removal of the marriage bar in the civil service. She also chaired the joint deputation to the prime minister but was unable to attend the April meeting with Ramsay MacDonald. Demands ranged from equal rights within the League of Nations to the minimum age of marriage and equal pay. Margaret told Baldwin about the two societies' differences in emphasis and support for issues and their own focus on equality issues alone.[57] In her view, for example, mixing up family allowances (a NUSEC demand) with equal pay would only 'queer the pitch for the latter'. She introduced the speakers, who included Holtby as a new voter (representing the SPG). Baldwin told the women that he had 'never heard a more business-like' deputation 'nor one that put their points more clearly, or with such brevity consistent with elucidation', and he admitted that they had raised some 'extraordinarily difficult questions'.[58]

Margaret chaired monthly meetings of the committee in 1929. Some continuity with her militant past in Wales was provided by Rachel Barrett, erstwhile Welsh organiser for the WSPU, becoming its secretary. By the autumn of 1930 it had been transmuted into the Equal Rights Committee. It had a wide range of demands, advocating equal pay and opportunities at home and (through Geneva) internationally, opposing the laws on solicitation, supporting peeresses sitting in the House of Lords, the separate taxation of married women and retention of their nationality on marriage.

The suffrage celebrations of 1928 had been tempered by the death of the movement's most famous figure: Emmeline Pankhurst. She had died of septicaemia on 14 June, a month short of her seventieth birthday. Drama attended her in death as in life for her funeral four days later coincided with the House of Lords endorsing the bill that would ensure that all British women finally had the right to vote.

Margaret was at the crowded service at St John's Church, Smith Square, Westminster. She became treasurer of the Pankhurst Memorial Fund. The moving spirit behind this was Kitty Marshall. She and her husband Arthur (Mrs Pankhurst's solicitor) had been close friends of the suffragette leader, who had left an estate worth only £86. Margaret, Kitty Marshall, Rosamund Massy (the Fund's secretary) and Rachel Barrett set about raising funds for a headstone for the grave in Brompton Cemetery and to purchase Georgina Brackenbury's portrait of Mrs Pankhurst for the National Portrait Gallery. They also commissioned a life-size statue of the suffragette leader with arms outstretched to be placed in Victoria Tower Gardens close to the House of Commons.[59] More than 700 people donated from Britain and Canada.

On 6 March 1930 a large crowd gathered to watch the prime minister unveil the statue which had been draped in a purple, white and green flag. Flora Drummond presided. Margaret and Frederick Pethick-Lawrence spoke from the platform. With delicious irony the composer and former suffragette prisoner Dame Ethel Smyth conducted the Metropolitan Police Band as they played her famous suffrage composition 'The March of the Women'. The Women's Auxiliary Police were in evidence too. Margaret held a dinner for Kitty Marshall, praising her initiative and energy. She called the event (which was broadcast) 'a very big thing for the feminist movement, for it does matter that success should be commemorated in bronze and stone'.[60]

Margaret also believed that international feminism mattered. On 7 April 1925 she had met Alice Paul, the American social worker and equal rights lawyer who had founded and chaired pre-war the militant American National Woman's Party. Gathered too in London's American Women's Club were seven other women prominent in advocating women's causes in Britain, including Robins and Emmeline Pethick-Lawrence[61]. They discussed international equal rights and formed a British committee of the National Woman's Party. Margaret helped to entertain Paul during her visit.

Although American women were now enfranchised there were deep divisions amongst feminists. The NWP was campaigning for an Equal Rights Amendment to the United States Constitution.[62] Such an amendment would render any women-specific legislation unconstitutional (and apply retrospectively). The NWP believed in complete equality with men in employment including, noted the *Daily*

Telegraph, the priesthood.[63] Yet many leading American feminists, notably the influential, much more moderate American League of Women Voters headed by Carrie Chapman Cott, favoured protective legislation. It was fundamentally challenged by the proposed amendment. The first statement from the new British group was to the American Association of University Women gathered at a convention in Indianapolis. Here they asserted their support for equal rights legislation and opposition to protective legislation.

In 1926 the NWP applied to join the International Woman Suffrage Alliance. Formed in 1904, the latter's president was currently the British woman Margery Corbett Ashby of NUSEC. Like Margaret she was the daughter of an erstwhile Liberal MP father and a mother who supported women's rights. Representing forty countries across the world it was not easy to demonstrate unity, though the alliance's very existence was significant. The NWP's application was considered at the alliance's congress in Paris in late May and early June 1926. Margaret was one of the twelve delegates from Britain to this congress. Her intervention there raised her profile as an international feminist.

The alliance's board (consisting of eleven women representing nine nationalities) recommended that the NWP application be rejected. As a result of this Margaret showed solidarity with the NWP by withdrawing the SPG application to affiliate, even though it had already been accepted. She wrote formally to Mrs Corbett Ashby saying the methods used in dealing with the NWP had left her no other option.[64] Eoff argues that Margaret's gesture marked her 'as a woman of principle and as a major force in the international women's movement'.[65] The *New York Post* announced 'British Leader Hits Woman's Party Ban'.[66] Margaret made an impassioned two-minute speech at the congress, summing up her appeal by declaring that:

> If you vote to keep the Woman's Party out you will be voting for the past. If you vote to take them in it will be a vote for the future.[67]

Emmeline Pethick-Lawrence (now president of the Women's Freedom League which the congress did accept) also supported the NWP, but Eleanor Rathbone pleaded with the delegates to accept the board's recommendation for rejection. A vote was taken and although a clear majority did so (49 favoured the NWP, 123 voted against it) three-quarters of the British delegates supported the NWP's admission. Margaret later argued that the alliance was wrong to have allowed themselves to be 'jockeyed into voting' against the NWP by the plea that a vote in the latter's favour would amount to a vote of no confidence in the alliance's board.[68]

Two days later the NWP held a hastily organised luncheon at the Restaurant Laurent in honour of Margaret and their benefactor Alva Belmont who had just arrived from the States. About 125 were present from fourteen nations including many Americans and women from France, Greece, Spain and Egypt. Margaret rose to the occasion. In rousing and provocative language she told the gathering that although the NWP had been accused of promoting itself unduly in the press coverage of the event (a claim that she dismissed), the real reason why they had been turned down was because they were feminists. Not all suffragists, she stressed, were feminists and the majority of delegates were actually social reformers.[69] The sight of feminists like themselves made 'the social welfarers shiver'.[70]

This was a scathing attack on these reformers. Very few, she claimed, were 'pure feminists' like members of the SPG and the NWP. They did not care 'two pence for equality for itself'.[71] The reformer was terrified lest

> instead of being allowed to potter away at welfare work, at protective work for women, she will be forced to move swiftly towards that complete equality of opportunity between men and women for which in her heart she is not ready.

Yet she suggested that the alliance's action had taught feminists a valuable lesson:

> However closely we may cooperate with the reformers in working for individual reforms, we must, if we are to keep our faith whole, actually work together with those of a like faith. We must separate the sheep from the goats... I think that this week's doings will have big results on the feminist movement the world over. They have shown us who are feminists, feminists first and last, where we were drifting to and where our spiritual home really lies. They have made us feel that we are one body, the feminists of the world'.[72]

Crystal Eastman, an American feminist and socialist lawyer who lived in both Britain and the United States, agreed that the majority had rejected them because they were feminists. She added that the British delegates (though clearly this did not apply to all) and the Scandinavians were as extreme in their feminism as the NWP, which was feared for the action it might take. She wrote later that the NWP had never had a tribute 'more generous, more deeply understanding' than Margaret's. She wanted readers of the paper *Equal Rights* to understand 'from what a background of power and distinction and achievement' Margaret was speaking and that:

> [w]hen she calls upon the real Feminists of the world to find each other it is the call of a comrade. Perhaps it is the call of a leader, too.[73]

However, her claim that Margaret had 'learned her feminism at the militant's school and has never lost their fire' only revealed one side of her. At home Margaret's speeches tended to be more measured as she held in tension a number of different roles. Her position as an eminent businesswoman was not always easily reconciled with her campaigning. It is perhaps no coincidence that the stirring rhetoric that seemed to flow so readily from Margaret at this luncheon was uttered not in London or Cardiff but in Paris before an international feminist audience.

The following summer thirty-five members of the NWP showed solidarity with the British suffrage cause by joining the demonstration in Hyde Park. At the end of August Margaret wrote to Alice Paul. She had attended the Amsterdam conference of the International Federation of University Women. It had not inspired her and she suggested that they 'could do with a considerable amount of waking up, which it might perhaps be possible to arrange...' She was, however, interested in what Dr Alfred Zimmern had said about the possibility of the League of Nations framing an international convention prohibiting the placing of legal disabilities on women's work.[74] Focusing attention on the League of Nations Assembly at Geneva now seemed the way forward.

Taking her cue from Margaret[75] and working with her and Doris Stevens, Paul drafted an Equal Rights Treaty outlawing discrimination against women. She then tirelessly advocated it. The idea of countries supporting an equality convention helped to put pressure on the United States to adopt the Equal Rights Amendment. For Margaret and the SPG it was a challenge to move beyond Britain in espousing the idea of equal rights. In the autumn of 1926 Margaret chaired an international committee of the SPG to promote the Equal Rights treaty in Europe. Brittain sounded the new approach in two SPG pamphlets, arguing that the time had come to move from the national to the international sphere 'and to endeavour to obtain by international agreement what national legislation has failed to accomplish'.[76] Brittain, Holtby and Margaret spoke at a series of weekly SPG meetings on international feminism in the autumn of 1928.

At the same time, Margaret was concerned not to deflect too much time and attention from her role as editor of *Time and Tide*. Eoff also points out some differences in priorities and tactics between Margaret and the NWP. On the vexed question of a woman's loss of nationality on marrying a foreigner, they proposed that

Margaret chair a World Committee on Nationality to prepare for raising the issue at the 1930 conference at The Hague on codifying international law. But Margaret did not see this as appropriate for The Hague (the situation was also complicated by Helen Archdale being involved with this). Margaret was more interested in directing attention to Assemblies of the League of Nations in Geneva. She also felt that Stevens and Paul were more committed to such matters and so better suited to chair a committee with worldwide implications. Disarmingly frank in her correspondence, she told Stevens: 'The laws against women in some small American Republic don't make me see *properly* red like they do you.'[77] She did, though, agree to chair the British support group.

In 1927 the French foreign minister Aristide Briand and Frank B. Kellogg, US Secretary of State, announced that France and the United States would sign a pact renouncing war and seeking the settlement of disputes by peaceful means. To gain support a conference of key nations would be held in Paris. Stevens desired a meeting between the Plenipotentiaries of the countries that would be signatories to the Kellogg-Briand Pact and equivalent women representatives to present the Equal Rights Treaty.[78]

Margaret accompanied Stevens to a meeting at the American Embassy in Paris in August 1928 just before the signing of the pact by fifteen Powers. She had tried (unsuccessfully) to recruit Brittain, Holtby, Lady Astor and others to attend too. Although initially she envisaged enormous 'world publicity'[79] for the Equal Rights Treaty, in the event Kellogg would not oblige and, to Margaret's embarrassment, the women then attempted and failed to put their case at the French president's summer chateau.[80] She did not accompany them but her name was linked with the affair and the episode dismissed by *The Times* as introducing 'extraneous matter' into the occasion.[81] Afterwards Margaret admitted to Brittain that although it would have been magnificent had they been able to argue their case, 'it was really about as likely as the Millennium!'[82] And the women should not, in her opinion, have persisted in their efforts. This was '[r]ather a damp squib opening' for the Treaty, both undignified and unsuitable. Militancy was correct 'after one has tried other methods'. But 'to open with militancy' was disastrous and Margaret found it humiliating to be linked with such actions.

In the following year the SPG lobbied unsuccessfully for the Treaty at the League of Nations Assembly. Margaret attended but, according to Betty Archdale, was 'most unenthusiastic'.[83] In order to have a more effective voice, preparations were now underway for a new organisation which would advocate the adoption of the Equal Rights Treaty by all nations. Margaret and Holtby joined Paul and others in Geneva in September 1930 on the eve of the opening of the League of Nations Assembly. The new body was called Equal Rights International.[84] It was the only organisation to recommend that the League of Nations adopt the Equal Rights Treaty. Its members canvassed government delegates during its annual Assembly meetings. Initial members included Paul, Australia's Jessie Street (its vice chairman) and Lily van der Schalk Schuster from Holland (treasurer). It had representation from as far afield as Romania and Cuba.

Although Margaret had been instrumental in its founding, chaired its first meeting and sat on its Council, she quickly withdrew from active involvement. Helen was elected its chairman. Given the breakdown in relations between the two women, Helen's prominence probably contributed to Margaret's low profile. In December, just a few months after its inauguration she wrote formally to Helen to resign from its Council, citing pressure of work for *Time and Tide* and business matters.[85] Worse was to follow as Paul also withdrew.

In 1929 another international group with SPG connections had been founded. This was Open Door International. It president was the Scottish-born (and St Leonards educated) barrister Chrystal Macmillan[86]. The organisation was dedicated to opposing protective legislation. Here again Margaret was a catalyst. Elizabeth Abbott along with Margaret, Archdale and Macmillan had started Britain's Open Door Council in May 1926 to advocate equal pay, status and opportunity for women. Although Abbott and Macmillan were initially NUSEC members, the following year they were part of a mass resignation of eleven out of the twenty-four members of its newly-elected executive committee, some of whom then defected to the Open Door Council executive.[87] A crucial difference between the NUSEC and the SPG concerned protective (or restrictive) legislation. This attracted considerable attention in the second half of the 1920s.[88]

Attempts were made through the Open Door Council, the SPG and the Equal Rights Committee to educate the public and put pressure on politicians not to focus on the sex of the worker when drafting legislation. In 1929 Margaret led a deputation of thirteen women's organisations (including Helen representing the SPG) to her father's erstwhile colleague J.R. Clynes, now the Home

Secretary. They wanted him to safeguard women's interests in industry and to repeal the Factories and Workshops Act of 1901, urging that legislation reflect the nature of the job.

Responding to Clynes' remark that in the past men had wished 'from a very fine sentiment' to protect women, Margaret suggested that 'often the very finest sentiments that people have are in fact some of the most dangerous'.[89] There were also campaigns to exclude women from the lead paint industry, from night work and to restrict hours of employment. Whereas Rathbone believed that each case should be judged on its merits, Margaret was adamant that the tag 'Women and Children First' should always arouse suspicion and argued for what she called 'the complete feminist case'.[90]

The Open Door Council challenged the claim that there was a direct correlation between the sex of the worker and the likelihood of industrial accidents. Dangerous and heavy work, it argued, was best tackled by selecting the best person for the job and training in the most appropriate manner. Committed to the notion that 'a woman shall be free to work and protected as a worker on the same terms as a man', it defended the right of women to work in industries such as coalmining, where British women were employed on the pit top.

In the 1930s Margaret contributed to letters in the press on topics such as pin money and equal pay.[91] She still expressed strong views in *Time and Tide*. For example, her views about protective legislation were unequivocal when it came to pensions for spinsters. She wrote in 1939 that '[t]he way to tackle the spinster problem is to give the same wages and conditions to women workers as to men, not to give them the status of a permanent semi-servile class that needs special protection'.[92]

But she had in effect bowed out of active leadership of the societies which she had been so instrumental in forming. From 1933 the SPG (working with the Open Door Council) actively advocated the rights of married women to work. Margaret became a vice-president of the SPG and eventually in 1955 'President of Honour'. By 1941, it was working in cooperation with The World Woman's Party for Equal Rights seeking to get equality recognised throughout the British Commonwealth. Its six points now encompassed political, occupational, moral, social, economic and legal equality. But Margaret's role had become largely titular. The SPG outlived her, lasting until 1983.

As early as 1937 Margaret was arguing that although still needed, instead of working flat out for equality of status, 'better results' could be obtained at present if women used the powers they possessed to do good in the world and to familiarise the general public with the idea of men and women working side by side 'regardless of sex and on equal terms for the general good'. She even suggested that there was a danger in equalitarian societies receiving too much publicity at present since they could perpetuate for the younger generation a picture of women 'as a class apart and inferior, always knocking outside the door, never doing, but always claiming the right to do...'[93]

Yet in many parts of the globe women did not possess power or influence. And within Britain where a notion of men and women working side by side with equal rights existed, it was as an ideal for some and as an uncomfortable thought for many more. It was far from the experience of industrial women workers in particular. They remained firmly 'outside the door'. Margaret's concept of the emancipated woman was essentially that of the professional, educated woman as was demonstrated in her publications and talks.

CHAPTER THIRTEEN

Reading Lady Rhondda

In August 1932 George Bernard Shaw read a copy of 'That Gadfly', Margaret's enthusiastic reaction to his latest play 'Too True to be Good'. He liked what he read, telling her: 'What a magnificent article! You CAN write. Even the best of the men's articles are intolerable and unreadable piffle after it.'[1]

Shaw's reaction was not a stock response to a flattering discussion of his work. He, of all people, was hardly in need of publicity or praise, and anyway Margaret had not written a straightforward appreciation of his talents. Her *Time and Tide* article opened with the claim that '[p]robably the most significant thing about Shaw... is that at seventy-six he still retains the capacity to exasperate almost beyond endurance both the world at large and half the younger writing men of today'.[2] As Margaret knew, he was more than capable of taking her to task if he felt she deserved it. His personal letters to her frequently proffered advice. But here he was praising her for a penetrating and intelligent understanding of his work. She was delighted. In a letter to Holtby she quoted his words, remarking that this was '[s]uch [underlined twice] a thrill!'³

Margaret is usually seen as the person who, as a newspaper owner and editor, enabled others to write. It is, however, worth considering her as an author and journalist in her own right, not least because, as Shaw recognised, she was capable of some fine writing. She had been penning articles for the press for many years and had become an influential editor who wrote rather more in her paper than was acknowledged. She also published three books.

She edited and wrote a substantial part of her first book, a memoir of her father.⁴ It was another dozen years before her best known work appeared. *This Was My World* is an autobiography with a difference: like Margaret's biography of D.A. it did not quite adhere to the conventional format. More than three hundred pages long and divided into four parts, it focused on the early part of her life. The final section is on 'The War – and After' but this was the First World War. It can hardly be called Margaret's life story. She lived for a further quarter of a century after it was published but chose not to produce a second volume. It concludes with a chapter called 'The Future' that, by the time it was written and read, was actually about the past.

Margaret's title was retrospective. It *was* her world. Her account ends in 1919, before the start of what is justifiably seen as her greatest achievement, the creation of *Time and Tide*. It could be argued that her paper then took her story forward and that by the time of its publication on 17 March 1933 (when she was in her fiftieth year) she was such a public figure that an account of her early life might seem more intriguing for the reading public than a focus on the present.

Margaret's explanation was the reasonable one of needing distance and perspective. She thought that she was too close to recent events to write about them: 'they have not yet arranged themselves into any pattern. They are still all tangled up.'[5] But there was more at stake here. Despite a need to keep her paper and causes in the public eye, Margaret was not keen to address publicly her private life. Writing about earlier days was safer and at a time when the future seemed uncertain both financially and personally, deflecting attention from the present and turning the spotlight on the recent past must have seemed appealing. To her alarm and annoyance, when the book appeared, 'RW' (probably Rebecca West) telephoned to 'sound me about any possible scandals in my family'.[6]

It was the fashion for former suffragettes to tell their stories in the interwar years. Titles were similar: Emmeline Pethick-Lawrence's *My Part in a Changing World* (1938) is not unlike Margaret's. Suffragette memoirs helped validate earlier activities and claim a historical role and hierarchy of authentic suffrage militancy, enabling the construction of a narrative that made sense of more recent feminist politics.[7] Margaret's story was an exemplar for the continued advocacy of equal rights feminism.

Robins' 'autobiography' a few years later covered only the years 1888 to 1890, when the young American actress first arrived in England.[8] At first glance her focus on the least auspicious period in the eminent life of this multi-talented international actress and writer seems perverse. But Robins knew what she was doing and by highlighting the ingénue waiting in the wings rather than the Ibsenite star, her *Both Sides of the Curtain* not only shielded her private (as opposed to professional self) from the public gaze but also revealed – though it was never spelt out – just how well-known she subsequently became.

An advance notice for Margaret's book in *The Times* claimed that it would show 'how a shy, dreamy Victorian child developed by the force of unusual circumstances into one of the outstanding personalities of post-war England'.[9] Its end leaves her poised for her bold step into journalism. By concentrating on a period prior to *Time and Tide*, before women had the vote, she demonstrated how dramatically the world had changed post-war and the impact made by forward-looking women through this review and organisations such as the SPG. Like Robins, Margaret used the past to illuminate the present, to show how women's lives and expectations were changing by implicitly contrasting the interwar years with the world she had known, a world that was being lost.

Margaret's introduction stressed that this was 'the autobiography of a normal person'. She was always critical of the idea of the exceptional woman. Her involvement in a popular movement like suffrage permitted identification with others of like mind,[10] though there is little sense of sister suffragettes in the book beyond family and Prid. But her privileged and supportive family meant that there was never a neat fit between Margaret's story and the opportunities provided for most women. And, as so often in her life, the shadow of D.A. was omnipresent. The *Monmouthshire Review* noted that here was the story of two people. It was evident that 'she shares the drama of living with her father, that she unfolds the secret of his psychology no less than her own. It is a remarkable achievement.'[11]

A number of reviewers specifically mentioned Margaret's candour, courage and frankness.[12] This was intended as a compliment, recognising that although she was a Victorian by birth, she was refreshingly modern in her approach.[13] Yet candour was surely an impression that she carefully sought, rather successfully, to suggest by her tone, which was one of assumed directness with Dear Reader. In practice she did not reveal much and what she did say tended to be about the young Margaret. Although she might not have been as disingenuous as Robins who openly admitted to 'cooking' accounts of her life, Margaret's little confessions about, for example, being greedy about food, served to endear her to readers at the same time as occluding more important revelations about her personal and business life. This experienced journalist seems to have been crafting her words and narrative strategies rather more assiduously than many imagined.

There are significant silences. The young Margaret might be prominent and her Haig aunts depicted with tender, loving care as well as an adoring and adored father but there is a notable sublimation of the self as the narrative proceeds. Margaret's war work is especially conspicuous by its absence. The chapter on the war is called 'London in War-Time' as though deliberately shifting attention from the self to the city. The wartime atmosphere is beautifully conveyed as is the story of the sinking of the *Lusitania* (largely reproduced from an earlier account), which could not fail to move readers, but

Margaret selected and shaped carefully what and how she wished to divulge.

Not surprisingly, it was Holtby who understood how little Margaret had revealed. Her review for *The Schoolmistress* was entitled 'The Unknown Lady Rhondda'. It praised her writing but whereas one review called it 'a memorable piece of self-portraiture'[14] Holtby recognised that it betrayed remarkably little about Margaret.[15] Unusually for an autobiography, Margaret's emphasis was on the word 'World' rather than 'My'.

Although Scotland and England are important, much of the story is centred on south-east Wales before the First World War. Historical accounts of early twentieth-century south Wales have tended to focus on miners and the coal industry which had made the Thomas fortunes and even gave them a new name. By contrast, Margaret usefully presents another perspective: a social and political world refracted through the lens of a woman who, although immensely privileged, nevertheless lacked the vote before 1918. *This Was My World* excels in what historians used to call 'the spirit of the age'. It is the changed spirit for educated women poised to take advantage of their new-found freedom that marks the end of Margaret's narrative.

Had her book been written a year or so later, it is likely to have had a less optimistic ending and reflected growing fears about world stability and peace. Margaret was working on it in the spring of 1931 though it did not appear for another two years. Hitler became Chancellor of Germany just weeks before Macmillan published it. The book cost 10/6d. Margaret offered to defray some of the advertising costs and told Macmillan that she was prepared to spend up to £200 – a hefty sum – for this purpose.[16]

Some reviewers could not resist a dig at the suffragettes, detecting hysteria and misguided actions. One assured readers that Margaret was 'much too charming and gentle a young woman ever to have been a success as a militant'.[17]

Nevertheless, reviews were largely positive. Margaret's style and wit pleased readers. Brittain, in the throes of completing her own autobiography, confessed to Holtby that 'whichever of our books is the better I shall be lucky if I get as good reviews as she seems to be getting'. Brittain had been surprised to read the *Daily Herald's* assessment ('No more honest, untheatrical or significant autobiography has been written in our time'). She conceded that Margaret's book was 'interesting, and full of ideas' but conscious that this maybe sounded overly enthusiastic, she modified this to 'or rather, perhaps, suggestions for ideas than the ideas themselves'.[18] But Holtby accepted that it was a challenging and readable book even if it hid as much as it revealed. Within three months it was in its third reprint and hailed by *The Times* as '[a] great and continuous success'.[19] A cheap edition appeared in the autumn of 1934.

Most of Margaret's other publications began as articles for *Time and Tide* but as the Appendix shows, there were a few exceptions. One was for the *Encyclopaedia Britannica*. It published in 1924 two large volumes entitled *These Eventful Years. The Twentieth Century in the Making* with chapters by 'the Makers of Current History'. They included Sigmund Freud, Bertrand Russell and H.G. Wells. Billed as 'The Book of the Century' and revealing 'What the Foremost Men of our Time Really Think', Margaret and Marie Curie were nonetheless listed as two of the most prominent contributors.

Entitled 'The Political Awakening of Women', Margaret's chapter (partly written in the south of France) focused on international demands for the vote since 1900 though the main emphasis was on 'The Anglo-Saxon Countries'.[20] Compared to her later writing it was a pedestrian piece, though a useful table showed how legislation (such as equal divorce laws) tended to follow the granting of the vote in different countries. It ended quite optimistically: leisured women of the wealthy classes, important shapers of public opinion, were poised for the world of work. Then 'the whole attitude of the well-to-do classes is likely to be altered'.[21]

'Women of the Leisured Classes' became the title of Margaret's six-part series in *Time and Tide* in the autumn of 1926.[22] She had been impressed by Thorstein Veblen's 1899 study of American society. In *The Theory of the Leisure Class* Veblen examined the development of a leisure class and critiqued the belief that true accomplishment lay in ostentatious wealth and status. He discussed those women who were 'excluded by the canons of good repute from all effectual work' and expected to live 'a life of leisure and conspicuous consumption' (it was Veblen who coined that term).[23]

Margaret adopted the pseudonym of Candida, borrowing the title of Shaw's early comedy with its eponymous heroine who challenged conventional representations of marriage and gender roles. The first article opened with a long quote from John Stuart Mill's *The Subjection of Women* (1869) which had influenced her when she first became a suffragette and began reading 'on new lines'.[24] Margaret argued that women were then regarded as inferior beings 'not far removed from a privileged slave class.' They were largely uneducated and 'carefully trained to think personally, never impersonally' and only about their own and their families' immediate interests. Women's influence was on their children. They had about as much impact on public opinion as dogs or horses.

In subsequent articles Margaret considered the changes of the past fifty years, stressing the decline in family size and the impact of women's demands on public life and politics. She provided facts and figures and stressed that there had not been much change in the training or thinking of most women of the leisured classes. In some heartfelt passages indirectly reflecting her own experience, she described the corrosive impact of 'a year or two of idle uselessness in the home'. Despite receiving an education, today's young woman was ultimately not much more advanced than her counterpart of 1870.

Most contentiously, Margaret scorned the notion of motherhood as destiny. Young ladies were taught that their first duty was not to community but to the home and that 'the one sacred thing in life is the maternal instinct'. However, she ventured:

> No one ever teaches them that the maternal instinct unregulated and unsublimated can be just as dangerous, just as anti-social and just as amoral as any other untaught and unregulated instinct.

Now that these women had smaller families, mothers tended to spoil children so they were growing up 'soft, expecting the best, as of right'. As for employment, the ideal remained unpaid charity work and even those who pursued a professional career – usually teaching – were still expected to sacrifice their career for male relatives.

In her final article Margaret suggested that the current situation was potentially more dangerous than that of 1870, since slave ideals of dependence, idleness and irresponsibility persisted, even though slaves had been set free. Given the influence of the leisured class on the whole community, the implications for all were evident. To improve the situation it must be recognised that motherhood was no longer a full-time job. Liberty needed to be accompanied by education and self-belief reflected in equal pay, conditions, respect and citizenship. Margaret ended on a suitably challenging note:

> The generation of 1870 set out to do a great service, but its task is not yet done, and if we of to-day leave that task unfinished we shall find that, so far from having saved society, the action of the early feminists has merely hastened its decay.

Margaret had, as she knew, generalised, exaggerated and simplified in order to make an impact about something that deeply concerned her. For example, families were indeed smaller than they had been, but to suggest that married women tended to have two children hardly reflected reality in 1926. Moreover her focus was only really on mothers with small families wealthy enough to employ servants and nurses. But Margaret was being deliberately provocative since she saw herself as having escaped the fate she described, even though her parents had been more enlightened than most and it had been her personal choice to opt out of higher education and marry an eligible bachelor. She regretted her youthful decisions and did not wish others to emulate them.

Time and Tide had just been through a crisis and needed to garner a wider readership and re-establish itself under its new editor. Margaret wrote to Robins in advance of the publication of the articles admitting that they were 'frankly and provocatively written', designed to 'make something of a stir'.[25] She sought 'a correspondence and, if possible, a controversy'. Her tactic paid off.

Letters poured in from men and women over subsequent months. They included stout defences of the status quo and statements about the sanctity of motherhood. It was argued that Margaret had underestimated the post-war expectations and training opportunities of the modern young woman. Others stressed the high standards of education in renowned public schools though Candida's critique had been primarily concerned with small private schools. Candida was, CMCB confidently asserted, very young and fifty years out of date.[26] H.F. Scott Stokes' emphasis on women's physical weakness received an indignant response from Brittain.[27] With correspondence generating further letters and the controversy also receiving attention in papers such as the *Evening Standard*, Margaret could feel satisfied that her articles had served their purpose. They were printed as a Hogarth Essay, and she persisted in stressing the corrosive effects of being a leisured woman, declaring for example in 1940 that 'the life led by the millionaire's daughters destroys them, body, soul and mind' and affected wider society.[28]

The subject was further stimulated by Margaret inviting G.K. Chesterton to express his views. Responding to what he called 'this delightful controversy', he challenged Candida's notion of servility, taking issue with the claim that motherhood was no longer a full-time job (he took particular exception to that word 'job').[29] Margaret argued that mothers might be devoted to their children 'but loving does not in itself constitute an occupation'. She also stated that since she believed the leisured woman to be 'one of the worst and least realised perils of our civilisation' she would like to challenge Chesterton to a public debate on the subject.[30] In the past an affronted gentleman might have invited his opponent to a duel. Abandoning anonymity, Margaret opted for words as her weapon, allowing Chesterton to choose when, where and how this modern battle would take place.

It was more of an engaging entertainment than a serious debate. The sell-out performance of 'The Menace of the Leisured Woman' took place in the Kingsway Hall on 27 January 1927 (Brittain and Holtby were stewards). It was chaired with 'puckish gravity' by Shaw.[31] Robins felt that he was 'the outshining star' of the evening.[32] Margaret was in a vulnerable position: Shaw and Chesterton had been sparring partners since 1911. She and Chesterton each spoke for twenty minutes. They had fifteen more minutes to reply to each other before Shaw summed up. Margaret criticised philanthropy as the sop for the unmarried woman and motherhood as the full-time occupation for the well-to-do mother of a small family. Chesterton glorified the home as a place of liberty.

The debate was on the radio (Shaw was a seasoned broadcaster and sat on the BBC's Pronunciation Committee). In a programme on early broadcasting at

Savoy Hill Lance Sieveking recalled this 'hair-raising' unscripted debate. The BBC had instructed him to warn the protagonists not to be too controversial. Sieveking knew this was an impossible request and inevitably they were 'brilliantly' controversial.[33]

The debate with Chesterton provoked a fascinating and remarkably outspoken exchange of letters between Margaret and Shaw. He was scornful of sweeping assertions and assumptions by both speakers: suggesting that it was equally idiotic to imply that a woman should spend all her time in either a nursery or an office. He also focused on her failure to develop some points. 'I think I'll give you a talking-to' was how he began three pages detailing the inadequacy of Margaret's performance.[34]

He roundly condemned her technique. Addressing her as though she were a young novice, he explained that if she was going into public life as a platform speaker she must appreciate that this was an art not a business. It required a thorough technique and one adjusted to her audience. Never one to mince his words, he declared that:

Your speaking at present is a perfect disgrace; lazy, slovenly... the speaking of a fine lady with an unattractive mouth and no consideration for the poor woman at the back of the hall who has paid her hard earned money to hear every syllable... Alas with no notion of what is wrong.

Shaw admitted that he had been a 'ghastly failure' the first time he had read a paper to an audience. A few weeks of exercises – mostly repeating the alphabet – would show Margaret what to do and 'a few months on the platform or in Hyde Park will get up your articulatory muscles'. He suggested that she listen to Annie Besant, the Fabian socialist turned theosophist, who, before devoting herself to India, had been renowned as England's greatest orator. Her 'quiet force', he wrote, was an inspiration. Shaw signed his letter 'too sincerely, I am afraid'.

More remarkable than Shaw's temerity was the manner in which Margaret responded. Used to addressing all kinds of meetings from vast suffrage demonstrations in her mid-twenties to, more recently, international conferences and UK boardrooms of influential businessmen – she was now President of the Institute of Directors – she did not rise to his bait. Instead she meekly accepted his criticisms. Her three-page reply displayed humility and gratitude. She admitted:

> Of course I knew before you wrote it that I was a bad speaker – I have always known it, though I think I have been inclined to drape the full extent of the badness from myself more than your letter did![35]

Her arguments were not very convincing. She suggested that her amateurishness was probably due to 'the fatal effect that being born a woman in a world where less is expected of women has on one's self respect and general standards of attainment'. And she attributed her difficulties to her personal upbringing:

> I was brought up in a quiet, virtuous household by a Mother whose chief view of young women was that they should never think about the effect they were producing; and all of a sudden, at the age of

> thirty odd, I found myself pitchforked, by luck
> rather than by management, into a public position...
> I felt speaking was a gift I had not got, and anyway
> it seemed too late, even then, to remedy my natural
> defect. And now when I'm forty odd you tell me
> there is still time to learn.

There was no reference to her father. Margaret was not in the habit of blaming him (a poor public speaker) for her perceived shortcomings. She seems to have accepted Shaw's advice because she valued his intellect and experience. She admired his outspokenness and honesty and whereas some of her friends were annoyed by his apparent flippancy, she was impressed by his advocacy of gender equality in civic life. She also appreciated how hard-working and generous he was.

The way Margaret's talks and speeches were reported in the press does not suggest that her style was a problem. Brittain was not prone to flatter Margaret, but she nevertheless recalled the 'surprised interest' with which she and Holtby had listened to her for the first time in 1922 at a mass meeting in London's Queen's Hall.[36] Lady Rhondda had, she wrote, a reputation as 'a harsh and pitiless feminist' and the two women were pleasantly surprised 'at the deprecating sweetness of her expression' and 'the mild earnestness of her hesitating voice' as she spoke of child assault. But just three months later, she and Holtby witnessed a very different performance. Gone was any suggestion of diffidence and sensitivity to a delicate subject-matter. 'No longer mild or deprecating', Margaret denounced the Sex Disqualification (Removal) Act before a small group of supportive women. Brittain noted her flushed face, indignant blue eyes and determination:

> as she spoke the combs fell out of her soft, exuberant hair and clattered to the floor, but she treated them with as much contemptuous indifference as if they had been the insolent witticisms of Lord Birkenhead.[37]

Margaret recognised that debating involved particular skills. Shaw had left her in no doubt that there was room for improvement but had stressed that she could succeed in the art of public speaking. He was a consummate performer.[38] She enjoyed a challenge, was accustomed to the best and appreciated how he had mastered his craft. So she was impressively eager to remedy the situation. She told Shaw that his letter had created 'a shower bath effect, and I have made up my mind to go and have elocution lessons'. She even asked him to show her some time how to practise saying the alphabet.

She was, though, less prepared to accept Shaw's attack on her subject-matter. She admitted that she had made the 'bad mistake' of not wanting to repeat what she had already written in her articles, but defended her arguments and once more ventilated her disdain for the popular view that married women from the age of twenty to seventy had 'a perpetual baby in arms in the house'.

Three months later Margaret participated in another debate. It was part of a hospital fund-raising series held at the London School of Economics. Her opponent was the clever but outspoken Ulsterman, St John Ervine. The tone of 'Are Women Fit Companions for Men?' was deliberately tongue-in-cheek and, suggested Margaret, the wrong way round. Perhaps taking her cue from Holtby's depiction of the Leisured Woman debate as a boxing match, the actress Edith Evans introduced the new combatants with 'On my left is the "Ulster Kid"; on my right the "Rhondda Daisy"'.[39]

Margaret continued to be in demand as a speaker. A letter from Shaw in October 1931 suggests that she had followed his advice.[40] Somewhat pleased with himself, he told her that he was 'greatly bucked' by her recent 'platform success'. He had

> felt sure that if you went through the necessary technical grinding, and thereby directed your will towards an athletic delivery for some time, you would unconsciously start a process which would end in your suddenly finding yourself with a new miraculous power.

Margaret made more than a dozen radio broadcasts from the mid-1920s.[41] But although her god-daughter remembers her 'beautiful speaking voice' and how others too thought she had a lovely voice, she recalls how upset she was when they listened together in 1950 to the BBC recording of her account of the sinking of the *Lusitania*. Margaret felt that her voice had been badly distorted though here and in the few recordings that have survived, she sounds assured, speaking slowly, clearly and with authority. She had, however, refused 'point blank' to do a live transmission and a few years earlier N.G. Luker (Talks Director) had noted that she was '*Not* a good broadcaster'[42].

Shaw had taken Margaret to task in his own inimitable and provocative way. She then turned a critical eye on his drama in six substantial articles that appeared in *Time and Tide* during March and April 1930. She had been deeply impressed by his work since first becoming a suffragette and had reviewed a number of his plays. From late 1921 for five years (more or less fortnightly) Margaret was a theatre reviewer for her paper under the pseudonym of Anne Doubleday.[43] She covered all manner of drama in London and even Paris, providing shrewd and forthright analyses from a feminist perspective. She was not afraid to call a play or its interpretation 'tosh' and was prepared to admit that 'my ribs ached and ached' after laughing at a light-hearted piece called 'Advertising April'.[44] She was impressed by seeing Sean O'Casey's 'The Plough and the Stars' but Shaw's 'St Joan' had a profound impact. Joan of Arc had played an important symbolic role in suffrage iconography and Margaret found the play:

> [m]oving, deeply moving, it... holds within itself some of the glory and the sunshine of the world. It is a great poetic drama... I stayed entranced, enchanted, betwitched.[45]

Described later by Tyrone Guthrie as the outstanding theatrical event of the 1920s, the eponymous heroine was played by Sybil Thorndike in a ground-breaking performance and the play earned Shaw the Nobel Prize for Literature.[46]

Margaret's articles focused on the women in Shaw's plays. She started from the premise that Shaw was the one male writer of recent decades who came close to 'drawing flesh and blood women with real reactions and real individualities'.[47] Shavian women 'are possible and even attractive' but precisely because of this Shaw needed watching.[48] A lot was being asked of him because he had given so much. Having appointed herself to undertake the watching, the well-mannered Margaret worried that this great supporter of her paper might take offence. So, just before the first article appeared, she hastily penned a letter in which she spelt out the situation:

> The fact is you see, you are the nearest approach to a feminist that exists in the masculine half of the world, so (on the same principle that proper revolutionaries always felt it more necessary to murder good kings than bad ones) you are the one person that needs criticising – the others aren't worth bothering about.[49]

She was, of course, also mindful of the fact that 'even mentioning your name has a wonderful effect on sales'.

Margaret appreciated that Shaw had, in her view, started out with the fundamental belief that humanity rather than the sex of a person was what mattered and sought to treat women as if they were 'as essentially part of creation as men'. But he was so influenced by the conventions of his early upbringing and 'the surface of things around him' that he found it impossible to allow 'for training, for environment, for suggestion'.[50] In other words he accepted the priority of nature over nurture.

Margaret's analysis of Shavian women hinges on the idea that their sole function was to act as conduit pipes (in effect, breeding machines). This image was taken from a speech in the House of Lords by the former Lord Chancellor Lord Birkenhead. It had a deeply personal meaning for

Margaret since Birkenhead had blocked her bid for herself and other women to sit in the Lords as peeresses in their own right.[51] He had described them as holders of privileges existing solely so that they could act as conduit pipes for perpetuating the blood of distinguished men. In other words they kept alive a family's title after its male possessor had died and ensured that it was then passed on through their own male offspring.

Margaret used Shaw's plays to argue that even this progressive playwright defined woman's place in conduit pipe terms. He responded by broadening the argument beyond physiological usage, claiming that in his religion of 'Creative Evolution' everyone was a means to an end: Epstein's mother was a conduit pipe for her son; he was one for the theory of relativity and a son of his might be merely the conduit pipe through which a future 'Great Woman' would be produced. And he teasingly asked Margaret (though she did not print this bit) whether she would not rather be considered a conduit pipe for *Time and Tide* 'than an attractive female with a morbid taste for business?'

She maintained that almost all men perceived women solely as physiological conduit pipes and although she conceded that Shaw did see some women as having the right to choose their function, he still 'in his heart' believed that most women were born to be only 'mother' conduit pipes. She thus detected biological determinism. What mattered for Margaret was women's choice over what kind of conduit pipe to be. It was vital that women recognised that 'on their shoulders also rests not merely the good physical continuance but the spiritual progress of the race'.

Margaret was using Shaw's plays as a peg on which to hang her beliefs about the need for a change in the role of the married woman in modern well-to-do households and so continue her Leisured Woman arguments. By presenting female characters such as Ann Whitefield (in 'Man and Superman') as out-of-date she could attack private girls' schools for grooming young ladies to become wives and mothers.

Shaw, Margaret felt, compartmentalised women, dividing female characters into recognisable types: mother and wife, mistress and those with 'some other big interest in life'. Although she thought that, unlike his fellow contemporaries, he could create independent women, even they were flawed since they lacked any 'surface deference' to men. In reality, she argued, women were more complex and contradictory than he suggested in plays such as 'Mrs Warren's Profession', and an amalgam of aspects of all his types. Given the society in which they lived, they were much more likely to be lacking in confidence than his bold creations though they might disguise this. She also noted the lack of comradeship between his women. However, in her review of 'Too True to be Good' two years later, she accepted that he had finally achieved this.[52]

Margaret celebrated 'St Joan' for breaking the mould. Shaw had made 'thrilling' a young woman 'whose head is in the stars instead of lying upon someone else's heart' and he understood that being attractive did not have to be synonymous with sexual attraction.[53] Only he was capable of drawing such a person. Yet Joan was not dreamed up by Shaw. She had existed so he was not entirely following his own instincts. And, Margaret noted, when Shaw did succeed in writing about women who appear human (most notably here and with Major Barbara) he made religion their inspiration. Joan was a genius and a saint. Shaw could 'see the exceptional woman as a human being: but what even he cannot yet quite see, is the ordinary woman as a human being'.

Shaw responded with the reasonable point that the essence of drama was conflict. This required shaping characters. So '[b]y all means insist that Ann is a cad [the title of one of her articles was 'Why Ann is a Cad'], or Iago a villain, or Autolycus a thief; but do not forget that they are so by dramatic necessity'.[54] He reminded Margaret that the author was 'only a poor devil faking up simulacra to give an illusion of life to the stage'.

Margaret underestimated the socialism at the heart of Shaw's plays such as 'Mrs Warren's Profession'. She was also selective in her choice of his writings, ignoring, for example his study 'The Quintessence of Ibsen', one of a handful of works that had been instrumental in shaping her views as a novice suffragette.[55] Here Shaw had declared that a life of domesticity was no more natural for all women than a military career was suitable for all men. But rather than accept Shaw's injunction that womanliness must be rejected for the sake of emancipation, feminists gave womanliness their own twist, subverting it in the way they thought most appropriate. Michael Holroyd has pointed out that 'protecting women against their protectors' appealed to Shaw.[56] It was less appreciated by Margaret.

The articles generated plenty of correspondence, most of it praising Margaret. One appreciative letter came from her erstwhile suffragette ally, Edith Lester Jones.[57] H.J.

Dion Byngham's correspondence struck a different note. He was deeply concerned about Margaret's apparent hatred of the maternal instinct, even though she had admitted that women wanted children 'a good deal more consciously than Shaw seems to realise' (her point had been that they wanted more than children).[58] Byngham saw Margaret as:

> ...typical of the dried up bloodlessness, the psychological hardening of arteries which is apt to overtake women who despise – or are disappointed in – their destiny as 'conduit-pipes' for the living blood. Oh for a good strong anti-social dose of D.H. Lawrence after this!... It seems to be a fact that women are constitutionally incapable of non-fanatical thinking, and intellectual women provide the most frightful examples of that fact.[59]

Inevitably this generated a reaction against what Monica Whately called 'fanatical, ill bred, and palaeontological criticism'.[60] Yet whereas Margaret had accorded many pages to Shaw's writing, she was chillingly brief in her own response to Byngham's letter: 'Does Mr Byngham hate everything that has danger in it? I do not.'[61]

Margaret's criticisms of Shaw did not affect their friendship.[62] In 1932 he wrote from South Africa, somewhat shaken after a car accident. He had been driving too fast and his wife Charlotte was injured. He called her 'dear Margaret' in this letter, adding 'for I also have bouts of affectionateness'.[63] He also chafed her about her background, asking in his response to her 'Gadfly' article; 'Are you sure you haven't a family habit of classing "poor devils with only ten thousand a year" as the poor?'[64] He visited Llanwern and, according to a relative, 'used to horrify poor Aunt Sybil with his remarks'.

Margaret may have depicted Shaw as an enlightened Victorian in relation to the women in his plays but he emerges as distinctly progressive and receptive to change in comparison with H.G. Wells. Her review of *Marriage* in 1912 had damned Wells's fictional representation of women. Although conceding that his disdain for spinsters was not quite so marked fifteen years later, she felt that he still saw women as inferior creatures.[65]

Margaret believed that Wells was essentially uninterested in women and even in relations between the sexes. Rather, he wished to secure for men the maximum use and value he could obtain from women. Focusing mainly on pre-war novels such as *Ann Veronica* with its 'pasteboard' heroine, she read his fictional women as victims of his sexism: 'emotional outlets for a violent and exasperated sex-antagonism'.[66]

Margaret stated unequivocally and provocatively that '[f]ew take Wells seriously on women'.[67] So why did she bother to devote four articles to him in 1930?[68] She did so because he was an important, influential and, in many ways, advanced thinker. She acknowledged his standing as a world citizen.[69] Yet she felt that only beautiful young women and mothers counted in his universe and questioned whether he even knew the meaning of the word feminist. Margaret found it depressing that such a figure was so prejudiced and seemingly unprepared to adapt to modernity in this one respect. She told Shaw that 'when Wells either talks or writes about women he does make me see red'.[70]

As for his personal relations with women, despite the fact that his lovers tended to be independent-minded individuals and not straightforward victims:

> When he takes a woman he *breaks* her somehow – takes all the self-confidence out of her, twists her till she sees life as something ugly. She's permanently maimed for having known him. I've seen that more than once.[71]

Wells believed that he was progressive. Margaret thought that he confused sexual freedom with women's rights. She was influenced by working with Rebecca West and Odette Keun. West (a director of *Time and Tide*) had been involved with Wells for a decade. Their son Anthony West claimed that Margaret angered his father when, in 1929, she encouraged Rebecca West to take legal action to make her Anthony West's sole legal guardian.[72] After Margaret's articles 'Wells on Women' appeared, Wells invited her to tea then claimed that he had made her 'properly sorry' about what she had written.[73] Margaret's version of this meeting, their first for some years, was that '[h]e was as charming as possible and I sat for two hours while he explained his point of view to me – but I remained of the same opinion still'.[74]

The journalist and translator Odette Keun realised that Wells had been hurt by the articles. She explained to Margaret that, as a result of the tea with Wells, he believed that Margaret had agreed that she had misapprehended the situation and that her assessment of him had been completely wrong.[75] Keun added that '[h]e believed that, because it hurt his vanity to believe anything else'. She had become Wells' mistress in the 1920s, living in their villa in Provence. Their tempestuous relationship ended bitterly in 1933 but lived on in print as they sought revenge on each other.

In *I Discover the English* (Margaret published extracts in the autumn of 1934 in *Time and Tide*), Keun rubbished the Englishman (for which, read Wells) as a lover, claiming that he made sex 'as flat, stale and deadly as a slab of one of his own cold suet puddings'.[76] Keun had already expressed her views frankly in letters that circulated in London. Brittain described one as '*delicious*' and commented, 'To think that the great Wells is so like the rest of human husbands!'[77]

In the same year Wells published his *Experiment in Autobiography*. It has been hailed as one of the great autobiographies of the twentieth century. Seeking a scoop, Margaret asked Odette Keun to review it for *Time and Tide*. Keun declined, telling Margaret that she would not have the book in her flat.[78] So Margaret suggested an essay on Wells. The result was three articles that appeared in October 1934.[79]

Keun painted a picture of a destructive personality, a man who lacked self-knowledge and whose book should be taken with 'the salt of the oceans'. She extended her experience of Wells the lover to his relationship with his readers, presenting him as vain, living for the moment and self-obsessed. It was 'in his bones' for this 'player' to be inconstant and life was, for him, a game.[80]

Her material had already been toned down. When the first article of 'H.G. Wells – The Player' reached the editorial office, Margaret was startled at its bitter tone. She, Holtby (who wrote the review of the book) and Cicely

Hamilton 'wrestled' with Keun over it. After several hours of heated discussion Keun admitted that 'it is all wrong in tone, it is the article of a discarded mistress'. She promised to rewrite it.[81] The printed version was, according to Margaret, 'very different', though the bitter tone remained.[82]

Margaret got her scoop and the articles were widely read and hotly debated. When Shaw suggested that she had been 'hitting below the belt' in printing what the paper called 'Madame Keun's analytical articles'[83], Margaret was worried both because she valued Shaw's opinions and since (although she would not admit it to others) she knew that her tactics had been questionable.[84] She told Shaw that the articles were 'simply by someone who has been hurt' and that Wells knew all too well about hitting below the belt himself. Wanting to salvage Keun's character, she stressed that she was training in maternity work for colonial social service and 'has a conscience the size of a house'.

Wells retaliated in *Apropos of Dolores* in which the eponymous heroine was so evidently Keun that Methuen withdrew from publishing it for fear of a libel case (Cape took over). He was furious that Margaret had given Keun space, questioning why she had printed something so abusive. Margaret claimed that she had simply provided a 'brilliant critical appreciation' of him as an author.[85]

In his novel *Brynhild* (1937) Wells ridiculed the pursuit of literary fame, publishing and reputation. He included a swipe at *Time and Tide* through his portrayal of *Wear and Tear*, a weekly paper voicing women's discontent.[86] It was run by Lady Roundabout and a group of women who appeared to delight in being disagreeable.

John Ruskin had written *Time and Tide by Weare and Tyne*
and the Welsh novelist Jack Jones, whose work Margaret
praised, had published his *Rhondda Roundabout* three
years before *Brynhild* appeared.

Addressing a Manchester luncheon club, Margaret
quipped:

> If I am supposed to be Lady Roundabout... and that
> is the purpose for which I am running the review,
> well, I ought to be in Colney Hatch.[87] And if 'Lady
> Roundabout' is an allusion to my figure, all I can say
> is that I would not change my figure for that of Mr
> Wells.[88]

Margaret was by no means the only feminist infuriated by
Wells' cavalier and public humiliation of women.[89] Robins
had crossed swords with him on a number of occasions
and was bitter about his treatment of his lover Amber
Reeves. Margaret had pointed out in *Time and Tide* that
Wells was not troubled by the idea of women remaining
ancillary to men.[90] In 1924 Robins published an
anonymous and angry volume entitled *Ancilla's Share*,
sub-titled *An Indictment of Sex Antagonism*. Wells was
presented here as 'the literary Grand Turk', a figure who
saw women's purpose as providing physical satisfaction
for men.[91]

Margaret reviewed Robins' book.[92] The author's
identity had been revealed the previous month. But
although the two women saw eye to eye over Wells and
worked closely together in the early stages of both the
paper and the SPG, Margaret had serious reservations
about Robins' polemic. The book's adversarial, staccato

style was uncompromising from the outset. Chapter 1 opens with the words: 'These pages are not addressed to the masculine mind'.[93] It ranged widely across time and place and analysed what today we would call sexist language, anticipating feminist writing of half a century later. Written with a sense of urgency in the wake of one war as militarism seemed to threaten future world stability, it argued that civilisation was threatened by war but that if harnessed in time, women could, as genuinely equal partners with men, make the vital difference in saving society.

Margaret had no difficulty with the idea that equal cooperation from both men and women was an essential prerequisite for civilisation's survival. Much of Robins' book traced the history of sex antagonism, including men's attitudes towards women's work. But although she conceded that equal cooperation certainly did not exist at present, Margaret did not see sex antagonism as fundamental or as widespread as Robins claimed.

Robins appeared to be advocating a separatist position for women (at least in the present), since in her phased plan for equality the ultimate cooperation of men and women needed to be preceded by different tactics: 'the short cut to real union lies through temporary abandonment of insistence on union'.[94] This notion of suspending, even temporarily, joint efforts between men and women struck Margaret as retrogressive, especially since women seemed to be making vital gains. She argued that their position in the west had changed dramatically in the past century, and pointed instead to men's amazing acquiescence rather than antagonism.

The American feminist Crystal Eastman claimed that

Ancilla's Share was fast becoming the feminist Bible.[95] But sales were poor and Robins' brave and angry words did not strike a chord with newly enfranchised women. Nevertheless, unlike Wells, Margaret did not altogether dismiss the book.[96] She found it a stimulating read and, loyal to one of her paper's founders, stressed the importance of its subject-matter.

Margaret's contributions to *Time and Tide* assumed various forms. She replied to letters criticising editorial opinion. Her habit of parrying attacks in paragraphs that accompanied a protesting letter placed her in an advantageous position since it would be at least a week before the reader could answer the editor. She wrote editorial comments (some signed) and Leaders. A number of people penned Leaders over the years including Holtby, Fenwick Gaye and Ellis Roberts. Later on R.T. Clark (of the BBC), the historian C.V. Wedgwood and Anthony Lejeune would write the lion's share.

It is difficult to ascertain exactly how much Leader and editorial comment was by Margaret, so the focus here is on what was indisputably her writing up to 1938. In early March 1933, after praising Holtby's contributions to the paper, Margaret sought her opinion on the latest issue for which she had written the Leader. She was concerned that, for all her efforts, it was 'pretty bad – a good deal below our standard'.[97] Her nervousness can probably be explained by the imminent publication of her autobiography, as well as the fact that Holtby had been unable to help steer the paper for two months. As Margaret put it, 'London & T&T go limping when you're away'.[98]

In 1932 Margaret wrote a signed article entitled 'Mrs

Mitchison and the Bishops', defending a controversial Victor Gollancz publication entitled *Outline for Boys and Girls and Their Parents* edited by Naomi Mitchison.[99] The book had provoked a letter of protest from eighteen men including an Archbishop, two Bishops and the headmasters of Eton and Harrow. It was criticised for not acknowledging the developmental role of Christianity and omitting the name of Christ (though Mohammed, Buddha and Lenin were named). It was also accused of endorsing Soviet attacks on the family.

Margaret countered the claims about Christianity, maintaining that it was mentioned frequently and with respect in the book. Although she became noted for her anti-Soviet views, here she defended Soviet educational institutions such as crèches and kindergartens. Unsurprisingly her claim that Christ was only '[r]ather half-heartedly, surely' on the side of the family, provoked in turn further indignant responses.[100]

Earlier that year Margaret signed a memorial on behalf of the Fight the Famine Council and European Reconstruction Council about famine conditions in Russia, calling for government cooperation with the United States.[101] She also took part in a demonstration at the Kingsway Hall to raise support for the famine districts. During the crisis of 1921-2 she had spoken about famine relief at a meeting organised by the Women's International League and donated £31.10/- to Russian Famine Relief.

Although never a pacifist, from the early 1930s Margaret's speeches and writings focused increasingly on the need for peace. A radio talk she broadcast in March 1934 (requested by Sir John Reith) as part of the 'Whither Britain?' series was printed in *The Listener*.[102] Here she outlined her ideal of a Britain 'fit to live in'. It would be part of a world 'from which fear of war on the grand scale has practically been banished'. There would be sufficient food, housing, warmth and comfort, good air and light for all and work for all with a reasonable amount of leisure and a healthy population. Britain would have no barriers: 'neither race nor class nor marriage nor any other irrelevant consideration' would impede full economic, political and social status and opportunity. Education would be given the place of honour. Equal consideration and opportunities for all would result in approximately equal wealth for all.

But she warned that it would not be possible to have what she wanted for Britain until the rest of the world got something similar. Equality was needed, not to make all the same but to set people free to be different and follow their own paths. Getting what one wanted involved, Margaret believed, three essential prerequisites. They were knowing what one wanted, knowing what getting one's own way involved and cost, and being prepared to pay the price for this.

Having outlined her vision, Margaret addressed the suggestions of earlier speakers in the series. She attacked splendid isolation, admitted to being a patriot but did not want peace at any price. She was especially critical of Winston Churchill, arguing that his plan for building up Britain's defences to create the world's strongest nation was flawed. Every other nation had come to the same conclusion and only one could be pre-eminent. It was unlikely to be Britain. Arming for strength had never prevented war and was expensive. Mr Churchill, Margaret concluded, 'is a romanticist, not a realist'.

Seeking to reconcile her love for her country and national pride[103] with her belief that another major war would be fatal to civilisation, Margaret advocated collective security. Strengthening the League of Nations was the way forward. Involvement in shaping a future on an international basis was essential for peace. Margaret struck a passionate and positive note for Britain's future. It involved, as she put it, getting in on the ground floor and (despite her earlier fear about Britain's global position) taking the lead in planning for 'world-control of labour, of commodities, of currency – and above all of tempers'. She ended with a wish: '[t]o make the writ of world-law run round the globe'.

Perhaps the wide-ranging nature of Margaret's topics and her ease of style were best expressed in her book of essays published by Macmillan in 1937 entitled *Notes on the Way*. This developed from the *Time and Tide* series started nine years earlier. The *Morning Post* had launched a series called 'Notes by the Way' by 'Men and Women of the Day' in the same year. Its 'daily miscellany' covered current affairs via well-known names, who each penned a paragraph. Margaret was advertised as a contributor.[104]

The *Time and Tide* column afforded writers a welcome free hand. They mused, in the tradition of newspaper Middles, on social, political, ethical and literary subjects triggered by topical events or even pet concerns. Margaret did her first stint for the month of May in 1933, wrote at least one series a year until the early 1940s, and still occasionally contributed them for years after that. 'Notes' came top in a questionnaire of 1939 asking readers to choose their favourite features, and Margaret was rated the third most popular writer for the newspaper.[105]

She originally planned to have fifty essays in her book under the headings of Places, Books, People, Manners, Politics and Meditation. Although the title and the bulk of the selection came from her 'Notes' articles, she included a few book reviews (ranging from Homer to Leonardo Da Vinci and one of her favourite modern authors, Gerald Heard) as well as her think pieces from the paper. Much of the Books section was cut from the final draft. She toyed with, though never developed, the idea of a separate volume about Shaw and more modern writers.

The collection cost six shillings, had a print run of two thousand and also sold in Canada. Clara Smith (who proofread for *Time and Tide*) helped prepare the manuscript. The *News Chronicle* remarked that it 'preserves the freshness and the stamp of a robust and individual judgment' whilst *The Times* noted that Margaret wrote with warmth, humour 'and a vitality both of the intellect and of human understanding'.[106] It was advertised, somewhat blandly, as '[c]risp comments on life in general and the way we live it' but it was difficult to sum up its eclectic mix, composed more for the moment than for posterity, and even Margaret admitted that she could not easily describe her volume.

She enjoyed confounding expectations. She defended the restraint of the popular press, suggesting that if *Daily Express* readers were asked to invite Ellen Wilkinson or Aneurin Bevan to put their points of view in the local village hall '[h]alf of them would jump hard the other way. What they would like to do would be to transport this pair of revolutionaries to Russia on the spot.'[107]

An essay on the difference between reputation and

character dismissed the popular notion of the lion as the bravest of animals. Seldom meeting its equal in strength, its courage is rarely put to the test. Margaret opted rather for the common housefly which:

> courts death again and again and again, second after second, for the sake of a taste of sugar, for the sake of an aroma of roast mutton, for the mere sake of the pleasure of perching upon one's leg... [108]

She included many aphorisms. We make other people's reputations subjectively and because we know that we can kill the fly and that the lion can slay us, the latter has the reputation for courage. Pointing out the dismissive saying that a person lacks the courage of a fly, Margaret remarked that '[o]ur judgment of people is just about as objective, unbiased and intelligent'.[109]

Attention was drawn to the use of language and what it suggested about a nation's sense of status and smug superiority. It was revealed, for example, in the short section in *The Times* on what it euphemistically called 'Faithful Service', with its recording of the working lives of dutiful domestic servants.[110] In the House of Commons, Margaret heard Anthony Eden refer to the 'foreign lives' saved by the British in Abyssinia. She cynically mused on 'the saving of a whole gradation of qualified lives' from 'black lives, native lives, foreign lives, American lives, leading up at last to the highest: British lives'.[111]

Margaret stressed the importance of democracy, yet questioned whether this was an accurate term, since government by the people in a state where all had equal rights hardly described the situation at home. Political democracy might have been achieved but what about social democracy? In any really civilised society she argued, 'it would not be possible that there should be gross arbitrary divisions of class, or inequalities of income'. Change was imperative. 'Absolute equality of educational opportunities' was of paramount importance otherwise the country would 'deserve to die'. She wanted 'no better label than that of democrat. But it must be in a real democracy.'

In November 1937 Margaret wrote in the paper's 'Notes' that '[w]e want to see an island free from those disgustingly vulgar distinctions of class and wealth which are so loathsome a feature of the semi-barbarian pseudo-democracy of today.'[112] Yet she had chosen to send her half-brother to Eton and she too had 'faithful servants' though she argued that the Left had 'an impregnable case' in believing in the 'abolition of all class, and of inequality of wealth as we have got it at present' and that 'no other Western nation is – superficially at least – as class ridden as ours'.[113]

Early in 1935 Margaret wrote that there were few more useful services than 'making people do a little hard thinking about peace and war and about the price which is worth paying for peace'.[114] Her writing for the paper was increasingly dominated by this concern and this found its way into her 'Notes' volume. In a signed article entitled 'Peace or Parsimony?' in 1930 she had predicted that disarmament would not succeed so long as the motive in favour of it was predominantly financial.[115] She also admitted that, much as she supported peace, if another war came which signalled the end of her country as a great nation, she would once again support her country.

The *Notes on the Way* volume inadvertently became notes on the way to war, a frozen snapshot of how Margaret saw her society in 1937. It included a carefully edited version of the 'Peace or Parsimony' article.[116] By the time Margaret was assembling the volume, the sentiments expressed in 1930 about the interlocking of nations and achieving safety by working towards a world community would have seemed impossibly idealistic so were eliminated. That November, sickened by recent events in Spain, Margaret declared that the ultimate objectives for which the paper stood were peace and democracy, but she applauded the Labour Party's reluctant decision that the rearmament programme must be accepted 'as a factor which makes for peace'.[117]

Margaret also wrote in a somewhat lighter vein.The year 1937 saw the start of an informal column as an antidote to the paper's serious political tone. It was initially signed by either Four Winds (with paragraphs usually composed by a few regulars) or a named wind such as Sirocco, Sou' Wester or West Wind. Playing on her initials, Ellen Wilkinson wrote the East Wind entries. Margaret was one of the Four Winds (this was also the name of a house close to her Surrey home). Before long this column was renamed a Diary, though still tended to be signed Four Winds. As with all weekly features, it must have been difficult at times to find sufficient material to fill the space. Alongside snippets of news and strong views on certain topics were personal anecdotes and stories of former travels. A humorous tale usually rounded off the column.

The Diary contained an element of well-informed upmarket gossip reminiscent of the social diaries of popular daily newspapers. It preserved some anonymity and avoided direct identification of people and places unless they were already in the public eye. Readers were told that information had been received from 'a friend' in Cairo, Paris, New York or Yorkshire. 'Vicky' drew witty cartoons to accompany the contents.

Although Margaret did not use her own name here, readers would have been well aware that it was their editor who was regaling them with an account of dining with the Roosevelts at an exclusive gathering at the White House.[118] Her signed writings elsewhere in the paper conveyed an undisputed authority. Yet at the same time the woman who signed her articles 'Rhondda' by virtue of being a member of the peerage was still denied the right to take her seat in the House of Lords. So before looking at the last two decades of Margaret's life, it is worth focusing on her sustained battle, over many years, to secure a place for women in that Upper House.

CHAPTER FOURTEEN

Entitlement: Viscountess Rhondda and the House of Lords

Imagine that Planet Earth has established regular communication with Planet Venus. Life there is remarkably similar to British society. But there is one essential difference: all political matters on Venus are managed by women. Only women have the right to vote or sit in the House of Commons. The House of Lords is composed of the eldest daughters of deceased peers.

This piece of science fiction was by the writer Bertha Thomas.[1] 'Latest Intelligence from the Planet Venus' was a witty pro-suffrage Victorian riposte to those who argued against giving women the vote (and evidence that Victorians envisaged even imagined societies to be structured in their own likeness). It was written in the decade before Margaret was born. In Thomas's tale, a clever female agitator audaciously advocates the enfranchisement of males on Venus. But although she has her supporters, the idea of admitting 'young cornets, cricketers and fops' to a share in the legislation and the prospect of parliamentary benches recruited from racecourses, hunts and billiard rooms is too much to contemplate for those running the country.[2] Why tamper with the foundations of society and disturb the laws of nature? So Venus shelves plans for enhancing male power.

Back in the realm of reality and almost half a century later, Margaret, the titled daughter of a deceased peer, became embroiled in a protracted battle to break the stranglehold of the male sex over control of the House of Lords. At times she must have wondered what planet she was on as she encountered antediluvian attitudes and inventive ploys to thwart her bid to allow her and a small group of peeresses[3] to take their seats.

She had succeeded to the peerage in July 1918 when the king agreed to settle the remainder of the Rhondda peerage on her. D.A. had wished his heir to enjoy what he saw as her due. Since Margaret had no children the title did not last beyond her generation, but she was determined that a peeress should be entitled to exercise the same rights as a peer.

Most hereditary peeresses were, unlike Margaret, from old English nobility. In 1924 she listed the current two dozen peeresses in their own right in England, Wales and Scotland.[4] The majority were baronesses. Three titles dated back to the thirteenth century. They were hardly a group renowned for shaking the establishment and it did not escape the notice of the press that it was an industrial magnate who 'sallied forth to do battle for her claim'.[5] Holtby noted that Margaret's lawsuit was seen as 'the ostentatious aggressiveness of a "nouveau aristot"'.[6]

The women's suffrage movement had concentrated on gaining the parliamentary vote, so the focus had been on the House of Commons. Once this was partially achieved in 1918, Viscount Haldane sought unsuccessfully to persuade the Lords that the right of women to sit in Parliament should apply to both Houses and to include them in the Parliament (Qualification of Women) Bill. A similar amendment in the Commons had been dropped on the understanding that the Lords would deal with it. The lack of election for the Lords (not a factor that usually exercised members) was of concern, as was a fear that introducing women at one fell swoop might 'swamp' the Upper House.[7]

Seeking to win the newly enfranchised women's vote, Lloyd George and Bonar Law had pledged to remove inequalities between men and women if returned to power in the general election of December 1918. Labour's Women's Emancipation Bill would have admitted the current hereditary peeresses but was superseded by the government's Sex Disqualification (Removal) Bill. This merely conceded that future titles by special remainder would encompass a seat and vote. However, even this was a step too far for some. The Lord Chancellor, Lord Finlay, moved an amendment in the House of Lords. He claimed that the clause relating to peeresses had only been inserted so that the Lords might express their views. This offending clause was dropped.

Margaret was critical of the new act's shortcomings quite apart from having a vested interest in its provisions. She noted wryly that the word 'Removal' had never managed to escape the brackets imposed on it. As a former suffragette and increasingly outspoken advocate of equal opportunities for women, it was hardly surprising that she should champion this cause. She also wanted to honour D.A.'s wishes. Margaret wasted no time, and on inheriting her title stated her intention to petition the king to receive a Writ of Summons to Parliament like other new Peers of the Realm.

Despite her disappointment with the 1919 act, its wording provided some leverage for a claim. Section 1 stated that:

[a] person shall not be disqualified by sex or marriage from the exercise of any public function, or from being appointed to or holding any civil or judicial office or post.[8]

Margaret and her lawyers chose to interpret sitting in the Lords as a public function and since no exemption was specified, argued that she was therefore entitled to a Writ.

Her timing looked good. Women were now being admitted to the legal profession. Margaret was a special guest at the celebratory dinner held at the House of Commons attended by women law students, the Lord Chancellor, the Attorney General, Solicitor General and Lord Chief Justice.[9] The advent of women MPs,[10] jurors, magistrates and the need for governments to appeal to women as voters, helped to ensure that their rights and responsibilities were kept in the public eye. From May 1920 the existence of *Time and Tide* meant that pressure was maintained.

But from the start Margaret was beset by bureaucracy and delays. The petition was referred to the Committee for Privileges of the House of Lords. On 2 March 1922 her case was heard before Viscount Hutchinson (the Earl of Donoughmore) and seven other peers. They were well placed to make a decision: three Law Lords, two other experienced lawyers, a lord with extensive administrative experience and one with special knowledge of cases involving complicated privileges. Margaret was accompanied by her Uncle Edric (Sybil was on holiday in South Africa). He confirmed that she was the only child of his sister and Viscount Rhondda. When she was asked, under oath, whether this was the only marriage of her father she answered in the affirmative and to the question 'Have you any brothers?' she replied 'No'. This was never queried.[11]

G.J. Talbot KC put the case for Margaret and had a good response. Sir Gordon Hewart KC, MP, the Attorney General, who had been in favour of women's suffrage, declared that he was 'very much in agreement with what has been urged' and could not imagine

> any sound agreement to the contrary of what is being asked by the petitioner. When one looks at the plain words of the Act, at the date of the Act, and at the legislation which has gone before, the conclusion would appear to be irresistible.[12]

The Committee decided to grant Margaret a Writ by a majority of seven to one.

Not surprisingly, there was jubilation amongst feminists. Using somewhat hyperbolic language, Lady Frances Balfour told the National Council of Women a week later that '[t]he collapse of the walls of Jericho was nothing to the way the walls of opposition fell down before Lady Rhondda'.[13] Margaret was fêted at the annual NUSEC conference a few days after the decision. Resolutions were passed congratulating her. She was presented with a big bouquet of mauve tulips by the SPG.

'Hail, Lady Rhondda', 'The Triumph of the Suffragette'

and other dramatic headlines were emblazoned across newspapers from Argentina to Ceylon. This one bit of news gave international recognition to the name Lady Rhondda. The *St Louis Post-Dispatch* spent one and a half pages outlining her success. It proclaimed that women were back in the House of Lords after five hundred years, though rather spoilt the effect by displaying a picture of Sybil instead of Margaret. The *Church Times* called it a remarkable triumph for feminism, especially since the Lords had not anticipated such a result when they passed the Sex Disqualification (Removal) Act. 'Shall we have a Lady Archbishop or Lord Chancellor?' hazarded the *Manchester Evening News*.

Such confidence was not surprising since no report from the Committee for Privileges had been resisted since 1869 and even then the motion had not been carried. The *Western Mail* thought it 'inconceivable that the House of Lords would reject the Committee's decision, based as it is on the interpretation of a statute'. The *Pall Mall Gazette* declared that 'it would have been impossible' for the Committee to have come to any other conclusion. The *Sunday Times* asked whether such drastic constitutional change had ever been accepted with so little difficulty. How wrong these papers were!

Yet one paper did not predict automatic success. *Time and Tide* suggested that 'backwoodsmen' amongst the peers would put up a strong fight.[14] And when St Loe Strachey, editor of the *Spectator*, prematurely congratulated Margaret on her victory on 9 March, she responded by correctly anticipating trouble: 'I am not in the House of Lords yet,' she warned, 'and I am afraid the Lord Chancellor is going to move against me.'[15]

When, on 30 March, Lord Donoughmore moved that the report be accepted by the Lords, the Lord Chancellor, the Earl of Birkenhead responded. Sitting, appropriately enough, in the Strangers' Gallery, Margaret heard him immediately oppose the motion. He moved an amendment to refer the request for a Writ back to the Committee for Privileges for 'reconsideration'.[16] Not only was this carried without a division, but Birkenhead also moved the goalposts. He requested that the committee be considerably enlarged and that he should sit on it.

He argued that the patent granted to Lord Rhondda and giving Margaret the peerage actually accorded the right to a seat in the House of Lords to 'those males who might hold the dignity after him', that is, to her male heirs but not to her. Birkenhead held that the patent denied this right to a female holder by its silence. The patent creating the peerage had been issued prior to the 1919 legislation which expressly did not include the right to sit in the Lords. In fact no peer during the 1919 debate on the bill had interpreted it to mean that peeresses in their own right were entitled to a seat. The 1919 Act removed disqualifications rather than conferring rights that had not previously existed.

Birkenhead also pointed out that although the original Committee for Privileges had heard what he called an 'ingenious' and 'full argument' in favour of the claim, they had not considered arguments to the contrary. He submitted that such arguments did exist. Clearly he intended to put them forward.

On 18 and 19 May a very nervous Margaret, accompanied by her mother and Robins, attended the House of Lords and sat in Black Rod's box. The *New York Times* described Margaret clutching her chair 'in an effort to restrain her militant tendencies'.[17] The situation was not helped by another petition with attendant publicity: earlier that month Margaret had appeared in the Divorce Court.[18]

Thirty men (including Lord Carson, erstwhile president of the National League for Opposing Woman Suffrage)) sat on the augmented Committee for Privileges. Unfortunately for Margaret, the sympathetic Sir Gordon Hewart was now Lord Chief Justice, and the new Attorney General Sir Ernest Pollock held very different views to his predecessor (and would soon head the SPG's Black List of political opponents of women's causes). Referring to the first section of the 1919 bill, that formed the grounds for Margaret's case, Pollock claimed that it was 'a confusion of thought to say that the holder of a peerage was exercising a public function by taking his seat in the House'.[19] What he viewed as 'a doubtful interpretation of an ambiguous word' was being used 'to make a vital alteration in the composition of their Lordships' House'. Such a sweeping alteration could never have been intended by 'mere general words'.

The *Manchester Guardian* noted that much highly technical and abstruse argument was adduced by the Lord Chancellor, who played a leading role in this expanded Committee.[20] Margaret stated that he 'frankly, unabashedly' and she conceded, most effectively, led the opposition throughout.[21]

The complicated arguments of constitutional law went down well with the dozen law lords but some others had difficulty following him. Much revolved around whether an act of Parliament was to be interpreted strictly according to its wording or whether the intentions of the legislators should also be taken into account. Margaret's claim was now rejected by a majority of twenty to four (there were some abstentions). Whereas the original Committee for Privileges report was 34 pages in length, the reconstituted Committee produced a report of 109 pages. Part of Birkenhead's concern was that serious constitutional change was involved without formal legislation.[22]

The Earl of Crawford noted later that Sir Ernest Pollock had been permitted to speak at great length against the petition, whereas Margaret's counsel was constantly interrupted.[23] Sir Frederick Pollock, who held somewhat different views from his namesake, wrote in the *Law Quarterly Review* that he agreed with the few dissenting speeches and that the argument drawn from 'the absence of positive enabling words' was sophistical.[24] He and his wife were close friends of Robins. She had personally observed that Margaret's counsel Talbot and Birkenhead seemed to be locked into a duel.[25] She also heard Haldane attempt to intervene. He later protested that they had been 'overwhelmed by numbers'.[26] He and Lord Wrenbury (who had chaired an enquiry in the Douglas-Pennant case) felt that Birkenhead prompted a decision before the evidence was fully considered.[27]

Yet there was no major challenge at the time to the Lord Chancellor who was both the presiding officer of the House of Lords and head of the judiciary. Haldane, Selbourne, Wrenbury and Ullswater were the only Lords to vote in favour of the claim. Millicent Fawcett called the situation 'simply scandalous'.[28] The CCWO chaired by Lady Astor sent a resolution to the solicitor general protesting against the situation but to no avail.[29]

On 27 June, over a month after this volte-face, Birkenhead finally spelt out to the House of Lords why Margaret's claim had been deemed invalid. His lengthy and clever judgment drew upon constitutional history and precedents going back to the 1620s.[30] He pointed out that the holder of a peerage who was a minor was not entitled to a Writ, but if he grew up he would become entitled. Felons and bankrupts were not entitled but the former might be pardoned and a bankrupt could be discharged. 'These things,' he stated, 'were possible in nature and permissible in law, but a person who was a female must remain a female till she died.'

Margaret had long been used to arguments about woman's nature and suffragettes were only too familiar with being classed with minors and criminals. But now they were being told that, unlike these categories, their sex placed them in an invidious and unalterable position. When Birkenhead told his fellow peers that Margaret's attempt to use the 1919 legislation had met with 'the discomfiture it deserved', he was received with laughter.[31]

Birkenhead's determination to intervene requires some explanation. A brilliant classicist and barrister who revelled in debating, this Lancashire Conservative had enjoyed a spectacular rise. At the end of the war, aged 46, he became the youngest Lord Chancellor since Judge Jeffreys. He had gained some notoriety for the way he had endorsed Ulster resistance to Irish Home Rule and for his prosecution of Roger Casement. Like D.A. he was highly intelligent, possessed great energy, had amassed great wealth and was known by his initials (F.E. as he was F.E. Smith). Yet although these men were linked through rumours of 'womanising' and both held strong views on many subjects, their outlooks were markedly different.

Margaret had encountered Birkenhead during her suffragette years. An eloquent man with a commanding physical presence, his attitude towards women was, even by the standards of the day, patronising and outmoded. His biographer John Campbell concedes that in his speeches on the subject he displayed an 'unusual lack of rigour and rationality' and that here was the one public question on which 'he could not think straight'.[32]

In 1910 he had led the attack in the Commons on the compromise proposal for suffrage known as the Conciliation Bill, challenging the automatic right of anybody, male or female, to a vote and arguing that women, protected by men, simply did not need the national vote and could anyway participate more appropriately in local politics. The effective running of the State depended on men, so the vote should be reserved for them. In his view, the judgments and opinions of the 'average' woman were 'more coloured by emotion and by personal considerations' than were the average man's and at times of crisis might 'prove a source of instability and disaster to the State'.[33]

The subject of women in the House of Lords touched a raw nerve. It symbolised for Margaret unfinished business and was a natural concomitant to the protracted struggle for the vote, completing women's struggle for parliamentary representation. For Birkenhead it was also linked to the past, reviving visceral sentiments about wild women activists. Resistance was especially important since women had just made so many gains in political and legal circles and entered 'The Other House'. A number of hitherto male preserves and privileges had been conceded. Margaret's bid for the peerage claim had begun just days after the first degrees were awarded to women at Oxford University.

The notion of women peers spelt much more of a threat to Birkenhead than had women's suffrage. For it struck at the heart of his world. It threatened the male establishment that this clubbable man most cherished, the space and place that nurtured, displayed and applauded his virtuoso performances and the seat of his authority. A verse in *Time and Tide* told of 'Bold Birkenhead' who thought:

> 't would put all Heaven in a rage,
> To see a Peeress in the Gilded Cage.[34]

He told Baroness Ravensdale (daughter of Lord Curzon but an active promoter of seats for women) that 'he would rather have us anywhere than in the House of Lords'.[35] The Rhondda Peerage Claim also afforded him an opportunity to demonstrate his erudition and power of advocacy.

Margaret stood for all that worried Birkenhead and vice versa. Unlike many in the Lords she had spent her adult life working and in the masculine world of business. A cartoon in the *Sunday Chronicle* depicted Birkenhead as a medieval Horatius holding the bridge as Lady Rhondda and her 'Amazonian cohorts' advanced.[36] His relentless attack on women's rights helped to ensure that Margaret persisted.

Press attitudes also fuelled her protest. Accompanying the cartoon was an article by Robert Blatchford entitled 'Why Not the House of Ladies?' Although Blatchford criticised the Lord Chancellor's opposition as illogical, ridiculous and futile and praised Margaret for acting bravely in a just cause, his remark that Birkenhead's conduct was 'ungallant' and that women would add a 'new grace and charm' inadvertently demonstrated the need to challenge attitudes in wider circles. One newspaper carried a picture of six of the women with the caption 'Who says Peeresses are ugly?'

In a signed *Time and Tide* article on 9 June, Margaret pointed out the government's culpability in the proceedings. Birkenhead was a leading member of the Coalition and 'it seems probable that no one less exalted than the Lord Chancellor himself could have exerted sufficient influence' to overturn a clear majority decision. 'Curious', she noted, somewhat disingenuously, that a leading member of the government that passed the 1919 Sex Disqualification (Removal) Act should also be the man responsible 'for preventing women benefiting by it'. This legislation had been rendered valueless. If the government wished to retain a reputation for intention of good faith, it should immediately introduce an amending act enabling peeresses in their own right to take up their rightful seats. As it was, the government did not last many more months.

In 1923 there were rumours that Margaret might try to stand for Parliament and her name was linked with the Pontypool seat in her home county. But Margaret was not interested. When St Loe Strachey suggested that she consider the House of Commons, she explained that she had spent twenty years as the daughter of an MP and it had taught her that the lot of an ordinary MP 'is a very dull one, that he is badly overworked, and has practically no power'.[37] The suffrage struggle had ensured that she was no longer a Liberal and she recognised that women were more likely to be elected if they had a party behind them. *Time and Tide* and its editor were resolutely non-party.

There was also the fact that Viscountess Astor was the first lady of the Commons. The two women did not always see eye to eye and Margaret would have been far happier carving out her own space in the Lords – she was, after all, very used to being the token woman on committees – than playing second fiddle to Lady Astor and the small number of women who followed her. Margaret instead attended debates weekly in the House of Commons as the *Time and Tide* editor. She was an assiduous reader of Hansard and actively sought to ease the way for other women to sit. She was also a founder member of the Women's Election Committee, which launched a million-shilling fund to help women stand for election. It entertained peeresses in their own right at a dinner at Frascati's restaurant in 1927 at which Margaret and Lady Ravensdale were speakers.

Margaret's decision to continue with her claim, despite the Lord Chancellor's judgment, says a lot about her. Her fight for peeresses in their own right would last for the rest of her life and earn her the sobriquet of 'The Persistent Peeress'.[38] Her determination was sharpened by the fact that she did not give up easily, was used to getting her own way and unafraid of taking on some of the country's most eminent figures. It also emanated from a conviction that the House of Lords, although dealt a blow in the constitutional crisis of 1910-11, remained a great national symbol.

As a journalist and businesswoman Margaret recognised

the value of the widespread publicity generated by the claim and its rebuttal. When a newspaper editor commented that she was making a great deal of capital out of her defeat, her response was: 'all the capital I know!'[39] Sitting in the Upper House would enable Margaret to carry on her father's links with Parliament, but in her own way. This was a legacy she was not prepared to abandon and she believed that she was fully entitled to enjoy it.

There was, however, an evident difficulty. The House of Lords had just confirmed that it was remote from everyday life and concerned with arcane precedents that appeared to matter little to the modern woman. The Duke of Rutland declared that if any women peeresses were to sit near him he would feel inclined to laugh. In 1957 the Earl of Glasgow could still claim that 'the emotional urge which exists in a woman's make-up does not help towards good judgment', adding that '[t]his is about the only place in the kingdom where men can meet without women. For heaven's sake let's keep it that way.'[40] It was easy to question what appeal this gentleman's club might hold for women.

Lady Ravensdale's autobiography recalls that although Baronesses Beaumont and Lucas were prepared to speak out alongside herself and Margaret, most 'never cared a jot for the principle of the thing'.[41] There is some truth here, but it is an exaggeration. For example, just two months after Margaret set the ball rolling, the Countess of Powis, Countess of Yarsborough and Viscountess Wolseley petitioned the king for Writs. The House of Lords did not proceed with their cases because of the lack of resolution in the Rhondda claim. Margaret called meetings with other peeresses in their own right in 1921 and 1924 and in the latter year about 90 peers were canvassed by them, the Countess of Powis writing many letters on behalf of the women.[42]

It could, however, certainly be asked how relevant peeresses were to working-class women. The birth control campaigner Stella Browne attacked the SPG for believing that Margaret's claim to sit and vote in the House of Lords was 'more urgent then working women's right to refuse to bear children they do not desire and cannot support'.[43]

Aware that she needed to demonstrate that the issue affected many more women than a couple of dozen peeresses, Margaret argued that the repercussions of the Lords' decision were serious: 'It has just slightly lowered the status of all women.' That use of 'just slightly' carefully avoided the charge of making a sweeping statement while permitting her to nevertheless suggest the gravity of the situation. The result, she explained, was 'that it is just a little more unlikely that any professional or working woman will get a fair chance ungoverned by the accident of her sex. *That* is why it matters.'[44]

In his novel *Brynhild,* H.G. Wells suggested that the only evident objective of the weekly paper *Wear and Tear* was to secure for Lady Roundabout a seat in the House of Lords where she would simply sit rather than do anything.[45] Wells's parody was inaccurate on several counts. Margaret was never passive and her claim was, as he knew, one of a number of equality issues dear to her in the 1920s and far from being for her own personal aggrandisement. But Margaret understood that she needed to rebut suggestions by individuals such as Lord Banbury that she sought 'small and petty advantage'.[46] She was well aware that she had enjoyed rare opportunities. As the *Sunday Chronicle* put it, 'there are not many Lady Rhonddas, and ninety women out of a hundred have never seen a bill of lading or a bill of exchange'.[47]

In an article on 'Women and the House of Lords' for the *Woman's Year Book* in 1923, and at a debate on 'This House approves the admission of women to the House of Lords' held at the University of London Union (which she won), Margaret pointed out that 'the eyes of the nation are focused upon Parliament'. Enabling women to sit in the Commons had been a reform of 'incalculable value'. They had already demonstrated the vital difference they could make to a legislative assembly. But 'in the view of the *ordinary* person, it is a reform which affects only the *outstanding* woman'. By describing the Commons in language that would normally be reserved for the Lords, she anticipated and weakened allegations that the latter was elitist.

Margaret argued that only exceptional women could get elected to the House of Commons. Throwing back at Birkenhead his emphasis on the 'average' woman, she claimed that the decision to admit women to the Lower House 'does not seriously affect the status of the average woman or the regard in which the average woman is held'. By contrast, the deliberate refusal on the sole grounds of sex to admit women to the House of Lords who were otherwise fully qualified was 'tantamount to saying that the average man is necessarily inferior in capacity to the average woman'.[48] This refusal, she stressed, 'must, and does, affect not only the status of the women directly concerned, but that of every woman throughout the country'.

This was a huge claim and far from the ordinary practical needs of women in the 1920s. But it was significant, as it sought to give women a further space and voice in shaping and making the laws of the land. As Cheryl Law has pointed out, 'it 'represented a symbol of women's entry to the ultimate seat of traditional political power... One of Lady Rhondda's many contributions to the movement was her insistence on testing the viability of operating a right when it had been won'.[49]

Through the SPG and other pressure groups Margaret attempted to integrate the cause of the peeresses into the wider struggle for women's rights. In the same week as her peerage claim had first been heard, Lord Knutsford sought to exclude future women medical students from the London Hospital. They had been welcomed when male students were absent during the war. In the deputation from 26 women's organisations to the Home Secretary of July 1923 protesting about the shortcomings of the 1919 Sex Disqualification (Removal) Act, Margaret was the SPG's spokesperson. She pointed out that the women who had worked for the Act had supposed that 'any public function' meant just that. She stressed how a short and simple government measure could secure peeresses the same rights and privileges as men.[50]

There was international interest in Margaret's case. In 1916 Emily Murphy of Alberta, the first woman magistrate in the British Empire, had been unsuccessfully challenged by a lawyer who claimed (based on an 1876 decision in an English court) that women 'are not persons in matters of rights and privileges'.[51] By the early 1920s there was widespread support for her to be appointed to the Canadian Senate, but women were not seen as 'qualified persons' under the British North America Act of 1867. The first woman was elected to the Canadian House of Commons in 1921 and the following year when the British Committee for Privileges first found in Margaret's favour, the Montreal Women's Club sent Margaret a letter of congratulations, seeing her triumph in Britain as helpful to the Canadian Senate bid. The franchise Committee of the club asked the Canadian prime minister whether, in view of Margaret's claim, women might be admitted to their senate. They were not.

Five Canadian women – known as the Famous Five – persevered, and although they were rebuffed in 1928, the following year what became known as the Persons Case was successful, the Judicial Committee of the British Privy Council deeming that women were persons in law and so could sit as senators. As Margaret had already found with the post of Attorney General, a change of minister made a difference. The Canadians were helped by the fact that Birkenhead was no longer Lord Chancellor. In his place was Lord Sankey, appointed by Ramsay Macdonald to liberalise the judiciary. British women were now fully enfranchised and there was a female cabinet minister.

But Margaret's struggle had still not been rewarded. And she now found that British newspapers were 'not biting' quite as well as she had expected. The press was 'so difficult to keep out of when you want to and so difficult to get into when you want to'.[52] Recognising that she needed to change tactics, she decided on a Private Member's Bill. One of her legal team W.A. Greene (later Lord Greene, Master of the Rolls) drafted the Parliament (Qualification of Peeresses) Bill. Frank Briant, Liberal MP for Lambeth introduced it in the House of Commons in

March 1924 under the ten-minute rule. It became known as Lady Rhondda's Bill and passed its first reading with a massive majority of 268. It sought to enable peeresses in their own right to receive their Writ of Summons to Parliament.[53]

It proposed (in the name of equality with their male counterparts) that peeresses would in future all be disqualified from voting in general elections. Women peers had been permitted to vote in the House of Commons due to an amendment to the Representation of the People Bill in January 1918 by Lord Desborough. Yet a private letter he sent to Lord Farrar in 1922 suggests that he might have contemplated wider implications. His letter expressed considerable doubt about whether Lady Rhondda would sit in the House of Lords, since he believed that a peeress should not have a seat there and also vote for a Member of Parliament if a peer could not do so.[54] This would not be equality but imply the unthinkable: women peers having greater privilege than their male counterparts.

Viscount Astor (whose elevation to the Lords had been the catalyst for his wife to seek election to the Commons) had a more difficult time championing the bill in the Lords. He argued that women voters deserved to have their views reflected there. However, demonstrating the narrow circles he moved in, Lord Banbury claimed that he had never met anybody who did not regret the presence of women in the House of Commons. They were dismissed as a 'ludicrous failure'. Women were not perceived as individuals: Lady Astor was known to interrupt and disregard parliamentary procedure, so it was presumed that all women would behave in the same way.

And there was the effect that they might have on peers: 'I do not say for a moment that by malice prepense [aforethought] she exercises that fascination which we all know women have over men, but she certainly does it unwittingly',[55] stated Banbury. He and other peers implied that men had difficulty concentrating and controlling their behaviour. Women were essentially sexual beings whose presence would fundamentally alter how gallant Lords behaved and so lower the dignity of their chamber. As on Planet Venus, the prospect of admitting the opposite sex raised elemental fears. Technical questions had given way to gendered issues of principle, custom and courtesy. The bid for legislation was proving to be as tricky as the petition.

The following year a letter to the press from notable women's organisations such as the Association of Head Mistresses and the BFUW cited the many countries where women were eligible to sit in their upper houses.[56] The bill now had the support of more than thirty national women's organisations. Margaret Wintringham (who had asked a question in Parliament in 1922 about the decision of the revised Committee for Privileges and the following year joined the board of *Time and Tide*) wrote to *The Times* in May 1925. She had experienced Commons support for measures demanded by women, only to see them stall in the Lords.[57] The presence of a handful of women in the latter chamber, she argued, could make a huge difference and ease the passage of reforms.

Margaret came close to success in this month. Viscount Astor sought again to have accepted a 'Bill to do justice to the other sex, and a Bill to do justice to this House'.[58] He pointed out that about one-third of the bills in the last session dealt with questions – such as legitimacy and guardianship of infants – especially relevant to women. Rejecting the bill, he argued, meant alienating a large number of thinking women.

Birkenhead (now Secretary of State for India) referred to the 'extreme impropriety' of a Private Member's bill dealing with this matter since it would put a group of women with only accidental claims or rights in an exceptionally privileged position. It was on this occasion that his language became especially offensive to Margaret and those in a similar position to herself. The proposal, he suggested, would admit a number of 'privileged ladies' who were merely physiological conduit pipes.[59]

Birkenhead's deep-seated opposition to change within the Lords was echoed by Lord Salisbury, who feared what it might mean for the country as a whole. The distinction between family and public life was of the greatest importance for women in his view, and when the Tory Primrose League had 'persuaded women to take part in public life' it had been the start of a slippery slope. Lord Merrivale negated Margaret's hard work in one breathtaking sentence, dismissing the bill as 'a frank and crude proposal' to give seats to persons who 'had never shown any particular interest in public affairs'.

However, the bill almost succeeded on this occasion and was only defeated by two votes. In an article called 'The Turning of the Tide', *Time and Tide* praised Astor's speech and declared that victory was within sight.[60] The renewed struggle to revive pressure for the enfranchisement of all women also gave Margaret an opportunity to publicise the case more widely. Each of the fifteen platforms at Hyde Park in the vast suffrage demonstration of July 1926 demanded seats for peeresses.[61]

Yet just before this the House of Lords rejected the Peeresses' Bill once again and by a significantly larger margin than the previous year. It was, suggested *Time and Tide* a reminder of how precarious was their newly won foothold in public life.[62]

This defeat (126 to 80) was one of the largest divisions of the inter war years.[63] Whereas 86 had voted the previous year, 206 voted in June 1926 (including five supportive bishops). The second reading was postponed twice, the first time due to the General Strike. Astor was supported by peers such as Lord Cecil of Chelwood and Lord Buckmaster (who had been the champion of legislation for female solicitors). The latter turned on its head the essentialist argument that women were unfit by nature for sitting in the Lords, arguing that, unlike the Commons where elections and long, hard hours of work were demanded, it would be a feeble creature indeed who could not manage to sit in the Lords. He asked whether there were any special grounds why women considered suitable for other political positions were deemed unfit for seats in the Lords.[64]

More than sixty women, including a number of peeresses, attended the debate, although Margaret was unable to be there (she was present the following month to see her old friend Seymour Berry ennobled). Birkenhead was as persistent as the women. He insisted that peeresses existed only because there was no other prospect of a male heir. Hope was founded on their 'physical fecundity' and many of them 'had disappointed that reasonable expectation'. He further insulted them by stating that 'not one of them would be nominated by any competent tribunal to sit in this or any other legislature'. In an article headed 'Lord Birkenhead's Bludgeon' the *Manchester Guardian* described the debate as sinking to 'the lowest level'.[65]

Astor gave Birkenhead's arguments a neat twist. His opposition to conferring rights on a very limited class of ladies with accidental claims or rights could, he argued, just as easily be applied to the Lords themselves who represented only a tiny fraction of males. They were mostly in the Lords by accident of birth and enjoyed an exceptional and privileged position. In an article in the *National Reformer* Astor stated that opponents' arguments amounted to an attack on the hereditary principle rather than the female sex.[66]

The third failure necessitated fresh drafting. Astor's bill of 1927 was a compromise, and one which would have excluded Margaret and other hereditary peeresses, instead empowering the king to create new peeresses, complete with the right to sit. Margaret accepted this as better than nothing but, as had happened with women's suffrage bills, the government pre-empted the situation by announcing wider proposals for reform. Astor's bill was withdrawn, and although he persisted for a few more years, the question became subsumed into the wider issue of reforming the House of Lords.

Margaret was wary of this from the start. As early as July 1922 Lord Peel had suggested a partially elected house with no provision for women. As a former suffragette Margaret was used to empty promises. She remarked as early as June 1922 that it was highly probable that reform of the Second Chamber would not take place 'till the Greek Kalends' and anyway

> To keep those who demand justice quiet by talking
> about justice in a dim, uncertain and speculative
> future is an old political trick. It has been tried too
> often.[67]

Margaret and eleven other hereditary peeresses signed a
letter to *The Times* in 1925, urging that their cause not
be mixed up with reform of the Lords, and correctly
anticipating that associating it with the problems of the
constitution and powers of the Upper House would mean
indefinite postponement of what was urgent to them.[68]
The situation was complicated by the fact that whereas
all political parties showed support (and some opposition)
for peeresses, each party had its own agenda for Lords
reform.

A new tactic was adopted in 1929. More than twenty
women's organisations came together in a Women Peers
Committee chaired by Helen Archdale and dedicated to
securing seats in the Lords for women peers.[69] The Equal
Rights Committee that Margaret now chaired demanded
as an 'immediate reform' that peeresses in their own right
sit and vote in the Lords before any other alteration in its
constitution so that they could participate in further
discussions on reform.

Deputations introduced by Margaret to each of the
political leaders in 1929 demanded a raft of equality
measures. They elicited different responses. Ramsay
MacDonald 'thoroughly agreed' with the proposals put
forward by Mrs Pethick-Lawrence to put 'the coping
stone' upon political democracy by admitting women
peeresses to the House of Lords.[70] Lloyd George (also in
opposition) could see no problem, but although the prime

minister Baldwin stressed that he was personally in favour, he refused to give his pledge, envisaging practical difficulties with opposition within the Lords and arguing that the issue should be part of wider reform of the Upper House.

Aware that much more interest was now being shown in life peerages than women peers, Margaret also began to adopt a more constructive approach to Lords reform, linking it to the women's claim In an editorial in *Time and Tide* in 1937,[71] she pointed out that life peerages were not universally popular, not least because some viewed them as an unwelcome boost to an anachronistic system. She suggested that supporters of life peerages stood their best chance of success if they united 'every possible progressive element behind their demand'. Allowing peeresses in their own right to sit and making women as well as men eligible for life peerages would, she argued, strengthen the Lords and bring on board many extra supporters for the life peerage camp. The net result would be that the Lords would become a truer reflection of the nation. Yet neither she nor other concerned peeresses were invited to contribute to government committees on the issue.

In the same year she attended the Coronation of King George VI and Queen Elizabeth in Westminster Abbey. Dressed in 'very solid red velvet' and tiara and all the pearls and diamonds she could muster, her account of the proceedings for *Time and Tide* carefully stressed her rank as a viscountess.[72] Guests had to be seated hours ahead of the ceremony and she reached the North Transept of the Abbey soon after 7.30am. Had she been in a theatre, Margaret explained, she would have been seated in the third row of the dress circle. In front were the duchesses and countesses and the baronesses were behind. In the South Transept *'on a level with ourselves* [my emphasis], were all the peers, their crimson velvet robes only visible here and there beneath the white ermine'. The two vacant thrones were just below, between the two Transepts.

The campaign for reform of the Lords was renewed after the end of the war by the elderly Cecil who moved motions for reform in 1946. He also wanted women to be eligible for peerages on the same terms as men.[73] But arguments about peeresses in their own right were beginning to sound somewhat dated in a post-war world. The State opening of Parliament that year issued invitations to peeresses but were meant for those whose husbands were currently members of the House of Lords.

In 1947 Margaret and several other peeresses sat on a new committee to secure the admission of women to the Lords on the same terms as men. It was chaired by Edward Iwi, a lawyer known for his letters to *The Times* on constitutional reform. The committee launched a campaign and organised a petition to the House of Lords, asking for a 'seat, place and voice' for women peers. Twenty-two of the twenty-four[74] current peeresses in their own right including Margaret and Viscountess Daventry (whose late husband had been the Speaker) would be included as well as future women peers. Support came from political parties, women's groups, local authorities and various religious organisations. Margaret addressed meetings about the petition, attended numerous meetings and canvassed potential supporters such as Lord Geddes and the Liberal leader Clement Davies. She told Violet Markham that they had received an extremely good

467

response and Markham in turn congratulated her on 'the weight and gravity of the language in which your petition is worded'.[75]

Although more than 50,000 signatures were collected and generated welcome publicity, there remained some unease about individuals like Margaret whose peerage was by special Remainder. A *Times* editorial advised that they had inherited their titles before the political emancipation of women so did not enjoy parliamentary privilege. The English law of hereditary succession privileged the male over the female, it was stressed, and arguments about sex equality could not logically be applied to its interpretation.[76]

Events once again overtook campaigning. Reform of the House of Lords was back on the agenda. A conference of party leaders in 1948 had accepted that women should be 'Lords of Parliament' on the same terms as men.[77] The following year Lord Reading, supported by the former suffrage activist Lord Pethick-Lawrence, moved the introduction of legislation to admit peeresses currently disqualified. Lord Badeley looked forward to seeing 'a charming lady on the woolsack'.[78] The motion was carried by 45 to 27.

However, this was a pyrrhic victory for the likes of Margaret. It was thirty years since the Sex Disqualification (Removal) Act that had been the basis for her claim. This was the first majority acceptance in the Lords of the principle of admitting women. But it had become clear during the debates that some Labour Lords were not happy with the idea of voting for something endorsing the hereditary principle.

Although earlier gendered protests had mellowed into a few predictable jibes, the spotlight was no longer on a couple of dozen of otherwise privileged peeresses who could be presented as anachronisms and would not be sitting on their own merits even though they might have deserved the honour for their own achievements. An abortive 1953 bill for the creation of life peers made no allowance for hereditary peeresses. It did, however, include provision for women to be created Lords on the same terms as men. This was finally achieved in the Life Peerages Act of 1958. The bill had attracted some protest, particularly from socialists in the House of Commons opposed to bicameralism. But it received Royal Assent on 30 April 1958.

Margaret was now in her mid-seventies. She would die less than three months later. The four women and ten men who became the first Life Peers included Mary Irene Curzon, Baroness Ravensdale of Kedleston.[79] She also happened to be a peeress in her own right by special Remainder. The public announcement of those selected was made the day before Margaret's funeral.

A seat in the Lords had eluded the woman who had exerted the most pressure and also boasted a very impressive record of public service. Yet, since it was the principle of having women in the Lords that Margaret had cared most about, it could be argued that her wish had at least been partially fulfilled.

It was not until five years later that the Peerages Act of 1963 (passed primarily to permit peers to disclaim their titles) finally accorded peeresses in their own right a place in the House of Lords. Only then was Britain permitted to sign up to the United Nations Convention on the Political Rights of Women.[80]

Margaret had campaigned for forty years. After the

high hopes of 1922, effectively dashed by the Lord Chancellor, she had encountered obfuscation and unconscionable behaviour from those peers who feared that their ancient rights and privileges might be threatened. The prospect of encountering Lady Rhondda there was seen as especially daunting by some. Years later Lady Violet Powell noted that it was known among the Lords that there was 'considerable nervousness as to what sort of shindy Lady Rhondda might raise'.[81]

Were she to return to Planet Earth today, though, Margaret might be cheered. The number of women in the House of Lords still by no means reflects wider society – in 2012 women comprised twenty-two per cent of membership – but there has nevertheless been a real shift in the gender composition of the Lords and evidence of women performing very active roles as members and Leaders of the House. Margaret would surely be especially pleased by one development: since 2006 the role of presiding officer in the House of Lords has not been undertaken by the Lord Chancellor but by the holder of the new post of Lord Speaker. The first holder of this elected position was Baroness Hayman, followed in 2011 by Baroness D'Souza.

In this same year, and ninety years after Margaret issued the petition which inaugurated the Rhondda Peerage Case, the Parliamentary Art Committee acquired the dignified Alice Burton oil painting of her that used to grace the offices of *Time and Tide*. It hangs in the middle of the Peers' Dining Room surrounded by portraits of former Lord Chancellors including her bête-noire, the Earl of Birkenhead.[82]

So there has been some belated recognition of

Margaret's entitlement. She may not have sat and deliberated in the Upper House and the title that Lord Rhondda passed on to her has become extinct. But in one sense Viscountess Rhondda now resides permanently in the House of Lords, keeping an eye on proceedings.

CHAPTER FIFTEEN

Friends and Foes: Politics and War

The last two decades of Margaret's life were simultaneously the most settled and unsettling of all her years. They were settled in that at her Surrey home Churt Halewell she enjoyed with Theodora a companionship and calm that she had long sought. At first, though, war posed a challenge. It also helped to cement a shift in Margaret's political thinking, which was reflected in *Time and Tide*.

Margaret and Theodora's leisurely Mediterranean cruise in the autumn of 1933 was not their first trip together. It had been preceded that Easter by a cruise on the *Homeric* – 'our floating island of peace' – to Madeira, Tenerife, Morocco and Gibraltar.[1] Margaret found the company and surroundings intellectually stimulating and mentioned in her 'Notes on the Way' column their discussions on the meanings of beauty. She did not, however, reveal there the name of her fellow traveller (beyond using the letter T) and the two women enjoyed a private joke when Theodora wrote a letter to the paper questioning the 'astounding view' of this subject held by Lady Rhondda's travelling companion.[2]

Margaret read *The Odyssey* for the first time on the spring cruise, appreciating how it allowed for the expression of emotions. This, her travels and the company prompted her to write, 'We stop up our natural emotional outlets far too much.'[3] Such a remark at such a time questions the standard image of Theodora as reserved, very serious and slightly forbidding. Some years later, Theodora movingly expressed what Margaret's companionship meant to her when she wrote that the difference between their London flat without her and with her was 'the difference between a pool of "static" water and a lake with a live stream running through it'.[4] Friends nicknamed them the Rondabouts.

During the autumn cruise, Margaret summarised what motivated her. Her written credo was articulated in Athens in October.[5] This statement reaffirmed her feminism at a time when it was no longer so prominent in her paper. It was a heartfelt and passionate personal commitment. She wished both to clarify her beliefs for herself and to appeal to Theodora to appreciate her priorities and recognise 'how I see my duty so long as I'm alive'. Her message was that women were at the centre of her endeavour: 'directly or indirectly everything I do must be tending towards that one end – must fit with what is my business to do'. *Time and Tide*, she suggested, was 'merely an instrument. A dozen other instruments would have served as well no doubt, and it is largely chance that this particular instrument shaped itself. If it failed tomorrow I should have to find another.'

'I believe', Margaret wrote, 'that everything I possess:

473

my brains, my strength, my health, my money, my reputation have to go to this one end.' Most importantly, Theodora could help her, and having her support would, her statement ended, 'make me happy'.

Before the first cruise Theodora had already admitted (to herself) that she was attracted by the young Tess Dillon. She noted, however, that 'at my time of life sexual adventures are not likely to be much in my way' and anyway reasoned that 'the Platonic ideal of *controlled* impulse is probably the ideal for friendship'.[6] Those two cruises were life-changing for Theodora as well as for Margaret.

Theodora had been born on 3 October 1880 at Sandown on the Isle of Wight where her father was a curate. She spent part of her childhood in Dorset and Devon. Her mother Gertrude died in her mid-forties in 1900 and her father Frederick C.T. Bosanquet remarried. When Theodora had lunch with her stepmother in 1945 it was their first meeting for some years. In 1958 when the television presenter Reginald Bosanquet did a programme with Margaret, Theodora discovered that he was a cousin.[7] Older relatives included the philosopher Bernard Bosanquet and his brother Charles, who founded the Charity Organisation Society. On her mother's side were even more illustrious connections: her maternal grandfather was Charles Darwin's second cousin.

Like Margaret, Theodora had the advantage of a good education. She attended Cheltenham Ladies' College before gaining a B.Sc. at University College, London, where she studied biology, geology and some physics. When she was twenty-seven she became Henry James's amanuensis, working with him for most of the last eight years of his life.[8]

She had been an indexer since at least 1901. From early 1907 she was working for Mary Petherbridge's Secretarial Bureau. That summer, when indexing the report of the Royal Commission on Soil Erosion, she discovered that James, one of her favourite authors, needed a 'literary secretary'. She promptly taught herself to use a Remington typewriter and was, to her delight, interviewed by 'The Master' himself. By mid-October Theodora was installed in lodgings that James had found for her at Marigold Cottage in Mermaid Street, Rye, and took daily dictation from him (seven mornings a week) at nearby Lamb House. The 'young boyish Miss Bosanquet' was, James told his brother, worth all his other secretaries put together.[9] They soon established a pleasing routine and constructive basis for work. They could be found in the Green Room in winter and the Garden Room in summer, with James pacing up and down as he composed and Theodora captured his convoluted sentences.

James called her 'the Remington priestess'.[10] She devoured books from his library. Her Hogarth Essay *Henry James at Work*, first published by Leonard and Virginia Woolf in 1924, is an evocative and perceptive account of her employer's working methods. It demonstrates a shrewd appreciation of James's fiction and stresses the significance of his later revisions (she had worked on these). Recently Theodora has received belated recognition as 'a pioneer critic-biographer' who helped to stimulate appreciation of the work of Henry James through her 'acute critical observations'.[11] She now features in several academic articles and in fiction.[12]

In Cynthia Ozick's short story of 2009 called 'Dictation', the scheming, spirited (in more than one sense) woman 'who served and observed'[13] James, conspires with Joseph Conrad's much more timid amanuensis to insert fragments of Conrad's writings into James's manuscript and vice versa. This secret transposition ensures that the women who played a part in the fashioning of their employers' reputations have left behind 'an immutable mark'. And in turn Ozick's witty tale has helped to perpetuate their significance in the twenty-first century.

The novel *The Typewriter's Tale* (2005) by the South African writer Michiel Heyns is loosely based on Theodora. Frieda Wroth, named after a suffragette aunt and raised in Chelsea then trained in Miss Petherbridge's Young Ladies Academy is Henry James's 'type writer' between 1907 and 1909.[14] But the plot is pure fiction. It has her seduced by the lover of the American novelist Edith Wharton, then asserting sexual equality and stealing for her lover incriminating letters that he had earlier sent to James.

Emma Tennant's haunting novel *The Beautiful Child* (2012) draws on James's *The Turn of the Screw* and the eponymous short story that he abandoned.[15] Theodora plays a key role in Tennant's layered tale – like a matryoshka doll – of fact and fiction, past and present. We even follow Theodora back to Lamb House in 1950 as she retrieves the manuscript of 'The Beautiful Child'. She is both a medium for communing with the long-dead Master and a medium for unfolding Tennant's story of the supernatural.

Early 1910 saw Theodora back in London sharing a flat at King's Cross Mansions with Nellie Bradley, daughter of James's walking companion in Rye. She was indexing for the *Encyclopaedia Britannica*. She resumed working for James, initially in two rooms behind her new flat in Lawrence Street, just off Chelsea's Cheyne Walk. James then moved to Carlyle Mansions in Cheyne Walk in early 1913. His health was deteriorating and on a number of occasions Theodora's diary records that he was feeling 'rather seedy'.[16] He dictated from his bedroom during his last months before his death in 1916. Edith Wharton (to whom Theodora had been reporting the state of James's health) offered her a secretarial post based in Paris but she declined. Theodora worked in the War Trade Intelligence Department then moved to D.A.'s former department, the Ministry of Food. For her war work Theodora received an MBE in 1919.

On leaving this job in 1920, she became executive secretary to the International Federation of University Women. This was probably how she and Margaret first met, perhaps through Cullis, who was its president. Theodora's conception of equal rights for women was not as broad as Margaret's. In September 1928 Doris Stevens stayed at Agay in France where Margaret was entertaining both Theodora and Dr Elen Gleditsch, president of the International Federation. Stevens noted that Theodora was opposed to the Federation undertaking anything not directly concerned with university women. She, Margaret and Gleditsch, however, discussed – when Theodora was not present – how it might nevertheless be possible for university women to support feminist proposals such as the equal rights treaty.[17]

Theodora had been reviewing regularly for *Time and Tide* since early 1927. She wrote reviews of works on French and British literature, art, biography and philosophy and valuable essays on James. She was well qualified to undertake this, having previously written for the *Saturday Westminster Gazette* and co-authored with Clara Smith (who edited Margaret's autobiography) an epistolary novel entitled *Spectators* published by Constable in 1916. It genuflected to James's style. Theodora also helped to edit James's posthumous publication and aided Percy Lubbock in preparing an edition of his letters.

In 1927 Theodora's study of Harriet Martineau was published (extracts appeared in advance in *Time and Tide*). This was a measured account, noting for example, that although Martineau did useful work in 'ventilating' Irish grievances, she 'had no natural understanding of the Irish temperament and measured everything by her English standards'.[18] But Theodora acknowledged that Martineau's later workload as a Leader writer for the *London Daily News* would have been impressive for a healthy man with full access to his sources. For an incurably sick woman living alone in a Westmorland village it represented 'an astonishing triumph of natural capacity over the disabilities of her position, her health and her sex'.[19]

In 1915 Theodora, the over-qualified secretary, had asked wistfully in her diary: 'Why can't one live by writing?'[20] Twenty years later she gave up her International Federation work to become literary editor of *Time and Tide*, a position she held for eight years. She subsequently sat on the Board of the paper for the rest of Margaret's life.

Theodora's diary shows that she copied out – with slight modifications – some of Margaret's articles.[21] Some even presumed she was Margaret's secretary. Nancy Lord found tall and thin 'Old Bosey' with her eye-glass, well-tailored tweed suits and sensible shoes intimidating at *Time and Tide*.[22] But C.V. Wedgwood's obituary for Theodora (in *The Times*) recalled how she encouraged young writers and hosted luncheons at Gourmets Restaurant.[23] Margaret felt that Theodora was not sufficiently appreciated and told Holtby that she 'is very fine I think in a lot of ways – finer than she gets the credit for being'.[24] The two women were, though, amused by Freya Stark's assessment. She felt that they were quite different and emphasised that Miss Bosanquet was both 'fastidious and amusing'. She nevertheless maintained that they 'go very well together'.[25]

There were some differences in their views on religion and spirituality. Margaret was nominally Church of England but did not see herself as a religious person. In 1937 she stated in print that she could not call herself a Christian,[26] though she sometimes attended church later in life. Theodora, a clergyman's daughter, went through an agnostic stage but was a committed High Church Anglican when she lived with Margaret. She was also deeply interested in mystical experience and psychical research. Theodora had done tarot readings in her youth and was elected an Associate of the Society for Psychical Research (SPR) in 1912. Formed in Cambridge in 1882, the SPR undertook scientific investigation of the paranormal, with an emphasis on spiritualism.

Theodora discussed the SPR report on automatic writing with Henry James's brother the psychologist William James who was the society's vice-president. In the latter part of the war she sat on its council. Pamela Thurschwell has shown how Theodora perpetuated her involvement in James's work through working with mediums and channelling him.[27] In her Hogarth Press pamphlet Theodora had described her work for James as '[t]he business of acting as a medium between the spoken and the typewritten word'.[28] By the 1930s she was practising automatic writing daily and contemplated (though never wrote) a book on the immortality of the soul.

Influenced by Theodora, Margaret attended some sittings. The medium Hester Dowden did automatic writing for her in 1933. There was also a family connection. Several of Margaret's relatives were spiritualists and Sybil was an SPR Associate in the 1920s. Sybil attended séances with the medium Gladys Leonard in 1938 and, through her spirit guide Feda, was told how happy her husband 'Davey' had become. Sybil was asked whether she knew 'an "E" on earth he is helping… someone he was very interested in'.[29] But since she had cousins called Ella and Ethel, she was unfazed.

Margaret too was 'connected' with D.A. Indeed, this was probably her chief motivation for her sittings. In February 1933 the medium Hester Dowden used the Ouija board then, through her spirit guide Johannes, contacted D.A. who warned Margaret about money matters and assured her that he would provide protection and care.[30] Margaret also sat with Mrs Leonard for sessions lasting up to two hours on at least four occasions in 1942. Both of her parents were now dead and she received encouraging messages. She was told that her 'real work' would be after the war. An elderly woman with the letter 'E' close to her was also evoked. Margaret's last recorded session was in December 1950 when she learned via the medium Muriel Hankey that her father predicted a very serious time ahead for her.

But although Margaret participated in a number of sittings, Theodora's notes imply that she was not fully committed.[31] Concerned about Margaret's intestinal problems in 1937, Theodora had noted her 'mental pulse' and her unfortunate 'inrush of other thought'. She believed that more could be done to help her '[b]ut we cannot do that if she thinks exclusively of her laborious life in the direction of Time and Tide'. Five years later she noted that it was still not possible for Feda to 'interpret very deeply' for her. Indeed Margaret could 'help her progenitors by entering a bit seriously into "their" game'.

Margaret's new life with Theodora had been confirmed by their move from Kent to the newly built Churt Halewell near Shere in Surrey. The house had cost Reginald Arthur Bray £3,617 to build.[32] Its architect Leonard Martin lived nearby and had been a student with Lutyens. Margaret was the third leaseholder, taking over the property and five and a half acres in 1937.[33] When Theodora first saw it that March she declared it '[a] delight. A pleasance. It will give unmixed satisfaction.'[34] Built of local green sandstone with a lovely garden and hidden walkways, it was surrounded by woods and offered privacy, comfort and space. Margaret added a pool. Her god-daughter recalls her swimming there with a 'beatific smile' on her face. In 1944 Margaret spent £17,000 purchasing land and property nearby: 245 acres that included an early eighteenth-century house called Cotterells with farm buildings. This she rented out.

Margaret and Theodora generally spent their weekends at Churt Halewell, leaving London on Thursday afternoons, armed with *Time and Tide* business. They returned to the office on Monday mornings. During the weekdays in London they lived in Hampstead before moving to 503 Keyes House, Dolphin Square in 1941. This imposing Pimlico complex – comprising Europe's largest self-contained blocks of flats – had only been completed in 1937. Being close to Westminster and, like Chelsea Court, on the Embankment, it attracted a number of MPs, including Ellen Wilkinson who also lived in Dolphin Square East (high up in Hood House). It may well have been Wilkinson who alerted Margaret to the opportunity to rent there. Two flats were taken to accommodate Margaret, Theodora, their housekeeper Annie New and any guests.

Like so many others, Margaret faced challenges simply by working and staying in wartime London. Wilkinson had moved to Dolphin Square after her home was bombed. But although parts of Hampstead had been blitzed from September 1940, Margaret and Theodora had been spared in Bay Tree Lodge. Dolphin Square was adapted to war demands. One part became the headquarters of the Free French in 1940, the square's garage was converted into an ambulance depot and the gymnasium became a hospital.

War brought family losses. Although she could not acknowledge it openly, Margaret's half-brother John died in France in 1940. Just over four years later she lost her intrepid explorer and ornithologist relative David Haig-Thomas (who wrote about the countryside for *Time and Tide*). He died in Normandy on D-Day. His bearskin rug, brought back from a polar expedition, was in use in Churt Halewell.

During the summer of 1944 new flying or buzz bombs

known as doodlebugs posed renewed dangers in the 'Little Blitz'. Margaret took to spending the night in the bathroom and Theodora slept on the floor in her bedroom though nearby Frobisher House had an underground air raid shelter. Travelling to and from Surrey was difficult due to petrol rationing, blackouts and transport shortages but at least they had their country home.

Time and Tide remained in Bloomsbury despite the dangers. During the blitz there were three or four air raid alarms daily and nightly raids. Eventually Margaret had to rely on writers who lived within walking distance so that they could bring in their own copy. Some contributors were no longer available anyway, so there was even more pressure on those who were handy.

After a raid in the city the assistant editor walked from Liverpool Street to the office through three miles of broken glass. Rose Macaulay would weave her way on her bicycle through glass-strewn roads to deliver her copy. One member of staff was bombed out three times. Margaret's secretary, Edna Burns, was bombed out of her home but was luckily away at the time. In June 1944 a flying bomb hit Russell Square. Staff felt the renewed strain. Wedgwood's hands shook after several near misses.

There were other pressures linked to censorship and paper shortages. *Time and Tide* was reduced from 36 to 28 pages in the spring of 1940. The Diary provided some light relief and stories designed to keep up morale. Wireless broadcasts were praised, especially J.B. Priestley's 'Postscripts', which an estimated twenty-nine per cent of the adult population heard on Sunday evenings. Margaret was an avid fan of the wireless.

Theodora's personal diary for 1943-5 suggests that the

two women continued to enjoy a comfortable existence. At weekends many friends visited Churt Halewell where Margaret and Theodora had their own cow called Bessie and a series of cats with witty names such as Vodka (a Russian Blue). Margaret was a great cat lover and once received a telegram from her diplomat friend Charles Peake in Belgrade informing her 'Tito sound on cats'. Mary Grieve, editor of *Woman* magazine, recalled visiting Margaret in her London flat. At about 10pm she moved from her wide armchair to a small, upholstered chair where her cat slept. She explained: 'I always sit here for half-an-hour before going to bed to warm the chair'.[35]

One regular visitor to Churt Halewell was Wilkinson. This friendship pre-dated being London neighbours. Eight years younger than Margaret and from a very different background,[36] 'Red Ellen' as she was known – a reference to both her socialism and her red hair – came from a working-class Methodist family in Manchester. Her father (a textile worker turned insurance clerk) was out of work for long periods and her mother suffered from chronic ill-health. Wilkinson was a clever scholarship girl who read History at Manchester University. Although she became a suffragist organiser before the war, unlike Margaret she was also deeply involved in other facets of radical politics, from student activism to trade union organisation. She helped to found the Communist Party in Britain and endorsed pacifism. It was into the Labour Party, however, that her politics became channelled.

She shared with Margaret a commitment to equal rights and was one of the early women MPs, representing Middlesbrough East in the turbulent years of 1924 to 1931. Not all women were enfranchised when she was elected. A number of issues she championed, such as women's position within the civil service, fitted the SPG agenda.

In 1931, when the Labour Party failed to win the election, she lost her seat. She then worked for a trade union, lectured, wrote books and newspaper articles and led, like Margaret, an extremely busy life. She devoted a considerable amount of her time to *Time and Tide* which printed her first signed review in December 1930. She also wrote features and even Leaders throughout the thirties, becoming one of the paper's 'best friends'.[37] Her ideas and advice were heeded at the weekly meetings and Margaret later recalled how Wilkinson 'cared about what she wrote more than the money she received and people and causes took precedence over her financial needs'.[38]

Wilkinson clearly appreciated Margaret as an editor, though at first Margaret found it difficult 'to persuade her into friendship', since she possessed 'a qualm of conscience about it, a cultivated Marxist class consciousness which made her tend to believe that there were barriers' that those on the left should never really cross.[39] Her novel *Clash* suggests something of this. But Wilkinson came to respect and to enjoy Margaret's company. Conscious that the older woman was better at listening than confiding, she told Holtby:

I like Lady Rhondda enormously, but always feel rather ashamed when I've left her. I feel as tho' I've talked her head off. She would have made a wonderful psycho-analyst. I find myself talking easily to her about anything that comes into my head. And I enjoy her delicious habit of accuracy. I say largely 'it's thirty miles', and she says 'well it's precisely 9 and a half'.[40]

Margaret in turn valued Wilkinson, and at this point was happy to support her. In June 1935 she explained to an American journalist friend that she was currently an ex-MP but 'she's a future MP too I think – she shall be in again next time *with any luck* [my emphasis]'.[41] Five months later Wilkinson was indeed back in Parliament and the best-known period of her life followed when, as Labour MP for the beleaguered north-eastern constituency of Jarrow, she helped to organise the famous march of unemployed workers to London. When training to be a barrister in the 1930s Betty Archdale worked for her – this may well have been Margaret's doing – and was deeply impressed by this tiny (four foot ten inches) bundle of energy.[42] Energy was a word a number of people associated with Wilkinson. When she died Margaret paid tribute to her 'warm-heartedness, energy, imagination and courage'.[43]

Wilkinson was a staunch anti-imperialist. A supporter of Indian nationalism, she was part of a delegation to India to study conditions there. She enjoyed what today we call networking, and when Jawaharlal Nehru visited London and was keen 'to meet people who are doing things', she suggested that Margaret host a small luncheon for him, adding, 'Theodora would like him, and I know you would.'[44]

Margaret and Wilkinson shared a commitment to oppose the spread of Fascism internationally. The latter was active in the Republican cause in the Spanish Civil War. Margaret signed a letter to the press in August 1936 about the rejection of individual liberty and destruction of political freedom in Europe, criticising in particular the way that the British press had misrepresented the struggle in Spain. It stressed that the Spanish government was democratically elected and affirmed sympathy with it and its people. She also lent her name to several letters condemning the bombing and slaughter of civilians and joined the group of MPs headed by Attlee and Wilkinson that called for the emergency conference on Spain that took place in the spring of 1938.[45]

Margaret, Wilkinson, Aneurin Bevan and Edith Summerskill were amongst the 200 British delegates at a vast congress, representing thirty countries, held by the International Peace Campaign in Paris to protest against the bombing of towns in the Spanish Civil War and urge peace. 'Four Winds' in *Time and Tide* hailed La Pasionaria (Dolores Ibárruri) as a genius, declaring that she possessed 'that indescribable, that inexplicable quality that moves men to their depths'.[46] But this famous Communist Spanish Republican was not permitted to address the audience, even though delegates had already heard speakers espousing a range of political and religious views. This was deplored by the paper as a serious denial of freedom of speech.

Wilkinson abandoned her earlier pacifism and as war loomed she and Margaret 'saw completely eye to eye'.[47] For Margaret the Munich Agreement of 30 September 1938 represented Britain's most shameful hour, as prime minister Neville Chamberlain and the French prime minister Deladier agreed with Hitler and Mussolini (but failed to consult the Czechs) about handing over German-speaking Sudetenland in Czechoslovakia to Germany. The day before

Chamberlain returned from Munich triumphantly celebrating what he called 'peace for our time' Wilkinson came into the *Time and Tide* office and 'howled' as she composed the Leader. Margaret's god-daughter who was working there recalled being sent with an office cup to a pub to fetch brandy. When she returned Wilkinson sat there with 'red hair, red eyes, red nose and sobbing and sniffing'. Meanwhile a very sombre Margaret was at the House of Commons.

Margaret and Wilkinson roundly condemned the Chamberlain government's policy of appeasement and the betrayal of the Czechs, which was cemented when Hitler broke the agreement in March 1939 and occupied the rest of their country. 'The odious little creature' was *Time and Tide's* sobriquet for the episode[48] and Margaret did not forgive *The Times* for its stance. Along with Wilkinson she actively supported the Master of Balliol College the socialist philosopher A.D. Lindsay when he stood as an 'Independent Progressive' on the anti-appeasement ticket during a by-election in Oxford. He was defeated but he halved the majority of the pro-appeasement Tory, Quintin Hogg. Margaret also appealed in *Time and Tide* for support for the Duchess of Atholl's by-election campaign. A former Conservative Parliamentary Secretary to the Board of Education, the 'Red Duchess' had resigned her Kinross and West Perthshire seat in opposition to appeasement and also stood unsuccessfully as an Independent.[49]

When they became neighbours in wartime London Margaret and Theodora spent a lot of time with Wilkinson. Theodora's diary shows them socialising together, whether taking coffee in Wilkinson's flat, enjoying weekly suppers at Keyes House or attending grand lunches with figures such as General Smuts. Like Margaret, Wilkinson was well read, loved the theatre and was highly sociable as well as dedicated to her work.

Wedgwood, who succeeded Theodora as literary editor and later became deputy editor, recalled weekends in Surrey with Wilkinson, the powerful Labour figure Herbert Morrison, who had led the London County Council, Richard Law (Conservative MP and minister and son of Bonar Law, a frequent contributor to the paper) and J.L. Hodson (Labour-supporting novelist and war correspondent). She found them friendly, espousing diverse political outlooks that were united by the paper and Margaret, who 'with skilful sympathy guided our discussions on the urgent politics of the moment'.[50]

Morrison seems to have been Wilkinson's married lover. The two spent many weekends at Churt Halewell. Margaret respected their privacy. When asked, just after Wilkinson's death, whether she had had a love life, she gave a deliberately vague answer.[51] Wilkinson had been parliamentary secretary to the Ministry of Pensions but then worked for Morrison who was Minister of Home Security in the wartime coalition. She was responsible for air raid shelters. It is surely no coincidence that in 1943 Margaret was attending monthly meetings of the Deep Shelter committee, a small group chaired by the Lord Mayor of London and supervising the building of new tube tunnel shelters. The whereabouts of these were secret during construction and the plan was that post-war they could be linked up to form part of a more modern underground railway.[52]

Wilkinson always insisted on seeing bomb damage for

herself as soon as possible. Margaret was full of admiration. The genuine sympathies and imagination of this 'deeply warm-hearted' woman meant, she stressed, that there was no better person to perform such a horrendous task. Selecting her for this job had been 'a stroke of genius'.[53]

Time and Tide's editor became privy to useful advance information thanks to her friends in high places. In early January 1943, for example, Morrison read Margaret a speech about the Empire that he was about to deliver.[54] Discussions at Churt Halewell with Margaret's friends in Parliament were often productive for developing her own ideas and writing. That May she wrote five articles on Empire prompted by talking to Morrison and Wilkinson, as well as reading a Leader in *The Times* entitled 'A Colonial Debate'. This had suggested that the words 'empire' and 'imperial' had 'distasteful' historical and so problematic contemporary associations for the Americans, Russians and Chinese.

These articles were turned into the first *Time and Tide* sixpenny pamphlet complete with the distinctive tomato-red cover that had been the hallmark of the paper. It was entitled *The Four Empires* and examined and compared the roots, motivations and consequences of expansion in American, Russia and China alongside the British Empire.[55] Margaret argued that all four Powers should be defined and recognised as empires with their possession of extensive territories and power. In her view the British Empire, though not free of autocratic control, was the least autocratic of the four. She suggested that a modern conscience about self-government should be combined with a self-confidence based on experience.

In March 1943 Morrison gave Margaret an advance

hearing of his Cabinet memorandum on communist activities which, given her intransigence on the subject and Wilkinson's views, led to a heated and stimulating debate.[56] Nevertheless, the two women respected how strongly each other felt about issues and continued to help each other. During the campaign that led to the sweeping Labour victory of 1945 Wilkinson used Margaret's car for electioneering.

When Wilkinson arrived at Margaret's flat for dinner on 1 August 1945 she announced that she was to be Minister of Education. She was the first woman to hold this post and only the second female cabinet minister. The following month she informed Margaret that she had been talking to the prime minister about her. Attlee had expressed his appreciation of *Time and Tide's* editor and agreed that she should be sitting in the Lords. He asked Wilkinson to see Margaret's old sparring partner Addison (now Leader of the House) to find out what might be done. Margaret was, reported Theodora, very pleased.[57]

In early 1946 Margaret and Ellen Wilkinson took a holiday together. They had been due to fly via Gibraltar on a scheduled flight but technical difficulties with the aircraft meant that they spent New Year together in Dolphin Square then travelled on a VIP Dakota from Hendon to Gibraltar and on to Tangier in an air sea rescue vessel (the cost of all this later prompted a question in the House of Commons).[58]

In French Morocco they were guests of Charles Peake, the Consul-General, another of Margaret's very close friends. He enjoyed a distinguished career in the diplomatic service, eventually becoming British Ambassador to Greece. He was knighted in 1948. Like Wilkinson, he had dined frequently with Margaret during the war, helping to ensure that she was signally up-to-date with international news. He did some writing for *Time and Tide* and, not long before he died, helped out as its general manager. On more than one occasion in the forties and fifties the paper was privy to the latest news and more akin to a daily newspaper than a weekly review. During the Suez Crisis, for example, on press day Peake dashed by taxi to the office to dictate information of the dramatic contents of a speech by Anthony Eden which Wedgwood then converted into a Leader.[59]

On the Moroccan trip Margaret and Wilkinson socialised at the consulate and visited Marrakesch. After years of rations, permits, queues and form-filling, they revelled in the sunshine, availability of luxury goods such as silk stockings, the profusion of oranges and delicious food. Their return home was a month later than originally planned and it was almost mid-February by the time they reached England. Margaret had raided the souks, filling her luggage with handkerchiefs, chocolates, lemons, bananas, fabrics and gloves.

Just under a year later Wilkinson was dead. She had been in very poor health: she had suffered from bronchial asthma and could not have sustained her lifestyle for much longer. Like Margaret, she burned the candle at both ends. 'At the end of a sixteen-hour day' wrote Margaret, 'she could no more resist the temptation of an amusing party than she could shirk yet another piece of gruelling hard work'.[60]

Asthma was not then recognised as an inflammatory disease but as a psychosomatic illness and patients were prescribed anti-depressants.[61] Whether Wilkinson's fatal injection on 6 February 1947 was with the intention of merely getting some sleep (she suffered from insomnia) or taking her life is not clear. The coroner's verdict was that it was an accidental drug overdose. She went into a coma and died in hospital. Edward MacLellan, the consultant surgeon who treated her regularly, confided to Margaret (who was also his long-term patient) that, contrary to reports, she was not at that point suffering from asthma or bronchitis. He had been told that she was 'very unhappy'.[62] Since mid-January Morrison had been seriously ill in hospital with a thrombosis in his leg with dangerous complications, a factor that could have affected Wilkinson's reasoning. Unlike her, he recovered.

During Wilkinson's last few years she was not as close to Margaret as she had once been. Gone were the blazing rows between two individuals who might not have seen eye to eye but nevertheless respected each other's passion and tenacity. Both women had become more careful to avoid controversial matters lest their friendship suffer. As with Holtby, who also died prematurely, Wilkinson evoked Margaret's more progressive side. But it was a side that was increasingly overshadowed as Margaret aged and observed how the modern world was changing.

Theodora recorded in her diary in April 1946 that Margaret and Morrison (now deputy prime minister) 'had a few frank words' at one of Wilkinson's cocktail parties. Margaret told him in her forthright, no nonsense manner that the present Labour government was 'a disaster for the country'.[63] It is tempting to ask what the long-term prognosis might have been for the friendship between the two women had Wilkinson not died when she did. Both were intensely loyal and had a catholic approach to friendships but their closeness had become strained due to widening political differences, even though Wilkinson's education policies in office appeared to be rather more moderate than her earlier left-wing beliefs had indicated.[64]

Another endangered friendship was with Bernard Shaw. Early in the war Margaret was prepared to be both diplomatic and understanding. In 1940 he had been invited to broadcast for the BBC on the Overseas Service. He submitted his script in advance. Its central plank was that lives must be risked in order to defeat anti-Semitism. Hitler was condemned for his persecution of the Jews but as a committed supporter of Stalin (and this was a year before Germany invaded the Soviet Union) Shaw stressed the importance of friendship with Russia. This script was peremptorily vetoed by the Ministry of Information, its parliamentary secretary explaining that Shaw's main theme was that 'the only thing Hitler has done wrong is to persecute the Jews'.[65] Although the Controller of the BBC intervened and Shaw seemed prepared to amend his script, the minister Duff Cooper was adamant, declaring 'I won't have that man on the air'.

Margaret told Shaw that she had read his script 'with enormous pleasure and satisfaction'.[66] She added that she loved what he said about the real quarrel with Hitler and agreed that 'the treatment of the Jews is the touchstone of the whole Hitler philosophy'. The following year she would state that 'The degree of anti-Semitism in any country is the measure of its civilisation and of the extent of its abandonment to the forces of barbarism'.[67] But she told Shaw that she doubted whether the public would have been happy with what would effectively be interpreted as qualified praise of Hitler. She knew the mood of the nation and of her friend:

> The country can't stand minority opinion just now. And however wholeheartedly you agree with the necessity for the war effort, you will always in every line you write express a minority point of view. How could it be otherwise? That after all is the reason for your existence.[68]

And even though she disliked Duff Cooper, Margaret admitted that, had she been in his position, she would reluctantly have decided that the broadcast could not go ahead.

Margaret and Shaw continued to communicate. Shaw's letter on New Year's Day 1945 begins 'Dear, Dear Rhondda'.[69] When his wife Charlotte died he sat talking about her to Margaret for several hours. So absorbed was he that, although a well-known vegetarian, he did not seem to notice that he had devoured an entire plate of ham and lettuce sandwiches. On a number of occasions Margaret stressed in print how utterly devoted he was to Charlotte, despite his public image.

After his death Margaret chose Shaw as the subject of what became her final three 'Notes on the Way' articles, written in the summer of 1956.[70] She saw him as essentially shy, like herself. In these articles she sought to unmask the 'real' Shaw, arguing that he had done himself a disservice for so long, perversely presenting himself in a bad light, that it eventually became a habit he could not shake off. She insisted that he was infinitely more generous and sensitive – even attuned to the supernatural

– than he appeared. And time and again she expressed her gratitude for his support back in *Time and Tide's* 'steep-climbing days'. Yet she found it harder and harder to accept his politics and apparent endorsement of dictators rather than democracy.[71]

In 1945 Margaret published her second *Time and Tide* pamphlet: a thirty-nine page disquisition on ideologies called *Men Not Masses*. It stressed that the fundamental question driving the century's conflicts had been and remained one of what would prevail in Europe and the world: the Atlantic tradition (with Britain as chief banner-bearer) or German ideals. Margaret was concerned about the struggle within Britain between forces standing for the totalitarian ideal and the democratic ideal. She discussed anti-democrats as she perceived them on both the extreme Left and extreme Right, nervous that what was being dangled as democracy with government of the people for the people or masses was not actually rule *by* the people and signified something far from true democracy.

Almost a third of the pamphlet exposed what she saw as the anti-democratic tendencies of one book: Shaw's 1944 publication *Everybody's Political What's What*. Written when he was in his mid-eighties, it sold 85,000 hardback copies in Britain in its first year. It should, suggested Margaret (playing on the title of Shaw's lengthy treatise of 1937, *The Intelligent Woman's Guide to Socialism and Capitalism, Sovietism and Fascism*) have been subtitled *The Intelligent Person's Guide to the Anti-Democrat*. She believed that Shaw demonstrated why no Planned State could be run without the effective abolition of democracy and substitution of an oligarchy amounting to dictatorship. As she put it: 'to make the omelette of a Collective State one must break the eggs of democracy'.

Margaret also suggested that the labels of Left and Right were outdated (though she continued to use them) and stressed that the current struggle was one for freedom against despotism. She was concerned about what Europe would view as the best pattern of government for the future, warning that although a democracy meant that the whole people were ruling, this 'no more absolves them from ruling for ends other than themselves than it does any other kind of rulers'.

The pamphlet strikes some shrill, even melodramatic, notes. Take, for example, her warning that 'everyone who passionately loves freedom and democracy and who wants to keep it safe' should read Shaw's book and be grateful for 'this Signpost to Hell'. Margaret's remarks were not particularly original but they indicate how her political perspectives were shifting as she grappled with questions about controlling the role of the State in a post war society.

Margaret's politics were transformed during the forties. According to her autobiography, when she was about twenty she had 'distinctly favoured' the 'socialist creed',[72] though it was into women's suffrage rather than socialist politics that she had put her faith. In the 1920s and 1930s she displayed a libertarian streak, supporting organisations and individuals that she would later attack. She was, for example, a vice-president of the (National) Council for Civil Liberties from its inception in February 1934 and signed a letter to the press complaining when the Albert Hall lessees refused to let the building for an anti-fascist meeting yet twice let it to Sir Oswald Mosley.[73] Fellow supporters included Bevan and Nevinson. She resigned, however in 1940 as she felt that the Council was controlled by communists and the following year the Four Winds column of *Time and Tide* expressed concern about the NCCL's communist links and suggested that it appeared to be totally unaware that there was a war in progress.[74]

Margaret had been attracted by the application of novel ideas. She had joined the Next Five Years group designed to advance broad political consensus around a progressive programme for social and economic reform and in 1936 sat on its executive committee. Founded by Clifford Allen who had been active in Left politics in the 1920s, it identified with Ramsay MacDonald and the National Labour group before seeking a different approach to progressive politics by harnessing 'middle opinion' from all parties.

In February 1934 Margaret supported an appeal by the German Refugees Assistance Fund. She was also one of those who signed the first of two manifestoes on 'Liberty and Democratic Leadership' organised by the Labour supporter Alfred Barratt Brown, principal of Ruskin College, Oxford.[75] This argued that a new wave of violence was evident in political thought and action and that democracy was threatened by both Fascism and Communism. Progressive literary and political figures such as Holtby, Sharp, George Lansbury, Ruth Fry, Sybil Thorndike and Laurence Housman were amongst the many signatories. But although some sought a centre party alliance that could challenge the National Government, the balance of the somewhat disparate group seems to have been towards a centre-right approach.

The following year its programme was published in a

320-page book. Harold Macmillan was, along with Allen and Arthur Salter (who had worked for the League of Nations) one of the main authors of *The Next Five Years*. It described itself as 'An Essay in Political Agreement', which embodied a 'far-reaching but attainable Programme of Action' and its printed list of 152 influential signatories, many of whom were academics and literary figures, included Margaret. The *News Chronicle* called them 'the most remarkable collection of experiences and talents which has ever proclaimed its agreement on so comprehensive and detailed a statement of policy'.[76] The book's twelve chapters included a series of progressive policies ranging from improving the collective peace system to economic planning at home. But as Daniel Ritschel has argued, the need to reconcile people with somewhat different ideologies resulted in a compromise that ensured that its economic policies did not match its more progressive social policies.[77]

Six weeks into the war Margaret remarked in 'Notes on the Way' that: 'One thing is certain, that if we had not fought, civilisation in our time would have gone.'[78] She commented bitterly on the depth of the roots of 'Hitlerism', presenting the Great War and the current conflict as one long period of warfare separated only by an uneasy truce. Had we, she suggested, 'put as much intelligent effort and capacity for self-sacrifice into making the peace as we did into making the war, we might not be fighting now'.

Two weeks later, Margaret presided at a Fabian Society lecture at Conway Hall where Richard Crossman spoke on 'The growth of nationalist and racial ideas'.[79] Just after this she signed a letter to the press urging support for the

Fabian Society[80] and stressing the importance of allowing voluntary societies to continue to provide a forum for free political research and education. The letter was also signed by thinkers such as Tawney, Laski and G.D.H. Cole as well as Attlee and Shaw. What is interesting is that Margaret was still at this stage prepared to append her name to a letter that stressed how the Fabians took a 'constructive socialist standpoint'. She had been disillusioned by socialism for many years, preferring to cast herself as a non-party democrat. Her association with the Fabians was due to her commitment to the importance of freedom of expression at a time when it was seriously threatened. The Margaret of the 1950s would not have contemplated allying herself with this group even for this end.

In 1936 she had stated that Britain was not a real democracy since gross inequalities of educational opportunities, of income and social prestige meant that real equal rights were non-existent.[81] At the end of 1940 she was suggesting how recent mistakes might be avoided in the future and advocating the abolition of class distinctions as a prerequisite for the civilised society she sought. Education was the key, so that 'all men and women are educated up to their capacity not of their pockets but of their brains'.[82] She proposed raising the school leaving age to sixteen, educating all children, regardless of income in local elementary schools until at least the age of thirteen. University education was not, though, in her opinion, appropriate for all. It should be reserved for those 'who can absorb it with advantage'. Yet she maintained that it should also be available 'for every single person' who was capable of this. Money spent on education would be 'money invested in the best possible security we possess'.

Margaret now interpreted the League of Nations as a great experiment but one that contained within it the seeds of failure. Its acceptance that all countries were equal and must have an equal say and equal rights and responsibilities in keeping peace, appeared to her as flawed and hopelessly idealistic.[83] She also feared that wars would not cease until the great peace-keeping powers accepted responsibility for stopping them. And by late 1941 it was the Atlantic Charter,[84] issued that summer by Roosevelt and Churchill that, in Margaret's view, appeared to provide some hope and a way forward.

In the past Margaret had been very critical of Winston Churchill. She had blamed him for the infamous Black Friday episode of 1910, which had disastrous consequences for one of her suffragette relatives. In the early 1930s she had questioned his views on rearmament and argued that he was not a realist. Yet she radically revised her opinions as she observed the wartime leader at work. He became 'the man whose genius could save his country and civilisation'.[85] The paper voiced some criticism in 1945 of his and Anthony Eden's lines on Yugoslavia and Poland.[86] *Time and Tide* was recognised as a pro-Polish paper and would continue to support Poland.[87] But Margaret came to represent Churchill as an indisputable international hero and world leader, the greatest statesman of her day and the politician she was prepared to support in peace as well as war.

Margaret's political shift never took her to the far right. Indeed she viewed Fascism and Communism as twin evils. In her *Men Not Masses* pamphlet she had noted that the far Left and far Right had much more in common in their ideological beliefs and methods than they would ever acknowledge. Tracing the effect of the Prussian militarism of Bismarck's time on Marxist and later Nazi beliefs, she conceded that Communism espoused a great ideal (though she was at pains to demonstrate that it was not matched by the practice). But she made it clear that was nothing noble about Nazism. It spelt 'the final degradation of humanity'.[88] Her belief in personal freedom was paramount.

There were some echoes of earlier feminist attitudes in her paper. Margaret's First World War experience prompted some critical comments in the summer of 1941 about the response to recent recruitment campaigns for women.[89] This was followed by a warning that publicity asking women to take subordinate jobs so that men could be set free for something better was outmoded and 'far from inspiring'.[90]

Although she no longer involved herself much with all-female organisations, Margaret did accept an invitation to become the first president of the Women's Press Club formed at a Fleet Street pub in April 1943 by *The Times* journalist Phyllis Deakin. Women journalists could not be members of the Press Club and wanted to pool information and ideas and provide hospitality to foreign visitors. From the autumn of 1944 they had their own premises in a former Lyons Corner House near the Law Courts, though its windows were blown out five times before it opened. Deakin later recalled that Margaret, who was president for three years, 'came up trumps. She gave us quite a bit of money and encouragement and a little knowledge of how to set about things. She was a very experienced editor by then. She really was very, very good.'[91]

In April 1934, Margaret had written in *Time and Tide* that the first action of most of the new Fascist governments of Europe was 'to return women to the *Kinder, Kirche und Küche*' (Children, Church and Kitchen) and that most women seemed on the whole quite willing to oblige. She pondered on what might be the case should Fascism or a suitably modified version of it, come to Britain. She feared that most women would embrace domestic ideology not least because comparatively few were already sufficiently liberated to enjoy any real freedom, let alone power. 'A vote is all very well' she admitted, 'but a vote doesn't make all that much difference – ask the unemployed'.[92] Nevertheless, the woman who had fought long and hard for the right to vote did acknowledge that it connoted citizenship and that, once granted, a citizen would not willingly surrender the symbol of the status of a human being.

A few former suffragettes such as Mary Richardson and Mary Allen embraced British Fascism.[93] In December 1936 after the Fascists had held a meeting at Pontypridd, the Welsh Communist and county councillor Lewis Jones addressed a crowd at Ferndale in the Rhondda, for which he was later charged with conduct likely to cause a breach of the peace. Here he threatened that if the Blackshirts attempted to return to the area, 'Mosley's bullies' would be stopped by force. 'Let there be a riot,' he proclaimed.[94] Jones also stated that on the night before their meeting Sir Oswald Mosley had dined with the chief constable of Glamorgan Colonel Lionel Lindsay at Lady Rhondda's house.

He was, however, referring to Margaret's mother rather than Margaret. Whether or not Mosley, Lindsay and Sybil dined at Llanwern is not clear, but it might well have happened. The politics of the widowed Sybil were far from the Liberal values she had espoused in D.A.'s time, and on a number of occasions Margaret sought to distance herself from them. As early as 1922, Margaret had admitted to Robins that her mother was 'a sound feminist' (though not au fait with all the modern developments) but she was

> inclined to regret what I think she regards as my Bolshevist tendencies, being herself what one might call a gentle and *very* inconsistent die-hard, but we do not allow our political differences to trouble us.[95]

On 26 November 1925, after lunch with Sybil, Margaret and a few of Margaret's friends, Robins noted in her diary that 'Mother R has joined the English Fascisti'.[96] Two years earlier twenty-six-year-old Rotha Linton-Orman had founded what was initially called the British Fascisti. Its name was later changed to the British Fascists. Fearing a Communist uprising, it sought to encourage patriotism, uphold the establishment and prevent the spread of Bolshevism and Communism. Robins did not elaborate on her terse statement, which suggests that Sybil joined this organisation. It does not appear to have been very influential and it was not until 1932 that a real Fascist programme was devised with the establishment of Mosley's British Union of Fascists.

There is no evidence that Sybil was ever a member of the latter, though a couple of her female relatives did join in mid-1934 when the movement was at its height and had attracted at least 40,000 members.[97] The following year, Sybil actively supported the successful Tory candidate for the constituency of Newport, and in 1936 she lent her motor car 'to stir up' Conservative voters in the municipal elections.

Her daughter was sometimes impatient with some of the more reactionary members of her large extended family. When she visited one cousin, Theodora noted with some relief that Margaret 'kept her desire for a classless society within bounds conversationally'.[98]

Margaret consistently condemned all forms of totalitarianism. Indeed, much of her difficulty with Shaw was that she perceived him being 'almost as polite to Fascism as to Communism'.[99] The SPG was affiliated to the British section of the Women's World Committee against War and Fascism and it and *Time and Tide* were very wary, as Holtby had been, of the insidious effects of Fascism on women.

When war looked increasingly likely, *Time and Tide's* Leader 'The Fifth Column' on 13 May 1939 stressed that London was 'the European danger-spot at this moment', with the resurrection of the 'poisonous influence' of people sympathetic to Nazi beliefs and ideals. The paper's pro-Jewish stance was well-known. Margaret was at pains to stress when Freud died (in the month that war broke out): 'I never met anyone easier to talk to, or more kind and fatherly to all younger acquaintances' than Sigmund Freud. He had been forced to leave Vienna the previous year and find asylum in London. Margaret, Wilkinson, Bonham-Carter and Rathbone had worked together in attempting (unsuccessfully) to get a reprieve for Liselotte Hermann who had been sentenced to death after attempting to publicise abroad evidence about Hitler's preparations for war.[100] When Margaret died the Israeli Ambassador made a point of attending her funeral.

In August 1940 as part of Hitler's invasion plans the Gestapo prepared a handbook listing those perceived to be a threat. *'Sonderfahndungsliste GB'*, known as the Black List, named 2,820 individuals to be automatically arrested. Margaret was included. She was described as a London journalist and her Hampstead address was given.[101] Wilkinson, Rose Macaulay and Rebecca West were named and *Time and Tide's* military correspondent. The paper was one of thirty-five to be banned and records confiscated.

War once more intensified Margaret's patriotism. This, her friendship with Peake and long-term difficulties with Brittain coalesced in an unfortunate episode. When Brittain's book was published in January 1940, Margaret visited Peake, who was then head of the News Department at the Foreign Office and Chief Adviser to the Ministry of Information. She informed him about a recent meeting of the Peace Pledge Union that had been addressed by Brittain, who was now on the point of leaving on a lecture tour of the United States. Margaret told Peake that she thought that Brittain was taking with her a resolution from that meeting. This stressed how English women were determined to secure peace.[102] It appealed to Eleanor Roosevelt (whom Brittain was due to meet) to do what she could to end the war by negotiation with Germany.

As a result of this information Peake reported in a Foreign Office Minute that 'Miss Vera Brittain is a determined pacifist and it is for consideration whether we ought to stop her going'. He was aware, though, that such intervention might succeed in giving the issue publicity, so suggested instead that the British Ambassador in Washington be told 'how little representative of British women Miss Brittain really is'. The Ambassador was asked to report on her activities but found nothing untoward.

How much Brittain learned of this episode is unclear but the *schadenfreude* implicit in her letters to Holtby was in later years untrammelled. In 1955 Brittain told Geoffrey Handley-Taylor (who co-edited Holtby's correspondence) that Margaret had suppressed her anger over much that *Testament of Friendship* had revealed about her. Margaret was, she wrote, 'my conscious and determined enemy' and her 'values and mine are just about opposite in every way; she is conservative, violently anti-pacifist, and has repudiated her feminism (or rather soft-pedals it) because it doesn't pay journalistically'.[103]

Brittain's anger had been stoked when *Time and Tide* printed in 1941 a long and somewhat critical review by Delafield of her wartime survey of life in London, *England's Hour*. Brittain believed, despite the fact that the paper had its own Literary Editor, that Margaret had arranged this and subsequent 'letters of abuse' by Rose Macaulay and others.[104] Brittain would, however, have been well aware that her pacifist perspectives were especially controversial at this time. In fact the book (which had suffered from the Ministry of Defence denying her access to places she needed to visit) received poor reviews from the UK press generally.[105] But Vera Brittain and Margaret had long since abandoned being reasonable in assessing each other's intentions.

Some also feared that Margaret was losing her sense

of perspective when it came to anything that smacked of Communism. Time and again editorials and the Diary lambasted all that the Soviet Union in particular stood for.[106] A letter in the paper in early 1941 by a member of the forces who was 'Lib-Lab' criticised *Time and Tide's* uncompromising attitudes (following numerous verbal attacks on the *Daily Worker*) and pointed out that there was much to admire in the internal planning and reconstruction of the USSR.[107] Margaret used her editorial privilege to retaliate. She stressed that Russia's current politics were nearer to National Socialism than real Socialism and emphasised the starvation of millions of peasants and liquidation of officials. There was indeed much to learn from 'the great Communist experiment', she thought, 'but mostly by way of warning'.

In 1944 Theodora noted that Margaret 'cannot see Russia as anything but a barbarous menace to civilisation'. The following year she told Theodora that 'Russian policy was to her the Devil'.[108] From the mid-forties the Cold War would certainly be waged in the columns of *Time and Tide*. In 1951 alone the paper carried fifteen articles on Communism abroad and ten at home. For Margaret personal freedom at home and abroad was the key to civilised society. This had become her priority and was the message she sought to convey as she and her paper faced the post-war world.

CHAPTER SIXTEEN

The Wrong Side of Time

As the war drew to a close, Margaret railed against bureaucracy and worried about threats to the freedom of the individual in a socialist Britain. In 1944 she purchased four copies of *The Road to Serfdom*, the influential study by the Austrian-born economist and political theorist Friedrich von Hayek. It warned of the danger of tyranny arising from government control of economic decision-making through central planning. For Hayek, who was at the London School of Economics, both Fascism and Socialism involved such dangers. In 1953, after moving to the University of Chicago, he wrote four articles for *Time and Tide*.

Margaret's 'Notes on the Way' articles in early 1947 (now signed 'by the Editor' rather than under her own name) made a clear assault on the concept of the Planned State.[1] She did not lay all the blame on its endorsement by the Labour government that had won a resounding victory at the end of the war. Rather, she argued that the ideal of the collective state had found supporters of different political complexions during the interwar years, even before the controls of wartime legislation put it into practice. But the critical response of Margaret and her fellow journalists towards, for example, the implementation of the National Health Service and their views on trade unions and the nationalisation of specific industries soon questioned the *Time and Tide* tag of 'Independent Non-Party'.

At first there was some caution. In September 1945 it was admitted that the sobriety of Prime Minister Attlee's tone 'and quiet incisive logic of his arguments are by no means ineffective'.[2] Then there was Margaret's residual loyalty. The Minister of Education's national training scheme was praised: 'Ellen Wilkinson will be blessed for introducing a ray of light onto what has always been a darker side of English life.'[3] And there was considerably more praise for Labour's foreign policy under Bevin than there had ever been for Chamberlain's in 1937 to 1939.

But the government's domestic policy became the target of severe criticism. Left-wing Labour Party members were especially derided. Long-term readers expressed their unease about the constant eulogising of Churchill and what seemed like a pronounced anti-Labour position. In the summer of 1946, letters asked what had happened to the old impartial paper. 'What has become of the *Time and Tide* of Winifred Holtby?' they wondered and regretted that it no longer seemed to be in the *Manchester Guardian* class (a newspaper that had long been respected by *Time and Tide* journalists).[4]

Margaret did not deny that her paper had been deeply critical of domestic issues. But she pointed out that British governments were elected and this did not mean that they must not be opposed. The Labour government had no special right to see itself as beyond reproach. Her opposition to the government at this point appears to have been stronger than that of at least one Leader-writer. She told Theodora that July that it had been 'a hell of a Wednesday [press day] – and R.T. Clark just couldn't write the sort of anti-Government Leader about the press that she had hoped for'.[5]

In 1936, Margaret had declared that, unlike most of her friends, she had no political label, though she would like to be able to call herself a democrat.[6] Two years later she stressed that *Time and Tide* was independent of all political parties, though this was not synonymous with not holding views.[7] Her paper came nearest, she thought, to an unofficial journal of the centre. Now, in 1946, a Leader declared that '[a]s an "independent" paper we respect all honestly-held opinions. We respect in others an "independent" point of view which may well not be our own. Indeed we exist for the defence of just such independence'.[8]

But such a position looked increasingly fragile. And after six years of Labour rule, just nineteen days before the 1951 General Election, *Time and Tide* admitted that it would be supporting the Conservatives. The 'Independent Non-Party' tag was to be replaced by 'The Independent Weekly'.[9] It suggested that this symbolised 'a change of expression' rather than of heart or principles. But although claiming to be tied to no party, this Leader added that they were firmly and resolutely opposed to the British Labour Party so long as it believed in 'nationalisation and totalitarian control'. In a sweeping statement it claimed that the country had been brought to the edge of disaster and that the only viable alternative to 'Socialist ruin' was offered by the Conservative Party. A Conservative majority was sought as a means to an end: the defeat of 'Socialism in our time'.

Churchill's new government was welcomed by the paper. It was regretted that public relations were not more effective, but there was little criticism of domestic policies and fulsome praise for its leader. Four years later the message was reiterated: all possible support was required for the Conservative Party since the Labour Party had not changed. There must be no return to policies which 'spell destruction for the nation'.[10] Indulging in a semantic high-wire act, the paper still claimed to be bound to no party. It could not promise unquestioning support for the government in future. Indeed, *Time and Tide* would be outspoken in its criticism of Conservative policy on the Middle East.

However, the understanding of who constituted the independent voter and what must be done was markedly different from the thinking that had underpinned the paper that Margaret had started in 1920. For this Leader ended by asserting that the independent was 'the man who values his own and other men's natural rights and long-established freedom' and that his vote must be cast for the Conservative candidate. In late 1957 an analysis of the views of 1,374 readers revealed that thirty-seven per cent of every hundred were Tories. A further nineteen per cent were disillusioned Tories. Thirty per cent belonged to no party. Liberals counted for eight per cent and a mere six per cent belonged to other parties, including Labour.[11]

More men than women completed the questionnaire.

The percentage of women (41.56%) appears disappointing when compared to the paper's female profile in the 1920s. But this needs to be viewed in the context of *Time and Tide* now being an international politics journal in which, despite continuity through a small number of writers such as Rose Macaulay and Rebecca West, male contributors were dominant.

One feature of the paper that increased post-war was the attention paid to Welsh affairs. This mirrored Margaret's greater involvement in her Welsh heritage as she aged and spent more time in Wales.

The elderly Sybil had died in March 1941. In her later years she was known for her economy drives. She only permitted one coal scuttle a day to warm her big old house. At the outbreak of war an invitation to the men of Llanwern village to a meeting to discuss the war effort added, to their amusement, 'ps bring your own sugar if you take it'.

Margaret had fulfilled her filial duty for decades but she had not lingered in Llanwern. She was now faced with the problem of what to do with her childhood home.[12] The army had requisitioned it, stationed troops there and erected some camouflaged buildings. A letter in *The Times* on 2 February 1943 from Lord Zetland, chairman of the National Trust, caught Margaret's eye. It suggested that some historic houses might be used as residential adult educational centres post-war. Sir Richard Livingstone, president of Corpus Christi College, Oxford and author of an influential book on the future of education, endorsed this suggestion, pointing out that only nine People's Colleges existed in Britain, compared with two hundred in Scandinavia with its much smaller population.

Margaret contacted Livingstone and the National Trust. At this stage her only other confidantes seem to have been Theodora and Janet Owen. She could no longer afford to endow such a venture but wanted the Trust to let the house to an educational body on a long-term full repair lease at a peppercorn rent. There was some hope – but no certainty – that the new education bill would help ease the financial burden for such ventures. The Trust suggested that Margaret make known her plans by writing to *The Times*. She obliged. Her letter made it clear how well-situated Llanwern was – close to the railway and centres of population yet with tranquil surroundings – and in need of funds.

She was not short of offers. The Workers' Educational Association, Britain's largest voluntary adult educational association, assured her that if they ran Llanwern she would be making 'a distinct contribution to the development of British democracy'. International Rotary was keen to develop a short course centre for United Nations students who were currently refugees. The Royal Society of Medicine suggested that it become a research centre.

Archie Lush, Monmouthshire's educational official responsible for youth work and adult education, had been an extra-mural student at Oxford and was joint secretary of Coleg Harlech. He asked Margaret to gift Llanwern to the Monmouthshire Education Committee if the education bill did not provide the finance for them to take it on. Monmouthshire also discussed leasing or buying the house to turn it into a nursery school. Further local interest came from Pontypool and Risca Settlements (offshoots of the Anglican Oxford House Settlement) seeking outposts for weekend schools. Margaret did not want her former home to be wholly in the hands of a local authority or to be a short course centre. A People's College was her goal.

Thomas Jones, secretary of the Pilgrim Trust and founder of north Wales's residential adult education college, had the most ambitious plans. He envisaged a Coleg Harlech Plus for south Wales, a multi-purpose college with a mixed governing body that included Newport Town Council, Monmouthshire County Council, the Workers' Educational Association and the University College in Cardiff, ideally with Board of Education finance and some pump priming from bodies such as the Nuffield and Carnegie Trusts.

But uncertainty about funding and the state of the house cut across such schemes. Jones discovered that it was rat-ridden and that the army had not been concerned about billeting men there. James Lees-Milne, the National Trust's Country Houses Secretary, went round Llanwern in September 1944. Although structurally sound he found that it had been sorely neglected and the army (no longer in residence but still in control) was ignoring basic problems such as leaking pipes. He told Margaret that 'The whole place is melancholy in the extreme'. He recommended that the Trust accept so long as an adult education institution was prepared to take it on and repair it but warned that it required 'urgent and immediate attention'.

Margaret visited in June 1944 to sort out the sale of furniture for auction in Newport. A Reubens painting was eventually sold at auction in London for £840 and the china was sold. Sybil's huge diamond brooch which had remained in the safe during the army's occupation was later retrieved for her daughter.

In early 1945 the Council of the University of Wales expressed interest in Llanwern. The National Trust agreed to hold the thirty-five roomed house and seventy-five acres of its park for the university, subject to a ninety-nine-year lease. But this plan also failed, as did Margaret's offer to the Ministry of Education for it to be used as a Training College for Teachers.

Over the following few years the house and gardens deteriorated further. A caretaker was installed in two rooms downstairs. Dry rot had set in and a staircase had to be removed. Ceilings were collapsing and wallpaper was hanging off the walls. The garden was a tangle of undergrowth and the lily pond full of slime. Lead was stripped by thieves from drainpipes. But Margaret did not have the money needed – now estimated at twenty thousand pounds – to begin to reverse the damage. The story was being repeated across Britain as country houses were derequisitioned. She told the local press, 'I've tried to sell it, I've tried to rent it, I've even tried to give it away'. In desperation, she sought a demolition order. But even here there was a problem. In January 1952 Llanwern was listed as a historic building under Section 30 of the 1947 Town and Country Planning Act so demolition was not permitted. Margaret eventually sold the house and land to a Newport resident. It was demolished in 1953. A local resident distinctly recalls returning by train from her annual summer holiday that August and the shock of seeing that half of the house had disappeared.[13]

For once Margaret had failed to get what she wanted. Her People's College did not materialise but in November

1950 she became the first woman president of a Welsh University College when she succeeded Viscount Kemsley (the one surviving Berry brother) as president of the University College of South Wales and Monmouthshire, the forerunner of Cardiff University. She had long enjoyed links with higher education in England and made her views known in the press. In April 1950, in response to the Lord Mayor's appeal for a National Thanksgiving Fund, she emphasised in a letter to *The Times* that a proposed residential centre for overseas students must show no race discrimination. Citing the war service of black students from Africa, the West Indies and America, she stressed that the British people must make 'a determined effort to stamp out all traces of a colour bar in this country'.[14]

Margaret sat on the Court of Governors of the London School of Economics from 1938 until the end of the 1951-2 session, but her Cardiff presidency was her first public indication of commitment to higher education within Wales. In her inaugural address she stressed that she was a Welshwoman and had grown up not far away. A *Western Mail* Leader praised Margaret's appointment since she had 'done so much in the past to break down the barriers of male exclusiveness'.[15] The Principal Anthony Steele saw her election as being 'in the best tradition of no sex discrimination in the college'.[16] He also drew attention to the inadequate recognition of university degrees in the recent Burnham scale award for teachers' pay. Margaret echoed this in *Time and Tide* the next week.[17]

During her five years in office Margaret presented degrees to students, for which she had to learn a few words of Welsh. In July 1955, though, it was her turn to be at the receiving end, and she travelled to Aberystwyth from Pen Ithon to receive an honorary doctorate from the University of Wales. Cardiff was a constituent college and Margaret had represented the college on the Court of the University of Wales since April 1951. The honorary graduands included Viscount Kilmuir, Admiral of the Fleet and the Liberal leader Clement Davies. Margaret was presented by the Rev. Professor Aubrey R. Johnson, a noted Hebrew scholar. She enjoyed talking to him later at the lunch in a building 'on top of a lovely hill', the new campus for the University College.[18]

With the ending of petrol rationing, Margaret spent more time at Pen Ithon Hall, scene of her fondest childhood memories. Surrey to Radnorshire entailed a long drive. They sometimes stayed in the Cotswolds to break the journey. She told Theodora that 'she quite realised that no sort of home would be nicer for the winter' than Pen Ithon with roaring fires.[19] But they usually visited in the summer and for a number of years Margaret spent at least part of July there. Haig cousins of all ages gathered there in time-honoured fashion. They took their meals at a suitably long table in the dining-room, relaxed in what they called the 'cat's parlour', danced Scottish reels, swam in the new pool, walked in the grounds and sat out on the front steps. Relatives remember Margaret blowing bubbles with the children and giving them all half a crown. Theodora described it as '[a] house of sincere affection – a refuge and – and above all a marriage between old and young'.[20]

In 1948, a limited company was created with shareholders and organised family rentals.[21] Margaret became the second chairman of Pen Ithon Estate Ltd. Her half-sister Janet had married and also lived in mid-Wales. She and her family used to come over to Pen Ithon and in July 1950 Theodora met Evelyn Salusbury for the first time. She described her as 'a smiling old lady in buff knitted skirt and jacket'.[22] Margaret's London friends such as Cicely Hamilton and Winifred Cullis also visited, as did school friends Prid and Gundreda Heyworth (who lived in Llangattock). There were also newer, younger house guests like Nancy Lord.

In June 1948, after a fortnight at Pen Ithon, Margaret wrote in *Time and Tide* about this remote corner of mid-Wales. She did not identify the exact location in her article. She made it clear, however, that local people felt they should manage their own affairs and resented Whitehall interference.[23] She detected 'a growing consciousness that Wales is their country and Welsh their language – a growing consciousness of their real nationality'. She applauded an interest in Welsh being taught in village schools. Her article generated a debate in the letters column between those who lauded the growth of cultural nationalism and others who feared its insidious effects. In 1955 an article on the National Eisteddfod was accompanied by an advertisement in Welsh encouraging supporters to subscribe to *Time and Tide*.[24]

Increased attention to Wales in the paper reflected contemporary debates about self-determination (Lady Megan Lloyd George wrote about the campaign for a Parliament for Wales in the independent 'Notes on the Way' section in 1954).[25] This chimed with Margaret's interest in international politics and forms of nationalism.

A focus on Wales also conveniently expressed Margaret's antipathy towards state control and centralisation by suggesting that the policies of the Labour government were inimical to the needs of small nations with distinctive cultures.

The views of members of Plaid [Genedlaethol] Cymru (The [National] Party of Wales) were aired in the paper. In 1949 Margaret discussed Wales and Welsh nationalism with the writer Richard Hughes[26] who claimed descent from an ancient king of Britain and immersed himself in Welsh affairs, even though his family had lived in England since the sixteenth century. *Time and Tide's* attention to things Welsh – in 1949 alone there were nine substantial articles on Wales – earned Margaret and her team praise since, as J. Wynne Lewis put it, 'It is so seldom that one finds in the London Press any indication that more than one nation occupies the area of England and Wales'.[27]

A Leader on Wales noted that, despite sending MPs to Westminster for more than four hundred years, only since 1944 had one day a year been devoted to Welsh affairs.[28] Walter Dowding, Welsh poet and social worker, wrote that '[r]eaders of *Time and Tide* will accept as axiomatic the statement that Wales is a nation'.[29] Unsigned articles such as 'Wales for the Welsh' criticised government proposals for a Council for Wales and Monmouthshire since they did not go far enough, though it was recognised that some Labour MPs were dissatisfied and sought greater autonomy. The Conservatives too were criticised. Their creation of a Minister for Welsh Affairs was seen as inadequate since a Secretary of State was needed. The Council's lack of effective power and the minister's role were criticised time and again, culminating in this attack on 10 August 1957:

What's the use of having a Minister for Welsh Affairs
if he stands idly by while Parliament decides to flood
a valley in Merioneth, washing away chapels and
churchyards and cottages, purely in order to slake
Liverpudlians' thirst?

Ten days earlier Royal Assent had been given to the
parliamentary Bill granting Liverpool Corporation the
right to have a reservoir in the Tryweryn Valley and in the
process to uproot the inhabitants of the village of Capel
Celyn and its surrounding farms. Not a single Welsh MP
had voted for the measure in the House of Commons.

As well as spending more time in Wales and on Welsh
matters, once the war was over Margaret resumed
travelling abroad. A proposed lecture tour to the United
States in the autumn of 1945 does not, however, seem to
have taken place. Margaret had been outraged to discover
that the American Embassy took a dim view of her
imprisonment in 1913.[30] She was also deterred by the
prospect of a heavy schedule addressing women's clubs.

In January 1949 she went on a cruise to South America
with Theodora. They were away for over five weeks, went
to Pen Ithon later in the year and cruised round
Scandinavia in the summer on the Norwegian *Stella Polaris*,
the world's sole vessel built especially for cruising.[31]

Margaret found the escape from austerity Britain
intoxicating. A winter holiday in the sun, by sea or air
became an annual event, whether to Madeira (where she
enjoyed staying at Reids Hotel) or further afield to
locations such as Bermuda and Jamaica. Theodora was not
always with her. Nancy Lord accompanied her on a few
voyages, as did Jean Press, a secretary and friend.

In 1949 Margaret and Theodora moved into a flat at
70 Arlington House, a highly desirable residence next
door-but-one to the Ritz Hotel in Piccadilly. It cost her
£1,750 a year: in 2010 one of the smaller apartments
there cost more than £1,000 a day to rent at the height
of the season. Their flat in this Art Deco building was on
the seventh floor with a long sitting room overlooking
Green Park. It was a good location for cocktail parties.
Theodora's diary records one such gathering in June
1951. Guests included Randolph Churchill, Herbert
Morrison, Osbert Lancaster, Cicely Hamilton and T.S.
Eliot.[32] Margaret attended a governors' meeting at the
London School of Economics beforehand, and she and
Theodora dined at Le Caprice afterwards. This restaurant
(conveniently below them in Arlington Street) had been
opened in 1948 by Mario Gallati, with financial help from
Margaret. Monsieur Mario had been the maitre d'Hotel
at the Ivy. Now Margaret conducted business meetings at
Le Caprice.

But business was by no means all pleasure. There were
serious financial and other strains on the paper that could
not be sustained indefinitely. Theodora's diary records a
management meeting about circulation difficulties in
March 1946 and another in October 1948 at which
economies worth £1,000 were agreed.[33] Just over a year
later the paper was still losing roughly £150 a week. By
early 1950 this had risen to £250 per issue. This did not,
however, stop Margaret going to Rio de Janeiro during the
winter.

Over the next few years potential wealthy backers were
targeted, but the fact that Margaret retained a controlling
interest did not augur well for securing solid financial

investment. Some were also wary of putting their faith in a woman, especially one who was now in her seventies.

Margaret remained committed to the paper but long cruises and increasing time away from London had an effect. When she returned from three months in Lisbon, South America and Madeira in 1955, Theodora remarked 'They don't welcome her back with flowers now as they used to do'.[34] When Margaret died, Rebecca West, a long-term director of the paper as well as contributor, remarked how nice she had been in the 1920s but in recent years she had become 'megalomaniac and fantastic', making demands that outraged her if they were not satisfied.[35] Many would not have agreed but it was nevertheless evident that Margaret held strong, increasingly inflexible, views.

A damning and very public critique came from John Betjeman in his poem 'Caprice'. Margaret would have been recognisable to his readers even though her name was not mentioned. It gives us his version of a lunch with Margaret on 1 December 1953 when he was peremptorily sacked as the paper's Literary Editor. He had held the post since 1950. Margaret felt that his focus was too narrowly defined for the paper as she now conceived it. Her account of events (refracted through Theodora's diary) is somewhat different.[36] Betjeman's title refers to the restaurant and alludes to Margaret's perceived capriciousness. Yet this witty reminiscence of wounded pride amongst the meringues acknowledges Margaret's indisputable dedication to the paper. The second verse states her intention:

'I'm making some changes next week in the organisation
  And though I admire
Your work for me, John, yet the need to increase circulation
  Means you must retire:
An outlook more global than yours is the qualification
  I really require'.[37]

The poem nevertheless suggests that, despite the sudden and personal betrayal, a friendship had existed. Margaret's god-daughter noticed that Betjeman was visibly upset at her funeral.

Some managerial problems were resolved after the recruitment of the young journalist Anthony Lejeune in 1955. John Connell, Leader writer for the *Evening News* and a director of *Time and Tide*, introduced him to Margaret. His mother was the *Observer* film critic C.A. Lejeune. His perspectives chimed well with Margaret's and he soon took over as deputy editor. His predecessor Philip Goodhart who had come from Fleet Street, had lasted just a few weeks. The following year Lejeune edited a *Time and Tide Anthology* published by André Deutsch and celebrating thirty-five years of the paper. It reproduced articles by contributors such as Graham Greene, Vita Sackville-West and L.P. Hartley. An Arts section included selections from Shaw and T.H. White. There were reviews by George Orwell and C. Day Lewis as well as Theodora and Holtby. Margaret wrote the introduction (which she dictated to Theodora) and the collection included her article 'The Pattern of Government', first published in 1945.

Time and Tide had survived against the odds. It had already outlived many of the weeklies that emerged after the First World War. Its ability to adapt and modernise had stood it in good stead. It prided itself on being, as one advertisement boasted, a paper 'for People who think'.[38] Neither was it afraid of changing its appearance. In April 1952 it appeared in a slightly smaller format but with thirty-five instead of twenty-three pages. It began a weekly column on chess.[39] A party at Arlington House in 1954 heralded a new turquoise cover.

Although radio, television and film all posed challenges to the press – between 1955 and 1959 the number of households with televisions more than doubled – the paper had long recognised the importance of film and television reviews. Margaret also made personal use of newer forms of media. She even appeared in Jill Craigie's documentary film 'To Be a Woman' narrated by Wendy Hiller. It made a cogent case for equal pay for women and featured Margaret standing on the steps of the *Time and Tide* offices. Margaret and Theodora were taken aback by how aggressive her words sounded. They thought she sounded very unlike her 'real' voice and that she looked at least a decade older than her mid-sixties.

Margaret had complained in the 1930s that the BBC neglected women broadcasters, particularly women writers.[40] But her fame and strong opinions ensured that she was in demand. BBC luminaries from Sir John Reith to Hilda Matheson were keen to engage her. The American broadcaster Ed Murrow specifically requested her to contribute to his CBS radio programme 'This I Believe', reputed to have the world's largest listening audience. Recording this in London, Margaret focused on meanings of freedom.

She participated in two programmes in the 'Editor's

Forum' series in 1947, debating current affairs with journal editors including Kingsley Martin of the *New Statesman* who was apparently reduced to 'trembling rage' by Margaret's anti-communist stance.[41] One of their topics was the current fuel crisis in the midst of the coldest winter in memory. Margaret claimed that it should be seen as part of a larger crisis due to the lack of manpower in the coalfields. It had already resulted in an unprecedented suspension of *Time and Tide* and all other periodicals for a fortnight (though papers such as the *Manchester Guardian* gave space to *Time and Tide* articles and comments). Here the journal editors were in agreement: this was an infringement of the freedom of the press.

In 1953 a Popular Television Association was formed to oppose the BBC monopoly in television and widen viewers' choices.[42] Vice-presidents included Lord Balfour, Valerie Hobson and Professor George Catlin (Brittain's husband) and Margaret. She was interviewed for the ITV News in 1958. She answered four questions about the problems facing *Time and Tide*.[43] She also discussed weekly papers for the BBC's *Panorama*. Her final appearance was on 30 April when she spoke about peeresses in the House of Lords for the BBC. But she did this with difficulty: she had a temperature and was seriously ill.

Margaret had not been fit for many years. Baroness Shirley Williams and her brother John Catlin have recalled how she would be accompanied by a large number of medicine bottles.[44] She had long suffered from bronchial problems. She sought both alternative and orthodox remedies for her ailments. On Theodora's advice she consulted the psychic Phoebe Payne in 1943. Payne told her that the nerves in her head were not shining as they should do. The same day her long-term medical consultant MacLellan diagnosed an enlarged gall bladder and prescribed a holiday. Margaret continued to suffer from gall bladder and duodenal trouble. A decade later she was seeing her doctor weekly and having frequent injections.

But it was from the start of 1957 that Margaret's health really deteriorated. She and Theodora were on a cruise to Australia. Betty Archdale, now principal of Women's College at the University of Sydney, was awaiting them. They never arrived. Once more a sea voyage resulted in disaster.

They were sailing on the *Iberia* towards the Cape of Good Hope and the ship was rolling slightly.[45] After pre-dinner drinks Margaret slipped on the steps coming down from the observation deck and fell onto the floor. She thought initially that she had not done much damage and went swimming. But she was forced to cut short her journey. The ship docked at Cape Town and she was taken by ambulance to the Monastery Nursing Home run by nuns and set in an idyllic spot halfway up the mountain at Sea Point. She had fractured her right femur and had an operation the following day. She was told that it would be at least four months before she could travel without being carried. In practice she was an invalid for the rest of her days.

At first she seemed to be making good progress. Theodora and Margaret's secretary Susan Cohen stayed in a nearby hotel and visited the patient. On 9 January Margaret dictated a strongly worded editorial telegram objecting to a sentence in a recent *Time and Tide* Leader.

But a month later Theodora was writing in her diary that it would be good if Margaret could recover a little more memory and speak more clearly. Her weight and adhesions caused by pleurisy the previous year hindered progress. It took two people to lift her though she began to use a wheelchair and sit on the verandah. She had physiotherapy but it was not until early April that she tried crutches. A few weeks later she was taken by nurses to the *Himalaya* and arrived at Tilbury on 29 April accompanied by Norah Kennedy, a nurse who had travelled with her from Cape Town. It was another month before she was taken by ambulance from Arlington House to Churt Halewell.

In July, Margaret was driven to Pen Ithon and joined cousins. The drawing room was converted into a bed-sitting room and a ramp now led from the study (known as the Old Bear's Den)[46] into the garden. By September, when she returned to Wales, her walking had improved. Kennedy and a West Indian nurse Mrs Everest Perry, were with her. Health problems were accompanied by health costs, with corresponding consequences. Margaret was increasingly distressed about the future of *Time and Tide* and she fretted about morale in the office. Her old friend Charles Peake was now the General Manager but seemed more concerned to sell off the paper and secure a financial future for Margaret than to save it. Theodora understood that although well-intentioned, this was misguided: without the paper 'Margaret wouldn't really have much to live for'.[47] Margaret invited Peake to Pen Ithon and told him not to spread gloom in the office. Before long ill-health forced him to withdraw and he died the following spring.

Margaret continued to canvas wealthy and influential friends but a weekly injection of £450 was now needed for *Time and Tide* to survive. On 15 February 1958 she announced in the paper that the next week's issue would be the final one unless financial support materialised. She admitted that, with the exception of the war years, it had been dependent on a subsidy that 'came out of my pocket, and I am no longer able to provide it'. Hundreds of letters and money poured in, from New Zealand to Ireland. Gertrude Caton-Thompson gave £1,000 and offered to repeat this for five years. Faithful readers enabled a 'period of grace'. Margaret expressed her gratitude and hope that the paper could be at least partly owned by its readers. A promise form and a covenant form (setting up a seven-year agreement for individuals to pay Margaret) appeared on 22nd March. T.S. Eliot declared that the termination of *Time and Tide* would be a disaster and Margaret appealed to him in New York to bring in some US dollars. Subscriptions were raised to £3 a year. They had increased the previous October too due to escalating postal costs and individual numbers now cost a shilling.

Margaret's lack of mobility meant that she spent most of her time at Churt Halewell. When the weather was fine she sat out in a secluded wooded part of the garden known as 'the hole'. She had a number of falls. Sisters from a local convent helped out. Her diet included yogurt. It had been recommended in South Africa but was, as yet, unfamiliar to most Britons. She had massages. But her accident was not her most pressing health worry. There were now ominous signs of serious abdominal problems. An investigatory operation was scheduled for March but then cancelled. Her doctor advised her not to go ahead due to the strain caused by worries about the paper. But Margaret also wanted to cancel it because, as Theodora put it, *Time and Tide* 'demanded her mind'.[48]

Lord Coleraine, one of the *Time and Tide* directors, came to see Margaret at the start of April. Theodora feared that they 'seemed to want to turn her [Margaret] out'.[49] There were a few tentative offers to buy the paper but they were either withdrawn once its financial state was made clear or they came with unacceptable strings attached. A Mr Vestey offered £5,000 pounds but only if four others put in the same amount and he was free of editorial control. Margaret even tried to contact Agatha Christie to see whether she could bail them out.

Margaret's personal finances were in a mess. Theodora admitted in mid-May that she was in a 'very worried financial flap'.[50] Never sufficiently careful about how much she had available, Margaret had spent rather more than she had realised. In December her jewellery had been valued at £2,700. Her pearls were sold at Christie's and she disposed of some items of furniture. She saw an estate agent about sub-letting the London flat. Theodora was convinced that they would soon have to leave Churt Halewell.

On 9 June, three days before her seventy-fifth birthday, MacLellan told Theodora that Margaret's heart was not strong and that he did not think she could endure much more '*Time and Tide* strain'. But she was already fatally ill with stomach cancer. She saw an abdominal specialist at Westminster Hospital on 25 June. She was taking a lot of sleeping tablets and was very confused. Janet rushed to London and this visit cheered her but Theodora's diary makes it plain that there were times when Margaret could no longer grasp or say much. By the end of the month she was bleeding profusely and in acute pain. She was taken by ambulance to Room 12, a private room on the sixth floor of Westminster Hospital.

On 2 July *The Times* reported that *Time and Tide's* weekly financial loss had been reduced by about £250. It added that Lady Rhondda was in hospital for 'rest and recuperation'. This was far from the case. She underwent radium treatment and had a blood transfusion. Flowers from Monsieur Mario decorated her room. The doctor suggested she might like Martini so Theodora took her a bottle. Margaret was anxious to see Janet, who dashed once more to her bedside as soon as Theodora telephoned her.

By mid-July the press was reporting on Margaret's serious condition.[51] Theodora visited hospital when permitted and tried to keep busy the rest of the time. She went to the office, attended the Marylebone Spiritualist Association and saw the foundation stone laid for the new wing of the BFUW's Crosby Hall. Margaret had been the honorary treasurer of the Crosby Hall Endowment Fund, which had raised the money for this since 1946. Theodora visited Margaret on 16 July but after that no visitors were permitted. Three days later, Theodora was briefly diverted by a murder at 38 Arlington House. She left a card for Margaret and was told that she was too weak to take food.

Theodora's entry for Sunday 20 July begins with the words 'Margaret died today'. She had passed away in her sleep at lunchtime. Her death was announced on the 6pm news. The following day Theodora saw her laid out in the hospital chapel. Janet, C.V. Wedgwood and Tess Dillon provided support for Theodora who felt ill but was kept busy. Margaret's solicitor C.G. Maby warned her of difficult problems to settle. She was helped by her faith. On the anniversary of Margaret's death she would write, 'I wonder how self-contained those who have recently passed over continue to be.'

The funeral was at Holy Trinity, Brompton in Knightsbridge on 25 July. Theodora and Tess Dillon walked behind the coffin which was covered with nine wreaths. Janet and her husband were behind them. The congregation included Haig descendants, *Time and Tide* directors such as Lord Coleraine, staff and contributors, Viscount Kemsley and journalists from other papers. Dilys Powell was there for the Women's Press Club. Charlotte Marsh represented the Suffragette Fellowship. The president of the Women's Freedom League attended, as did representatives from bodies such as International P.E.N., the University College of South Wales and Monmouthshire, the National Union of Women Teachers and the BFUW.

There was a choir of eight but no Address. Theodora hoped that Margaret could see from her 'etheric' position. She did not accompany Janet to the private crematorium at Putney Vale. On the same day burglars, taking advantage of the staff attending the funeral broke into Churt Halewell and removed rugs and jewellery in a furniture van.

There was considerable publicity surrounding Margaret's death, but Theodora was relieved that there was 'no scandal about Janet'. After her accident on board ship Margaret had been anxious to contact Janet. Her secretary had been puzzled about this connection so she had been told that Janet was 'an illegitimate relation on the Thomas side'.[52] Margaret respected her father's wishes and took his secret with her to her grave.

The committal took place on 29 July in Wales. And so we return to where this biography began: Llanwern. Some villagers were there. One of them remembers it as an impersonal, perfunctory event. A taxi arrived outside the church. It had come from London with the urn. Theodora was not there. Margaret's parents were long dead. Her half-sister was present but unacknowledged as such. The old home was no longer standing. But Margaret had been Viscountess Rhondda of Llanwern, had grown up there and had chosen for her ashes to be buried there with those of her parents even though she had made her life elsewhere.

That week, the cover of *Time and Tide* displayed a photograph of Margaret. Inside were tributes from Anthony Lejeune (who assumed the mantle of editor), Wedgwood and Connell.[53] Lejeune evoked Margaret's commitment and control over thirty-eight years: 'not an article, not a leader, not a diary paragraph, not so much as an italic note went into the paper without her personal approval'. Wedgwood's warm words recalled her unquenchable zest for life and 'wonderfully quick and clear mind with a capacity for singling out the essentials in a complex argument'. Connell, the consummate Fleet Street writer, called Margaret 'an Editor of genius, firm in her judgments, clear in her decision' but he focused on her at Pen Ithon since '[h]er heart's home was there'.

Margaret had witnessed tumultuous changes over the past seventy-five years. Rebecca West noted that she was 'one of the last women whom Charlotte Brontë foresaw in *Shirley*: daughters of the men who had made great fortunes from modern industry, who were resolved to give more service to society than had been the habit of rich women'.[54] She had been infinitely more privileged than the majority of her contemporaries yet, as a woman, she was long denied a number of basic rights. She dedicated many years to challenging outmoded laws and attitudes, through the written and spoken word, and even by direct action resulting in a prison sentence. She made as well as edited news. And she was remarkably successful. Her *Times* obituary was headed 'Champion of her Sex'.[55]

It is tempting, though, to consider some of the 'What ifs?' Had her parents had a son, what would her inheritance have been? Had she had children of her own, how big a part might she have been able to play in public life? Had D.A. not died when he did, how might her role in business and familial responsibilities been affected? Had Theodora taken up Edith Wharton's offer of a job in Paris, how different might Margaret's lifestyle have been? Had *Time and Tide* not survived its early years, what might have become the central focus of her life?

But counterfactual history is well named and none of this happened. Margaret had been a survivor and a courageous one. She fought against serious illnesses. She spent much of two world wars in London and, most remarkably, experienced the sinking of the *Lusitania*. She spoke out against prejudice as she saw it and battled for women's equality for decades. She addressed her youthful rejection of higher education by supporting it wherever possible and was sociable as well as serious, generous to a fault and deeply loyal to her many and varied friends. As T.S. Eliot put it, 'Among other excellences Viscountess Rhondda had the great and rare virtue of magnanimity.'[56]

Margaret also had the courage of her convictions. As an older woman she was not afraid of expressing views that challenged many of her earlier political beliefs, so risking the loss of support from many who had once admired her. Wary of the concept of the exceptional woman, Margaret nevertheless deserved the sobriquet.

Although far from representative of most women's lives, her achievements are a reminder of the broad social trends of her era. Margaret was a product of late Victorian society, albeit a very successful, progressive element of it. Her actions both before and after the First World War were symptomatic of the wider demands for women's legal, political and social rights that were effectively challenging long-established beliefs. At the same time her bid to sit in the House of Lords illustrates the entrenched power of tradition in Britain and the dominance of incremental rather than dramatic change. Her industrial career reflected the decline in heavy industry.

Margaret's focus on change within Britain broadened as Europe posed challenges to personal liberty and the rights of the individual. She became increasingly concerned about the rights of small nations, including her own. She also displayed intolerance of collectivist solutions and ideas that did not fit her increasingly rigid perspectives. She had, however, embraced modernity in a number of forms, from the motor car to the aeroplane and from radio and television to film. From the 1920s to the late 1950s she commanded an older form of communication: the weekly review. Its successes, adaptations and struggles for survival encapsulated the changes within the modern media.

It took a lot to deter Margaret, and that dogged persistence – which some, especially in her later years, called obduracy – helped to ensure the longevity of the paper that came to define her. One of its numerous correspondents summed up the sentiments of many when he wrote that, although he had never met her, he felt her death as a personal loss. 'Lady Rhondda was *Time and Tide*', he wrote, and the paper served her cause which was 'the cause of every thinking man and woman in our tumbling world'.[57]

Its dependence on Margaret, however, ensured that ultimately a reckoning would come. That it was somehow still in existence when she died speaks volumes about what she had created and sustained. It was far from being her only significant achievement, but it effectively symbolises how, in many different ways and over decades, Lady Rhondda sought to turn the tide of public opinion in twentieth-century Britain.

POSTSCRIPT:
Later

Margaret made her will in January 1956, a month after suffering from pneumonia. Anyone reading it without knowing her and her circumstances could be forgiven for surmising not just that she was a generous woman, but also that her finances were in a healthy state. She left Theodora an annuity. She could continue living at Churt Halewell for her lifetime. Codicils stipulated that her rent should be paid out of the general estate and permitted her to stay at Arlington House for two months rent-free. Janet and the son of Janet's late brother John were the other main beneficiaries. Janet, Theodora, Cyril Maby (of Lewis and Lewis Solicitors) and Charles Peake were named executors, though Peake predeceased Margaret. Annie New was left £1,000 and other employees were remembered. There was even a life annuity of £26 for Mrs Thursby of the Clapham Road, 'who has kept me supplied with matches for some fifteen years'.

Margaret's interest in the Time and Tide Publishing Company and £15,000 on trust was left to Theodora, C.V. Wedgwood and Maby, and £1,000 for them to divide amongst current and former staff as they thought fit. The University College of South Wales and Monmouthshire would receive £1,000 and the same amount was to create the Sir Thomas More Fellowship for women graduates needing help to become journalists.

But in practice there was not enough money to go around. The gross value of Margaret's estate was £85,458.1sh but the net value £27,995.13sh. When

Time and Tide's debts and obligations were taken into account there was not enough left to honour the bequests. Two godchildren had been left £1,000 each, but were asked to forego this 'to provide something for poor old Theodora'. The president of the BFUW, Margaret Peacocke and Mary Grieve had been named as the trustees to distribute the fellowship for aspiring women journalists. But the money was not forthcoming. A bequest was, however, made by a friend of Margaret's to the Women's Press Club. The Society of Authors currently administers the Margaret Rhondda Award, which assists professional freelance women journalists (whose main occupation is writing books) who are in needy circumstances. Other legatees lost out too.

And 'poor old Theodora' was just that. Margaret had died on 20 July. Just over two weeks later Theodora learned that Cotterells was to be sold (it was on the market the following month) and she was advised to give up Churt Halewell soon. On 21 August a sad diary note records 'I am pretty well ordered to clear out'. She left the Surrey house where she had lived for more than twenty years, and took a solitary room in the BFUW's Crosby Hall where she had worked in the 1920s. Theodora had returned to Chelsea. She died on 1 June 1961. A bursary was founded in her memory in 1973 for women scholars or postgraduates needing to spend a summer at a London hall of residence while undertaking research in History or English Literature.

As for *Time and Tide*, it survived for a while. In mid-August 1958 the new Trustees agreed to sell the paper to L.M. Skevington. His managing director Ernest Kay was soon occupying Margaret's room. Anthony Lejeune edited the paper. By 1960 the Anglican clergyman and church reformer Timothy Beaumont owned the paper and reinvented it. Two years later it was bought by W.J. Brittain. It was now barely recognisable: when asked why there were not more articles on women (it had started a fashion page) the response was a series on 'The women behind the men who rule the world'.

In the 1970s the *Time and Tide* title was owned by Sidgwick and Jackson, a subsidiary of Trust House Forte. It called itself 'The world's longest established news magazine founded in 1920 by Viscountess Rhondda'. In 1979 it became a glossy monthly and was then absorbed into a magazine called *Panache*. A quarterly review with the title *Time and Tide* edited by the *Spectator*'s former editor Alexander Chancellor appeared in the mid-1980s, still financed by the hotel baron Lord Forte but with no reference to the woman who had started it all.

APPENDIX

PUBLICATIONS AND BROADCASTS

(excluding contributions to newspapers
and *Time and Tide* articles)

A. Books

D.A. Thomas. Viscount Rhondda, Longmans, Green, and
Co, 1921

This Was My World, Macmillan, 1933

Notes on the Way, Macmillan, 1937

B. Contributions to Books

'The Political Awakening of Women' in *These Eventful
Years. The Twentieth Century in the Making As Told by
Many of the Makers*, vol.2, *Encyclopaedia Britannica*,
1924

'Women and the House of Lords' in *The Woman's Year
Book 1923-4*, G. Evelyn Gates (ed.), Women Publishers,
1924

'Business and Commerce' in *Careers for Girls*, J.A.R.
Cairns (ed.), Hutchinson, 1928

Introduction and 'The Pattern of Government' (1945) in
Time & Tide Anthology, Anthony Lejeune (ed.), André
Deutsch, 1956

C. Essays and Pamphlets

Leisured Women, Hogarth Essays, 1928 (also reprinted in *Century* 115, April 1928)

The Four Empires, Time and Tide Publishing Co Pamphlet 1, 1943

Men not Masses, Time and Tide Publishing Co Pamphlet 2, 1945

Some Notable Letters on the National Egg Collection (contributor), 1918

D. Articles

'National Service for the Women of Wales' *Welsh Outlook* iv, July 1917

'The Business Career for Women', *Ladies Field* 28 August 1917

'The Women of Great Britain', *Overseas*, 3 August 1918

'May 7th 1915', *Spectator* 15 May 1923

'Whither Britain? – ix', *The Listener*, xi, 7 March 1934

'The World As I Want It', *Forum,* 93, April 1935

E. Radio Broadcasts

Time and Tide's Fifth Birthday, 1925

Imperial Baby Week, 1925

The Menace of the Leisured Woman (debate), 1927

Mrs Pankhurst's Statue, 1930

Whither Britain? 1934

The Changing Status of Women 1934 (for US conference)

Shopping Tomorrow (A Nation of Shoppers series), 1937

As I Have Seen Things (Wales Service), 1938

For You Madame: Too Old At – , 1939

Britain's Food Controller, 1939

Time and Tide (in Women Generally Speaking series, Far Eastern transmission), 1942

Residents versus Editors Quiz, 1946

Five Editors (Editor's Forum), 1947

I Was There. The Sinking of the Lusitania, 1950

This I Believe (North American transmission), 1953

NOTES

Introduction

Place of publication is London unless otherwise stated. Sources are referenced throughout except where material uses private family papers and personal testimony. Full titles of Margaret's publications are provided in the Appendix. Abbreviations: MR (Margaret Rhondda); *MG* (*Manchester Guardian*), SWDN (*South Wales Daily News*), *T&T* (*Time and Tide*), *WM* (*Western Mail*); BLPES (British Library of Political and Economic Science Archives Division); BD (Theodora Bosanquet Diaries, Bosanquet Collection, Houghton Library, Harvard University, Cambridge, Massachusetts); VB Papers (Vera Brittain Papers, Mills Memorial Library, McMaster University, Hamilton, Ontario); C8/C9, D.A., NLW (Scrapbooks in D.A. Thomas Papers, Llyfrgell Genedlaethol Cymru/National Library of Wales, Aberystwyth); RP (Elizabeth Robins Papers, Fales Library, New York University); HRC (Harry Ransom Center, University of Texas at Austin); NATS, NA (National Service Department, The National Archives, Kew); ND (Nevinson Diaries, H.W. Nevinson Papers, Department of Special Collections, Bodleian Libraries, University of Oxford); WH (Winifred Holtby Collection, Hull History Centre); SPG/ERI, WL (Six Point Group Papers/Equal Rights International Papers, Women's Library @ LSE); WWC, IWM (Women's Work Collection, Imperial War Museum, London).

[1] *T&T* 9 December 1927. She founded it in 1920 and became editor in 1926.

[2] *Writing Lives. Conversations between Women Writers*, Mary Chamberlain (ed.), Virago Press, 1988, p. 239.

[3] Virginia Woolf, *A Writer's Diary*, Leonard Woolf (ed.), Triad Grafton, 1985 edition, p. 265.

[4] *Time & Tide Anthology*, Anthony Lejeune (ed.), Andre Deutsch, 1956, p. 17.

[5] *My World*, p. 120.

[6] C8, D.A.

[7] *Daily Herald* 18 April 1927.

[8] Dale Spender, *Time and Tide Wait for No Man*, Pandora Press, 1984, challenges the view, still quite common in the early 1980s, that the women's movement was quiescent in the interwar years.

[9] Shirley M. Eoff, *Viscountess Rhondda, Equalitarian Feminist*, Columbus Ohio, Ohio State University Press, 1991, p. ix. See also Muriel Mellown, 'Lady Rhondda and the changing Face of British Feminism', *Frontiers* ix/2, 1987, pp. 7-13.

[10] Clay is currently writing *Time and Tide: Feminism, Journalism and British Literary Culture, A Story of Time and Tide 1920-1945*.

[11] Winifred Holtby, *South Riding. An English Landscape*, Fontana, 1974 edition, p. 179.

[12] First names have been used only for those with whom Margaret lived.

[13] David Lodge, *Author, Author*, Penguin, 2005 edition. See Chapter 15.

[14] Dai Smith is writing a novel to be published in 2013 in which Margaret will feature.

[15] *www.100welshheroes.com* and Culturenet Cymru, 100 Arwyr Cymru/Welsh Heroes, National Library of Wales, 2004, pp. 146-7.

[16] A description used in 1923. C8, D.A.

[17] Deirdre Beddoe, 'Waiting for No Man: Lady Rhondda and *Time and Tide*, *New Welsh Review* 45, summer 1999, pp. 35-8.

[18] *Independent* 2 June 2009.

[19] See Angela V. John, 'Lifers: Modern Welsh History and the Writing of Biography', *Welsh History Review*, 25/2, December 2010, pp. 251-272.

[20] C8, D.A.

[21] Freya Stark, *The Coast of Incense. Autobiography 1933-1939*, John Murray, 1953, p. 121.

[22] Malcolm Muggeridge, *Chronicles of Wasted Time. Volume 2. The Infernal Grove*, Collins, 1973, p. 63.

[23] On 7 January 1957 Theodora's diary refers to Margaret's 'diary'. This does not seem to have survived and might have been merely an appointments diary or a holiday diary (they were in South Africa).

[24] Theodora's notes from the 1930s are in the Society for Psychical Research archives, Cambridge University Library.

[25] Barbara Caine, *Biography and History*, Palgrave Macmillan, 2010, p. 5. See too Alice Kessler-Harris, 'Why biography?' in 'AHR Roundtable. Historians and Biography', *American Historical Review* 114/3, 2009, pp. 625-30.

Chapter 1

[1] *D.A. Thomas*, p. 52; *My World,* p. 6; Chris Lyes, 'Llanwern House. The Early History', *Gwent Local History*, 77, p. 49; Thomas Lloyd, *The Lost Houses of Wales. A Survey of County Houses in Wales demolished since c1900*, SAVE Britain's Heritage, 1989 edition, pp. 103, 125; Sir Joseph Bradney, *A History of Monmouthshire. Volume 4 Part 2*, Merton Priory Press reprint, 1994, pp. 246-56; Sale Catalogue Llanwern House, NMR 45098, Royal Commission on the Ancient and Historical Monuments of Wales, Aberystwyth. There has been speculation about its origins. Charles Van may have built the modern house, perhaps utilising exterior walls from an earlier Tudor house (see *Cardiff Times and South Wales Weekly News* 14 January 1911). It has also been suggested that Margaret's home was the third house on this site, a moated manor house having stood on what became the kitchen garden. The estate passed to the Salusbury family after Katherine Van married Sir Robert Salusbury in 1780. See Chapter 7.

[2] *D.A. Thomas*, p. 52.

[3] Oswald Milne (1881-1967) worked for Lutyens before setting up his own practice in 1905. He became an expert in the remodelling of mansions. His finest work is considered to be Coleton Fishacre, the Devon holiday home he designed in the 1920s for the D'Oyly Carte family. He was responsible for Llanwern's Village Institute and other arts and crafts

style cottages named after shrubs and Margaret's home Oaklands.

[4] See H. Avray Tipping, 'Llanwern Park, Monmouthshire. The Seat of Lord Rhondda', *Country Life*, Xl11, 15 December 1917, pp. 580-5.

[5] Quoted in *D.A. Thomas*, p.16.

[6] Ibid.

[7] *T&T*, p. 88.

[8] See *http://www.oxforddnb.com/view/article/58913* by Deirdre Beddoe, accessed 17 March 2008.

[9] They were Charles Edwin 1849-1917, Janet Augusta 1850-1928, Edith Caroline 1852-1924, Rose Helen 1853-1942, Alexander (Alec) 1855-1940, Sybil Margaret 1857-1941, Charlotte Wolseley 1858-1937, Rodolf Wolseley 1860-1876 (paralysed after a fall aged twelve, he died in France in 1876, having spent the rest of his short life in a bath chair), Cecil 1862-1947 and Edric Wolseley 1865-1938.

[10] *My World*, p. 18; D.A. Thomas, p. 4.

[11] Gorsedd Beirdd Ynys Prydain (literally meaning the throne of bards of the Isle of Britain) was founded in the late eighteenth century by Iolo Morganwg to promote the Welsh literary tradition. Since 1819 it has been part of the National Eisteddfod. Rachel Thomas was initiated into the Order of Ovate at the Aberdare Eisteddfod in 1885.

[12] *Aberdare Times* 28 March 1896; *Merthyr Express* 28 March 1896.

[13] *D.A. Thomas*, p. 58.

[14] David Evans, *Viscount Rhondda. A Memoir*, Cardiff, South Wales Printing & Publishing Co 1919, p.12.

[15] *My World*, p. 173.

[16] *Merthyr Express* 22 June 1895.

[17] *My World*, p. 36.

[18] G.A. Haig's Will did not give preferential treatment to his eldest son. Instead he left the estate he had carefully cultivated

to be divided equally amongst his nine surviving sons and daughters. Between 1912 and 1927, Sybil and D.A. rented Pen Ithon, using it as a holiday home. It remained in family hands.

[19] Ibid., p. 23.

[20] Although Margaret and Sybil spelt her name as Lotty, she signed herself as Lottie.

[21] For details of D.A.'s political career see Gerard Charmley, '"The Little White Father". The Impact of D.A. Thomas on the Politics of South Wales 1888-1918', Swansea University Ph.D, 2010 and *The Little White Father. A Political Life of D.A. Thomas,* forthcoming.

[22] Elizabeth Phillips, *Pioneers of the Welsh Coalfield*, Cardiff, Western Mail Ltd, 1925, p. 213.

[23] Rev. J. Vyrnwy Morgan, *Life of Viscount Rhondda*, H.R. Allenson, 1918, pp. 194-5.

[24] *T&T*, 28 October 1927.

[25] Ibid., 30 September 1927.

[26] Janet Courtney, *The Women of My Time*, Lovat Dickson, 1934, p. 21.

[27] Other former pupils also expressed appreciation. *S.L.S. Gazette* June 1930, St Leonards School Archives.

[28] Angela V. John, *Evelyn Sharp. Rebel Woman 1869-1955*, Manchester, Manchester University Press, 2009.

[29] *My World*, pp. 80-1.

[30] *S.L.S. Gazette* December 1958.

[31] Betty Archdale, *Indiscretions of a Headmistress,* Sydney, Australia, Angus & Robertson, 1972, pp. 8-9

[32] Quoted in Deirdre Mcpherson, *The Suffragette's Daughter. Betty Archdale. Her Life of Feminism, Cricket, War and Education*, Duval, NSW, Australia, Rosenberg, 2002, p. 62.

[33] *My World,* p. 82.

[34] Ibid., p. 84.

[35] Ibid., p. 87.

[36] *T&T* 18 August 1934.

[37] E.M. Delafield, *Thank Heaven Fasting*, Virago Press edition, 1988.

[38] See Perry Williams, 'Pioneer Women Students at Cambridge, 1869-81' in Felicity Hunt (ed.), *Lessons For Life. The Schooling of Girls and Women 1850-1950*, Oxford, Basil Blackwell, 1987, p. 190.

[39] *My World,* p. 107 and College Register 1879-1971, Somerville College, nd, p.43; Report on Students' work, 1904-6, Somerville College Archives, Oxford University.

[40] Winifred Peck, *A Little Learning or a Victorian Childhood*, Faber & Faber, 1952, p. 158.

[41] *My World*, p. 107.

[42] Vera Brittain, *Testament of Youth*, Virago Press edition, 1978, p. 76.

[43] Ibid., p.108.

[44] Muriel St. Clare Byrne & Catherine Hope Maitland, *Somerville College. 1879-1921*, Oxford, Oxford University Press, 1922, p. 20.

[45] *My World*, p. 52.

[46] *T&T* 28 January 1921.

[47] C8, D.A.

[48] *T&T* 26 September 1924.

[49] WH/5/5.17/04/01h, MR to WH, 17 October 1933, HP.

[50] Vera Brittain, *The Women at Oxford*, George G. Harrap, 1960, p. 179.

[51] *My World,* p. 105.

[52] Ibid., p. 104.

Chapter 2

[1] *My World*, p. 80.

[2] *WM* 14 October 1909.

[3] *My World*, p. 110.

[4] Christchurch was her parish since Llanwern House was technically in Milton rather than the tiny Llanwern village.

[5] *WM* 10 July 1908.

[6] *My World*, p.108.

[7] John Newman, *The Buildings of Wales. Gwent/Monmouthshire* Penguin/University of Wales Press, 2000, pp. 67, 320.

[8] *My World*, p. 117.

[9] Ibid., p. 111.

[10] Ursula Masson (ed.), *'Women's Rights And Womanly Duties': The Aberdare Women's Liberal Association, 1891-1910*, Cardiff, South Wales Record Society, 2005, pp. 48-9.

[11] Ibid., p. 169.

[12] K. Bradley, '"Odd Men". The Role of Men in the Oxford Suffrage and Anti Suffrage Societies 1870-1914', paper given at the 'Seeing through Suffrage' conference, University of Greenwich, 1996; June Balshaw, 'Suffrage, Solidarity and Strife: Political Partnerships and the Women's Movement 1880-1930', Ph.D, University of Greenwich, 1998.

[13] Ryland Wallace, *The Women's Suffrage Movement in Wales 1866-1928*, Cardiff, University of Wales Press, 2009, pp. 18, 118.

[14] She was Margaret's second cousin.

[15] For the Haigs see Elizabeth Crawford, *The Women's Suffrage Movement. A Reference Guide 1866-1928*, Routledge edition, 2001, pp. 256-7, 2 and Idem, *The Women's Suffrage Movement in Britain and Ireland. A Regional Survey*, Routledge, 2006, pp. 180, 182.

[16] Quoted in Antonia Raeburn, *The Militant Suffragettes*, Michael Joseph, 1973, p. 49. Campbell-Bannerman was prime minister.

[17] Kabi Hartman considers how suffragette narrative appropriated the spiritual autobiography in 'What made me a suffragette': the New Woman and the new (?) conversion narrative', *Women's History Review* 12/1, 2003, pp. 35-50.

[18] See Lisa Tickner, *The Spectacle of Women*, Chatto & Windus,

pp. 90-8; Diane Atkinson, *The Purple White and Green. Suffragettes in London 1906-14*, Museum of London, 1992, pp. 15-18.

[19] See Wallace, *The Women's Suffrage Movement*, Chapter 1. Lady Amberley, first President of the Bristol and West of England Society for Women's Suffrage (encompassing south Wales and Monmouthshire) established in 1871 the affiliated Monmouthshire Committee (the first Welsh suffrage committee). By the late 1870s Newport had its own committee.

[20] *My World*, p. 119.

[21] Ibid., p. 120.

[22] Graham Martin, 'The Culture of the Women's Suffrage movement: The evidence of the McKenzie Letters', *Llafur*, 7/3&4, 1998-9, p. 110.

[23] *T&T* 6 February 1943.

[24] 'The Political Awakening of Women', p. 560.

[25] *My World*, p. 121.

[26] Quoted in Masson, *'Women's Rights And Womanly Duties'*, pp. 88-9.

[27] See *WM* 1, 3, 4 November 1910.

[28] Ibid., 29 December 1911.

[29] See Angela V. John and Claire Eustance (eds), *The Men's Share? Masculinities, Male Support and Women's Suffrage in Britain, 1890-1920*, Routledge, 1997.

[30] *Men's League for Women's Suffrage* (newspaper) 38 November 1912. D.A. was also following some other pro-suffrage industrialists such as the Cory Brothers of Cardiff.

[31] *WM* 18 November 1909.

[32] See Ursula Masson, *'For Women, for Wales and for Liberalism'. Women in Liberal Politics in Wales 1880-1914*, Cardiff, University of Wales Press, 2010, pp. 119-121. Masson argues (p. 156) that open-air suffrage speakers tended to get off more lightly than those at indoor events who were 'subject to organized wrecking by Liberal supporters'.

[33] For this episode see *WM* 19 November 1909, *Merthyr Express* 27 November 1909; *Aberdare Leader* 27 November 1909. See too Jon Lawrence, 'Contesting the Male Polity: The Suffragettes and the Politics of Disruption in Edwardian Britain' in Amanda Vickery ed, *Women, Privilege and Power: British Politics, 1750 to the Present*, Stanford, California, Stanford University Press, 2001, pp. 201-26.

[34] Elizabeth Andrews, *A Woman's Work Is Never Done*, Dinas Powys, Honno, 2006 edition, p. 16.

[35] *Aberdare Leader* 4 December 1909.

[36] Ibid., 2 October 1909.

[37] *My World*, p. 123.

[38] Ibid., pp. 121, 124.

[39] *WM* 14, 21 October 1909.

[40] *Votes for Women* 7, 21, 28 May, 18, 25 June, 23 July, 17 September, 1, 8, 15, 29 October 1909.

[41] *T&T* 6 February 1943.

[42] *My World*, p. 123.

[43] *WM* 20 April 1909.

[44] *My World*, pp. 124-5.

[45] Lady Osborne Morgan, the sole identifiably Welsh woman who signed this Appeal, was a vice president of the Welsh Union of Women's Liberal Associations but Sybil was at pains to point out in the English press that her views were not representative of that society. Masson, *For Women*, Chapter 2.

[46] *My World*, p. 169; *South Wales Argus* 13 September 1909.

[47] Mary Richardson, *Laugh a Defiance*, Weidenfeld, 1953, p. 51.

[48] *Votes for Women* 17 September 1909; Crawford, *The Women's Suffrage Movement*, p. 752.

[49] *WM* 23 February 1910, 11 February 1911; *Votes for Women* 13 May 1910.

[50] Krista Cowman, '"Crossing the Great Divide"; Interorganizational Suffrage relationships on Merseyside, 1895-1914' in

Claire Eustance, Joan Ryan and Laura Ugolini (eds.), *A Suffrage reader. Charting Directions in British Suffrage History*, Leicester University Press, 2000, pp. 37-52.

[51] *Monmouthshire Weekly Post* 6 November 1912.

[52] *D.A. Thomas*, p. 185.

[53] *Monmouthshire Weekly Post* 3 November 1911.

[54] Ibid., 20 July 1912.

[55] *T&T* 19 October 1928.

[56] Ibid., 31 October 1924; *My World*, pp. 131-2.

[57] The first signed article was on 4 May but her 'Woman's Cause' column began on 27 April and she may also have written the suffrage article (to which she later referred) on 20 April.

[58] *Monmouthshire Weekly Post* 13 July 1912.

[59] Ibid., 27 June 1913.

[60] Sybil had been a supporter since the 1880s of social (sexual) purity, with its focus on regulating prostitution and protective surveillance of the working class.

[61] *WM* 14 September 1912.

[62] *Monmouthshire Evening Post* 15 June 1912.

[63] *WM* 14 August 1912.

[64] Evelyn Sharp, *Rebel Women*, Warrington, Portrayer Publishers edition, 2003, p. 82.

[65] *Votes for Women* 14 June 1912. Maria Di Cenzo, 'Gender Politics: women newsies and the suffrage press', *Women's History Review* 12/1, 2003, pp. 31-2 suggests that Margaret viewed this activity in a more positive light than did many.

[66] ND e616/1, 14 April 1910.

[67] *SWDN* 19 June 1911.

[68] Ibid., 15 November 1909.

[69] *My World,* p. 136; *Votes for Women* 2 September 1910.

[70] *WM* 13 October 1913.

[71] *The Scotsman* 20 January 1910.

[72] See *My World*, pp. 144-8; *T&T* 6 February 1943.

[73] Lewis Jones, *Cwmardy*, Lawrence & Wishart 1978 edition, p. 240.

[74] There were, for example, important connections with the ILP in 1906. Some of its female members were active in the early WSPU in south Wales. During the First World War Sylvia Pankhurst was involved in anti-conscription work in the Rhondda and worked closely with the miners. South Wales was the one region beyond London where her Workers' Suffrage Federation was active. See Wallace, *The Women's Suffrage Movement*, pp. 54-5, 234-5.

[75] See Neil Evans and Kay Cook, '"The Petty Antics of the Bell-ringing Boisterous Band"? The Women's Suffrage Movement in Wales, 1890-1918' in Angela V. John (ed.), *Our Mothers' Land. Chapters in Welsh Women's History 1830-1939*, Cardiff, University of Wales Press, 2011 edition, p. 174.

Chapter 3

[1] This was the title of Evelyn Sharp's short story, based on experience. Sharp, *Rebel Women*, pp. 20-6.

[2] Laurence Housman, *The Unexpected Years*, Jonathan Cape, 1937, p. 273. See too Maroula Joannou, 'Gender, Militancy and Warfare' in Julia Swindells ed., *The Uses of Autobiography*, Taylor & Francis, 1995, p. 31. His sister Clemence designed suffrage banners with Florence Haig.

[3] See Chapter 13 for a discussion of *This Was My World*.

[4] Wallace, *The Women's Suffrage Movement*, pp. 76-7, 81.

[5] *WM* 8 March 1912 and *Suffragette* 4 April 1913 for Margaret Llewhellin's imprisonment.

[6] Angela V. John, 'Carmarthen and the Cause: the Suffragettes who got away', *Carmarthenshire Life*, 126, December 2008, pp. 28-9.

[7] *South Wales Worker* 19 July, 23 October 1913.

[8] Elsie McKenzie and Vera Wentworth were held in custody at Swansea gaol for two days after breaking into Swansea's Albert

Hall in advance of Lloyd George speaking there. *WM* 31 December 1909. See Wallace, *The Women's Suffrage Movement*, pp. 91-3 for the forcible feeding in Caernarfon Gaol of Phyllis North and 'Georgina Lloyd'.

[9] He was not Margaret's MP. This was the Liberal Lewis Haslam, who represented Monmouthshire Boroughs from 1906.

[10] Reported in *WM* 18 November 1911.

[11] *Monmouthshire Evening Post* 20 July 1912.

[12] *WM* 14 August 1912.

[13] See David Powell, *The Edwardian Crisis. Britain, 1901-1914*, Macmillan, 1996.

[14] Florence Haig Papers. 96.103, Museum of London.

[15] Chris Williams, *Capitalism, Community and Conflict. The South Wales Coalfield 1898-1947*, Cardiff, University of Wales Press, p. 17.

[16] K.O. Morgan, *Wales 1880-1980. Rebirth of a Nation*, Oxford, The Clarendon Press/University of Wales Press, 1981, p. 152.

[17] Idem., 'D.A. Thomas: the Industrialist as Politician' in Idem, *Modern Wales: Politics, Places and People*, Cardiff, University of Wales Press, p. 430.

[18] Reported in *WM* 29 February 1912.

[19] Ibid., 2 March 1912.

[20] *Monmouthshire Weekly Post* 29 June, 20 July 1912.

[21] *WM* 14 August 1912. Comparing perceptions and treatment of militancy was popular in the suffrage press. Pictures of Carson (represented as licensed to break the law) and Mrs Pankhurst (being persecuted because of her conscience) headed 'The Two Militants' appeared in the *Suffragette* 27 March 1914.

[22] *WM* 13 June 1914.

[23] Ibid., 22 December 1909.

[24] Ibid., 1 May 1913.

[25] Ibid., 29 July 1913.

[26] Ibid., 1, 3, 4 April 1911.

[27] Ibid., 30 December 1912.

[28] The situation was further complicated by the fact that the editor William Davies was a personal friend of Mrs Pankhurst's.

[29] *WM* 21 April 1913.

[30] Ibid., 21 January 1913.

[31] *My World*, p. 161.

[32] Ibid., p. 149.

[33] Ibid., p. 161.

[34] Ibid.

[35] Ibid., p. 163.

[36] Ibid.

[37] D2, D.A. Thomas Papers.

[38] See Caroline Morrell *'Black Friday'. Violence against women in the suffragette movement*, Women's Research and Resources Centre pamphlet, 1981.

[39] Elizabeth Robins, *Way Stations*, Hodder & Stoughton, 1913, pp. 241-4; Angela V. John, *Elizabeth Robins. Staging A Life*, Tempus/History Press edition, 2007, pp. 220-1.

[40] *My World,* p. 161.

[41] Morrell, *'Black Friday'*, p. 35.

[42] Ibid., p. 41.

[43] *Votes for Women* 5 January 1912.

[44] Sylvia Pankhurst, *The Suffragette Movement*, Virago edition, 1977, p. 343.

[45] Reproduced in B.M. Willmott Dobbie, *A Nest of Suffragettes in Somerset*, The Batheaston Society, Ralph Allen Press, Bath, 1979, pp. 45, 51.

[46] *My World*, p. 165.

[47] Robins, *Way Stations*, p. 244.

[48] BBC Wales Radio interview with Edith Lester Jones, 31 March 1965. I am grateful to Ryland Wallace for this material.

[49] *WM* 28 October 1912.

[50] Norman Watson, *Suffragettes and the Post*, published privately, 2010, p. 26.

[51] See Angela V. John, '"Run Like Blazes". The Suffragettes and Welshness', *Llafur*, 6/3, 1994, p. 31; Kay Cook and Neil Evans, '"The Petty Antics"' pp. 176-7. The concept of a 'Woman's War' was deployed by suffragettes.

[52] *WM* 22 May 1913.

[53] Ibid., 4 September 1913.

[54] Quoted in June Purvis, *Emmeline Pankhurst. A Biography*, Routledge, 2002, p. 262. See too Martin Farr, *Reginald McKenna. Financier among Statesmen 1863-1916*, Routledge, 2008, p. 239.

[55] For Margaret's imprisonment and its aftermath see *My World*, pp. 150-161; *WM* 27 June -26 July 1913; *Cardiff Times and South Wales Daily News* 19 July 1913; *Votes for Women* 1 August 1913; *The Times* 28 June, 12 July 1913; *South Wales Argus* 22 April, 26 June-19 July 1913; *Suffragette* 20 June-17 July 1913; *Monmouthshire Evening Post* 26-7 June 1913; *Monmouthshire Weekly Post* 19 July 1913; Wallace, *The Women's Suffrage Movement*, pp. 87, 211-2.

[56] *Monmouthshire Weekly Post* 20 April 1912.

[57] For example, *South Wales Argus* 28 December 1912.

[58] BBC interview, Edith Lester Jones.

[59] Watson, *Suffragettes and the Post*, p. 28.

[60] O. Wynne Hughes, *Every Day was Summer. Childhood memories of Edwardian days in a small Welsh town*, Llandysul, Gomer Press 1990, p. 4; Angela V. John, '"Run Like Blazes". The Suffragettes and Welshness', *Llafur. Journal of Welsh Labour History*, 6/3, 1994, p. 29.

[61] *WM* 18 July 1913.

[62] Angela V. John, '"Behind the Locked Door": Evelyn Sharp, suffragette and rebel journalist', *Women's History Review*, 12/1, 2003, pp. 5-13.

[63] *My World*, p. 121.

[64] Florence Haig Papers, 96.103.

[65] Rule 243a March 1910. For prison life and forcible feeding see June Purvis, 'The Prison Experiences of the Suffragettes in Edwardian Britain', *Women's History Review* 4/1, 1995, pp. 103-132; J.F. Geddes, 'Culpable Complicity: the medical profession and the forcible feeding of suffragettes, 1909-1914', Ibid, 17/1, 2008, pp. 79-94.

[66] Crawford, *The Women's Suffrage Movement*, pp. 241-2 and Wallace, *The Women's Suffrage Movement,* pp. 91, 93.

[67] She could not resist a long, scathing reply to an article in the local press by the leading local opponent of women's suffrage. Gwladys Gladstone Solomon had claimed that '[t]here is no more misunderstood person in the world than the anti-suffragist'. *South Wales Weekly Argus* 2, 9 September 1912.

[68] For suffrage societies within Wales in these years see Wallace, *The Women's Suffrage Movement.*

[69] John, *Evelyn Sharp*, p. 72.

[70] See Michelle Elizabeth Tusan, *Women Making News. Gender and Journalism in Modern Britain*, Urbana and Chicago, University of Illinois Press, 2005, pp. 176-186. Sybil's own copies of the *Suffragette* are in the National Library of Wales.

[71] *My World*, p. 132.

[72] For the petition and subsequent events see D2, D.A. (Handwritten Petition and letter of 12 February 1914 from Israel Zangwill); *Votes for Women* 27 February 1914; ND e618/2 24-27 February 1914; H.W. Nevinson, *More Changes. More Chances*, Nisbet, 1925, pp. 334-5; *Suffragette* 27 February 1914; *WM* 25, 28 February 1914; *My World*, pp. 167-70; Wallace, *The Women's Suffrage Movement,* p.72; Housman, *The Unexpected Years*, pp. 282-3.

[73] *WM* 19 March 1914.

[74] This was the name for the Central Society for Women's Suffrage from 1907.

[75] She had been president of the London Welsh society, the Cymric Suffrage Union, from its inception in 1911, but did not

hold office in its successor the Forward Cymric Suffrage Union. She was also briefly treasurer of Sylvia Pankhurst's East London Federation of the Suffragettes in 1914.

Chapter 4

[1] *Votes for Women* 18, 25 December 1914, 8 January 1915; WM 25 November, 11 December 1914; John, *Evelyn Sharp*, p. 80.

[2] *My World*, pp. 275-6.

[3] For the *Lusitania* and its sinking see: *My World*, Chapter xvi; D.A. Thomas, pp. 196-200; WM 8-13 May 1915, 19 December 1921, *The Times* 18 June1915; *Spectator* 5 May 1923; Margaret Haig Thomas, *Sinking of the Lusitania* ICD0177201, BD9, 1950 BBC, National Sound Archive, British Library; Des Hickey and Gus Smith, *Seven Days to Disaster. The true story of the sinking of the Lusitania,* Fontana, 1982 edition; Colin Simpson, *Lusitania,* Longman, 1972; Robert Ballard, *Lusitania,* Haynes Publishing, Yeovil, 2009 edition; Diana Preston, *Wilful Murder. The Sinking of the Lusitania*, Corgi edition, 2003, Thomas A. Bailey and Paul B. Ryan, *The Lusitania Disaster. An Episode in Modern Warfare and Diplomacy*, Collier Macmillan, 1975; *Dark secrets of the Lusitania*. TV Documentary, National Geographic Channel, 15 July 2012.

[4] For some time his favourite hymn had been the Rev. David Williams's 'Yn y dyfroedd mawr a'r tonnau' ('In the mighty waters and the waves') about Christ's support for the drowning man.

[5] It has also been alleged that the British Navy later deliberately sought to destroy evidence by bombing part of the shipwreck on the sea bed.

[6] A Boston bookseller and seasoned traveller observed that more than half the passengers had not adjusted their life belts properly. There had been no demonstrations showing how to adjust them.

[7] It too was a Boddy belt. It is preserved in the National Library of Wales.

[8] He is somewhat conspicuous by his absence from her accounts. Margaret had mentioned in her 1921 memoir of her father that D.A.'s secretary had 'leant forward and warmly grasped his hand' as he settled into the lifeboat. Evans took exception to this as he felt it implied that he had hastened to secure his safety regardless of others. He assured the *WM* (on 19 December 1921) that he had helped people to fasten their lifebelts and been precipitated into the sea then hauled into a boat. He was dazed by a blow on the head. Margaret replied that she was sorry that he had interpreted her thus and stressed that nobody could have been accused of undue haste.

[9] *MG* 7 May 1940.

[10] The official list left out three prisoners.

[11] Elizabeth Robins, *The Messenger*, Hodder & Stoughton, 1919, p. 233.

[12] He had complained to the press (*Morning Post* 10 May 1915) that the vessel had been travelling too slowly and was not properly protected, that the crew had only been concerned for its own safety and that panic had ensued. At the time he had complained that the fog horns (sounded regularly for three hours from 8am on the morning of the disaster) had betrayed their whereabouts.

[13] *Monmouthshire Weekly Post* 4 May 1912.

[14] *T&T* 15 April 1939.

[15] *Daily Chronicle* 15 August 1922.

[16] *Selected Letters of Winifred Holtby and Vera Brittain*, Vera Brittain and Geoffrey Handley-Taylor (eds.), Hull, A. Brown & Sons, 1960, p. 64.

[17] Application Form signed 14 July 1999, St Leonards School Archives.

[18] Manuscript copy of Octavia Wilberforce's autobiography 'The Eighth Child', p. 228 in the author's possession.

[19] *A Reflection of the Other Person. The Letters of Virginia Woolf. Volume 1 1929-1931*, Nigel Nicolson (ed.), Chatto & Windus, 1981 edition, p. 235.

[20] *Notes*, pp. 161-2.

Chapter 5

[1] *Suffragette* 23 May, 11 June 1915.

[2] Margaret sent £5 towards the WSPU's new Home for Babies. Sybil contributed £25 and £50 to support the patriotic line taken by the *Suffragette*. See Paula Bartley, *Emmeline Pankhurst*, Routledge, 2002, p. 195; Purvis, *Emmeline Pankhurst*, pp. 279-280 for the war baby scheme.

[3] *Britannia* 14 April 1916. See Angela K. Smith, 'The Pankhursts and the War: suffrage magazines and First World War propaganda', *Women's History Review*, 12/1, 2003, pp. 103-118.

[4] *My World,* p. 268. Eoff, *Viscountess Rhondda*, pp. 40-1 does, however, briefly discuss this.

[5] YR/30, R/232 and BEL 6177.3, WWC, IWM.

[6] See too *D.A. Thomas*, pp. 201-3.

[7] See Chapter 7.

[8] Charmley, '"The Little White Father"'.

[9] Quoted in *D.A. Thomas*, p. 202.

[10] *My World*, p. 207.

[11] In *SWDN* 7 July 1917. For the WAAC see Elizabeth Crosthwait, '"The Girl Behind the Man Behind the Gun": The Women's Army Auxiliary Corps, 1914-18' in L. Davidoff, b. Westover (eds.), *Our Work, Our Lives, Our Words: Women's History and Women's Work,* Macmillan, 1986, pp. 161-81; Arthur Marwick, *Women at War 1914-1918*, Fontana edition, 1977; Roy Terry, *Women in Khaki. The Story of the British Woman Soldier*, Columbus Books, 1988; Doron Lamm, 'Emily Goes to War. Explaining the Recruitment to the Women's Army Auxiliary Corps in World War 1' in Billie Melman (ed.), *Borderlines. Genders and Identities in War and Peace. 1870-1930*, Routledge, 1998, pp. 377-95.

[12] National Service Department, Women's Section, NATS 1/1114, NA.

[13] *SWDN* 29 January 1917.

[14] *The Times* 19 March 1917.

[15] She had changed her views about the right to the franchise but still maintained, as she had in a speech at the Albert Hall on 28 February 1912, that 'men and women are different – not similar beings, with talents that are complementary, not identical'. 'Woman's Sphere', The National League for Opposing Woman Suffrage Pamphlet, 1912.

[16] NATS 1/1297.

[17] See Ibid., 1/1306.

[18] Quoted in Helen Jones (ed.), *Duty and Citizenship: the correspondence and political papers of Violet Markham*, The Historian's Press, 1994, p. 85.

[19] Ibid., p. 10.

[20] See, for example, her comments to Alfred Zimmern and Tennant, Ibid, pp. 84 and 86.

[21] Margaret was secretary of Abergavenny's sub-committee of Monmouthshire's Women's War Agricultural Committee.

[22] NATS 1/1297.

[23] Deirdre Beddoe, *Out of the Shadows. A History of Women in Twentieth-Century Wales*, Cardiff, University of Wales Press, 2000, pp. 66-8; *WM* 6 March 1915. Winifred Coombe Tennant who sat on a Welsh Women's War Agricultural Committee had addressed a Board of Agriculture conference at the House of Commons in 1916 emphasising that Glamorgan farmers 'would rather do anything than employ women'. Peter Lord, *Winifred Coombe Tennant: A Diary of Emancipation*, Aberystwyth, National Library of Wales, 2011, p. 200.

[24] For this section see NATS 1/1307.

[25] *SWDN* 7 July 1917.

[26] Crosthwait, '"The Girl Behind The Man"', p. 163.

[27] *SWDN* 7 July 1917.

[28] 'National Service for the Women of Wales', *Welsh Outlook* iv July 1917.

[29] *SWDN* 17 July 1917.

[30] *Welsh Outlook* iv July 1917.

[31] For example, *SWDN* 4 May 1917.

[32] For the relative attraction of clerical over domestic work see Lamm, 'Emily Goes to War', pp. 380-4.

[33] For this discussion see NATS 1/1268.

[34] NATS 1/1307, 18 and 19 June 1917.

[35] *Daily Mirror* 30 June 1917.

[36] As president of the Local Government Board, D.A. had actively endorsed the idea that one or more women should sit on these committees.

[37] Beddoe, *Out of the Shadows*, p. 68.

[38] NATS 1/1305.

[39] Ibid.

[40] NATS 1/1268.

[41] Jones, *Duty and Citizenship*, p. 85.

[42] Ibid., p. 87. For the difficulties dogging the department generally see David Dilks, *Neville Chamberlain. Volume 1. Pioneering and reform. 1869-1929*, Cambridge, Cambridge University Press, pp. 199-250.

[43] Jones, *Duty and Citizenship* p. 91; Violet Markham, *Return Passage*, Oxford, Oxford University Press, 1953, pp. 151-4.

[44] See Chapter 9.

[45] *WM* 15 November 1917.

[46] *South Wales Argus* 2 November 1918.

[47] *SWDN* 24 January 1918.

[48] A new order under the Defence of the Realm Act made it a penal offence to communicate a venereal disease to an officer. Some soldiers in France began making charges against WAACs. Marwick, *Women at War*, p. 125.

[49] Terry, *Women in Khaki*, p. 70.

[50] NATS 1/1297, Report of Commission of Inquiry on alleged immoral conduct in the WAAC.

[51] Lamm, 'Emily Goes to War'.

[52] *South Wales News* 23-28 April 1918.

[53] *The Times* 11 June 1918; *WM* 11 June 1918.

[54] *My World*, p. 268.

[55] Ibid.

Chapter 6

[1] Markham Papers 4/9, National Service 1917-18, 18 January 1918, BLPES.

[2] Ibid., 15 January 1918.

[3] Ibid., 21 January 1918.

[4] *Queen* 14 January 1918.

[5] *Sketch* 23 January 1918.

[6] SUPP 46/156, WWC.

[7] See NATS 1/11272.

[8] Ibid., 1/1267, 13 June 1918.

[9] *My World*, p. 268.

[10] Markham Papers, 12 April, 4 July 1918; NATS 1/1267 16 April 1918.

[11] Dame Katharine Furse, *Hearts and Pomegranates: the story of forty-five years, 1875 to 1920*, Peter Davies, 1940, pp. 382-3.

[12] NATS 1/1290.

[13] Ibid., The original title was 'Women's Share in the War'.

[14] http://www.oxforddnb.com/view/article/67667, accessed 23 June 1910.

[15] PP. Cmd. 243, December 1919. Select Committee on the Women's Royal Air Force: Inquiry on Miss Douglas-Pennant, Appendix 7, p. 403.

[16] Hansard, House of Commons 5th Series CIX, 5 August 1918, pp. 925-6.

[17] The two women were currently sitting on the Women's Panel of the Staff Investigation Committee. Strachey was Margaret's nominee. See Chapter 8.

[18] Dame Helen Gwynne-Vaughan, former chief controller of the WAAC in France, became the third commandant.

[19] In Letter of 2 September 1918, Douglas-Pennant to Lord Weir. Reproduced in PP. Cmd. 813, Air Ministry Correspondence, May 1919.

[20] *The Times* 3 June 1919.

[21] Helen Archdale had attended in her absence. This section is based on PP, Cmd. 243, December 1919.

[22] Violet Douglas-Pennant, *Under the Search-Light*, George Allen & Unwin, 1922, p. 178.

[23] As revealed in the *MG* 11 June 1925. For the report see PP Cmd. 254, Air Ministry. Further correspondence relating to the termination of the appointment of the Hon Violet Douglas-Pennant as Commandant of the Women's Royal Air Force, p. 13.

[24] Two colonels subsequently sued successfully for libel.

[25] *The Times* 9 December 1919.

[26] T1/12437. Air Ministry, NA.

[27] Unless otherwise indicated the following section is based on Douglas-Pennant, *Under the Search-Light*.

[28] HU22/LSE Pamphlets. A Brief History of the Douglas-Pennant Case, BLPES.

[29] *Liverpool Post and Mercury* 6 April 1922.

[30] See too David Mitchell, *Women on the Warpath. The Story of the Women of the First World War*, Jonathan Cape, 1966, pp. 236-7.

[31] *MG* 10-13 June 1925.

[32] Ibid., 13 June 1925.

[33] Ibid., 12 June 1925.

[34] Ibid., 12 June 1925.

[35] Nina Boyle was to have written an article but C.P. Scott insisted that Nevinson take it on. ND e623/5, 9 April, 22 May 1925; Angela V. John, *War, Journalism and the Shaping of the Twentieth Century. The Life and Times of Henry W. Nevinson*, I.B. Tauris, 2006.

[36] ND, e623/5, 14 May 1925.

[37] *MG* 15 June 1925.

[38] ND, e623/5, 13 May 1925.

[39] Ibid., 20 December 1925.

[40] Ibid., 26 December 1925.

[41] JF (42) D144, LSE Pamphlets, BLPES.

[42] ND, e625/2, 17 February 1931.

[43] *MG* 3 July 1931.

[44] JF (42) D144, LSE Pamphlets.

[45] ND, e626/1, 25 September 1934.

[46] Markham Papers, 4/16, Letter of 14 September 1918.

[47] Ibid., 28 February 1920.

[48] Eoff, *Viscountess Rhondda*, p. 44.

[49] ND, e623/6, 31 December 1925.

Chapter 7

[1] *My World,* p. 173.

[2] *D. A. Thomas*, p. 91.

[3] *WM* 10 May 1915.

[4] Quoted in Evans, *Viscount Rhondda*, p. 83.

[5] Transcript of *Britain's Food Controller*, BBC Home Service Broadcast, 13 December 1939, BBC Written Archives, Caversham.

[6] M.H. Mackworth to D. Lloyd George, 31 March 1918, Lloyd George Papers, LG/ F/43/5/64, Parliamentary Archives.

[7] Quoted in *D.A. Thomas,* p. 273.

[8] *The Times* 8 July 1918; *South Wales News* 15 July 1918.

[9] Quoted in *D.A. Thomas*, p. 273.

[10] Quoted in Evans. *Viscount Rhondda*, p. 40.

[11] Ibid., p. 76.

[12] *Merthyr Express* 16 July 1918.

[13] Quoted in Evans, *Viscount Rhondda*, p. 58.

[14] See Chapter 9.

[15] 3409/1, National Trust Reports 1935-6, p.8; *National Trust News* February 1936, The National Trust, Heelis, Swindon.

[16] For example, she was one of ten contributors to a publication of 'Notable Letters' about the importance of the national egg collection that supplied eggs weekly to wounded soldiers and sailors. The actress Lena Ashwell was the only other female contributor.

[17] See Chapter 8.

[18] *Queen* 5 April 1919.

[19] *The Times* 12 July, 25 October 1918.

[20] Angela Gaffney, '"A National Valhalla for Wales". D.A. Thomas and the Welsh Historical Sculpture Scheme, 1910-1916', *Transactions of the Honourable Society of Cymmrodorion 1998*, ns. 5, 1999, pp. 131-44.

[21] Dai Smith, *Aneurin Bevan and the World of South Wales*, Cardiff, University of Wales Press, 1993, p. 110.

[22] The few references to Margaret were tentative: 'She *appears* to have inherited in a large measure her father's business and organizing ability' and '*It is said* that she is chairman of not less than seven limited companies...' [my italics]. J. Vyrnwy Morgan, *Life of Viscount Rhondda*, H.R. Allenson, 1918, p. 84. See too Gerard Charmley, 'J. Vyrnwy Morgan (1861-1925): Wales in another light', *Welsh History Review*, 24/2, 2008, pp. 20-43.

[23] Seven Appendices supplied further reminiscences.

[24] By contrast, Gerald Charmley's twenty-first century analysis portrays D.A.'s career as an illuminating example of the changing relationship between capital and labour in late Victorian and Edwardian society. Charmley, '"The Little White Father"', p. 347.

[25] *D.A.Thomas,* p.vii. There seems to have been a disagreement with D.A.'s brother, John Howard Thomas, over this. See Charmley, 'The Little White Father', p. 337.

[26] Beveridge Papers 4/25. 11 August 1919. Ministry of Food, BLPES.

27 Ibid., 13 August 1919.

28 *T&T* 4 November 1919.

29 MR to ER, 13 January 1921, series 2B, Box 20, folder 150, RP.

30 'Diligentia Absque Timore', *The Contemporary Review*, 120/2, December 1921, p.856; MR to ER, 17 December 1921, Series 2B. Box 20, folder 150, RP.

31 Quoted in *T&T* 11 November 1919.

32 C8, D.A.

33 Ibid.

34 Ibid.

35 *London Mercury* V, December 1921, pp. 214-5.

36 *D.A. Thomas*, p. 43.

37 Kenneth O. Morgan, 'D.A. Thomas: The Industrialist as Politician' in Idem, *Modern Wales: Politics, Places and People*, Cardiff, University of Wales Press, 1995, pp. 424-434. See too Martin Daunton,'D.A. Thomas. 1ˢᵗ Viscount Rhondda 1856-1918' in *Dictionary of Business Biography* V, Butterworth, 1986, pp. 473-80.

38 H.O 45/10743, NA.

39 *Suffragette* 7 December 1917.

40 *Daily Mail* 16 February 1918.

41 *WM* 11 May 1915.

42 *D.A. Thomas*, p. 308.

43 The 1911 census records her at Llanwern as a visitor. She travelled (as Mrs. Owen) from Glasgow to New York. The *George Washington's* manifest has her destination as Manhattan's luxury hotel, the Endicott. *http://www.ellisisland.org*.

44 Copy of D.A.'s Will, Merthyr Tydfil Central Library.

45 Register, St Leonards School Archives.

46 Ibid., Council Minutes 22 October 1929, 21 October 1930.

47 See Chapter 9.

48 *Daily Express* 14 September 1926; James Hepburn, *Letters of*

Arnold Bennett vol.3., 1916-1931, Oxford University Press, 1970, p. 238; Margaret Drabble, *Arnold Bennett*, Harmondsworth, Penguin edition, 1985, pp. 300-03, 315-6.

[49] *Nation and Athenaeum* 16 October 1926.

[50] This is not included in the UK edition of Bennett's journals but appears in the US edition: *The Journal of Arnold Bennett 1896-1928*, Viking Press, New York, 1933, pp. 803-4, 806-7.

[51] A University of Paris Ph.D thesis includes a close textual reading of the comparisons between Bennett's journal and D.A.'s life. See Louis Tillier, *Studies in the Sources of Arnold Bennett's Novels*, Paris, Didier, 1969, Chapter X 'Is Lord Raingo a Roman à Clef?' It is worth noting, however, that although Tillier matches the facts of D.A.'s life against the entries in Bennett's journals, he has no information to offer about the woman neither does he make any suggestion that D.A. had a mistress.

[52] J.A.Turner 'The formation of Lloyd George's "Garden Suburb": "Fabian-Like Milnerite Penetration"?', *Historical Journal* 20/1, 1977, p. 172 claims that 'Rhondda's personal morals were little different from Lloyd George's, though exercised with less discretion'. This seems to have been based on David Davies of Llandinam having warned Lloyd George in 1916 that Rhondda stood as the negation of the moral sense of the nation, a comment that was not about personal morals.

[53] *The Journals of Arnold Bennett 111. 1921-8*, Newman Flower (ed.), Cassell, 1933, pp. 108, 200.

[54] John Campbell, *F.E.Smith. First Earl of Birkenhead*, Jonathan Cape, 1983, pp. 691-2; *Daily Mail* 23, 25, 29, 30 November 1926. Bennett enjoyed the publicity this generated.

[55] A.J.P. Taylor, *Beaverbrook*, Harmondsworth, Penguin edition, 1974, p. 316.

[56] See Chapter 14.

Chapter 8

[1] Interviewed for *Great Thoughts* 6 October 1917.

[2] Cheryl Law, *Suffrage and Power. The Women's Movement 1918-1928,* I.B. Tauris, 1997, pp. 182-3.

[3] 'The Political Awakening of Women', p. 563.

[4] See MUN 5/27. Minutes of the Meetings of the Staff Investigation Committee. Final Report. Appendix 1, NA; Helen Jones, *Women in British Public Life. 1914-50. Gender, Power and Social Policy*, Harlow, Pearson, 2000, p. 25.

[5] Kenneth O. Morgan and Jane Morgan, *Portrait of a Progressive: the political career of Christopher, Viscount Addison*, Oxford, The Clarendon Press, 1980, pp. 70-94.

[6] RECO 1/751, NA.

[7] Cmd. 67, Report of the Women's Advisory Committee on the Domestic Service Problem, 1918; RECO 1/751, NA.

[8] *T&T* 22 June 1923.

[9] *MG* 21 June 1923.

[10] *The Times* 20 June 1923.

[11] Domestic service was defined as a skilled occupation for which training was essential. It advocated a gender-based solution: prescribing domestic science for all elementary schoolgirls aged twelve to fourteen and further instruction in central and secondary schools with funding for specialised training. Recognising the importance of raising the status of the profession, it advocated pension provision and the extension of unemployment benefit to those in private service, as well as the vote on the same residential basis as men.

[12] *MG* 11 November 1923; *T&T* 9 November 1923.

[13] For this see *The Times* 7, 8 December 1918; 17 February, 20 June, 10 July 1919; *MG* 18 December 1918; Emp. 71/2, 71/6, SUPP 31/199, 48/4, 48/76, 48/195, WWC, IWM.

[14] *Queen* 5 April 1919.

[15] Memorial to the prime minister on the future employment of women in Industry, 1918.

[16] Law, *Suffrage and Power*, p. 57.

[17] She addressed Edinburgh women on the new Whitley

Councils. They were designed to resolve labour disputes by arbitration through Joint Industrial Councils, with employer and employee representation at different levels. Here Margaret argued that the interests of capital and labour were in many respects identical. *The Scotsman* 14 November 1918.

[18] *MG* 18 December 1918.

[19] See, for example, *Pall Mall Gazette* 8 November 1918.

[20] *Daily Express* 10 December 1919.

[21] Quoted in Law, *Suffrage and Power*, p. 80.

[22] Forty-six pages of *D.A. Thomas* were devoted to his letters and press controversies.

[23] Martin Pugh, *Women and the Women's Movement in Britain*, Basingstoke, Macmillan, 2000 edition, p.89.

[24] He went on a deputation to Lloyd George about this in October 1917.

[25] Morgan and Morgan, *Portrait of a Progressive*, pp. 75-81.

[26] *WM* 14 November 1918.

[27] *The Times* 4 February 1919.

[28] *Ibid.,* 3 March 1919.

[29] Ibid., 21 and 26 March 1919.

[30] *T&T* noted on 8 April 1921 that Addison had refused to put a woman on the Welsh Board of Health which replaced the Welsh Insurance Commission. The latter had included a woman member paid at the same rate as the men.

[31] *The Times* 25 March 1919. Robins' letter was reprinted as a broadside by the Watching Council.

[32] Ibid., 17 May 1918.

[33] *Pall Mall Gazette* 8 November 1918.

[34] Quoted in the *Observer* 9 March 1919.

[35] *MG* 13 February 1919.

[36] *The Times* 14 February 1920.

[37] Mrs Ogilvie Gordon. Quoted in *Monmouthshire Evening Post* 1 July 1921.

[38] *Welsh Outlook* November 1922.

[39] *Daily Sketch* 19 February 1923 in C8, D.A.

[40] Addison, the first Minister of Health was succeeded by Sir Alfred Mond, Margaret's business colleague in south Wales. In 1968 the Ministry of Health was amalgamated with the Ministry of Social Security. In 1974 Barbara Castle became Secretary of State for Social Services.

[41] Anne Logan, 'Making Women Magistrates: Feminism, Citizenship and Justice in England and Wales 1918-1950', Ph.D, University of Greenwich, 2002.

[42] Lord, *Winifred Coombe Tennant*.

[43] *My World*, p. 275.

[44] Ibid., p. 201.

[45] George Bernard Shaw to MR, 12 August 1932, HRC.

[46] *T&T* 28 November 1942.

[47] *WM* 30 September 1921.

[48] Ibid. 24 February 1922. Information for this and the following paragraph comes from newspaper cuttings in C8, D.A.

[49] *T&T* 7 March 1924 and 21 May 1938.

[50] See Oliver Fairclough (ed.), *'Things of Beauty'. What Two Sisters did for Wales,* Cardiff, National Museum Wales, 2007, also Peter Lord, *Winifred Coombe Tennant: A Life through Art*, Aberystwyth, National Library of Wales, 2007.

[51] *T&T* 2 September 1927.

[52] Ibid., 6 November 1937.

[53] But see Chapter 16.

[54] *My World*, p. 294.

[55] Macpherson, *The Suffragette's Daughter.* p. 64.

[56] *T&T* 1 December 1922, 6 February 1925.

[57] *Suffragette* 13 December 1912.

[58] *T&T* 14 November 1936.

[59] Ibid., 28 May 1938. See too her Anne Doubleday letter on 19 December 1936.

[60] *My World*, p.xi. Margaret later called her paper an infant and claimed that seeing a weekly through the first years of its life was 'almost as difficult as to bring up a baby'. *T&T* 5 October 1935. Sec Catherine Clay, *British Women writers 1914-1945. Professional Work and Friendship*, Ashgate, 2006, pp. 52-5.

[61] Quoted in *Selected Letters,* Brittain and Handley-Taylor (eds.), p. 161.

[62] *My World*, p. 108.

[63] WH to VB 6/6.1/07/06a, 2 May [1926], HP.

[64] See below.

[65] Diary 2 January 1922, RP.

[66] *My World*, p.295.

[67] Between 1921 and 1925, 59% of British divorce cases were instigated by women. See Lesley A. Hall, *Sex, Gender and Social Change in Britain since 1880*, Macmillan, 2000, pp. 104-5.

[68] For court proceedings see *The Times* 1 May, 22 December 1922; *WM* 2 May, 22 December 1922; *South Wales Argus* 21 December 1922.

[69] MR to ER, 21 December 1921, HRC.

[70] Ibid. In *My World*, p, vi, she called it 'the plain and simple story of a misfit'.

[71] Diary, 2 January 1922, RP.

[72] Lucy Bland, '"Hunnish Scenes" and a "Virgin Birth": a 1920s Case of Sexual and Bodily Ignorance', *History Workshop Journal* 73/1, Spring 2012, pp. 144-69.

[73] MR to ER, 21 December 1921, 1 May 1922, HRC.

[74] The destination was South Africa but Margaret may have only gone to the Balearic Islands.

[75] Letter of 23 December 1922 quoted in *Selected Letters of Winifred Holtby*, Brittain and Handley-Taylor eds, p. 21.

[76] They lived in Usk. Margaret was upset when Humphrey died in 1948.

[77] *T&T* 13 July 1923.

[78] Diary 10 and 11 January 1922, RP.

[79] For Mrs Archdale see Helen A. Archdale, 'An Interfering Female'; Archdale, *Indiscretions of a Headmistress*; Leah Leneman, *The Scottish Suffragettes*, Edinburgh, NMS Publishing, 2000, pp. 50-1; Purvis, *Emmeline Pankhurst*, pp. 191-2, 213-4, 233, 402; *http://www.oxforddnb.com/view/article/58331*, accessed 3 Dec 2010; NATS 1/1309; ND e624/4, 25 April 1928.

[80] Archdale, 'An Interfering Female', Chapter 1, p. 5.

[81] See Jill Liddington and Elizabeth Crawford, 'Women do not count, neither shall they be counted': Suffrage, Citizenship and the Battle for the 1911 Census', *History Workshop Journal*, 72/2, Spring 2011, p. 21 for their group census evasion.

[82] *S.L.S. Gazette*, May 1915, St Leonards School Archives.

[83] Quoted in Macpherson, *The Suffragette's Daughter*, p. 54.

[84] Archdale, *Indiscretions of a Headmistress*, p. 9.

[85] ND, e624/4, 25 April 1928.

[86] The telephone directory records her living at 12, Chelsea Court from 1922.

[87] The following account is based on descriptions in C8, D.A.

[88] Archdale, 'an Interfering Female', Chapter 13, p. 3.

Chapter 9

[1] This was how the *New York Times* described Margaret, 25 May 1924.

[2] *The Times* 20 March 1919. This company had 1,694 shareholders, a number of whom were coalminers.

[3] But see *http://www.oxforddnb.com/view/article/47974*, accessed 7 July 2009.

[4] David Painter, *Amy Dillwyn*, Cardiff, University of Wales Press, 1987.

[5] See Swansea University's Dillwyn Project: *http://www.swan.ac.uk/crew/researchprojects/dillwyn*

[6] Revel Guest and Angela V. John, *Lady Charlotte. An*

Extraordinary Life, Tempus edition, 2007, especially Chapters 6 and 8.

[7] He replaced Ivor Churchill Guest (who became Lord Wimborne) as MP for Cardiff in 1910.

[8] *My World*, p. 217.

[9] Ibid., p. 95.

[10] *WM* 18 November 1916.

[11] *D.A. Thomas*, p. 23.

[12] *My World*, p. 240.

[13] C9, D.A.

[14] *My World*, p. 263.

[15] Quoted in *D.A. Thomas*, p. 216.

[16] The following account is largely based on Chapter xviii in *My World*.

[17] She called it 'a reasonable sized boat' but the website for the Peace River Centennial Museum describes it as 'one of the largest steamers ever to ply inland Canadian waters'. The Hudson Bay Company acquired it but it was taken out of service in 1930. *http://www.telusplanet.net/public/prcma/webdoc3.html*.

[18] *D.A. Thomas*, pp. 137-8; Aled Jones, *Press, Politics and Society. A History of Journalism in Wales*, Cardiff, University of Wales Press, 1993, p. 210.

[19] Deian Hopkin, 'The Membership of the Independent Labour Party 1904-10. A spatial and occupational analysis', *International Review of Social History*, 20, 1975, p. 185.

[20] 5 ERI/Box 331, WL.

[21] *D.A. Thomas*, p.138.

[22] For this see *The Times* 16 April 1919, 18 March 1920; Joanne Cayford, 'The *Western Mail* 1869-1914. A study in the Politics and Management of a Provincial Newspaper', Ph.D, 1992, Aberystwyth University.

[23] *My World*, p. 263.

[24] *T&T* 28 March 1924.

[25] Smith, *Aneurin Bevan*, pp. 109-112.

[26] Ibid., p. 110.

[27] It influenced the 1902 Budget. D.A.'s 1902 monograph on coal exports won him the Guy Medal of the Royal Statistical Society.

[28] *WM* 10 September 1910.

[29] Daunton, 'D.A. Thomas', pp. 473-80.

[30] *D.A. Thomas*, p. 140.

[31] *Daily Express* 20 December 1917.

[32] *Ladies Field* 28 April 1917.

[33] *Directory of Directors*, Thomas Skinner & Co, 1918, p. 706. In 1911 he had accompanied D.A. and Sybil on a three-month business tour of South America and the West Indies.

[34] *Notes on the Way*, p. 69.

[35] EMP.48.411, WWC, IWM.

[36] *WM* 10 May 1915.

[37] Morgan, 'D.A. Thomas', pp. 419-20.

[38] *Colliery Guardian* 3 January 1919.

[39] *My World*, p. 230.

[40] Ibid., p. 233.

[41] *Sketch* 3 October 1917.

[42] Katharine Graham, *Personal History*, Phoenix edition, 2001, p. 626.

[43] See *Who's Who in Wales*, Cardiff, *WM*, 1921, p. 402.

[44] *The Times* 20 March 1919. North's Navigation bought the Celtic Collieries in 1920. The Imperial Coal Company took over the Cynon Colliery Company but was later absorbed into North's Navigation.

[45] *Directory of Directors*, 1923, p. 1202.

[46] D.J. Williams, *Capitalist Combination in the Coal Trade*, Labour Publishing Co. Ltd, 1924, p. 118.

[47] Ibid., p. 141.

[48] *The Times* 11 September 1919.

[49] Edgar Jones, *A History of GKN. Volume 2. The Growth of a Business 1918-1945*, Macmillan, 1990, pp. 95-8.

[50] Chris Williams, *Capitalism, Community and Conflict. The South Wales Coalfield*, Cardiff, University of Wales Press, 1998, pp. 32-3.

[51] Jones, *A History of GKN,* p. 59.

[52] Research is revealing a number of nineteenth century female ship owners. Helen Doe, *Enterprising Women and Shipping in the Nineteenth Century*, Woodbridge, The Boydell Press, 2009.

[53] *Financial News* 2 March 1922. Margaret gave evidence at the winding up court.

[54] *The Times* 16 April 1920, 23 March 1923.

[55] *Colliery Guardian* 3 January 1919.

[56] Williams, *Capitalism, Community and Conflict*, p. 34.

[57] *WM* 31 March 1922.

[58] *Sunday Times* 30 March 1924.

[59] E.D. Lewis, *The Rhondda Valleys. A Study in Industrial Development, 1800 to the present day*, Phoenix House, 1959, p. 253.

[60] *Morning Post* 9 March 1922.

[61] *T&T* 23 March 1923.

[62] *South Wales Journal of Commerce* 1 March 1923.

[63] *Brooklyn Eagle* 9 May 1926 in C9, D.A. See Margaret Morris, *The General Strike*, Harmondsworth, Penguin, 1976, p. 252 for the Organisation for the Maintenance of Supplies. The following year Margaret gave up thee premises and conducted business from the *Time and Tide* office in Fleet Street.

[64] *Daily Herald* 28 April 1927.

[65] See the annual *Colliery Year Book and Coal Trades Directory*, Louis Cassier. Co. for 1924-1937.

[66] List of Members 1926 and 1929, Institute of Directors, Pall Mall, London. Amalgamations camouflage the extent of Margaret's control.

[67] *The Times* 24 December 1923; *Daily News* 27 December 1923.

[68] *T&T* 25 June, 17 September 1920.

[69] Ibid., 7 July 1926, 7 August 1925 on the south Wales coal owners' proposals for family allowances.

[70] C9, D.A.

[71] Quoted in *D.A. Thomas*, p. 187.

[72] C9, D.A.

[73] *Daily Sketch* 2 December 1926 in Ibid.

[74] *The Times* 15 July 1925; *MG* 16 July 1925.

[75] C8, D.A.

[76] Ibid.

[77] 'Business and Commerce', pp. 58-64.

[78] Miss Gordon Holmes, *In Love with Life*, Hollis & Carter, 1994, p. 64. See too *http://.www.addidi.com/awards/profile_bgh.asp*.

[79] *WM* 2 December 1926.

[80] Ibid., 29 July 1926; Minute Book 1911-1933, *List of Members* 1924-9; *Annual Reports and Accounts* 1944; *The Director* 11/5, November 1958, p. 405, Institute of Directors. Cockburn saw the vote as a key to strengthening family life. In 1935 Margaret sat on the tribunal established by the Retail Trading Standards Association to ensure that descriptions were used consistently.

[81] C8, D.A; The *Times* 20 June 1935.

[82] Mrs Margaret Dinah Thomas was a director of the Mumbles Railway and Pier Company in the 1890s. D/D 5B 9/417; D/D58 9/437. Records of Swansea and Mumbles Railway, West Glamorgan Archives.

[83] *Guardian* 15 October 2011. A 30 Percent Club exists to increase the number of women directors. *Independent* 1 December 2012.

[84] C8 D.A.; *WM* 16 October 1923.

[85] *T&T* 4 May 1923. The *South Wales Argus* also ran these articles.

[86] *Daily Express* 20 December 1917.

[87] *The Times* 18 July 1924.

[88] Ibid. 13 June 1931 She was active in the Advertising Association and the Women's Advertising Club.

[89] *Daily Chronicle* 23 November 1926.

[90] *Notes*, p. 193. She spoke at the Efficiency Exhibition (run by the Office Appliances Trade Association) in Cardiff in 1923 and at the Birmingham Business Club in 1926. *WM* 16 October 1923; C9, D.A.

[91] *My World*, pp. 267-8.

[92] Ibid., pp. 295-7.

Chapter 10

[1] See, for example, Philip Gibbs, *The Journalist's London*, Allan Wingate, 1952.

[2] *My World*, p. 39.

[3] Ibid.

[4] Ibid., pp.40-1.

[5] Christine Pullen, *The Woman Who Dared. A Biography of Amy Levy*, Kingston University Press, 2010, p. 18.

[6] *My World,* p. 40.

[7] *T&T* 14 May 1920.

[8] Ibid., 8 October 1920.

[9] Her actor husband had drowned himself in Boston's River Charles. Series 1A, Box 7, 9 June 1920, RP.

[10] The Haig family seat in Berwickshire.

[11] MR to ER, 4 and 16 February 1920 Series 2A, Box 29, folder 12, RP.

[12] Post-war it reinvented itself as the *Woman's Leader* and Margaret left the board.

[13] 14 July, 6, 8 December 1919, Series 2B, Box 20, folder 150, RP. Author's copy of Wilberforce's Ms 'The Eighth Child'. Wilberforce's dating of some letters is inaccurate and she

confuses letters about *Common Cause* with the establishment of *Time and Tide*.

¹⁴ See Sian Rhiannon Williams, 'The True "Cymraes": Images of Women in Women's Nineteenth Century Welsh Periodicals' in John (ed.), *Our Mothers' Land*, pp. 73-94. Britain's first feminist journal, the *English Woman's Journal*, was established in London in 1858.

¹⁵ *My World*, pp. 128, 304-5. See too her Introduction to *Time and Tide Anthology*, Lejeune (ed.), p. 11 where she stressed the importance of 'a first-class review' and an elite but influential readership.

¹⁶ *T&T* 9 December 1927.

¹⁷ For the 'Little Magazine' see *The Oxford Critical and Cultural History of Modernist Magazines. Vol 11. Britain and Ireland 1880-1955,* Peter Brooker and Andrew Thacker (eds.), Oxford, Oxford University Press, 2009, especially pp. 11-25 and section V11.

¹⁸ See *The Letters of T.S. Eliot. Vol 1 1898-1922,* Valerie Eliot and Hugh Haughton (eds.), Faber & Faber, 2009.

¹⁹ *Notes* p. 49.

²⁰ See Catherine Clay, '"WHAT WE MIGHT EXPECT – If the Highbrow Weeklies Advertised like the Patent Foods": *Time and Tide*, Advertising and the "Battle of the Brows"', *Modernist Cultures* 6/1, (2011), pp. 60-95.

²¹ *T&T* 19 March 1926.

²² Quoted in Tusan, *Women Making News.* p. 222.

²³ See Lucy Delap, '"Philosophical vacuity and political ineptitude": The *Freewoman's* critique of the suffrage movement', *Women's History Review* 11/4, 2002, pp. 613-630.

²⁴ David Doughan, Denise Sanchez, *Feminist Periodicals 1855-1984. An Annotated Critical Bibliography of British, Irish, Commonwealth and International Titles*, Brighton, Harvester Press, 1987, p. xv.

²⁵ Tusan, *Women Making News*, p. 222.

[26] *My World*, p. 300.

[27] Wilberforce, 'The Eighth Child', p. 228.

[28] Ibid., p. 227.

[29] Series 2c, Box 29, folder 12, 1 December 1919, RP.

[30] *T&T* 31 October 1924.

[31] In the 1890s the heiress Rachel Beer, married to the owner of the *Observer*, bought the *Sunday Times* and for a short period edited both papers. She penned 3,000-word weekly columns, some of which promoted women's rights. In France Marguerite Durand established a feminist newspaper run and written by women. A decade earlier Elizabeth Johnson had established England's first Sunday newspaper the *British Gazette and Sunday Monitor*. Eilat Negev & Yehuda Koren, *First Lady of Fleet Street. The Life, Fortune and Tragedy of Rachel Beer,* JR Books, 2011.

[32] *T&T* 8 July 1927.

[33] Series 1A, Box 7, 25 March 1920, RP.

[34] Ibid., 12 May 1920.

[35] Ibid., 16 May 1920.

[36] In *Home and Country* 3/1, 1 May 1920.

[37] *T&T* 31 October 1924.

[38] MR to ER, Series 2B, Box 20, folder 150, 30 April 1920, RP.

[39] Ibid., Series 2C, Box 29, folder 12, 22 February 1920.

[40] *T&T* 4 June 1920.

[41] *Time and Tide*, BBC Broadcast, Eastern Service, 6 May 1942, BBC Written Archives Centre, Caversham Park, Reading.

[42] *My World,* p. 302; Vera Laughton Mathews, *Blue Tapestry*, Hollis & Carter, 1948, p. 35.

[43] Series 1A, Box 7, 14 June 1920, RP. Robins' diary refers to Archdale complaining about Laughton.

[44] Ibid., MR to ER, Series 2B, Box 20, folder 150, 27 July 1920.

[45] Eoff, *Viscountess Rhondda*, p. 221.

[46] *T&T* 16 March 1928.

[47] Ibid., 13 July 1928.

[48] Ibid., 16 March 1928. This was in the form of a letter signed 'Independent Press'. It may have been written by Margaret.

[49] MR to ER, Series 2B, Box 20, folder 150, 13 August 1920, RP.

[50] Ibid.

[51] Ibid.

[52] Ibid., MR to ER, 3 June 1922.

[53] Ibid., MR to ER, Series 2C, Box 20, folder 150, 2 September 1920, 13 January 1921.

[54] Ibid., 15 June 1921.

[55] Ibid., Series 1A, Box 7, 14 December 1922, 3 May 1923 Diary; Series 2B, ER to Archdale, Box 6, folder 1A, 13 August 1926.

[56] Cicely Hamilton, *Life Errant*, J.M. Dent, 1935, p. 207.

[57] Muriel J. Mellown, *'Time and Tide'* in *British Literary Magazines. The Modern Age, 1914-1984*, Alvin Sullivan (ed.), Westport, Ct., Greenwood Press, 1986, p. 442.

[58] MR to ER, Series 2B, Box 20, folder 150, 13 August 1920, RP.

[59] Catherine Clay, 'Not Forgetting "the importance of everything else". Feminism, Modernism and *Time and Tide*', *Key Words: A journal of cultural materialism* (2009), pp. 20-37 and Johanna Alberti, 'The Turn of the Tide: sexuality and politics, 1928-31' in *Women's History Review* 3/2, 1994, pp. 169-190.

[60] See Dowson, 'Interventions in the Public Sphere', pp. 530-551. This compares the first decade of *Time and Tide* and *The Bermondsey Book* a quarterly edited by Ethel Gutman between 1923 and 1930; Clay, 'Not Forgetting', pp. 26-9 and Mellown, *'Time and Tide'*, pp. 441-452 assess it as a literary magazine.

[61] Waste Paper Bin. Quoted in *Time & Tide Anthology*, Lejeune (ed.), p. 13. The book was dedicated to the paper's editor and directors.

[62] *T&T* 22, 29 November 1929. Woolf had published 'The Sun

and the Fish' in *T&T* on 3 February 1928.

[63] Ibid., 10 May 1929.

[64] MR to ER, Series 2B, Box 20, folder 150, 14 March 1928, RP.

[65] Clay, 'WHAT WE MIGHT EXPECT', p. 68.

[66] Dowson, 'Interventions in the Public Sphere', pp. 540-3; Clay, 'Not Forgetting', pp. 26-29.

[67] L WH/5/5.17/03/01r, 4 March 1933, HP.

[68] Winifred Holtby, *Letters To A Friend*, Alice Holtby and Jean McWilliam (eds.), Collins, 1938 edition, p. 177.

[69] Ibid., p. 240. For Margaret's friendship with Holtby see Chapter 11.

[70] *T&T* 5 October 1935.

[71] Holtby, *Letters*, p. 429.

[72] *T&T* 17 May 1941.

[73] Ibid., 29 June 1940.

[74] See Chapter 13.

[75] GBS to MR, Box 40, Folder 40.4, 9 February 1927, HRC.

[76] *T&T* 24 September 1938. See Chapter 13 for Margaret's own contributions.

[77] Spender, *Time and Tide Wait for No Man*.

[78] Eoff, *Viscountess Rhondda*, pp. 132-133.

[79] Clay, *British Women Writers*, p. 58.

[80] Idem, 'Winifred Holtby, Journalist: Rehabilitating Journalism in the Modernist Ferment' in *Winifred Holtby 'A Woman In Her Time': Critical Essays*, Lisa Regan (ed.), Newcastle upon Tyne, Cambridge Scholars Publishing, 210, p. 72.

[81] *T&T* 17 May 1941.

[82] Based on personal communication with Clay in January 2012.

[83] Quoted in Eoff, *Viscountess Rhondda*, p. 96.

[84] *T&T* 4 July 1936.

[85] Mellown, *'Time and Tide'*, p. 447.

[86] *The Time and Tide Album*, E.M. Delafield (ed.), Hamish Hamilton, 1932.

[87] *T&T* 14, 21, 28 July, 4 August 1934.

[88] Mellown, '*Time and Tide*, p. 448.

[89] *T&T* 23 November 1938.

[90] Ibid., 10 October 1931.

[91] Tusan, *Women Making News*, pp. 230-1.

[92] Pugh, *Women and the Women's Movement*, p. 49.

[93] In *The Four Empires,* p. 33.

[94] '*Time and Tide*' Broadcast.

[95] In 1939 music, ballet, theatre and finance had male editors. Advertisement managers were male.

[96] *T&T* 2 November 1923.

[97] Vera Brittain, *Chronicle of Friendship. Vera Brittain's Diary of the Thirties 1932-1939,* Alan Bishop (ed.), Gollancz, 1986, p. 104.

[98] *T&T* 6 November 1937.

[99] Ibid., 23 May 1931. See also Margaret's article on the limitations of big circulations on 13 July 1930.

[100] Ibid., 15 July 1944.

[101] L WH/5/5.24/04/05a, 6 September 1933, HP.

[102] MR to Marie Mattingly Meloney, 24 June 1935, Marie Mattingly Meloney Papers, Rare Book and Manuscript Library, Columbia University in the City of New York.

[103] Ibid., 31 December [1937].

[104] *The Schoolmistress* 16 March 1933.

[105] Quoted in *Selected Letters*, Brittain and Handley-Taylor, p. 201.

[106] Marion Shaw, *The Clear Stream. A Life of Winifred Holtby*, Virago Press, 200 edition, pp. 162-3.

[107] WH/5/5/17/ 04/01a, HP.

[108] Ibid., WH/5/5/17/04/01h.

[109] Vera Brittain, *Testament of Friendship*, Virago Press, 1980

edition, p. 265. See Chapter 11.

[110] *T&T* 13 October 1934.

[111] Ibid., 17 May 1941.

[112] Ibid. She did, however, annoy Margaret when she asked for one manuscript to be returned in order to make amendments but then sent it to the *New Statesman*.

[113] *Observer* 26 February 1933.

[114] Quoted in *Time & Tide Anthology*, Lejeune (ed.), p. 16.

[115] *Notes*, p. 52. Virginia Woolf's impression in 1933 was that Ellis Roberts influenced Margaret. He had recently joined the staff after being literary editor of the *New Statesman*. *The Diary of Virginia Woolf. Volume 4 1931-5*, Anne Oliver Bell (ed.), Penguin, 1983, p. 149.

[116] *Notes*, p. 52.

[117] *T&T* 4 July 1936.

[118] Ibid., 10 June 1933.

[119] Ibid., 20, 27 May, 3 June 1933.

[120] Virginia Woolf to MR, Box 1, folder 10, 10 June 1938, HRC.

[121] Quoted in *Virginia Woolf. A Writer's Diary*, p. 279. Margaret had written 'I don't know how to tell you how exciting I found it or how profoundly it moved me'. MR to Virginia Woolf, 23 May 1938, Monks House Papers, University of Sussex.

[122] WH/5/5/17/03/0/5, HP.

[123] MR to Virginia Woolf, 2 June 1938, Monks House Papers.

[124] *T&T* 4 June 1938 written by Theodora.

[125] Viscount Camrose, *British Newspapers and their Controllers*, Cassell & Co, 1947, p. 150.

[126] *MG* 21 February 1947.

[127] Mellown, '*Time and Tide*', pp. 441, 452. See too *Chambers Biographical Dictionary of Women,* Edinburgh, 1996, p.555 for comments on its representation of a cross-section of British intellectual life.

[128] MR to Virginia Woolf, 23 May 1938 Monks House Papers.

[129] Virginia Woolf to MR, Box 10, folder 1, 24 May 1938, HRC.

[130] MR to Virginia Woolf, 2 June 1938, Monks House Papers.

[131] Ibid.

[132] MR to ER 23 April, 28 July 1936, Series 2B, Box 20, folder 150, RP.

[133] *T&T* 23 October 1937.

[134] See Chapter 12.

[135] See Chapter 14.

[136] *Herald Tribune* 8 October 1934. Her voice was unintelligible across the airwaves but an advance copy of her speech was read out.

[138] *T&T* 27 January 1934.

Chapter 11

[1] Holtby, *Letters*, p. 429.

[2] E.M. Delafield, *The Provincial Lady Goes Further* in *The Diary of a Provincial Lady*, Virago Press edition, 2008, pp. 228-9.

[3] She spoke at a temperance meeting in Hull in 1922.

[4] Naomi Mitchison, *You May Well Ask. A Memoir. 1920-40*, Victor Gollancz, 1986 edition, p. 169.

[5] C8, D.A.

[6] *Wesleyan Methodist Magazine* in Supp 46/3 WWC, IWM.

[7] Muggeridge, *Chronicles*, p. 63.

[8] Winifred Holtby, 'Mother Knows Best', *Lovat Dickson's Magazine*, December 1934 in *Testament of a Generation: The journalism of Vera Brittain and Winifred Holtby*, Paul Berry and Alan Bishop (eds.), p. 275: Holtby, *Letters*, p. 419.

[9] Holtby, *Letters,* p. 335.

[10] Delafield, *The Provincial Lady*, p. 169.

[11] Ellen Wilkinson, *Clash*, Nottingham, Trent Editions, 2004, p. 9

[12] Ibid.

13 Ibid., p. 10.

14 L WH/5/5.17/01/01b, HP.

15 Maroula Joannou, 'Reclaiming the Romance: Ellen Wilkinson's *Clash* and the cultural legacy of socialist-feminism' in David Margolies and Maroula Joannou, *Heart of the Heartless World. Essays in Cultural Resistance in memory of Margot Heinemann*, Pluto Press, 1995, p. 152.

16 Wilkinson, *Clash*, p. 90.

17 Brittain, *Testament of Friendship*, p. 177.

18 Wilkinson, *Clash*, p. 9.

19 Cullis was the first holder of the Sophia Jex-Blake chair at the University of London. She worked at the London School of Medicine for almost twenty-five years and was head of the physiology department. She sat on the executive of the SPG, helped found and was president of the BFUW.

20 L WH/5/5.3/01a, HP.

21 C8, D.A.

22 Secretary of the P.E.N. Club to MR, P.E.N. Box, HRC.

23 Glyn Jones to Keidrych Rees, Wales Papers, MS.22745-D, NLW.

24 Ibid., Glyn Jones to MR. 14 July 1934, MS. 21711E.f.64. This is a draft letter so Margaret may have received a more circumspect version.

25 *The Times* 15 February 1921.

26 Ibid., 25 March 1931.

27 Paul Fussell, *Abroad. British Literary Travelling Between the Wars*, Oxford, Oxford University Press, 1982 edition, p. 72.

28 Series 2B, Box 20, folder 150, 19 September 1927, RP.

29 L WH/5/5.17/03/01l, HP.

30 Ibid., L WH/5/5.17/01/01b; *T&T* 8 October 1949.

31 Quoted in *The Diary of Virginia Woolf*, Bell, p. 149.

32 *MG* 3 August 1928.

33 Brittain, *Chronicle of Friendship,* p. 104.

[34] See Chapter 13.

[35] MR to VB 6 and 8 September 1931, VB.

[36] See Chapter 10 and below.

[37] Brittain, *Chronicle of Friendship,* pp. 34, 48.

[38] Fenja Gunn, *Lost Gardens of Gertrude Jekyll*, Charles Letts, 1991, p. 52.

[39] See Jean Fox, David Williams, Peter Mountfield, *Seal. The History of a Parish*, Phillimore & Co. Ltd, 2007, pp. 88-9. Particulars for the sale of the Kemsing Estate in 1919 describe it as a fourteenth century manor house.

[40] Gunn, *Lost Gardens*, pp. 99-101; *http://www.ced. berkeley.edu/cedarchives/*. Both Margaret and Helen were named as clients.

[41] Archdale, *Indiscretions of a Headmistress*, p. 10.

[42] Quoted in *Selected Letters,* Brittain and Handley-Taylor (eds.), pp. 63-4; *Holtby, Letters*, p. 387.

[43] Brittain, *Testament of Friendship*, p. 177.

[44] L WH6/6.1/03a, 2 April 1927, HP.

[45] *S.L.S. Gazette* November 1928, St Leonards School Archives.

[46] 29 October 1930, HA to Lily van der Schalk Schuster, 5ERI/Box 331, WL.

[47] Ibid., 5 August 1931.

[48] Archdale, 'An Interfering Female', Chapter xi, p. 8.

[49] MS 546, Box 60, folder 16, Helen Archdale to Doris Stevens, 9 April 1939, Stevens Collection, Schlesinger Library, Radcliffe Institute, Harvard University.

[50] Quoted in Macpherson, *The Suffragette's Daughter*, p. 171.

[51] Archdale, 'An Interfering Female', Chapter viii, p. 2.

[52] Series 1B, Box 7, 17 May 1922, RP.

[53] It is possible that her companion was Cicely Hamilton. Both Hamiltons (no relation – Cicely's real surname was Hammill) were friends and wrote for her paper but Margaret refers, in a letter to Robins sent on this holiday, to a scheme for supporting

Hamilton as a parliamentary candidate. M.A. Hamilton became a Labour MP and was probably the holiday companion on this occasion. Series 2B, Box 20, folder 150, 9 January 1922, RP.

[54] Ibid.

[55] *http://content.cdlib.org/view?docId=kt6x0nb1ts&brand=callisphere &doc.view=entire_text*. She became Rebecca Hourwich Reyher.

[56] In C9, D.A.

[57] *Christian Science Monitor* 29 August 1922.

[58] Series 2B, Box 20, folder 150, 28 August 1922, RP.

[59] C8, D.A. Unless otherwise indicated quotations in the following section are from this source.

[60] In Brittain, *Testament of Friendship*, p. 177.

[61] Lord, *Between Two Worlds*, p. 269.

[62] In Supp 24/77, WWC,/WM.

[63] See Katherine Holden, *The Shadow of Marriage: Singleness in England, 1914-60*, Manchester, Manchester University Press, 2007, pp. 99-103, Alison Oram, 'The Spinster in Inter-War Feminist Discourse', *Women's History Review* 1/3, 1992, pp. 413-31.

[64] Quoted in Leila J. Rupp, *Worlds of Women. The Making of an International Women's Movement,* Princeton NJ, Princeton University Press, 1987, p. 100.

[65] *My World*, pp. 126-7.

[66] Ibid.

[67] See Lucy Bland and Laura Doan (eds.) *Sexology in Culture: Labelling Bodies and Desires*, Cambridge, Polity Press, 1998; Liz Stanley, 'Romantic Friendship? Some Issues in Researching Lesbian History and Biography', *Women's History Review*, 1 / 2 1992, pp. 193-216 and Chiara Beccalossi, *Female Sexual Inversion. Same-Sex Desires in Italian and British Sexology, c1870-1920*, Palgrave Macmillan, 2012.

[68] Wilberforce, 'The Eighth Child'. Quote in letter from MR of 17 August 1920 reproduced on p. 235.

[69] Ibid., letter of 24 August 1920 reproduced on p. 236.

[70] *Notes,* p. 72.

[71] Ibid., p. 73.

[72] L WH 6/6.1/10/O3a, August 1929, HP.

[73] Winifred Holtby, *Women and a Changing Civilisation*, The Bodley Head, 1941 edition, p. 132.

[74] *Notes,* p. 19.

[75] See Martha Vicinus, *Intimate Friends. Women who loved women 1778-1928*, Chicago, University of Chicago Press, 2004, p. xxiv.

[76] Laura Doan, *Fashioning Sapphism. The Origins of a Modern English Lesbian Culture, New York, Columbia University Press,* 2000, p. 30.

[77] *T&T* 22 November 1928.

[78] Radclyffe Hall, *The Well of Loneliness*, Century Hutchinson edition, 1986, pp. 209, 210.

[79] See Chapter 15 for Margaret's life with Theodora. See too Susan Pedersen, *Eleanor Rathbone and the Politics of Conscience,* New Haven, CT, Yale University Press, 2004, Chapter 9 for a discussion of the relationship between Rathbone and Elizabeth MacAdam. See too Louise W. Knight, *Jane Addams,* New York, W.W. Norton & Company, 2011, especially pp. 262-3.

[80] Eoff, *Viscountess Rhondda*, p. 108.

[81] L WH 5/5.17/O1e, 27 January 1931, HP.

[82] *Notes*, p. 213.

[83] Shaw, *The Clear Stream.*

[84] *Selected Letters*, Brittain and Handley-Taylor, p. 240.

[85] *Yorkshire Post* 7 March 1933.

[86] *Selected Letters,* Brittain and Handley-Taylor, p. 251.

[87] Ibid., p. 252.

[88] L WH 6/6.1/10/O3a, August 1929, HP.

[89] Quoted in *Selected Letters,* Brittain and Handley-Taylor, p. 217.

[90] In Brittain, *Chronicle of Friendship*, p. 61.

[91] MR to VB, 20 July 1933, VB.

[92] Brittain, *Chronicle of Friendship*, p. 338.

[93] MR to VB, 16 October 1935 and 28 March 1936, VB.

[94] Ibid., 28 March 1936.

[95] Ibid., 13 April 1936.

[96] Brittain, *Testament of Friendship*, p. 440.

[97] MR to VB, 27 December 1939, VB.

[98] Brittain, *Chronicle of Friendship,* p. 338. On 19 February 19 1939 she wrote in her diary that Edith de Coundouroff (who had lived with the Holtbys from 1916) agreed with her about this.

[99] L WH 5/5.45/03g, 6 September 1955, HP.

[100] Ibid., L WH/7/7.38/02/09a. Written on 18 February 1937 but posted two years later.

[101] Gill Fildes, 'Winifred Holtby and "The Voice of God". A Writer's View of Radio and Cinema Between the Wars' in *Winifred Holtby*, Regan, p. 96.

[102] Quoted in Ibid., p. 7.

[103] *T&T* 4 April 1936.

[104] *Selected Letters*, Brittain and Handley-Taylor, p. 455.

[105] *T&T* 5 October 1935.

[106] Ibid., 25 April 1925.

[107] *Sunday Times* 6 October 1935.

[108] L WH5/5.17/03/01f, 3 August 1932, HP.

[109] Quoted in *T&T* 11 April 1926.

[110] Ibid.

[111] L WH 5/5.17/01c, 10 May 1930, HP.

[112] Quoted in *T&T* 25 April 1936.

[113] Holtby, *Letters*, p. 188.

[114] Winifred Holtby, *Mandoa, Mandoa!*, Virago Press edition, 1982, p. 40.

[115] L WH/11/11.3/01/04a, HP.

[116] Brittain, *Testament of Friendship*, p. 295.

[117] Ibid., p. 328. See too Berry and Bostridge, *Vera Brittain*, pp. 273-5, 546 and Clay, *British Women Writers*, pp. 37-40.

[118] See Shaw, *The Clear Stream*, pp. 285-93 and Margaret's comments in *T&T* 6 January 1940.

[119] Holtby, *Women*, p. 192.

[120] L WH 6/6.1/09/02a, 21 August 1928, HP.

[121] Clay, *British Women Writers*, p. 15.

[122] L WH 5/5.17/04/01c, 21 September 1933, HP.

[123] Ibid., L WH 5/5.17/04/01f, 6 October 1933.

[124] Ibid., L WH 5/5.17/04/o1r, 19 November 1933.

[125] Ibid., MR to WH 5/5.17/04/01h, 17 October 1933.

[126] Ms Eng misc.f407, Holiday Diaries, 20 April 1937, Evelyn Sharp Papers, Bodleian Libraries, University of Oxford.

[127] Clay, *British Women Writers*, p. 67.

[128] L WH 5/5.17/04/01h, 17 October 1933, HP.

[129] Clay, *British Women Writers*, p. 68.

[130] *T&T* 18 April 1936.

[131] L WH 5/5.17/04/01a, September 1933, HP.

[132] Clay, *British Women Writers*, p. 65.

[133] L WH, 5/5.17/04/ o1r, 19 November 1933, HP.

[134] Ibid., L WH, 5/5.17/04/01p, 19 March 1935.

[135] In *T&T* 25 April 1936.

[136] L WH 5/5.17/04/01h, 17 October 1933, HP.

Chapter 12

[1] Dorothy E. Evans and Claire Madden, 'Six Point Group. A Brief Account of its National and International Work', 1946 pamphlet, p. 1, WL.

[2] *T&T* 16 February 1923.

[3] Ibid., 25 February 1921.

[4] For feminist societies and policies see Cheryl Law, '"The old

faith living and the old power there". The movement to extend women's suffrage' in Maroula Joannou and June Purvis eds. *The Women's Suffrage Movement. New Feminist Perspectives*, Manchester, Manchester University Press, 1998, p. 203; Law, *Suffrage and Power*; Harold L. Smith 'British Feminism in the 1920s' in Idem, *British Feminism in the Twentieth Century*, Aldershot, Edward Elgar, 1990; Susan Kingsley Kent, 'The Politics of Sexual Difference: World War 1 and the Demise of British Feminism', *Journal of British Studies*, 27/3, July 1988, pp. 232-53; Pugh, *Women and the Women's Movement*; Joanna Alberti, *Beyond Suffrage. Feminists in War and Peace 1914-28*, Macmillan 1989 and Idem, '"A Symbol and a Key". The Suffrage Movement in Britain, 1918-1928' in June Purvis and Sandra Holton, *Votes for Women*, Routledge, 2000.

[5] *T&T* 22 October 1920.

[6] Ibid., 5 November 1920.

[7] Brittain, *Testament of Youth*, p. 585.

[8] Smith, 'British Feminism in the 1920s', p. 52.

[9] *Daily Sketch* 16 October 1922.

[10] Brittain, *Testament of Youth*, p. 587.

[11] *MG* 2 November 1922.

[12] See Pat Thane, 'What Difference Did the Vote Make?' in Vickery (ed,) *Women, Privilege and Power*, pp. 252-288.

[13] *T&T* 3 August 1923; *MG* 28 July 1923.

[14] Published in *The Times* 26 November 1923.

[15] *T&T* 10 August 1923.

[16] Ibid., 16 February 1923.

[17] Ibid., 25 June 1920.

[18] *The Vote* 9 February 1923.

[19] Ibid., 2 March 1923.

[20] See Hilda Kean, *Deeds Not Words*, Pluto Press, 1990, p. 97.

[21] *Home and Country*, 3/5, 1 July 1921, p. 8.

[22] *T&T* 9 December 1921.

Notes

[23] Lord, *Winifred Coombe Tennant*, 2012, p. 339.

[24] For the effect of the lists on results, see Pugh, *Women and the Women's Movement*, pp. 142-5.

[25] Brittain, *Testament of Youth*, p. 592; *T&T* 13 July 1923.

[26] Quoted in Eoff, *Viscountess Rhondda*, pp. 72-3.

[27] *Dundee Advertiser* 20 February 1924.

[28] *T&T* 23 November 1923.

[29] Letter in *WM* 17 March 1922. Margaret was only briefly associated with NUSEC.

[30] Eoff, *Viscountess Rhondda*, p. 76.

[31] Lord, *Winifred Coombe Tennant*, 2012, p. 245.

[32] *The Vote* 20 June 1924. The formal letter signed by Margaret (for the SPG) and other representatives of women's groups was in the *MG* 17 April 1924.

[33] *T&T* 4 July 1924.

[34] Smith, 'British Feminism', p. 54.

[35] *T&T* 5 March 1926.

[36] Ibid., 12 March 1926.

[37] Ibid., 2 March 1923.

[38] W.M. Adamson's Bill with the support of a former suffragette Dorothy Jewson MP.

[39] *T&T* 15 October 1926.

[40] Ibid., 12, 19 March.

[41] Ibid., 19 January 1923.

[42] Emmeline Pankhurst to MR, 30 November 1925 quoted in Ethel Smyth, *Female Pipings in Eden,* Edinburgh, Peter Davies, 1933, p. 260.

[43] Quoted in Blanche Wiesen Cook (ed), *Crystal Eastman on Women and Revolution*, New York, Oxford University Press, 1978, pp. 121-4.

[44] Astor Papers MS 1416/1/2/36, Reading University.

[45] Bartley, *Emmeline Pankhurst,* p. 226.

595

[46] *T&T* 6 July 1928.

[47] Ibid., 9 July 1926.

[48] The EPRCC minutes are in the folder of Minutes for 1927 and in the Minutes of the General Committee folder in 5ERI, FL 335, WL. For the activities of other groups see Law, *Suffrage and Power*, Chapter 10 and Alberti, 'A Symbol and a Key'.

[49] 20 January 1927, 5ERI, FL335, WL.

[50] Law, *Suffrage and Power,* p. 217.

[51] *T&T* 6 July 1928.

[52] For example in the *Nation* 6 January 1912.

[53] *Cambrian News* 18 January 1924.

[54] See Alberti, *Beyond Suffrage,* p.87.

[55] *T&T* 19 October 1928.

[56] Quoted in Wallace, *The Women's Suffrage Movement,* p. 292. See too 5ERI, FL336, WL.

[57] Other demands encompassed the abolition of solicitation laws, rights of married women, need for women police and peers, and protective legislation issues. Not supported by Margaret, the ERGECC and its allied groups were NUSEC's demands for family allowances, the peaceful settlement of international disputes and birth control, issues perceived to be more social than feminist despite being generally supported by them as individuals (though the Catholic St Joan's Social and Political Alliance opposed the last demand).

[58] Deputation to PM folder, 19 April 1929, in 5ERI, FL 335, WL.

[59] In the mid-1950s it was moved to an even more prominent position. *The Times* 7 March 1930.

[60] Microfiche Box 2 v.i-v.6, WL.

[61] *Equal Rights* 9 May 1925. Paul's organisation was initially called the Congressional Committee. The others were Dr Louisa Martindale who ran the Women's Hospital in Brighton, Dorothy Evans of the Women's Civil Servants Association, Alison Neilans of the British Association for Social and Moral Hygiene, Dr

Elizabeth Knight of the Women's Freedom League and Virginia Crawford of the St Joan's Social and Political Alliance.

[62] The 19th Amendment assuring women the right to vote had been ratified in August 1920. Paul had drafted the Equal Rights Amendment in 1923.

[63] *Daily Telegraph* 2 June 1926.

[64] MR to Mrs Corbett Ashby 30 May 1926, reproduced in Cook, *Crystal Eastman*, p. 200.

[65] Eoff, *Viscountess Rhondda,* p. 92; Alberti, *Beyond Suffrage*, pp. 201-10.

[66] See Rupp, *Worlds of Women*, pp. 141-2, 271.

[67] *Equal Rights* 26 June 1926. See too 3 July 1926 for a slightly different wording. Both are reproduced in Cook, *Crystal Eastman*, pp. 206-7.

[68] *T&T* 18 June 1926.

[69] *The World* 27 June 1926 quoted in Cook, *Crystal Eastman,* pp. 193-4.

[70] Quoted in Pedersen, *Eleanor Rathbone and the Politics of Conscience*, p. 190.

[71] A letter from Edith How Martyn in *Time and Tide* (26 November 1926) stressed that she would enjoy the paper more if Margaret stopped criticising NUSEC for 'activities you don't think are feminist'.

[72] Ibid., 11 June 1926. See Marie Sandell, *The Rise of Women's International Activism. Identity and Sisterhood Between the World Wars*, I.B. Tauris, forthcoming.

[73] *Equal Rights* 3 July 1926. Margaret and Rathbone expressed their very different interpretations of events in *T&T* 18 June 1926.

[74] MR to Alice Paul, 31 August 1926, Equal Rights Treaty Formation of International, folder in 5ERI, FL 331, WL.

[75] Carol Miller, 'Inter-War Feminists and the League of Nations' in *Women's History Review* 3/2 (1994), p. 221.

[76] Ibid., p. 221. See too Deborah Gorham, *Vera Brittain. A Feminist Life*, Oxford, Basil Blackwell, 1996, Chapter 8.

[77] Quoted in Eoff, *Viscountess Rhondda*, p. 94. Betty Archdale played an important role in drafting legislation in 1937 on British nationality and the status of aliens.

[78] For Equal Rights International and its internal conflicts see Miller, 'Inter-War Feminists', pp. 224-6.

[79] MR to VB, 20 August 1928, VB.

[80] Ibid., pp. 94-5; *The Times* 27 August 1928. The SPG was represented by Brittain.

[81] For Doris Stevens' much more upbeat interpretation of the effect on the Plenipotentiaries and indirectly on events at Geneva see her letter to Betty Archdale, 5 October 1929 in the Jane Norman Smith Papers, Box 5A-116, folder 125, Schlesinger Library, Radcliffe Institute, Harvard University.

[82] MR to VB, 4 September 1928, VB.

[83] Betty Archdale to Doris Stevens, 24 September 1929, Box 5 A-116, folder 125, Smith Papers, Schlesinger Library.

[84] For the origins of this see Equal Rights Treaty Formation of International folder in 5ERI, FL331, WL.

[85] Ibid., MR to Helen Archdale, 9 December 1930, FL 334.

[86] An ex-suffragist, she had been a central figure in the formation of the Women's International League for Peace and Freedom.

[87] In a letter to Helen, Margaret criticised Abbott and the Open Door Council's approach in Geneva in 1928, as exhibiting 'the usual mole like qualities' of NUSEC: although it purported to be representing five societies including the SPG, the impression they conveyed was that the other four were 'politically inexperienced'. MR to Helen Archdale, 13 July 1928, Doris Stevens Papers, Box 60, Folder 15, Schlesinger Library.

[88] For differences between the SPG/*T&T* and NUSEC see Alberti, *Beyond Suffrage,* Chapter 7.

[89] Deputation to Home Secretary from the Equal Rights Committee 4 November 1929 in 5ERI, FL335. WL.

[90] Letter to *T&T* 27 January 1927. The issue of women's equal nationality seems to have been much less divisive in terms of cooperation between the SPG and NUSEC after 1928. See M.

Page Baldwin, 'Subject to Empire: Married Women and the British Nationality and Status of Aliens Act', *Journal of British Studies*, 40/4, October 2001, p. 532; 5ERI, Box 335, ERC report, 1929, WL.

[91] See Eoff, *Viscountess Rhondda*, pp. 80-1. Not until 1975 when the 1970 Equal Pay Act was implemented would equal pay exist (in theory).

[92] *T&T* 29 April 1939.

[93] Ibid., 23 October 1937.

Chapter 13

[1] GBS to MR, Box 40.4, 12 August 1932, HRC.

[2] *T&T* 13 August 1932.

[3] LWH 17/03/01L, 20 August 1932, HP.

[4] See Chapter 7.

[5] *My World*, p. xiii.

[6] L WH, WH/5/5.17/03/0/r, 4 March 1933, HP.

[7] See Hilda Kean, 'Searching for the Past in Present defeat: the construction of historical and political identity in British feminism in the 1920s and 1930s', *Women's History Review* 3/1, 1994, pp. 56-80 and Laura E. Nym Mayhall, 'Creating the "Suffragette Spirit": British feminism and the historical imagination', Ibid., 4/3, 1995, pp. 319-44.

[8] See John, *Elizabeth Robins*, Introduction.

[9] *The Times* 17 January 1933.

[10] See Regenia Gagnier, *Subjectivities. A History of Self-Representation in Britain, 1932-1920,* Oxford, Oxford University Press, 1991, p. 203.

[11] *Monmouthshire Review* 1/2, April 1933.

[12] See the selection at the end of *Notes*.

[13] For Victorian autobiographies see Sally Mitchell, 'Frances Power Cobbe's *Life* and the Rules for Women's autobiography', *English Literature in Transition 1880-1920*, 50/2, 2007, pp. 131-57.

[14] *T&T* 1 April 1933.

[15] *The Schoolmistress* 16 March 1933. Janet E. Courtney wrote a perceptive review in the *Fortnightly Review* 33, April 1933, p. 536.

[16] 147/246, MR to H. Macmillan, Macmillan Archive, Reading University.

[17] *Bookman* 84/499, April 1933.

[18] *Selected Letters*, Brittain and Handley-Taylor, pp. 237, 240.

[19] *The Times* 12 May 1933.

[20] 'The Political Awakening of Women', pp. 557-570.

[21] Ibid., p. 569.

[22] Starting on 15 October.

[23] Thorstein Veblen, *The Theory of the Leisure Class*, Constable, Dover edition, 1994, p. 218.

[24] *My World*, p. 125.

[25] MR to ER, 5 April 1926, Series 2B, Box 20, folder 150, RP.

[26] *T&T* 19 November 1926.

[27] Ibid., 12, 19 November 1926.

[28] *T&T* 31 August 1940.

[29] Ibid., 3 December 1926.

[30] Ibid., 10 December 1926.

[31] Holtby's description in *T&T* 4 February 1927.

[32] Diary, 27 January 1927, RP.

[33] 'Radio Portraits of Savoy Hill', 24 April 1959, 24912(1), BBC Written Archives Centre.

[34] GBS to MR, Box 40.4, 9 February 1927, HRC.

[35] Ibid., MR to GBS, Box 51.6, 17 February 1927.

[36] Brittain, *Testament of Youth*, p. 583.

[37] Ibid., p. 584. See Chapter 14 for Birkenhead.

[38] Michael Holroyd, *Bernard Shaw. Volume 1 1856-1898. The Search for Love*, Penguin, 1990 edition, pp. 192-7.

[39] *MG* 25 May 1927.

[40] GBS to MR, Box 40.4, 5 October 1931, HRC.

[41] See Appendix.

[42] Rhondda File, 910, BBC Written Archives Centre.

[43] After 1926 they only appeared occasionally. As Anne Doubleday she penned a few reviews and letters.

[44] *T&T* 9 February 1923.

[45] Ibid., 4 April 1924.

[46] Jonathan Croall, *Sybil Thorndike. A Star of Life*, Haus Publishing, 2008, p. 180.

[47] *T&T* 14 March 1930.

[48] Ibid., 7 March 1930.

[49] MR to GBS, Box 51.6, 2 March 1930, HRC.

[50] *T&T* 4 April 1930.

[51] See Chapter 14. For the conduit pipe arguments see *T&T* 28 March, 5 July 1930; GBS to MR, Box 40.4, Easter Sunday 1930, HRC.

[52] *T&T* 13 August 1932.

[53] Ibid., 11 April 1930.

[54] GBS to MR, Box 40.4, 16 March 1930, HRC.

[55] *My World*, p. 125.

[56] Michael Holroyd, 'George Bernard Shaw. Women and the Body Politic', *Critical Inquiry*, 6/1, Autumn 1979, p. 122.

[57] *T&T* 18 April 1930.

[58] Ibid., 21 March 1930.

[59] Ibid., 2 May 1930.

[60] Ibid., 9 May 1930.

[61] Ibid., 2 May 1930.

[62] But see Chapter 15 for her attack on his politics in the 1940s.

[63] GBS to MR, Box 40.4, 15 February 1932, HRC.

[64] Ibid., 12 August 1932.

[65] *T&T* 30 September 1927.

[66] Ibid., 8 November 1930.

[67] Ibid., 7 March 1930.

[68] Ibid., 25 October-15 November 1930.

[69] See Lesley Hall, 'An Ambiguous idol: H.G. Wells inspiring and infuriating women', *The Wellsian* 34, 2011, pp. 68-75. Margaret supported his parliamentary candidature (Labour Party) for the University of London in the 1922 election.

[70] MR to GBS, Box 51.6, 1 November 1934, HRC.

[71] Ibid.

[72] Anthony West, *H.G. Wells: Aspects of a Life*, Penguin edition, 1984, p. 136.

[73] H.G. Wells to Amber Reeves, October 1930, 3329, H.G. Wells Papers, Library of the University of Illinois at Urbana-Champaign.

[74] 23 April 1936, Series 2B, Box 20, folder 150, RP. The following year Margaret called on Wells when they were both in France.

[75] This and the following quote are in L WH/5/5.14/01/06f, nd, HP.

[76] Quoted in David Smith, *H.G. Wells. Desperately Mortal*, Yale University Press, 1986, p. 411.

[77] *Selected Letters*, Brittain and Handley-Taylor, (eds.), p. 202.

[78] According to Margaret, MR to GBS, Box 51.6, 1 November 1927, HRC. It seems from a letter Holtby wrote to Brittain (17 September 1934) that Keun had initially intended to write a review providing she could do so 'with detachment so that no one can accuse her of bitterness'. *Selected Letters*, Brittain and Handley-Taylor (eds.), p. 294.

[79] *T&T* 13, 20, 27 October 1934.

[80] Ibid., 27 October 1934.

[81] MR to GBS, Box 51.6, 1 November 1934, HRC.

[82] See Holtby's comments *Selected Letters*, Brittain and Handley-Taylor (eds.), p. 306.

[83] *T&T* 20 October 1934.

[84] MR to GBS, Box 51.6, 1 November 1934, HRC.

[85] Quoted in *MG* 12 October 1937.

[86] H.G. Wells, *Brynhild*, Thirsk, House of Stratus edition, 2002, p. 168.

[87] Colney Hatch was a famous lunatic asylum.

[88] *MG* 12 October 1937.

[89] See Hall, 'An ambiguous idol' for how Wells could both impress and infuriate.

[90] *T&T* 8 November 1930.

[91] See John, *Elizabeth Robins,* pp. 173-4.

[92] *T&T* 27 June 1924.

[93] Anonymous, *Ancilla's Share*, Hutchinson, 1924, p. 47.

[94] Ibid., p. 48. See too Sue Thomas, 'Miss Robins and Mrs Brown', *Tulsa Studies in English Literature* 20/1, Spring 2001, p. 47.

[95] Quoted in Cook, *Crystal Eastman*, p. 166.

[96] See John, *Elizabeth Robins*, pp. 212-4.

[97] L WH/5/5.17/03/01r, 4 March 1933, HP.

[98] Ibid.

[99] *T&T* 15 October 1922.

[100] Ibid., 22 October 1922. Margaret did not write much about the Church though a Leader of 17 February 1934 attacked it as a slum landlord in Paddington and urged it to take action. Margaret's involvement with housing was via the Women's Pioneer Housing organisation to provide women workers with housing tailored to their needs. She opened their first venture in 1921: a house in Holland Park converted into self-contained flats. She sat on their council until 1930.

[101] *Daily Herald* 6 March 1932.

[102] Cullis chaired the programme sub-committee of the Central Council for Broadcast Adult Education and was keen for Margaret to participate. Rhondda file, 910, BBC Written Archives Centre.

[103] During wartime this was not voiced as Wales or even Britain but as England.

[104] *Morning Post* 15 February 1926.

[105] *T&T* 29 July 1939. Norman Angell headed the list followed by Malcolm Muggeridge.

[106] Ibid., 4 October 1937, *The Times* 12 November 1937; Macmillan Archives 212/18 and 167/187, Reading University.

[107] *Notes*, p. 58.

[108] Ibid., p. 45.

[109] Ibid., p. 46.

[110] Ibid., pp. 118-22.

[111] Ibid., p. 165.

[112] *T&T* 6 November 1937. See her admission in *T&T* 14 May 1938 that democracy had advanced apace.

[113] *Notes*, p. 126; *T&T* 21 May 1938, 30 November 1940.

[114] Her 'Notes' in *T&T* during February 1935 need to be read in response to T.S. Eliot's 'Notes' of 12 January 1935 and subsequent letters.

[115] Ibid., 31 January 1930.

[116] *Notes*, pp. 144-9.

[117] *T&T* 6 November 1937.

[118] Ibid., 23 January 1937.

Chapter 14

[1] Bertha Thomas (1845-1918) was a popular writer. Her maternal grandfather had been the Archbishop of Canterbury and her father came from a well-connected Carmarthenshire family. Her satire first appeared in *Fraser's Magazine* in 1874 and was published as a pamphlet the following year.

[2] Reprinted in Kirsti Bohata (ed.), *Stranger Within The Gates. A collection of short stories by Bertha Thomas,* Dinas Powys, Honno Press, 2008, pp. 263-9.

[3] Unlike the modern meaning of the term which describes the wives of peers, it used to mean hereditary women peers.

[4] Rhondda, 'Women and the House of Lords', p. 85. The numbers of peeresses in their own right fluctuated slightly over the years but there were usually about two dozen. See too Eoff, *Viscountess Rhondda*, pp. 81-8. For details of the three ways in which women could succeed to a peerage and the history of them see Duncan Sutherland, 'Peeresses, Parliament, and Prejudice: The Admission of Women to the House of Lords 1900-1963, Ph.D, University of Cambridge, 2000, Chapters 1 and 2.

[5] *MG* 3 March 1922.

[6] Holtby, *Letters*, p. 186.

[7] See Duncan Sutherland, 'Peeresses, Parliament and prejudice: the admission of women to the House of Lords, 1918-1963', *Parliaments, Estates and Representation* 20, November 2000, pp. 215-31.

[8] HL/PO/DC/CP/4153, Parliamentary Archives.

[9] *The Times* 6 March 1920.

[10] American-born Nancy Astor was the first woman to take her seat. She won her by-election by a thousand votes.

[11] See HL/PO/DC/CP/3/86, Minutes and Proceedings of the Committee for Privileges and the Case in Support of the Petition, 1922, Parliamentary Archives.

[12] Rhondda, 'Women and the House of Lords', p. 83; *MG* 3 March 1922.

[13] This and subsequent newspaper responses to the news are, unless otherwise noted, in C8, D.A.

[14] *T&T* 10 March 1922.

[15] John St Loe Strachey to MR, 9 March 1922, STR/19/4/8a, Parliamentary Archives.

[16] Hansard, House of Lords debates, xxxix, col.1015, 30 March 1922; Rhondda, 'Women and the House of Lords', p. 83.

[17] *New York Times* 25 May 1924.

[18] Robins wrote articles on the subject for three daily papers but

they did not accept them. She was successful with the Sunday paper, the *Observer*. Diary 7, 11, 13, 15 June 1922, RP.

[19] Rhondda, 'Women and the House of Lords', p. 84.

[20] *MG* 31 March 1922.

[21] *T&T* 9 June 1922.

[22] Duncan Sutherland suggests that King George V was concerned. After the first Committee for Privileges met his private secretary asked Birkenhead whether the king would now have to issue Writs. He was told that Birkenhead would be challenging the situation. Sutherland thesis, p. 138.

[23] See Idem., 'Peeresses, Parliament and Prejudice' (article), pp. 220-1.

[24] 'Notes' in *Law Quarterly Review,* CL111, January 1923, p. 3.

[25] Diary 18 May 1922, RP.

[26] Hansard, Lords Debates, LIV, col. 586, 24 June 1926.

[27] Sutherland, 'Peeresses, Parliament and Prejudice', p. 221.

[28] This was in a letter to *The Times* 14 June 1922.

[29] Eoff, *Viscountess Rhondda*, p. 87.

[30] F.E. Smith, Earl of Birkenhead, *Judgments delivered by Lord Chancellor Birkenhead 1919-1922*, HMSO, 1923, pp. 467-491; Rhondda, 'Women and the House of Lords', p. 84.

[31] *MG* 5 July 1922.

[32] Campbell, *F.E. Smith,* p. 281.

[33] Quoted in Ibid., p. 280.

[34] *T&T* 15 July 1927.

[35] Baroness Ravensdale, *In Many Rhythms*, Weidenfeld & Nicolson, 1953, p. 95.

[36] *Sunday Chronicle* 14 March 1922 in C8, D.A.

[37] MR to John St Loe Strachey 5/19/4/8d, 6 July 1922, Parliamentary Archives.

[38] Alice Fraser, '"The Persistent Peeress", *Independent Woman,* December 1948, pp. 346-48.

[39] MR to ER, 17 June 1922, Series 2B, Box 20, folder 150, RP.

[40] *Evening News* 7 March 1922; Hansard, Lords Debates CCV, col.690, 31 October 1957.

[41] Ravensdale, *In Many Rhythms*, p. 96.

[42] Sutherland (thesis), p. 151.

[43] Quoted in Lesley A. Hall, 'Stella Browne, '"What a Lot There Is Still to Do": Stella Browne (1880-1955) – Carrying the Struggle Ever Onward' in Eustance, Ryan and Ugolini, *A Suffrage Reader*, p. 198; *The New York Times* 12 November 1922.

[44] *T&T* 9 June 1922.

[45] Wells, *Brynhild*, p. 168.

[46] Quoted in *Evening Standard* 18 July 1924 in C8, D.A.

[47] *Sunday Chronicle* 13 May 1923.

[48] Rhondda, 'Women and the House of Lords', p. 84.

[49] Law, *Suffrage and Power*, p. 112.

[50] *T&T* 3 August 1923.

[51] See Vivien Hughes, 'How the Famous Five in Canada Won Personhood for Women', paper given at the Women's History Network Tenth Anniversary Conference, September 2001; National Archives of Canada, 'The "Persons" Case', Ottawa, 2000, *WM* 25 March 1922 and C8, D.A..

[52] MR to ER, 8 June 1922, Series 2B, Box 20, folder 150, RP.

[53] This was the request for England and Wales. It sought for Scottish and Irish peeresses voting rights at the election of Representative Peers and their own election.

[54] Lord Desborough to Lord Farrer, 8 March 1922, 2572/1/82, Letter Book of T.C. Farrer, Surrey History Centre, Woking.

[55] Quoted in *Evening Standard* 18 July 1924 in C8, D.A.

[56] *MG* 18 May 1925.

[57] *The Times* 16 May 1925.

[58] Hansard, Lords Debates, LXI, cols. 428-471, 21 May 1925 and *The Times* 22 May 1925; Pamela Brookes, *Women at Westminster. An Account of Women in the British Parliament 1918-66*, Peter Davies, 1967, pp. 205-213.

[59] See Chapter 13 above.

[60] *T&T.*, 22 May 1925.

[61] Ibid., 9 July 1926.

[62] Ibid., 2 July 1926.

[63] Sutherland, 'Peeresses, Parliament and Prejudice', p. 222.

[64] For this debate see Hansard, Lords Debates, LXIV, cols.568-610, 24 June 1926.

[65] *MG* 25 June 1926. Birkenhead died in 1930. Both his son and daughter married the children of Lord Camrose, Margaret's childhood friend. There was a further twist as Birkenhead's eldest son became a director of *Time and Tide* in the 1950s.

[66] July 1925. In Astor Papers, MS1416/1/1/313, Reading University.

[67] *T&T* 9 June 1922.

[68] *The Times* 15 May 1925.

[69] Advertisement in *T&T* 10 May 1929.

[70] 5 ERI /1/A, Box 335, WL.

[71] *T&T* 3 April 1937.

[72] Ibid., 15 May 1937. Also published as 'In the Abbey', a T&T Coronation Day supplement. Compare this with Lady Ravensdale's more irreverent account, describing 'rabbit and cotton-velvet robes' and the 'slow stream of Peeresses to the Elsan lavatories at the back'. Ravensdale, *In Many Rhythms,* p.203.

[73] *The Times* 5 March 1946.

[74] One was ineligible as a minor, the other as a member of the royal family.

[75] 6, 12 June 1947, Markham Papers 25/82, BLPES; Edward F. Iwi, 'Women and the House of Lords' in Sydney Dawson Bailey, *The Future of the House of Lords: a Symposium*, Hansard Society, 1954, pp. 104-7.

[76] *The Times* 27 July 1949.

[77] Iwi, 'Women and the House of Lords', p.107.

[78] *MG* 28 July 1949.

[79] The others were Baroness Swanborough (Dame Stella Isaacs, Marchioness of Reading and the first woman to take her seat), Baroness Elliot of Harwood (Dame Katharine Elliot) and Baroness Wootton of Abinger, (Barbara Wootton, who been president of the Young Suffragists, was the first woman to receive her letters patent and become deputy speaker). In 2012 181 women had seats in the Lords.

[80] Mari Takayanagi, 'A Changing House: The Life Peerages Act 1958', *Parliamentary History* 27/3, 2008, p. 390. Baroness Strange of Knokin was the first hereditary woman peer to take her seat (in November 1963). Since then 25 female hereditary peers have sat in the Lords.

[81] Violet Powell, *The Life of a Provincial Lady*, Heinemann, 1998, p. 74.

[82] The Commons Tea Room displays Ivan Gregorewitch Olinsky's portrait of D.A. Lady Astor's portrait was hung in the Commons in 1924. Adrian Fort, *Nancy: The Story of Lady Astor*, Jonathan Cape, 2012, p. 209.

Chapter 15

[1] *T&T* 6 May 1933.

[2] Ibid., 13 May 1933.

[3] Ibid., 20 May 1933.

[4] bMS Eng 1213.1, 28 July 1949, BD.

[5] SPR archives MS 7/11/14, Cambridge University Library.

[6] SPR MS 7/2/X and 7/2/9. Theodora's diary included later references to Tessa Dillon, (sister of the London bookshop owner Una Dillon), visiting her and Margaret at Churt Halewell and Pen Ithon. She accompanied them on several cruises to Madeira in the 1950s.

[7] Ibid., 27 September 1945; 20 January 1958. Theodora was also related to the Bosanquets of Dingestow Court, Monmouthshire whom Sybil knew.

[8] *T&T* 3, 10 July 1954.

[9] Leon Edel, *Henry James. A Life*, New York, Harper & Row, 1977 edition, pp. 634-7.

[10] Quoted in Bosanquet, *Henry James at Work*, ed. Lyall H. Powers, Ann Arbour, University of Michigan Press, 2006, p. 75.

[11] Ibid., p. 27.

[12] Pamela Thurschwell, 'The Typist's Remains: Theodora Bosanquet in Recent Fiction', *The Henry James Review* 32/1, Winter 2011, pp. 1-11.

[13] Cynthia Ozick, 'Dictation' in *Dictation*, New York, Mariner Books, 2009, pp. 15 and 49.

[14] Michiel Heyns, *The Typewriter's Tale, Johannesburg, Jonathan Ball, 2005.*

[15] Emma Tennant, *The Beautiful Child,* Peter Owen, 2012.

[16] For example on 26 August 1915, bMS Eng 1213.1, BD.

[17] See Chapter 12. Doris Stevens to Jane Norman Smith, 13 September 1928, Jane Norman Smith Papers, Box 5A-116, folder 125, Schlesinger Library.

[18] Theodora Bosanquet, *Harriet Martineau. An Essay in Comprehension,* Etchells & Macdonald, 1927, p. 194. The Hogarth Press published her 1933 study of Paul Valéry, French poet and essayist. Valéry called it 'exact et excellent'. Quoted in Bosanquet, *Henry James at Work* (2006), p. 123.

[19] Ibid., p. 211.

[20] 5 September 1915, bMS1213.1, BD.

[21] Ibid. See, for example, 30, April and 8 December 1943.

[22] Macpherson, *The Suffragette's Daughter*, p. 120.

[23] *The Times* 3 June 1961. Wedgwood and Theodora were distantly related.

[24] L WH, 17/03/01u, 23 April 1933, HP.

[25] Stark, *The Coast of Incense*, pp. 121-2.

[26] *T&T* 13 February 1937 in a review of Gerald Heard's book *The Third Morality*. In *My World*, (Chapter VII) Margaret was at

pains to stress the doubts that assailed her as a teenager preparing for Confirmation.

[27] Pamela Thurschwell, *Literature, Technology and Magical Thinking, 1880-1920*, Cambridge, Cambridge University Press, 2005 edition, Chapter 4.

[28] Bosanquet, *Henry James at Work* (2006), p. 34.

[29] SPR MS. 7/9/1.

[30] Ibid., MS7/3/2.

[31] Ibid., MS 7/9/7, 7/9/2, 7/6/122.

[32] He was part of an important local landowning family.

[33] Information from the Bray family and Surrey History Centre shows that Angela Blakeney-Booth was the first owner from 1930 to 1931 followed by Edgar McIntyre who surrendered his lease after a few years. Margaret and Theodora rented a furnished house (Glasson) for a few months before moving.

[34] SPR MS 7/6/27.

[35] Mary Grieve, *Millions Made My Story*, Victor Gollancz, 1964, p. 144.

[36] See Betty D. Vernon, *Ellen Wilkinson*, 1982.

[37] *T&T* 17 May 1941.

[38] Ibid., 15 February 1947.

[39] Ibid.

[40] L WH/3/3/27.034, nd but 1933, HP.

[41] 24 June 1935, Marie Mattingly Meloney Papers, Columbia University.

[42] Macpherson, *The Suffragette's Daughter*, p. 115.

[43] *T&T* 15 February 1947.

[44] Quoted in Ibid., 17 May 1941.

[45] *MG* 10 February, 16 March, 14 June 1938.

[46] Ibid., 25 July 1938; *T&T* 30 July 1938.

[47] *T&T* 30 July 1938.

[48] Ibid., 15 April 1939.

[49] Ibid., 10, 17 December 1938; *The Times* 22 October 1938.

[50] *T&T* 19 April 1958. Wedgwood ceased being an editor in 1949 but still worked for the paper when possible and became Deputy Chairman.

[51] bMS Eng 1213.1, 11 February 1947, BD.

[52] Markham also sat on this committee.

[53] *T&T* 6 January 1945.

[54] bMS Eng 1213.1, 7 January 1943, BD.

[55] *The Four Empires*, pp. 1-2. She had earlier been active in the British Commonwealth League.

[56] bMS Eng 1213.1,13 March 1943, BD. Morrison wrote occasionally for *Time and Tide*.

[57] Ibid., 24 September 1945. Addison acknowledged the injustice of excluding peeresses. The Labour government was prepared to support their bid if the House as a whole agreed.

[58] See the correspondence from Anthony Part in ED136/764, NA.

[59] bMS Eng 1213.1, 12 September 1956, BD. Towards the end of the war Peake was political adviser to the Supreme Commander of the Allied Expeditionary Force and later served in Belgrade.

[60] *T&T* 15 February 1947.

[61] See Paula Bartley, *From Communist Suffragist to Cabinet Minister*, Pluto Press, forthcoming.

[62] bMS Eng 1213.1, 11 February 1947, BD.

[63] Ibid., 9 April 1946.

[64] See Bernard Donoughue and G.W. Jones, *Herbert Morrison. Portrait of a Politician*, Weidenfeld & Nicolson, 1973, p. 340.

[65] Quoted in Michael Holroyd, *Bernard Shaw. Volume 3 1918-1950. The Lure of Fantasy*, Penguin, 1991, pp. 432-3.

[66] MR to GBS, Box 51.6, 17 June 1940, HRC.

[67] *T&T* 29 November 1941.

[68] MR to GBS, Box 51.6, 17 June 1940, HRC.

[69] In *Collected Letters. 1926-1950. Bernard Shaw.Volume 4*, Dan H. Laurence (ed.), Max Reinhardt, 1988, p. 35.

[70] *T&T* 28 July, 4, 11 August 1956.

[71] Ibid., 11 November 1950, 16 September 1944.

[72] *My World*, p. 86.

[73] NCCL Papers, Annual Reports DCL/73A (ii), Hull History Centre.

[74] *T&T* 21, 28 June 1941.

[75] *The Times* 15 February 1934.

[76] Quoted on dust jacket of *The Next Five Years*.

[77] *http://www.oxforddnb.com/templates/theme-print.jsp-print.jsp? articleid=92516*. Accessed 26 July 2009. A Federal Union of Democratic Countries with its headquarters in Bloomsbury was formed in the summer of 1939. It saw itself as the nucleus of a future world federation. Margaret supported it as did figures such as Cecil, A.D. Lindsay, Nevinson, Sharp, Violet Bonham-Carter and Lord Astor. *MG* 29 June 1939.

[78] *T&T* 14 October 1939.

[79] *MG* 7 October 1939.

[80] Ibid., 31 October 1939.

[81] *T&T* 21 November 1936.

[82] Ibid., 30 November 1940.

[83] Ibid., 4 October 1941.

[84] This declaration of aspirations embraced eight principles including the right for people to choose their own forms of government and enjoy much fuller international economic cooperation.

[85] *T&T* 2 October 1948. See also her article on 'Churchill and the Nation' on 9 October 1948.

[86] Ibid., 27 January 1945.

[87] See, for example, articles on 1, 8 June 1946.

[88] *Men Not Masses*, p. 27.

[89] *T&T* 26 July 1941

[90] Ibid., 23 August 1941.

[91] Phyllis Deakin, interviewed by Alex Bennion, 1990, *National*

Life Stories Fawcett Collection, British Library Sound & Moving Image reference: C468/001, 1990.

[92] *T&T* 21 April 1934.

[93] See *A Suffrage Reader*, Eustance, Ryan and Ugolini, Chapters 6 and 10.

[94] *WM* 21 January 1937.

[95] MR to ER, 18 April 1922, Series 2B, Box 20, folder 150, RP.

[96] Ibid., Diary 26 November 1925.

[97] *Blackshirt* 15, 22 June 1934. Martin Durham, *Women and Fascism*, Routledge, 1998; Julie Gottlieb, *Feminine Fascism*, I. B. Tauris, 2000, pp. 74, 307.

[98] bMS Eng 1213.1,16 January 1943, BD.

[99] *T&T* 11 November 1950.

[100] Johanna Alberti, 'British Feminists and Anti-fascism in the 1930s' in Sybil Oldfield (ed.) *This Working-Day World. Women's Lives and Culture(s) in Britain 1914-1945*, Taylor & Francis, 1994, pp. 114-121.

[101] This was revealed in September 1945. *T&T* 22 September 1945; *MG* 14 September 1945; David Lampe, *The Last Ditch. Britain's Secret Resistance and the Nazi Invasion Plan*, Greenhill Books, 2007, p. 192.

[102] See Berry and Bostridge, *Vera Brittain*, pp. 392-3.

[103] L WH/5/5.45/03g, 6 September 1955, HP.

[104] Although it seems unlikely that *Time and Tide* would have 'fixed' two weeks of letters, like other papers it was not above facilitating responses. Margery Allingham, best remembered for her crime fiction, reviewed novels regularly for *Time and Tide*. In 1940, encouraged by Theodora, she wrote to the paper about the need for the Church to play an active role in the spiritual defence of the country. Theodora sent advance copies of this letter to those she hoped would respond in print. Julia Jones, *The Adventures of Margery Allingham*, Golden Duck, Chelmsford, 2009, pp. 230-1.

[105] Berry and Bostridge, *Vera Brittain*, pp. 401-2, 409-10.

[106] In 1930 she had joined Holtby and others protesting against

a ban on the showing of Soviet-produced films by a working-class film society, a position she would not have endorsed post-war. See Fildes, 'Winifred Holtby and "The Voice of God" p. 108.

[107] *T&T* 1 February 1941.

[108] bMS Eng 1213.1,6 March 1944, 20 December 1945, BD.

Chapter 16

[1] *T&T* 25 January, 8 February, 8 March 1947.

[2] Ibid., 8 September 1945.

[3] Ibid., 1 June 1946.

[4] Ibid., 17, 31 August, 7 September 1946.

[5] bMS Eng 1213.1,17 July 1946, BD. In the local elections of that summer Margaret placed what Theodora described as 'an anti-Labour vote' in Holborn. Ibid., 20 August 1946.

[6] *T&T* 21 November 1936.

[7] Ibid., 29 October 1938.

[8] Ibid., 24 August 1946.

[9] Ibid., and *The Times* 6 October 1951.

[10] *T&T* 23 April 1955 and Margaret's response to letters in Ibid 4 June 1951.

[11] Ibid., 30 November 1957.

[12] For Llanwern's fate see JLM/MR/1355, The National Trust; Thomas Jones Papers, Class D, vol.7, 133-162, Class W, vol.10, 88, NLW; E.L. Ellis, *T.J. A Life of Dr Thomas Jones, CH*, Cardiff, University of Wales Press, 1992, pp. 478-9; *South Wales Argus* 22 February, 8 March 1952; CADW, Rural District Magor and St Mellons HLG 2295, Listing and delisting schedules 8 January 1952, 2 October 1953.

[13] CADW's delisting schedule is, however, dated 2 October 1953 and describes the house as 'unoccupied' so demolition may not have been completed until later.

[14] *The Times* 14 April 1950.

[15] *WM* 17 November 1950.

[16] Ibid. Cardiff boasted Britain's second hall of residence for women students. Millicent McKenzie, the first woman member of the Senate, was a pioneer female professor who trained women teachers. The ex-suffragist Mabel Howell whom Margaret had known before and during the First World War was a governor when Margaret was appointed. The Minute Book of the Court of Governors (1929-1958) at Cardiff University shows that Margaret did not attend governors' meetings.

[17] *T&T* 25 November 1950.

[18] 19 July 1955, BD; *Cambrian News* 26 July 1955.

[19] bMS Eng 1213.1, 9 November 1946, BD.

[20] SPR MS 7/1/2.

[21] In the 1920s the Pen Ithon Estate became a Trust. Margaret inherited her mother's share of the estate when Sybil died. Alec Haig, who had in effect run the estate, died in the same year. All but the house and a hundred acres was sold off in the 1940s though just three farms passed out of family control. Margaret purchased two farms.

[22] bMS Eng 1213.1, 5 July 1950, BD.

[23] *T&T* 26 June 1948.

[24] Ibid., 6 August 1955.

[25] Ibid., 27 February 1954.

[26] 5 December 1949, BD. He was a founder of the Portmadoc Players supported by Margaret in the 1920s.

[27] *T&T* 21 May 1949.

[28] Ibid., 2 November 1946.

[29] Ibid., 12 April 1947.

[30] bMS Eng 1213.1, 20 August, 3 September 1945, BD.

[31] Most passengers were American and Margaret compared British and American attitudes as well as considering post-war Norway, Sweden and Denmark in three articles: *T&T*, 1, 8, 15 October 1949.

[32] bMS Eng 1213.1, 28 June 1951, BD.

[33] Ibid., 1 March 1946, 22 October 1948.

[34] Ibid., 30 March 1955.

[35] Carl Rollyson, *Rebecca West. A Saga of the Century,* Hodder & Stoughton, 1955, p. 279.

[36] Theodora's diary suggests that although the infamous lunch took place on 1 December 1953, difficulties were eased by some excellent claret 'and all was well in the end'. A week later Betjeman was apparently still hoping to 'dominate the reviewing', but by 14 December he was spreading news of his 'resignation' and the following day Margaret told him (by telephone) what she thought of his behaviour. On 29th a letter from Betjeman arrived severing his connection with *Time and Tide*.

[37] John Betjeman, *Collected Poems*, John Murray, 2006 edition, p. 291. See too Eoff, *Viscountess Rhondda,* p. 131.

[38] *T&T* 22 November 1952.

[39] From June 1955 this was edited by D.J. Morgan Chairman of the Chess Education Society and father of the historian Professor Lord Morgan.

[40] To Phyllis Bentley, L WH/5/5.23/05/06f, 23 May 1933, HP.

[41] Editors' Forum, 21 February 1957, 823483, BBC Written Archives Centre.

[42] *The Times* 23 July 1953. Lord Derby was its president.

[43] For her television appearances see 20 February, 3 March and 30 April 1958, BD.

[44] Shirley Williams, *Climbing the Bookshelves. Shirley Williams. The Autobiography,* Virago Press, 2009, p. 8; John Catlin, *Family Quartet: Vera Brittain and her Family*, Hamish Hamilton, 1987, p. 155.

[45] This account is based on Theodora's diary for 1957, BD.

[46] The centre from which George Augustus Haig had operated his careful management of the estate.

[47] bMS Eng 1213.1, 2 August 1957, BD.

[48] Ibid., 11 July 1958.

[49] Ibid., 1 April 1958.

[50] Ibid., 14 May 1958.

[51] For example, *Daily Express* 15 July 1958.

[52] bMS Eng 1213.1, 26 January 1956, BD.

[53] *T&T* 26 July 1958.

[54] Ibid.

[55] *The Times* 21 July 1958.

[56] *T&T* 26 July 1958.

[57] Ibid., 2 August 1958 by Walter Sachs.

INDEX

The index does not include references to the illustrated material or the endnotes. 'Mac', 'Mc' and 'St' have been filed as they are written.

Index

Mosley, Sir Oswald 497, 503–4
Moullin, Charles Mansell 98
Moullin, Edith Mansell 98
Moxon, John 102–3
Muggeridge, Malcolm 21, 307, 326
Mumbles Railway and Pier Company 281
Munich Agreement (1938) 487–8
Murphy, Emily 458
Murray, Flora 381
Murray, Jessie 93

Nation 290
National Baby Week 219–20
National Council for Civil Liberties 497–8
National Council of Women 224, 276, 299, 445
National Eisteddfod 229, 519
  Abergavenny 110, 111
  Wrexham 110–11
National Federation of Business and Professional Women's Clubs of Great Britain and Northern Ireland 279
National Federation of Women Workers 214
National Health Service 220, 510
National Kitchens movement 159, 195
National League for Opposing Woman Suffrage 97, 375, 448
National Magazine Company 282

National Service Department (NSD) 141–2, 145, 155, 156
National Thanksgiving Fund 517
National Trust 187–8, 513–14, 515, 516
National Union of Societies for Equal Citizenship (NUSEC) 237, 301, 369, 375, 376, 377, 378–9, 384, 387, 389, 392, 399, 445
National Union of Women Teachers 369, 373, 377, 532
National Union of Women's Suffrage Societies (NUWSS) 56, 61, 78, 88, 89, 103, 110, 237, 289, 376, 378
National War Savings Committee 159
National Woman's Party (of America) (NWP) 16, 344, 391–5
  International Advisory Committee 22
National Women Citizens' Association 359–60, 379
Naval Colliery Co Ltd (Penygraig) 52, 256
Naylor, Marie 55, 66
Nevinson, Henry W. 77, 115, 116, 117, 176–7, 178, 180, 181, 241, 386, 497
New Freewoman 291
New Statesman 298, 312, 526
New, Annie 482, 537
Newport and District Women Citizens' Association 383

prostitution 74, 113, 119–20,
371
Provisional Club 279

Queen Mary's Army Auxiliary
Corps (QMAAC) 158, 164,
171, 172

R. Marten and Co Ltd 267–8
Rahil Morganwg *see* Thomas,
Rachel (Rahil Morganwg)
Rathbone, Eleanor 275, 376,
378, 380, 387, 393, 400,
505
Ravensdale, Baroness of
Kedleston 452, 454, 455,
469
Reading, Lord 468
Rees, Sarah Jane (Cranogwen)
289
Reeves, Amber 430
Reeves, Maud Pember 213
Reith, Sir John 433, 525
Representation of the People Act
(1918) 211–12, 460
Representation of the People
(Equal Franchise) Act (1928)
385
Rhondda Engineering and Mining
Company 263
Rhondda, 2nd Viscountess
(Margaret Haig Thomas)
Addidi Inspiration Award for
Female Entrepreneurs (2009)
19
as Anne Doubleday 230, 327,
420

as Mrs M. H. Mackworth 73,
89, 151
'At the Half Way House' 367,
368
author and journalist 285–
324, 332, 404–40, 478, 488,
490, 499–503, 509–10
birth 33
'Business and Commerce'
277–8
businesswoman 15, 19, 243–
84
Canadian ventures 249–51
Chief Controller of women's
recruitment 16, 161–82
commissioner of Women's
National Service for Wales and
Monmouthshire 142
*D. A. Thomas. Viscount
Rhondda* (1921) 190, 191–5,
197
debate with G. K. Chesterton
413–15
debating skills 417–19
debutante 41–2
'Diary' / 'Four Winds' column
439
divorce 17, 175, 229–30,
232–8, 343, 352, 448
Douglas-Pennant affair 168–
82, 184, 201, 262, 449
'Dying and Killing' (essay)
135–6
editor of *Time and Tide* 285–
6, 303–23, 325, 508–36; see
also *Time and Tide*
education 34–5, 37–41

Lightning Source UK Ltd.
Milton Keynes UK
UKOW02f1314280415

250495UK00002B/22/P